ISBN 978-1-5284-0696-3
PIBN 10914289

FB &c Ltd, Dalton House, 60 Windsor Avenue, London, SW19 2RR.
Company number 08720141. Registered in England and Wales.

For support please visit www.forgottenbooks.com

ANNUAL REPORT

OF THE

ADJUTANT GENERAL

OF THE

STATE OF NORTH CAROLINA

FOR THE

YEAR 1910

RALEIGH:
EDWARDS & BROUGHTON PRINTING CO., STATE PRINTERS
1911.

CONTENTS

PAGE

North Carolina National Guard.................................. 5
Report of Quartermaster General 12
Report of Inspector General 80
Report of Surgeon General 85
Report of Paymaster General 96
Report of Commissary General 99
Report of Chief of Ordnance 103
Report of Brigade Commander 114
Report of Commanding Officer First Infantry 116
Report of Commanding Officer Second Infantry 118
Report of Commanding Officer Third Infantry 121
Report of Commanding Officer Coast Artillery Corps............ 126
Report of Commanding Officer Naval Brigade 130
Report of Commander C. D. Bradham of sail of U. S. T. B. *Dupont* from Charleston, S. C., Navy Yard to home station, New Bern, N. C. 132
Return of strength .... folder
Return of publications 135
Report of small arms firing............................... 136-137
General Orders 138
Roster of active officers..................................... 175
Roster of retired officers.................................... 189

ANNUAL REPORT

OF THE

ADJUTANT GENERAL

STATE OF NORTH CAROLINA,
ADJUTANT GENERAL'S DEPARTMENT,
RALEIGH, December 31, 1910.

To His Excellency, HONORABLE WILLIAM W. KITCHIN, GOVERNOR AND COMMANDER IN CHIEF.

SIR:—I have the honor to submit herewith annual report of the operations of the Military Department for the year ending December 31, 1910.

The following changes have been made in the organization of the Guard since the last annual report:

The Battery of Field Artillery, located at Charlotte, N. C., has been transferred to the Coast Artillery Corps and assigned as Fifth Company.

Company D, First Infantry, located at Charlotte, having fallen below the standard of efficiency required by law and regulations, was mustered out of the service May 5th.

In accordance with request of Company and Regimental Commanders and the approval of the Brigade Commander the home station of Company B, First Infantry, was transferred from Dallas, Gaston County, to Gastonia, Gaston County.

One hospital corps detachment was mustered into the service at Kinston, N. C., May 16, 1910.

One division of naval militia was mustered in at Hertford, N. C.

The strength of the Guard shows the following:

LAND FORCES:

Commissioned officers	222	
Enlisted men	2,268	
Total, land forces		2,490

NAVAL MILITIA:

Commissioned officers	39	
Enlisted men	298	
Total, Naval Militia		337
Total, all arms		2,827
Aggregate strength exceeding previous year		112

Owing to your active interest in the improvement and welfare of the Guard, and under the wise administration of my predecessor, the lamented General Armfield, who had the hearty co-operation of the officers and enlisted men, the Guard made much progress during the past year and is now in a better state of efficiency and comes nearer filling its mission than at any time in its history.

FIRST REGIMENT.

The First Regiment of Infantry participated in joint maneuvers with the organizations of the regular army at Chickamauga Park, Ga., for ten days, July 11th to 20th. The regiment performed all duties promptly and thoroughly while at Chickamauga, and I was told by an officer of high rank in the regular army who observed the conduct of this organization that it made a very fine showing.

SECOND REGIMENT.

The Second Regiment of Infantry engaged in rifle practice and field instruction at Camp Glenn for eight days, July 19th to 26th. This regiment showed much energy and interest in their work, qualifying three expert rifleman, two sharpshooters, 147 marksmen, making a great increase in figure of merit and improvement in marksmanship. The field instruction was progressive and included from squad drill to battle exercise by the entire regiment. On the return trip from camp this regiment, upon invitation, stopped over at New Bern and participated in exercises incident to the celebration of the 200th anniversary of the settlement of New Bern.

THIRD REGIMENT.

The Third Regiment of Infantry engaged in rifle practice and field instruction at Camp Glenn for eight days, July 6th to 13th. This regiment entered into their work with zest and promptness and showed marked improvement in marksmanship, qualifying three sharpshooters, 114 marksmen and other classes to such an extent that the regimental figure of merit was materially increased. On account of poor train service, causing the troops to arrive in camp late, this regiment lost almost an entire day's work.

COAST ARTILLERY CORPS.

The five companies and field and staff of the Coast Artillery Corps engaged in joint coast defense exercises at Fort Caswell, August 5th to 15th, and according to reports of Commanding Officer Artillery, District of Cape Fear, this organization, both officers and men, showed such diligent application, that the ultimate results surpassed the high standard set last year.

NAVAL BRIGADE.

The Naval Brigade shows progress. Nearly all the divisions have reached the maximum strength allowed by law. During the year the Navy Department has loaned the State the Torpedo Boat *Dupont*. This with the U. S. S. *Elfrida* gives the Naval Brigade two vessels for use in the practice cruises. During the summer each division performed service afloat, either on the *Elfrida* or the *Dupont,* and for these exercises Lieut. C. H. Shaw, U. S. Navy, was detailed by the Navy Department as instructor. Lieut. Shaw reported for duty July 1, and remained on duty with Naval Brigade until August 15th. Target practice with small arms and one pounders was engaged in by all the divisions. Divisional and deck duty was performed by the officers of the division; the routine ship duties of the regular navy performed by the enlisted men.

MEDICAL CORPS.

The Medical Corps performed satisfactory and efficient service at Camp Glenn, Fort Caswell and Chickamauga. The

Charlotte Detachment was on duty at Chickamauga with the First Infantry, and at Fort Caswell with the C. A. C. The Reidsville Detachment was on duty with the Third Infantry at Camp Glenn, and the Kinston Detachment was on duty at Camp Glenn with the Second Infantry. The Kinston detachment was also on duty with the Second Infantry while at New Bern and rendered prompt aid to the sick who were overcome with heat and fatigue.

This branch of the service is not as large as it should be for the number of troops it has to serve. It is hoped that during the coming year this arm can be increased in enlisted strength to the proper number of sanitary troops for a brigade of infantry and the coast artillery corps.

ARMS AND EQUIPMENT.

The arms and equipment of all branches of the service is complete and of modern pattern required by the War Department.

ORGANIZATION.

Our present organizations of one brigade of Infantry, Coast Artillery Corps, Hospital Corps Detachment, is in accordance with requirements of the War Department for such organizations of the Militia.

RIFLE PRACTICE.

During the year a silver cup designated "Dupont Trophy," was competed for at gallery shooting by teams of five officers, and men from each company of infantry. Company L team Second Infantry won the trophy, making a total score of 332 out of a possible 350.

More interest is being taken in gallery practice and first class outdoor ranges of one thousand yards each have been established at Goldsboro, Raleigh and Gastonia. These ranges have a capacity of three targets, and will be the means of stimulating much interest in rifle practice, and will provide ready accommodation for regimental competion and raise the standard of marksmanship in the Guard.

These ranges were constructed by the sacrifice of time and money of officers and the men of the Guard and without State aid, and much credit is due the patriotic members of the Guard who accomplished such good work.

INSPECTIONS.

The Inspector General inspected the Guard and his notes of inspection have been published in circular form, and each officer furnished with a copy of the same. Lieut. C. M. Butler, Seventeenth Infantry, U. S. A., representing the United States, inspected the Infantry organizations on the same dates as the Inspector General.

Capt. Gwyn R. Hancock, representing the United States, inspected the Coast Artillery Corps. Maj. William Lyster, Medical Corps, U. S. A., inspected the Medical Corps. Lieut. Col. Henry D. Harper, Assistant Inspector General, inspected the Naval Brigade.

Capt. Marcus B. Stokes, U. S. A., was on duty with the Second and Third Regiments at Camp Glenn during the period of encampment, representing the United States in the dual capacity of Instructor and Inspector. His work was very helpful to our troops and much appreciated by all.

The report of the Inspector General shows the Guard to be better equipped and in a better state of efficiency than ever before.

The work of Sergeant John Wadington, Company C, Second Infantry, U. S. A., detailed by the War Department to instruct the enlisted men, has been most satisfactory.

RECOMMENDATIONS.

I have the honor to make the following recommendations: That another mess pavilion be built at Camp Glenn of sufficient size to accommodate 14 company organizations; that the water supply be increased to be adequate for the necessities of a brigade of infantry; that driveways and walkways be laid off in company streets and around the grounds at Camp Glenn and covered with oyster shells, macadam or hard clay, and made suitable for walking and necessary wagon service in camp. As it is now after a few days in camp the sand becomes very deep, heavy and unsanitary.

That store room for quartermaster's, subsistence and ordnance supplies be built to properly handle and care for this property.

That the appropriation for the North Carolina National Guard be increased so as to allow $50 per annum to company and division commanders for expenses in carrying out the duties of their offices and $50 per annum be allowed company quartermaster sergeants for caring for government property and company quarters.

That the sum of twenty-five hundred dollars per annum additional appropriation be allowed for the Naval Brigade to defray expenses of transportation, subsistence and maintenance of ship during the summer cruise.

APPROPRIATIONS.

Federal appropriations for the organized militia of this State for 1911 is as follows:

Arms, equipment and camp purposes	$35,210.14
Promotion of rifle practice	11,736.71
Equipment and ammunition	30,161.84

In addition to above mentioned Federal allotment the allowance for pay, subsistence and transportation for an encampment for a period of twelve days each year for the Coast Artillery Corps is paid by the United States out of special funds provided for the coast defense service.

The U. S. Navy Department has loaned the State two vessels, U. S. S. *Elfrida* and the *Dupont* for the instruction of our Naval Brigade. Nearly all the cost of maintenance for these vessels is borne by the Federal government.

Due to the splendid administration of my predecessor, this report is almost an unbroken record of progress in every department of the service, yet it must be saddened by announcement of the loss by death of two of our best and most capable officers, Col. J. G. Hollingsworth, late Paymaster General, who died in hospital, Richmond, Va., September 5th, and Brigadier General J. F. Armfield, late Adjutant General, who died at his home in Statesville, October 12th. Suitable announcements of the decease of these officers were published in General Orders.

Both of these officers responded promptly to the call of the President for volunteers in the war with Spain, and served throughout the war with credit to themselves and to the State. While as soldiers they represented different types of men, yet they were alike in lofty patriotism, promptness, high sense of duty and cheerful obedience to orders; respectful to superiors in office, and considerate of inferiors; as citizens and as soldiers ever faithful and true. They have gone from amongst us, but the record of their lives will ever be an inspiration to the citizen soldiers of our State.

I desire to recommend that some suitable text-book setting forth the organization, aims and purposes of the military establishment of our State and the United States be taught in all our schools. I am prompted to make this recommendation because of the great lack of information on military matters by the general public.

It is desired in presenting this report in behalf of this Department and of the officers and enlisted men of the North Carolina National Guard to express grateful appreciation for the sincere interest you have taken and shown in everything which tended towards the welfare and improvement of the military and naval service of the State.

Very respectfully,

R. L. LEINSTER,
The Adjutant General.

Report of Quartermaster General

STATE OF NORTH CAROLINA,
OFFICE OF QUARTERMASTER GENERAL,
HENDERSON, December 31, 1910.

ADJUTANT GENERAL,
Raleigh, N. C.

SIR:—I have the honor to submit the annual report of the operations of the Quartermaster's Department for the year ending November 30, 1910.

For convenience the report is divided into the following:

Abstract A, serviceable property, 1st Regiment.
Abstract B, serviceable property, 2d Regiment.
Abstract C, serviceable property, 3d Regiment.
Abstract D, unserviceable property, 1st Regiment.
Abstract E, unserviceable property, 2d Regiment.
Abstract F, unserviceable property, 3d Regiment.
Abstract G, serviceable property, Coast Artillery Corps.
Abstract H, unserviceable property, Coast Artillery Corps.
Abstract I, statement of all property, both serviceable and unserviceable, for the three regiments and the Military Supply Depot, and the Coast Artillery Corps.

PROPERTY RETURNS.

The tardiness with which the officers submit annual returns absolutely precludes the possibility of the examination expected of this office prior to the rendition of the Quartermaster General's annual report. It is for this reason that I am unable to furnish the information desired in this connection at this time. I am enabled to state, however, that from the examination it has been possible to make, I find that the discrepancies noted are due generally to errors rather than to shortage. Attention will be called to the irregularities with a view to obtaining accurate information for future use and a report to your office.

INSURANCE.

General Orders No. 17, September 6, 1901, requiring the organizations to which State funds are appropriated, to insure the military property in their possession, is still in effect, and whilst the necessity for this requirement has not existed for several years past, owing to the fact that the orders have not been revoked, a few company commanders very properly acquit themselves of the obligation imposed by promptly forwarding their insurance policies to this office. Under the circumstances attending the matter of insurance, with especial reference to my former reports and recommendations, all of which have been officially promulgated to the Guard, I am not insensible to the fact that, even though the officers who keep up the insurance do so at a sacrifice and are deserving of commendation therefor, the others are not censurable for an apparent disobedience to orders.

When the order was issued the law provided that the cost of insurance should be a charge against company appropriations, but the militia law of 1903 increased the Federal appropriation to the Guard to the extent of advancing our resources to a considerable degree of self-protection, therefore, the need for insurance protection was correspondingly lessened. By reason of this the Legislature of 1904 repealed the insurance requirement in question. The Militia Act of 1908 removed the necessity for insurance on the property in the possession of the companies.

In view of the foregoing, together with the fact that to relieve the company appropriations of the cost of insurance premiums would in effect increase these appropriations, I respectfully recommend that General Orders No. 17, September 6, 1901, be revoked.

DEPARTMENT INSURANCE.

The property which would be destroyed by burning of a Company Armory could be replaced from the Military Supply Depot, and the Depot would, in turn, replenish by requisition against the credit to the appropriation to the State. The cost of a few such fires could be easily borne by either appropriation, or if necessary by both appropriations, consequently the possibility of inconvenience arising in a general way by reason of such fires as these is not apparent. On the other hand, so long as the general supply should consist of property equivalent in value to the amount of, at least, one or both annual appropriations it is imperative that our interests be protected by a reasonable amount of insurance. The approximate value of the property stored in the Military Supply Depot is $15,000, and at Camp Site (Camp Glenn), $45,000 to $50,000. On the former we have $5,250 insurance, and on the latter $6,325.

CAMP GLENN.

The plans of Colonel Ludlow provide for extensive grading. We have reached the point in the work of constructing and preparation where, if done at all, this grading must be done now. It is estimated that this work can be done for not less than $8,000 under contract. The amount is so great and the prospects of securing it so remotely possible that I have not seriously considered the attempt. However, it is important that the grounds should be graded and leveled so that the work may go ahead without unnecessary delay in preparing the soil, sowing grass, and building streets, etc., etc.

I respectfully recommend that arrangements be made for the grading to be done by convict labor. It would seem that such an arrangement could be easily made, and I desire to be of service in an endeavor to perfect same.

Respectfully,

FRANCIS A. MACON,

Quartermaster General, N. C. N. G.

ABSTRACT A.—SERVICEABLE PROPERTY, FIRST REGIMENT.

Serviceable Property as per Companies' Returns.	QUARTERMASTER'S SUPPLIES. Tableware and Cooking Utensils. Table Forks.	Table Knives.	Teaspoons.	Field Range, Complete.	Clothing. Blankets, Woolen.	Coats, Cotton Khaki.	Coats, Olive Drab.	Breeches, Khaki.	Breeches, Olive Drab.	Trousers, Khaki.	Trousers, Olive Drab.	Blouses, Blue.	Trousers, Blue.	Caps, Olive Drab.	Caps, Khaki.	Caps, Dress.
Major Fisst Infantry																
Company A, 1st Inf., Hickory					50	61	50	41	50			49	46	50		
Company B, 1st Inf., Dallas	49	52	53		53	55	55	110	55					55		
Company C, 1st Inf., [illegible]on					43	59	50	125	50			50	34	50		48
Company D, 1st Inf., Charlotte																
Company E, 1st Inf., Statesville					48	68	58	126	58			81	51	58		49
Company F, 1st Inf., [illegible]le					50	75	50	109	50			19	30	50		36
Company G, 1st Inf., Shelby					50	70	57	182	56			43	36	58		35
[illegible]y H, 1st Inf., Waynesville				1	51	56	50	105	50			45	52	50		47
Company I, 1st Inf., Mt Airy	53	53	53		53	75	50	53	50		50	54	51	50		52
Company K, 1st Inf., Asheville					49	80	50	120	50			60	38	50		47
Company L, 1st Inf., Concord					64	68	57	114			58	55	53	53		52
[illegible]y M, 1st Inf., High Point	1	1	1		88	72	50	8	45	47		50	60	50		50
Band, 1st Inf.	28	28			28	35	28	33	28			26	27	28		21
[illegible], 1st Regt.					16	9	6	8	7			8	6			9
Hospital Detachment					8	12	10	12	12	12		12	12		12	
Total	131	134	107	1	651	795	621	1,246	561	59	108	552	496	602	12	446

ABSTRACT A—CONTINUED.

QUARTERMASTER'S SUPPLIES.

CLOTHING.

Serviceable Property as per Companies' Returns.	Cap Ornaments.	Chevrons, Cloth, Pairs.							Chevrons for Field Uniforms, Pairs.				Gloves, Berlin, Pairs.	Hats, Campaign.	Hat Cords.	Leggings, Pairs.
		N. C. S. Colors and First Sergeants.	Sergeants.	Corporals.	Cooks.	Saddlers.	Service.	Signal.	N. C. S. Colors and 1st Sergeants.	Sergeants.	Corporals.	Cooks.				
Major First Infantry																
Company A, 1st Inf., Hickory	62		6	6						6	6			34	15	46
Company B, 1st Inf., Dallas	60		6	6	2								60	52	70	55
Company C, 1st Inf., Winston	50	1	5	6					2	10	12	4		56	42	58
Company D, 1st Inf., Charlotte																
Company E, 1st Inf., Statesville			6	6	2								80	47	50	52
Company F, 1st Inf., Asheville			6	6	2				1	5		2	50	60	50	50
Company G, 1st Inf., Shelby			1	4	6	2	1	2					9	55	52	60
Company H, 1st Inf., [illegible]			18	17	2								48	44	50	56
Company I, 1st Inf., Mt Airy	50		6	6	2									43	53	94
Company K, 1st Inf., Asheville	62	1	5	6	2									69	27	54
Company L, 1st Inf., Concord			6	6						6	6		58	58	51	58
Company M, 1st Inf., High Point		2	6	6					3	12	12	2	100	54	50	69
Band, 1st Inf.			6	8										31		33
Colonel 1st Regt.		16												10	9	9
Hospital D[illegible]													12	12		15
Total	284	20	77	83	18	2	1	2	6	39	36	8	417	625	519	709

ABSTRACT A—CONTINUED.

Serviceable Property as per Companies' Returns.	Quartermaster's Supplies.														
	Clothing.													Equipage.	
		Shirts.								Trouser Stripes, Pairs.					
	Ponchos.	Chambray.	Flannel, Heavy.	Flannel, Light.	Cooking Outfit, Co.	First Aid Pockets.	First Aid Pouches.	Housewives.	Overcoats, Blue.	Musicians.	N. C. S. and H. C.	Sergeants.	Corporals.	Axes.	Axe Helves.
Major First Infantry															
Company A, 1st Inf., Hickory	48	39		50	1	48	48	48						4	
Company B, 1st Inf., Dallas	49		55			1	59	58	43						
Company C, 1st Inf., Winston	45	17		50		48	48	48		1	1	5	6		
Company D, 1st Inf., [illegible]															
Company E, 1st Inf., Statesville	67	21				50	50	25							
Company F, 1st Inf., Asheville	50			50		50	50	50							
Company G, 1st Inf., Shelby	69			53		50	50	50						4	4
Company H, 1st Inf., Waynesville	45	20		53		50	50	50							
Company I, 1st Inf., Mount Airy	53	22	53		1	50	50	50							
Company K, 1st Inf., Asheville	41			47		45		44							
Company L, 1st Inf., [illegible]rd	57		61		1			58		2		6	6		
Company M, 1st Inf., High Point	53	48		56	1	50	50	50				6	6		
Band 1st Inf.	28			28				28							
Colonel 1st Regt.	12			23				1							
Hospital Detachment	12		12			12		12						2	
Total	629	167	181	410	4	454	455	572	43	3	1	17	18	10	4

ABSTRACT A—CONTINUED.

Serviceable Property as per Companies' Returns.	QUARTERMASTER'S SUPPLIES.																
	EQUIPAGE.																
						Books, Company.							Flags, etc.				
													Colors.				
	Axe Slings.	Barracks Bags.	Bed Sacks.	Bed Sheets.		Letters Received.	Order.	Index Received.	Letters Sent.	Index Sent.	Desks, Field.	Drums.	Belt and Sling.	Cases.	National.	Regi-mental.	Field Hospital.
Major First Infantry																	
Company A, 1st Inf., Hickory	4										1						
Company B, 1st Inf., Dallas											1						
Company C, 1st Inf., Winston											1						
Company D, 1st Inf., Charlotte																	
Company E, 1st Inf., Statesville							1	1	1	1	1						
Company F, 1st Inf., [illegible]le																	
Company G, 1st Inf., Shelby	4	3	5	15	1	1	1	1	1		1						
Company H, 1st Inf., Waynesville						1	1		1		1						
Company L 1st Inf., Mt Airy						1	1	1	1	1	1						
Company K, 1st Inf., Asheville						1			1		1						
Company L, 1st Inf., Concord						1		1	1		1						
Company M, 1st Inf., High Point											1						
Band, 1st Inf.												2					
Colonel, 1st Regt.													2	2	1	1	
Hospital Detachment															1		1
Total	8	3	5	15	1	5	4	4	6	2	10	2	2	2	2	1	1

ABSTRACT A—CONTINUED.

Serviceable Property as per Companies' Returns.	QUARTERMASTER'S SUPPLIES.														
	EQUIPAGE.														
	Shelter Tents, Halves.	Trumpets, with E. M. P.	Trumpet Cords and Tassels.	Trumpet Mouthpieces.	Whistles.	Shelter Tent Pins.	2 foot Folding Rules.	Hand Axes with Carriers.	Pick Mattocks with Carriers.	Intrenching Shovels with Carriers.	Wire Cutters.	Collar Ornaments.	Barracks Cleaning Rod.	Web Belts, Revolver.	Blanket Bag Straps.
Major First Infantry															
Company A, 1st Inf., Hickory	84	2	1												
Company B, 1st Inf., Dallas			2	1											
Company C, 1st Inf., [illegible]	48	2	2	2											
Company D, 1st Inf., Charlotte															
Company E, 1st Inf., Statesville	25		4	4											
Company F, 1st Inf., Asheville	56	2	2												
Company G, 1st Inf., Shelby	57					569									
Company H, 1st Inf., Waynesville	50	3	1	3											
Company I, 1st Inf., Mount Airy	50	2	2	2											
Company K, 1st Inf., Asheville	48	1			1	1	4	6	18	1	120	10	3	1	1
Company L, 1st Inf., Concord	58	2	2												
Company M, 1st Inf., High Point	50	2	2												
Band, 1st Inf.	1														
[illegible] 1st Regt.	8														
Hospital Detachment															
Total	535	16	18	12	1	570	4	6	18	1	120	10	3	1	1

ABSTRACT A—CONTINUED.

Serviceable Property as per Companies' Returns.	QUARTERMASTER'S SUPPLIES.														
		Musical Instruments and Supplies.													
	Sight Covers.	Cymbals, Pairs.	Drums, Bass.	Flutes.	Piccolos.	Triangles.	Music Stands.	Drum Major Baton.	E flat Bass.	B flat Barritone.	Saxaphone.	Helicon.	Altos.	Oboe.	Trumpets.
Major First Infantry															
Company A, 1st Inf., Hickory															
Company B, 1st Inf., Dallas															
Company C, 1st Inf., [illegible]															
Company D, 1st Inf., [illegible]															
Company E, 1st Inf., [illegible]															
Company F, 1st Inf., Asheville								3	2						
Company G, 1st Inf., [illegible]															
Company H, 1st Inf., [illegible]															
Company I, 1st Inf., [illegible]															
Company K, 1st Inf., Asheville	26							2	51	50	50	50	50	50	1,000
Company L, 1st Inf., [illegible]															
Company M, 1st Inf., High Point															
Band, 1st Inf.		1	1	2	1	3	1	1	2	2	1		4	1	2
[illegible], 1st Regt.								1	1						
Hospital D[illegible]															
Total	26	1	1	2	1	3	1	7	56	52	51	50	54	51	1,002

ABSTRACT A—CONTINUED.

Serviceable Property as per Companies' Returns.	QUARTERMASTER'S SUPPLIES.														
	MUSICAL INSTRUMENTS AND SUPPLIES.														
	Cornets.	Clarionets, B flat.	Clarions, E flat.	Regulation, Army.	Regulation, Malitia.	Regulation, National Guard.	Drill Regulation, Infantry.	Drill Regulation, Coast Artillery.	Drill Regulation, Field Artillery.	Field Service Regulation.	Firing Regulation, Small Arms.	Manual of Guard Duty.	Manual of Pay Department.	Manual Q. M. Department.	Manual Subsistence Department.
Major First Infantry				1		1	1			1					
Company A, 1st Inf., Hickory				1			3			1	3	1			
Company B, 1st Inf., Dallas					1	3	3			9	3	3			
Company C, 1st Inf., [illegible]				1	1	1	3			1	3				
Company D, 1st Inf., [illegible]															
Company E, 1st Inf., [illegible]				1	1	1	4			1	1				
Company F, 1st Inf., Asheville				1	1	1	3			3	5	1			
Company G, 1st Inf., Shelby															
Company H, 1st Inf., [illegible]															
Company H, 1st Inf., Mt Airy					1	1	3			3	1				
Company K, 1st Inf., Asheville		1,000	6,000	1	1	3	3			1	4	1			
Company L, 1st Inf., Concord				1		3					1				
Company M, 1st Inf., High Point				1	1	2	3			3	3	3			
Band 1st Inf.	2	3	1												
Colonel 1st Regt.				6	6	5	7				4	1	1	1	4
Hospital D[illegible]t				1	1		12	10	12		11	6	11	8	11
Total	2	1,003	6,001	15	14	21	45	10	12	23	39	17	12	9	15

ABSTRACT A—Continued.

Serviceable Property as per Companies' Returns.	Inf. Manual Private.	Map Reading.	Bayonet Exercise.	Shovels.	Picks.	Axes.	Rule.	Pliers.	Picks, Mattocks and Carriers.	Intrenching Shovels and Carriers.	Wire Cutters.	Rule.	Pans.	Potato Mashers.	Spoons, Large Cooking	Pans, Small.
	QUARTERMASTER'S SUPPLIES.															
Major First Regimznt																
Company A, 1st Inf., Hickory																
Company B, 1st Inf., Dallas																
Company C, 1st Inf., [illegible]	12	3	1													
Company D, 1st Inf., [illegible]																
Company E, 1st Inf., Statesville																
Company F, 1st Inf., [illegible]	1	2	2	18	6	3	1	1								
Company G, 1st Inf., Shelby													1	2	1	1
Company H, 1st Inf., Waynesville																
Company I, 1st Inf., Mt Airy																
Company K, 1st Inf., Asheville																
Company L, 1st Inf., Concord																
Company M, 1st Inf., High Point	12								4	5	15	3	1			
Band, 1st Inf.,																
Colonel, 1st Regt.	15	15	2													
Hospital Detachment	1	1														
Total	41	21	5	18	6	3	1	1	4	5	15	3	2	2	1	1

ABSTRACT A—CONTINUED.

Serviceable Property as per Companies' Returns.	QUARTERMASTER'S SUPPLIES. Ice Hook.	Coffe Pot.	Dippers.	Meat Chopper.	Sifters.	Pots.	ORDNANCE AND ORDNANCE STORES. Rifles, Gallery, Cal. 22.	Rifles, Cal. 30.	Bayonets.	Bayonet Scabbards.	Gun Slings.	Rifle Cartridge Belts.	Rifle Cartridge Belt Suspenders.
Major First Infantry													
Company A, 1st Inf., [illegible]							2	51	50	50	50	50	50
Company B, 1st Inf., Dallas							2	50	50	50	50	50	50
Company C, 1st Inf., [illegible]							2	50	50	50	50	50	50
Company D, 1st Inf., [illegible]													
Company E, 1st Inf., [illegible]							2	50	50	50	50	50	50
Company F, 1st Inf., Asheville							2	50	50	50	50	50	50
Company G, 1st Inf., Shelby	1	2	1	1	1	2	2	50	50	50	50	50	50
Company H, 1st Inf., Waynesville							2	50	50	50	50	50	50
Company I, 1st Inf., Mt. [illegible]							2	50	50	50	50	50	50
Company K, 1st Inf., Asheville													
Company L, 1st Inf., Concord							2	56	56	56	56	56	56
Company M, 1st Inf., High Point							2	49	49	49	49	49	50
Band, 1st Inf.													
[illegible] 1st Regt.								1					
Hospital D[illegible]ment													
Total	1	2	1	1	1	2	20	507	505	505	505	505	503

ABSTRACT A—CONRINUED.

Serviceable Property as per Companies' Returns.	ORDNANCE AND CRDNANCE STORES.														
	CARTRIDGES.														
	Rifle, Ball, Cal. 30.	Rifle, Blank, Cal. 30.	Guard, Cal. 30.	Gallery, Cal. 22.	Revolver, Cal. 38.	Gun Caps.	Frost, Sight Arm.	Target Outfit.	Revolver, Cal. 38.	Revolver Holsters.	Clips.	Canteens.	Canteen Straps.	Haversacks.	Haversack Hooks.
Major First Infantry															
Company A, 1st Inf., Hickory	2,400	500		8,000	300				3	3		48	48	51	51
Company B, 1st Inf., Dallas	1,400			2,500	100	1	1	50	3	3		55	55	52	
Company C, 1st Inf., Winston	600	75	400	1,000		1	1		3	3		43	50	49	
Company D, 1st Inf.,															
Company E, 1st Inf., Statesville	400	1, 00		1,000					3	3		50	83	58	60
Company F, 1st Inf., Asheville	1,360	1,000	460	1,000					3	3		49	50	50	120
Company G, 1st Inf., Shelby	772	3,382	480	1, 00	5	21	14	1			63			59	59
Company H, 1st Inf.,	50	1,030	800		3,850				1	2		50	70	50	
Company I, 1st Inf., Mt Airy	2,460	520	280						3	3		53	50	44	50
Company K, 1st Inf., Asheville									3	3		48	42	50	10
Company L, 1st Inf., Concord	1,200			5,500	200				3	3		58		57	116
Company M, 1st Inf., High	1,200	500	460	2,000					3	3		58		58	150
Band, 1st Inf.		120			20							27	27	28	28
Colonel, 1st									12	12	4	16	8	9	8
Hospital D															
Total	11,892	8,127	2,880	22,000	4,475	23	13	51	40	41	70	560	483	615	652

ABSTRACT A—CONTINUED.

Serviceable Property as per Companies' Returns.	ORDNANCE AND ORDNANCE STORES.														
	Tin Cups.	Knives.	Forks.	Spoons.	Meat Cans.	Saber, Officers.	Saber Belt, Officers.	Saber Belt Slings.	Blanket Roll Straps.	Arm Chest.	Screw Drivers.	Saddles, complete.	Bridles.	Saddle Blankets.	Spurs, pairs.
Major First Infantry															
[illegible] A, 1st Inf., [illegible]	45	48	48	48	49	3	3	3		5	4				
[illegible] B, 1st Inf., Dallas	53	52	49	51	53	2	2		55						
[illegible] C, 1st Inf., [illegible]	50	48	50	48	48				47	5	10				
[illegible] D, 1st Inf., [illegible]															
[illegible] E, 1st Inf., [illegible]	50	50	52	62	59	3	3		5	10					
[illegible] F, 1st Inf., Asheville	46	50	50	50	50	3	3		50	5					
[illegible] G, 1st Inf., Shelby	60	54				2	1		50	5	10				
[illegible] H, 1st Inf., [illegible]	50	50	55	54	56	3	3	3	50	5	10				
[illegible] I, 1st Inf., [illegible]	53	53	53	53	53	2	2	2	50	5	3				
[illegible] K, 1st Inf., Asheville	50	50	51	50	50	3	3	3	50	5					
[illegible] L, 1st Inf., [illegible]	58	58	58	58	58	2	2	2	58	5					
[illegible] M, 1st Inf., High Point	44	67	67	58	54	3	3	2	50	5					
[illegible], 1st Inf.	28	28	28	28	28				27						
[illegible], 1st [illegible]	16	16	16	16	16	6	6					16	11	2	8
[illegible]												1	1		
Total	603	624	577	576	574	32	31	15	492	55	37	17	12	2	8

ABSTRACT A—Continued.

Serviceable Property as per Companies' Returns.	ORDNANCE AND ORDNANCE STOEE.															
	Non. Com. Swords.	Field Range.	Hand Axes.	Pickers and Covers.	Shovel and Covers.	Wire Cutters.	Folding Rules.	Officers Field Desk.	Trenching Shovels.	First Aid Pockets.	Pick Mattocks.	Ladle.	Pair Ice Hooks.	Spoons.	Boiler.	Copper Pot.
Major First Infantry																
Company A, 1st Inf., [illegible]																
Company B, 1st Inf., Dallas																
Company C, 1st Inf., [illegible]n		1	4	6	18	3	1									
Company D, 1st Inf., Charlotte																
Company E, 1st Inf., Statesville												1	1	1	1	1
Company F, 1st Inf., Asheville																
Company G, 1st Inf., [illegible]								1								
Company H, 1st Inf., Waynesville																
Company I, 1st Inf., Mt. Airy																
Company K, 1st Inf., [illegible]																
Company L, 1st Inf., [illegible]		1	4			3			18	58	6					
Company M, 1st Inf., High Point																
Band, 1st Inf.		1														
Col., 1st Regt.	4															
Hospital Detachment																
Total	4	3	8	6	18	6	1	1	18	53	6	1	1	1	1	1

ABSTRACT A—CONTINUED.

Serviceable Property as per Companies' Returns.	ORDNANCE AND ORDNANCE STORES.															
	Potato Masher.	Pans.	Dipper.	Knife.	Tifles.	Pie cans.	Rules.	Hand Axes.	Carriers.	Pick Mattocks.	Carriers.	Intrenching Shovels.	Carriers.	Wire Cutters.	Box Metal and Folding Holders.	Barracks Cleaning Rods.
Major First Infantry																
Company A, 1st Inf., Hickory																
Company B, 1st Inf., Dallas																
Company C, 1st Inf., [illegible]																
Company D, 1st Inf., [illegible]																
Company E, 1st Inf., [illegible]	1	1	1	1	1	2	1	4	4	5	5	15	15	3	1	12
Company F, 1st Inf., Asheville																
Company G, 1st Inf., Shelby																
Company H, 1st Inf., Waynesville																
Company I, 1st Inf., [illegible]																
Company K, 1st Inf., [illegible]																
Company L, 1st Inf., Concord																
Company M, 1st Inf., High Point																
Band, 1st Inf.																
Colonel, 1st Regt.																
Hospital Detachment																
Total	1	1	1	1	1	2	1	4	4	5	5	15	15	3	1	12

ABSTRACT B.—SERVICEABLE PROPERTY, SECOND REGIMENT.

Serviceable Property as per Companies' Returns.	Quartermaster's Supplies. Tableware and Cooking Utensils. Table Forks.	Table Knives.	Teaspoons.	Field Range.	Clothing. Belts, Waist.	Blankets, Woolen.	Coats, Cotton Khaki.	Cotas, Olive Drab.	Breeches, Khaki.	Breeches, Olive Drab.	Trousers, Khaki.	Trousers, Olive Drab.	Blouses, Blue.	Trousers, Blue.	Caps, Olive Drab.
SECOND INFANTRY:															
[illegible] Second Infantry						2									
[illegible] A, Tarboro	50	48				40	47	50	100	50		50	61	60	50
[illegible] B, Kinston						48	110	60		60	75		58	73	61
[illegible] C, [illegible]	55	55	55			48	59	60	57	60					60
[illegible] D, [illegible]						68	62	58	129	60					57
[illegible] E, [illegible]						64	104	60	177	60			64	60	60
[illegible] F, Fayetteville	27	25	43			40	58	50			46	50		50	50
[illegible] G, [illegible]						51	64	53	85	53	51		66	74	53
[illegible] H, [illegible]						60	73	65	100	65			59	50	65
[illegible] I, [illegible]	53	47	56			43	65	48	120	48			64	45	48
Company K, Wilson	45	45	60			33	71	50	53	50	4	1	74	75	50
[illegible] L, Lumber Bridge	60	60	60			45	50	65	50	65			50	40	65
[illegible] M, [illegible]	2	4		1	5	52	57	46	66	39					51
Band, Second Infantry	23	14				41	13	28	15	28	15	26	16	15	28
Total	315	298	274	1	5	637	838	693	952	638	191	127	512	542	698

ABSTRACT B—CONTINUED.

Serviceable Property as per Companies' Returns.	QUARTERMASTER'S SUPPLIES. — CLOTHING.														
			Chevrons, Cloth, Pairs.					Chevrons for Field Uniform, Pairs.							
	Caps, Dress.	Cap Ornaments.	N. C. S. Colors and 1st Sergeants.	Sergeants.	Corporals.	Cooks.	Saddlers.	Sergeants.	Corporals.	Cooks.	Gloves, Berlin, Pairs.	Hats, Campaign.	Hat Cords.	Hat Ornaments.	Leggins, Pairs.
SECOND INFANTRY:															
M[illegible]r Second [illegible]y												1			
Company A, Tarboro	45	50		6	4	1						38	43		38
Company B, Kinston	47			1	5	6	2					50	52		51
Company C, [illegible]y M[illegible]t				6	6	2		6	6	2	60	60			63
Company D, [illegible]o	45			6	6	2						35			60
Company E, [illegible]o	62	10										74	56		91
Company F, Fayetteville				6	6									50	44
Company G, [illegible]n	61			1	5	6	2								58
Company H, [illegible]n	58		1	5	6	2						15	15		60
Company I, [illegible]n	50			6	6	2						45			54
Company K, [illegible]n	45	50		4	4	2		4	4	2		48	50		47
Company L, [illegible]r Bridge	50	100		15	18	2						50	20	12	60
Company M, [illegible]o				12	10	4						51	32		98
Band, Second [illegible]y	16			4								11	5		30
Total	479	210	1	72	76	29	4	10	10	4	60	478	273	62	754

ABSTRACT B—CONTINUED.

Serviceable Property as per Companies' Returns.	QUARTERMASTER'S SUPPLIES.														
	CLOTHING.													EQUIPAGE.	
		Shirts.									Trouser Stripes, Pairs.				
	Ponchos.	Chambray.	Flannel, Heavy.	Flannel, Light.	Gingham.	Cooking Outfit, Co.	First Aid Pockets.	First Aid Pouches.	Housewives.	Overcoats, Blue.	Sergeants.	Corporals.	Cartridge Belt.	Axes.	Axe Helves.
SECOND INFANTRY:															
Mr Second Hy	1												1		
Gy A, aBo	32			45			43		38						
Gy B, Kinston	51						50	50	50						
Gy C, Hy Mt	60	60	60			1	55	55	55					4	4
Gy D, Go	31	54		60		1	43	43	45						
Gy E, Go	62	80	58				58	58	58					4	4
Gy F, e	12	6				1	53		53						
Gy G, n	48		53				50	50	50					4	4
Gy H, Gn	46	60		53		1	61	61	61	23					
Gy I, n	20	34		42	35	1	48	48	46					6	6
Gy K, n	30	45	45			1	48		33					2	2
Gy L, Lumber Bridge	55	35			33		56	56	58		5	8			
Gy M, o	56	44					48	48	48					3	3
Band, Second y	20			18			20	20	20						
Total	524	418	216	218	68	6	638	489	615	23	5	8	1	23	23

ABSTRACT B—CONTINUED.

Serviceable Property as per Companies' Returns.	QUARTERMASTER'S SUPPLIES. Equipage. Axe Slings.	Bed Sacks.	Books, Company. Letters Received.	Books, Company. Order.	Desks, Field.	Drums, Etc. Drums.	Drums, Etc. Heads, Snare.	Drums, Etc. Sticks, Pairs.	Flags, Etc. Colors. Belt and Sling.	Flags, Etc. Colors. National.	Mess Pans.	Stencil, Alphabet, sets.	Stencil, Numbers, sets.	Shelter Tents, Halves.	Trumpets, with E. M. P.
SECOND INFANTRY:															
Major Second [illegible]y															
Company A, [illegible]o			1		1									40	2
Company B, [illegible]n														41	
Company C, [illegible]y [illegible]t	4													60	2
Company D, [illegible]o			1	3	1									60	3
Company E, [illegible]o	4				1									58	4
Company F, Fayetteville														44	1
Company G, [illegible]n	4				1									60	
Company H, [illegible]n														62	2
Company I, [illegible]n		6									54			41	
Company K, [illegible]	2				1	1	1	1	1	1		1	1	32	
Company L, [illegible]r Bridge					1									40	
Company M, [illegible]o	4				1										
[illegible], [illegible] [illegible]y											20			27	
Total	18	6	2	3	7	1	1	1	1	1	74	1	1	565	14

ABSTRACT B—CONTINUED.

Serviceable Property as per Companies' Returns.	QUARTERMASTER'S SUPPLIES. Equipage.											Musical Instruments and Supplies.			
	Trumpet Cords and Tassels.	Trumpet Mouthpieces.	Whistles.	Intrenching Rule.	Wire Cutters.	Hand Axes and Carriers.	Pick Mattocks and Carriers.	Intrenching Shovels and Carriers.	Aiken Target.	Field Ranges.	Khaki Shirts.	Cymbals, Pairs.	Drums, Bass.	Drums, Snare.	Triangle.
SECOND INFANTRY:															
M[illegible]jor Second [illegible]y															
[illegible]y A, [illegible]o	2	2													
[illegible]y B, [illegible]n	2										2				
[illegible]y C, Rocky M[illegible]t.	2														
[illegible]y D, [illegible]o	3	2													
[illegible]y E, [illegible]o	3	3		1	3										
Company F, [illegible]e	2														
[illegible]y G, [illegible]n															
[illegible]y H, [illegible]n	2	2													
[illegible]y I, [illegible]n															
[illegible]y K, [illegible]n		2	1											1	
[illegible]y L, [illegible]r Bridge				1	3	4	7	21	1	1					
[illegible]y M, Wadesboro															
Band, Second [illegible]y												1	1	1	1
To[illegible]al	16	11	1	2	6	4	7	21	1	1	2	1	1	2	1

ABSTRACT B—CONTINUED.

Serviceable Property as per Companies' Returns.	QUARTERMASTER'S SUPPLIES.														
	Musical Instruments and Supplies.														
	Trombones.	Bags.	Cases.	Bugles.	Cords.	Music Stands.	Regulation, Army.	Regulation, Militia.	Regulation, National Guard.	Drill Regulation, Infantry.	Field Service Regulation.	Firing Regulation, Snall Arms.	Manual of Guard Duty.	Officers Manual.	Map Reading.
SECOND INFANTRY:															
[illegible]								1	1		1			1	1
[illegible]y A, [illegible]o							1	1	1	3	3	3			
[illegible]y B, [illegible]n							1	1	4	2	2	3	2		
[illegible]y C, Rocky [illegible]t							1		3	3	3	3	3		
[illegible]y D, [illegible]o							1	1	3	4		3	4		
[illegible]y E, [illegible]o							1	1	3	3		3	3		
[illegible]y F, [illegible]e								1	1	3	1	3	2		
[illegible]y G, Washington							1	1	2	1	3	1	1		
[illegible]y H, [illegible]n							1	1		4	3	3	3		
[illegible]y I, [illegible]n				3	2		1		1	1	1	1	1		
[illegible]y K, [illegible]n							15		1	10	2	2	10		
[illegible]y L, Lumber [illegible]e							1		1	3	3	3	3		
[illegible]y M, [illegible]o															
Band, Second Infantry	2	2	7			3									
Total	2	2	7	3	2	3	24	8	21	37	22	28	32	1	1

ABSTRACT B—CONTINUED.

Serviceable Property as per Companies' Returns.	QUARTERMASTER'S SUPPLIES.												ORDNANCE AND ORDNANCE STORES.		
	Correspondence Book.	Descriptive and Property Book.	Sick Report.	Descriptive Book.	Manual Army Cook.	Drill Report.	U. S. Magazine Rifle.	Company Order Book.	Map Reading.	Minor Tactics.	Bayonet Exercise.	First Sergeant's Book.	Rifles, Gallery, Cal. 22.	Rifles, Cal. 30.	Bayonets.
SECOND INFANTRY:															
Major [illegible]														1	
Company A, Tarboro													2	50	60
Company B, Kinston	1	1	2	2	2	1	3	3	3	3	1	1	2	56	57
Company C, [illegible]													2	55	55
Company D, [illegible]															
Company E, [illegible]													2	61	60
Company F, [illegible]														58	58
Company G, [illegible]													2	49	50
Company H, [illegible]													2	61	60
Company I, [illegible]													2	50	49
Company K, [illegible]													2	50	50
Company L, [illegible]													2	59	58
Company M, [illegible]													2	61	59
Band, Second Infantry															
Total	1	1	2	2	2	1	3	3	3	3	1	1	20	611	616

ABSTRACT B—CONTINUED.

Serviceable Property as per Companies' Returns.	ORDNANCE AND ORDNANCE STORES.													
					CARTRIDGES.									
	Bayonet Scabbards.	Gun Slings.	Rifle Cartridge Belts.	Rifle Cartridge Belt Suspenders.	Rifle Ball, Cal. 30.	Rifle, Blank, Cal. 30.	Guard, Cal. 30.	Gallery, Cal. 22.	Revolver, Blank, Cal. 30.	Revolver, Cal. 38.	Revolver Holsters.	Canteens.	Canteen Straps.	Haversacks.
SECOND INFANTRY:														
Major Second Infantry									1	1	1	1	1	1
Company A, Tarboro	50	50	50	50	400	200	240	200		3	3	44	44	48
Company B, [illegible]	57	56	57	57	1,200	2,000	460	4,600		2	2	52	48	49
Company C, Rocky Mt.	55	55	55	55	1,200		286	4,000		3	3	60		45
Company D, Goldsboro														
Company E, [illegible]	60	62	58	60	2,400	1,000	320	3,100		3	3	62	6	60
Company F, [illegible]	58	49	58	58	500					3	3	61		52
Company G, [illegible]	50	49	50	50		3,000	480	4,000		4	4	52	22	62
Company H, [illegible]	60	60	60	60	500			1,000		3	3	60	60	53
Company I, [illegible]	47	50	47	43	332	2,193	194	2,550		3	3	39		53
Company K, [illegible]	50	50	50	50	300	450		1,000		3	3	55	50	75
Company L, Lumber Bridge	58	58	58	58	1,700		500			3	3	60		60
Company M, [illegible]	59	61	61	61			350	5,050		3	3	61	58	65
Band, Second Infantry												15	15	17
Total	604	600	604	602	8,532	8,843	2,830	27,300	1	34	34	622	304	640

ABSTRACT B—CONTINUED.

ORDNANCE AND ORDNANCE STORES.

Serviceable Property as per Companies' Returns.	Haversack Hooks.	Tin Cups.	Knives.	Forks.	Spoons.	Meat Cans.	Saber, Officer's.	Saber Belt, Officer's.	Saber Belt Slings.	Blanket Roll Straps.	Arm Chest.	Screw Drivers.	Handspikes, Maneuvering.	Saddles, complete.	Briddles.
SECOND INFANTRY:															
Major [illegible] Infantry	1	1	1	1	1	1				1				1	1
[Company] A, [illegible]	48	41	48	50	68	51	3	3	3		5	5			
[Company] B, [illegible]		68	51	49	71	59	2	2			6	2			
[Company] C, Rocky [illegible]		60				60	3	3	3	60	6	11			
[Company] D, [illegible]															
[Company] E, [illegible]		64			61	60	3	3		53	6				
[Company] F, [illegible]		21				62	3	3			7				
[Company] G, [illegible]		61	52	41	39	57	3	3	3	53	5	1			
[Company] H, [illegible]	120	60	60	60	60	60	3	3	3	60	6				
[Company] I, [illegible]	53	50					3	3	3						
[Company] K, [illegible]		42	46	45	60	51	3	2			5		6		
[Company] L, Lumber Bridge	60	58	60	60	60	60	3	3		38					
[Company] M, [illegible]	65	62	63	66	71	65	3	3	3			2			
[Band], Second Infantry	17	20	14	23	20	20									
Total	364	608	395	395	511	606	32	31	18	265	46	21	6	1	1

ABSTRACT B—CONTINUED.

Serviceable Property as per Companies' Returns.	ORDNANCE AND ORDNANCE STORES.														
	Target F. A. R · es.	Pairs Plyers.	Pick Mattocks.	Holders.	Shovels.	Shovel Holders.	Rifle Cleaning Racks.	Winder Targets.	Sight Covers.	Two-foot Folding Rule.	Hand Axes with Carriers.	Pick Mattocks with Carriers.	Intrenching Shovels with Carriers.	Wire Cutters.	Cartridge Belt Revolver Covers.
SECOND INFANTRY:															
M[illegible]r Second [illegible]y															
[illegible]y A, [illegible]o															
[illegible]y B, [illegible]n									11	1	4	5	15	3	2
[illegible]C, [illegible]y M[illegible]nt															
[illegible]y D, [illegible]o															
[illegible]y E, [illegible]o															
[illegible]y F, [illegible]le															
[illegible]y G, Washington															
[illegible]y H, Cl[illegible]n															
[illegible]y I, Edenton															
[illegible]y K, [illegible]n															
[illegible]y L, Lumber Bridge															
[illegible]y M, [illegible]o	2	2	4	5	4	5	13	1							
Band, Second Infantry															
Total	2	2	4	5	4	5	13	1	11	1	4	5	15	3	2

ABSTRACT C.—SERVICEABLE PROPERTY, THIRD REGIMENT.

Serviceable Property as per Companies' Returns.	Quartermaster's Supplies. Tableware and Cooking Utensils. Table Forks.	Table Knives.	Teaspoons.		Clothing. Bandages, Abdominal.	Belts, Waist.	Blankets, Woolen.	Coats, Cotton Khaki.	Coats, Olive Drab.	Breeches, Khaki.	Breeches, Olive Drab.	Trousers, Khaki.	Trousers, Olive Drab.	Blouses, Blue.	Trousers, Blue.
Major 3rd Inf.								2	1	2	1				1
Hospital Corps, 3d Inf.	10	10	9				14	17	10		10	17		15	13
Comp'y A, 3rd Inf., Lexington	51	50	51				50	98	50	90	50			50	45
Comp'y B, 3rd Inf., Raleigh						2	65	89	65	150	65			63	60
Comp'y C, 3rd Inf., [illegible]															
Comp'y D, 3rd Inf., Louisburg	41	37	45		53		70	54				130	54	66	65
Comp'y E, 3rd Inf., Oxford	7	10		2			49	74	50	106			49	63	55
Comp'y F, 3rd Inf., [illegible]	44	49	57				52	94	53	90	53			55	52
Comp'y G, 3rd Inf., Reidsville	43	43	43				42	97	45			144	45	81	68
Comp'y H, 3rd Inf., [illegible]	49	47					50	75	49	110	49				65
Comp'y I, 3rd Inf., Burlington							57	100	58	138	58			65	55
Comp'y K, 3rd Inf., [illegible]	45	47	49				50	48	55	89	55				
Comp'y L, 3rd Inf., Thomasville	50	40	40				49	50	50	60	50				51
Comp'y M, 3rd Inf., Durham	58	58	58				50	90	50	116	56			52	55
Band, 3rd Inf.							21	29	28	36	28	28	28	28	28
Colonel 3rd Inf.							18	8	5	5	33	7	5	4	4
Total	392	391	352	2	53	2	637	925	569	992	503	326	181	542	617

ABSTRACT C—CONTINUED.

Serviceable Property as per Companies' Returns.	Caps, Olive Drab.	Caps, Dress.	Cap Ornaments.	Chevrons, Cloth, Pairs.					Chevrons for Field Uniforms, Pairs.					Gauntlets, Gold Lace.	Gloves, Berlin, Pairs.	Hats, Campaign.
				N. C. S. Colors and 1st Sergeants.	Sergeants.	Corporals.	Cooks.	Saddlers.	N. C. S. Colors and 1st Sergeants.	Sergeants.	Corporals.	Corporals, Lance.	Cooks.			
Major 3rd Inf.		1	1		4										1	1
Hospital Corps, 3rd Inf.	12	14	12		3	3									12	11
Company A, 3rd Inf., [illegible]	50	45	50		12	12	2									46
Company B, 3rd Inf., [illegible]	65	65			2	2										
Company C, 3rd Inf., [illegible]																
Company D, 3rd Inf., [illegible]	54	44	52													53
Company E, 3rd Inf., Oxford	50	57		1	5	6										57
Company F, 3rd Inf., [illegible]	53	52			1	5	5	2	1	5	5		2			62
Company G 3rd Inf., Reidsville	45	49	62		6	6	2								40	44
Company H, 3rd Inf., [illegible]	49			3	15	18	2									62
Company I, 3rd Inf., Burlington	58		63												50	51
Company K, 3rd Inf., [illegible]	58			1	5	6	2								48	58
Company L, 3rd Inf., [illegible]			60		2	6	2									48
Company M, 3rd Inf., [illegible]	50									6	6	1	2			46
Band, 3rd Inf.	28															25
Colonel 3rd Inf.	3	32												5		4
Total	575	359	300	5	56	64	15	2	1	11	11	1	4	5	151	568

ABSTRACT C—CONTINUED.

Serviceable Property as per Companies' Returns.	QUARTERMASTER'S SUPPLIES. Clothing. Hat Cords.	Hat Numbers.	Leggings, Pairs.	Mittens, Canvas, Pairs.	Ponchos.	Shirts. Chambray.	Shirts. Flannel, Heavy.	Shirts. Flannel, Light.	Shirts. Gingham.	Shirts. Muslin.	Cooking Outfit, Co.	First Aid Pockets.	First Aid Pouches.	Housewives.	Overcoats, Blue.	Musicians' Trouser Stripes, pairs.
Major 3rd Inf.	1		1		1	1	1						9			
[illegible] [illegible]s, 3rd Inf.			17		6	12			12							
Company A, 3rd Inf., Lexington	50		59		48	31							50	50	50	
Company B, 3rd Inf., Ral[illegible]	56		65		58	74	40	62					58	58	58	
Company C, 3rd Inf., Henderson																
Company D, 3rd Inf., Louisburg	60		56		48	104		52			1	50	50	50		1
Company E, 3rd Inf., [illegible]rd	37		54	48	38	50	51				1	48		48	13	2
Company F, 3rd Inf., Franklinton	63		69		59	58	42				1	50	50	50		
Company G, 3rd Inf., Reidsville			81		46	55						45	45	45		
Company R, 3rd Inf., [illegible]	41		62			16	15					50	50	50		
Company I, 3rd Inf., [illegible]	55	48	101		52	60	50			30	1	58	58	58		
Company K, 3rd Inf., [illegible]	53	43	103		55	80	38				1	50	50	50	52	
Company L, 3rd Inf., Thomasville	48		50		50	50	50				1	50	50	50		
Company M, 3rd Inf., Durham	50		50		43	33	46				1	50		49		1
Band, 3rd Inf.			28		22							28		28		
Colonel 3rd Inf.			7		27	2			2							
Total	519	96	804	48	558	626	333	114	14	30	7	479	470	586	173	4

ABSTRACT C—CONTINUED.

Serviceable Property as per Companies' Returns.	QUARTERMASTER'S SUPPLIES.														
	CLOTHING.		EQUIPAGE.												
	Trouser Stripes, pairs.														
	Sergeants.	Corporals.	2-foot Rule.	Axes.	Axe Helves.	Axe Slings.	Barrack Bags.	Bed Sacks.	Bed Sheets.	Sets of Entrenching Tools.	Order Books, Regimental.	Letters Received.	Desks, Field.	Drums.	Belt and Sling.	Cases.
Major 3rd Inf.	1												1			
Hospital Corps, 3rd Inf.				2				24								
Company A, 3rd Inf., [illegible]n				4	4	4		63					1			
Company B, 3rd Inf., [illegible]h				1	1			48								
Company C, 3rd Inf., [illegible]n																
Company D, 3rd Inf., Louisburg	6	6												1		
Company E, 3rd Inf., Oxford	6	6		4	1	4	5	15	13				1			
Company F, 3rd Inf., [illegible]n				1	1			32					1	1		
Company G, 3rd Inf., [illegible]e																
Company H, 3rd Inf., [illegible]n													1			
Company I, 3rd Inf., [illegible]n				1							1	1	1			
Company K, 3rd Inf., [illegible]n				4		4	7	21	3			1	1			
Company L, 3rd Inf., Thomasville			1							2			1			
Company M, 3rd Inf., Durham	8	8		4	4	4							1			
Band, 3rd Inf.				1				24								
Colonel 3rd Inf.														1	2	2
Total	21	20	1	22	11	16	12	227	16	2	1	2	9	3	2	2

ABSTRACT C—CONTINUED.

Serviceable Property as per Companies' Returns.	QUARTERMASTER'S SUPPLIES.															
	EQUIPAGE.															
	National Colors.	Regimental Colors.	Field Hospital Flag.	Mattress Covers.	Mess Pans.	Music Pouches.	Shelter Tents, Halves.	Trumpets, with E. M. P.	Trumpet Cords and Tassels.	Trumpet Mouthpeice.	Whistles.	2-Ft. Folding Rules.	Hand Axes with Carriers.	Pick Mattocks with Carriers.	Intrenching Shovels with Carriers.	Wire Cutters.
Major 3rd Inf.																
Hospital Corps, 3rd Inf.	1		1	12	12											
Company A, 3rd Inf., [illegible]					51		40	3	3							
Company B, 3rd Inf., [illegible]							54	2	2	2						
Company C, 3rd Inf., Henderson																
Company D, 3rd Inf., Louisburg				41	46				1							
Company E, 3rd Inf., [illegible]							66	2	1							
Company F, 3rd Inf., [illegible]					52		44	2	1	2	1	1	4	5	15	3
Company G, 3rd Inf., Reidsville							21	2	2							
Company H, 3rd Inf., [illegible]					88		44									
Company I, 3rd Inf., [illegible]							44	2		2						
Company K, 3rd Inf., [illegible]									2	4						
Company L, 3rd Inf., [illegible]							50	2	2							
Company M, 3rd Inf., Durham					50		50	3								
Band, 3rd Inf.						28	24									
Colonel 3rd Inf.		1														
Total	1	1	1	53	299	23	437	18	14	10	1	1	4	5	15	3

ABSTRACT C—CONTINUED.

Serviceable Property as per Companies' Returns.	QUARTERMASTER'S SUPPLIES. Equipage.							Musical Instruments and Supplies.								
	Canteen, Haversacks and Straps.	Canteen Strap Web.	Old Web Revolver Belts.	Tan Leather Belts.	Poles.	Pins.	Field Desk.	Cymbals, Pairs.	Drums, Bass.	Drums, Snare.	Flutes.	Piccolos.	Triangles.	Trombones.	Clarinets.	Cornets.
Major 3rd Infantry																
[illegible] Corps, 3rd. Inf.																
Company A, 3rd Inf., [illegible]																
Company B, 3rd Inf., [illegible]																
Company C, 3rd Inf., [illegible]																
Company D, 3rd Inf., [illegible]																
Company E, 3rd Inf., [illegible]																
Company F, 3rd Inf., [illegible]	10	52	3	46	54	270	1									
Company G, 3rd Inf., Reidsville																
Company H, 3rd Inf., [illegible]																
Company I, 3rd Inf., [illegible]																
Company K, 3rd Inf., [illegible]																
Company L, 3rd Inf., [illegible]																
Company M, 3rd Inf., Durham																
Band, 3rd Inf.								1		3		1	1	3	8	7
Col[illegible] 3rd Inf.								1	1	2	1	1	1	1	12	28
Total	10	52	3	46	54	270	1	2	1	5	1	2	2	4	20	35

ABSTRACT C—CONTINUED.

Serviceable Property as per Companies' Returns.	QUARTERMASTER'S SUPPLIES.															
	MUSICAL INSTRUMENTS AND SUPPLIES.															
	Tuba.	Baritone.	Altos.	Saxaphone.	Helicon.	Oboe.	Shakos.	Baton.	Regulation, Army.	Regulation Militia.	Regulation, National Guard.	Drill Regulation, Infantry.	Field Service Regulation.	Firing Regulation, Small Arms.	Manual of Guard Duty.	Map Reading.
Major 3rd Inf.									1		1	1	1	1		
[illegible] Corps, 3rd Inf.																
Company A, 3rd Inf., [illegible]									1	1	3	3	4	6	1	
Company B, 3rd Inf., [illegible]									1	1	1	3	1	1	2	
Company C, 3rd Inf., [illegible]																
Company D, 3rd Inf., [illegible]										1	3	3	1	3		
Company E, 3rd Inf., [illegible]										1	1	3	1	4	1	
Company F, 3rd Inf., [illegible]										1	1	3	1	3	4	
Company G, 3rd Inf., [illegible]																
Company H, 3rd Inf., Warrenton									1	1	3	3	4	1	1	
Company I, 3rd Inf., [illegible]									1		3	4	1	3	2	
Company K, 3rd Inf., [illegible]									1		3	3		1	3	
Company L, 3rd Inf., [illegible]									1	1	3	3	3			3
Company M, 3rd Inf., Durham									1	1	3	3	1	1	1	
Band, 3rd Inf.	3	2	3	3	1	1	1	1								
[illegible] 3rd Inf.				28					1	1	1	1	1	1	1	
Total	3	2	3	31	1	1	1	1	9	9	26	33	19	30	16	3

ABSTRACT C—CONTINUED.

Serviceable Property as per Companies' Returns.	QUARTERMASTER'S SUPPLIES.														
	Manual of Arms.	Manual Subsistence Dept.	Cprrespondence Book.	Descriptive Book.	Report Target Firing.	Sick Report.	Descriptive Book.	Report Target Firing.	First Sergeant's Book.	Drill Report Book.	U. S. Magazine Rifle.	Spades.	Spade Cases.	Rule.	Pliers.
Major 3rd Inf.															
Hospital Corps, 3rd Inf.															
Company A, 3rd Inf., [illegible]															
Company B, 3rd Inf., Raleigh															
Company C, 3rc Inf., [illegible]															
Company D, 3rd Inf., [illegible]															
Company E, 3rd Inf., [illegible]															
Company F, 3rd Inf., [illegible]			1	1	1	2	2	1	1	1	6				
Company G, 3rd Inf., [illegible]															
Company H, 3rd Inf., [illegible]															
Company I, 3rd Inf., [illegible]		1	3	3	1	12	1								
Company K, 3rd Inf., [illegible]															
Company L, 3rd Inf., [illegible]	3					3	15	3	2						
Company M, 3rd Inf., [illegible]												15	15	1	3
Band, 3rd Inf.															
Colonel 3rd Inf.															
Total	3	1	4	4	2	17	18	4	3	1	6	15	15	1	3

ABSTRACT C—CONTINUED.

Serviceable Property as per Companies' Returns.	QUARTERMASTER'S SUPPLIES. Musical Instruments and Supplies.											ORDNANCE AND ORDNANCE STORES.				
	Cornets.	Tubas.	Baritone.	Tattoo.	Helicons.	Clarinets.	Saxaphone.	Oboe.	Tenors.	Shakos.	Baton.	Rifles, Gallery, Cal. 22.	Rifles, Cal. 30.	Bayonets.	Bayonet Scabbards.	Gun Slings.
Major 3rd Inf.																
Hospital Corps, 3rd Inf.																
Company A, 3rd Inf., [illegible]												2	50	51	51	53
Company B, 3rd Inf., Raleigh												2	62	60	60	60
Company C, 3rd Inf., [illegible]																
Company D, 3rd Inf., Louisburg												2	50	50	50	50
Company E, 3rd Inf., Oxford												2	50	50	50	50
Company F, 3rd Inf., Fr[illegible]												2	61	60	60	60
Company G, 3rd Inf., Reidsville												2	50	50	50	50
Company H, 3rd Inf., [illegible]												2	50	50	50	47
Company I, 3rd Inf., [illegible]												2	50	50	50	50
Company K, 3rd Inf., [illegible]												2	60	60	60	60
Company L, 3rd Inf., [illegible]												2	50	50	50	50
Company M, 3rd Inf., Durham												2	50	50	50	
Band, 3rd Inf.	5	2	2	4	1	9	3									
Colonel 3rd Inf.	5	2	2	4	1	9	3	1	2	1	1		1			
Total	10	4	4	8	2	18	6	1	2	1	1	22	584	581	581	530

ABSTRACT C—CONTINUED.

Serviceable Property as per Companies' Returns.	ORDNANCE AND ORDNANCE STORES.													
			CARTRIDGES.											
	Rifle Cartridge Belts.	Rifle Cartridge Belt Suspenders.	Rifle, Ball, Cal. 30.	Rifle, Blank, Cal. 30.	Guard, Cal. 30.	Gallery, Cal. 22.	Revolver, Cal. 38.	Ball.	Revolver, Cal. 38.	Revolver Holsters.	Canteens.	Canteen Straps.	Haversacks.	Haversack Hooks.
Major 3rd Inf.														
Hospital Corps, 3rd Inf.														
Company A, 3rd Inf., Lexington	52	50	500		340	500					12	12	12	
Company B, 3rd Inf., [illegible]h	60	60		800	500				3	3	50		52	
Company C, 3rd Inf., [illegible]n									3	3	65		59	
Company D, 3rd Inf., [illegible]g	50	50	480	1,000	500	300								
Company E, 3rd Inf., Oxford	50	50	480	1,420	460	10,400			3	3	43		49	
Company F, 3rd Inf., [illegible]n	60	60	3,000			6,500			3	3	50		52	
Company G, 3rd Inf., Reidsville	50	50	500	1,000	480	900			3	3	44		40	50
Company H, 3rd Inf., Warrenton	49	48	1,680	1,000	500	500			2	2	43	55	47	27
Company I, 3rd Inf., [illegible]n	60	62			250	2,000			3	3	55	55	52	
Company K, 3rd Inf., [illegible]n	56	56	540	400	400	2,000			3	3	52		50	100
Company L, 3rd Inf., [illegible]e	50	50	900			700	28	1,000	2	2	50	50	50	50
Company M, 3rd Inf., Durham	50	50	1,200	500					3	3	50	58	42	84
Band, 3rd Inf.											28	28	28	28
Colonel 3rd Inf.							15		15	15				
Total	587	586	9,280	6,120	3,430	23,800	43	1,000	43	43	542	258	533	339

ABSTRACT C—CONTINUED.

Serviceable Property as per Companies' Returns.	Tin Cups.	Knives.	Forks.	Spoons.	Meat Cans.	Saber, Officer's.	Saber Belt, Officer's.	Saber Belt Slings.	Blanket Roll Straps.	Arm Chest.	Screw Drivers.	Curb Bridle.	Non-Com. Sword.	Saddles, complete.	Bridles.	Spurs, pairs.
	ORDNANCE AND ORDNANCE STORES.															
Major 3rd Inf.														1	1	1
[illegible], 3rd Inf.	12	11	10	9	12	1						1		1		
[illegible] A, 3rd Inf., [illegible]	52								50	5	2					
[illegible] B, 3rd Inf., [illegible]	58	56	58	55	65	3	3	3	64	6						
[illegible] C, 3rd Inf., [illegible]																
[illegible] D, 3rd Inf., [illegible]																
[illegible] E, 3rd Inf., Oxford	46	62	63	80	64	3	3			5	9					
[illegible] F, 3rd Inf., Franklinton	58					3	3			6	12					
[illegible] G, 3rd Inf., Reidsville	43	43	43	43	45	3	3			5						
[illegible] H, 3rd Inf., [illegible]	40				2	3	3	3		5						
[illegible] L 3rd Inf., [illegible]	55	58	59	54	55	3	3	3		5						
[illegible] K, 3rd Inf., [illegible]	43	47	45	49	48	3	3			6						
[illegible] L, 3rd Inf., Thomasville	47				50	3	3	3								
[illegible] M, 3rd Inf., Durham	50	58	58	58												
Band, 3rd Inf.	28	28	26	28	28											
Col[illegible]l 3rd Inf.						14	14						5	10	9	7
Total	532	363	362	376	369	39	38	12	114	43	23	1	5	12	10	8

ABSTRACT C—CONTINUED.

Serviceable Property as per Companies' Returns.	ORDNANCE AND ORDNANCE STORES.										MEDICAL PROPERTY AND MEDICINES.					
	Axes with Carriers.	Barracks Cleaning Rod.	Sight Covers.	Intrenching Rods.	Hand Axes and Carriers.	Picks, Mattocks, and Carriers.	Intrenching Shovels and Carriers.	Set O. D. Chevrons.	Wire Cutters.	Non-Com. Officers Sword.	Reg. Chest Surgical.	Medical and Surgical Chest.	Regular Chest Sterilizer.	Mess Chest, Small.	Tool Chest.	Miscellaneous Chest.
Major 3rd Inf.																
Hospital Corps, 3rd Inf.											1	1	1	1	1	1
Company A, 3rd Inf., [illegible]																
Company B, 3rd Inf., Raleigh	1															
Company C, 3rd Inf., [illegible]																
Company D, 3rd Inf., [illegible]																
Company E, 3rd Inf., Oxford																
Company F, 3rd Inf., [illegible]		14	6													
Company G, 3rd Inf., Reidsville																
Company H, 3rd Inf., [illegible]				1	4	6	18	1	3							
Company I, 3rd Inf., Burlington																
Company K, 3rd Inf., [illegible]																
Company L, 3rd Inf., [illegible]																
Company M, 3rd Inf., Durham																
Band, 3rd Inf.																
Colonel 3rd Inf.										5						
Total	1	14	6	1	4	6	18	1	3	5	1	1	1	1	1	1

ABSTRACT G—CONTINUED.

Serviceable Property as per Companies' Returns.	Dressing Chest.	Furniture Rolls.	Bedding Rolls.	Tent Poles, common.	Reg. Chest Medicine.	Hospital Tent and Poles.	Hospital Tent Flies.	Brooms.	Spades.	Commode.	Bales.	Pick.	Fitters.	Acetylene Gas Light	Dry Carbide Boxes.
	MEDICAL PROPERTY AND MEDICINES.														
Major 3rd Inf.															
[illegible]s, 3rd Inf.	1	2	2	12	1	3	3	3	2	1	2	1	1	1	1
Company A, 3rd Inf., Lexington															
Company B, 3rd Inf., [illegible]h															
Company C, 3rd Inf., Henderson															
Company D, 3rd Inf., Louisburg															
Company E, 3rd Inf., Oxford															
Company F, 3rd Inf., [illegible]n															
Company G, 3rd Inf., Reidsville															
Company H, 3rd Inf., Warrenton															
Company I, 3rd Inf., Burlington															
Company K, 3rd Inf., Weldon															
Company L, 3rd Inf., [illegible]e															
Company M, 3rd Inf., Durham															
Band, 3rd Inf.															
Col[illegible]l 3rd Inf.															
Total	1	2	2	12	1	3	3	3	2	1	2	1	1	1	1

ABSTRACT G.—SERVICEABLE PROPERTY, COAST ARTILLERY CORPS.

Serviceable Property as per Companies' Returns.	QUARTERMASTER'S SUPPLIES.														
	TABLEWARE AND COOKING UTENSILS.			CLOTHING.											
	Table Forks.	Table Knives.	Teaspoons.	Blankets, Woolen.	Coats, Cotton Khaki.	Coats, Olive Drab.	Breeches, Khaki.	Breeches, Olive Drab.	Trousers, Khaki.	Trousers, Olive Drab.	Blouses, Blue.	Trousers, Blue.	Caps, Olive Drab.	Caps, Dress.	Cap Ornaments.
Headquarters Coast Artillery Corps															
1st Co., Coast Artillery Corps				60	67	52			67	59			65		57
2nd Co., Coast Artillery Corps				50	70	63	49	68			62	65	63	74	63
3rd Co., Coast Artillery Corps	81	71	74	55	118	50	154	50			69	79	50	51	50
4th Co., Coast Artillery Corps				61	20	63	5	63	10		49	41	73	51	55
5th Co., Coast Artillery Corps				62	65	59	90	54			65	75	62	65	
6th Co., Coast Artillery Corps															
Total	81	71	74	288	340	287	289	235	77	59	245	260	313	241	162

ABSTRACT G—CONTINUED.

Serviceable Property as per Companies' Returns.	QUARTERMASTER'S SUPPLIES. CLOTHING. Chevrons, Cloth, Pairs. N. C. S. Colors and First Sergeants.	Sergeants.	Corporals.	Cooks.	Chevrons, for Field Uniforms, Pairs. N. C. S. Colors and First Sergeants.	Sergeants.	Corporals.	Corporals, Lance.	Cooks.	Gloves, Berlin, Pairs.	Hats, Campaign.	Hat Cords.	Helmet Trimmings, Bands.	Leggings, Pairs.	Mittens, Woolen, Pairs.	Ponchos.
Headquarters Coast Artillery Corps																
1st Co., Coast Artillery Corps	1	5	6		1	4	6		2		43	43		54	58	
2d Co., Coast Artillery Corps		6	6		12	12		2			28			60	30	
3rd Co., Coast Artillery Corps	1	4	6			4	6			72	86	97	37	120	50	43
4th Co., Coast Artillery Corps	3	6	6	2							80	60		70		55
5th Co., Coast Artillery Corps											20			65	64	
6th Co., Coast Artillery Corps																
Total	5	21	24	2	13	20	12	2	2	72	257	200	37	369	202	98

ABSTRACT G—CONTINUED.

Serviceable Property as per Companies' Returns.	QUARTERMASTER'S SUPPLIES.															
	CLOTHING.										EQUIPAGE.					
	Shirts.								Trouser Stripes, pairs.			Books, Regimental.		Books, Company.		
	Chambray.	Flannel, Light.	Muslin.	Cooking Outfit, Co.	First Aid Pockets.	First Aid Pouches.	Housewives.	Overcoats, Blue.	Sergeants.	Corporals.	Bed Sacks.	Fund, Descriptive.	Letters Sent, Correspondence.	Letters Received.	Letters Sent.	Index Sent.
Headquarters Coast Artillery Corps	4											1	1			
1st Co., Coast Artillery Corps	114				65	65	65								1	
2nd Co., Coast Artillery Corps		60			50	50	50	65	6	6						
3rd Co., Coast Artillery Corpt	53	17	1		50	50	50		6	6	54					
4th Co., Coast Artillery Corps	57			1	56	50										
5th Co., Coast Artillery Corps	66			1	63	63	60							1		1
6th Co., Coast Artillery Corps																
Total	294	77	1	2	284	278	226	65	12	12	54	1	1	1	1	1

ABSTRACT G—CONTINUED.

Serviceable Property as per Companies' Returns.	QUARTERMASTER'S SUPPLIES.															
	EQUIPAGE.															
		Flags, Etc.														
		Colors.														
	Desks, Field.	Cases.	National.	Standards.	Staffs.	Mess Pans.	Shelter Tents, Halves.	Trumpets, with E. M. P.	Trumpet Cords and Tassels.	Trumpet Mouthpieces.	Whistles.	Commissary Chests.	Regulation, Army.	Regulation, Militia.	Regulation, National Guard.	Drill Regulation, Infantry.
Headquarters Coast Artillery Corps	2	2	1	1	2							1	1	1	1	
1st Co., Coast Artillery Corps	1						64		2					1	1	1
2nd Co., Coast Artillery Corps						43		2	2		1			1	1	1
3rd Co., Coast Artillery Corps	1					58	40	1	3	2		80	3	2	2	3
4th Co., Coast Artillery Corps							58	1	2				1	1	1	3
5th Co., Coast Artillery Corps							62						2	2	1	
6th Co., Coast Artillery Corps																
Total	4	2	1	1	2	101	224	4	9	2	1	81	7	8	7	7

ABSTRACT G—CONTINUED.

Serviceable Property as per Companies' Returns.	QUARTERMASTER'S SUPPLIES.															
	Drill Regulation, Coast Artillery.	Field Service Regulation.	Firing Regulation, Small Arms.	Manual of Guard Duty.	Manual Subsistence Department.	M. S. Cook Book.	Morning Report Book.	Des. and Clothing Book.	Duty Roster.	Description Book of U. S. Rifle.	Military Map Reading.	Minor Tactics.	Sick Report Book.	First Sergeant's Book.	Sick Report Pamphlet.	Money Pamphlet.
Headquarters Coast Artillery Corps	1				1											
1st Co., Coast Artillery Corps	15			5												
2nd Co., Coast Artillery Corps	16	1	1	1												
3rd Co., Coast Artillery Corps	16	1	3	2		1	2	2	1	6	3	3	2	1	1	1
4th Co., Coast Artillery Corps	15	1	3													
5th Co., Coast Artillery Corps			1													
6th Co., Coast Artillery Corps																
Total	63	3	8	8	1	1	2	2	1	6	3	3	2	1	1	1

ABSTRACT G—CONTINUED.

Serviceable Property as per Companies' Returns.	Quartermaster's Supplies.			ORDNANCE AND ORDNANCE STORES.										
												CARTRIDGES.		
	Correspondence Book.	Manual for Privates.	Manual for Bayonet Exercise.	Rifles, Cal. 48.	Rifles, Gallery, Cal. 22.	Rifles, Cal. 30.	Bayonets.	Bayonet Scabbards.	Gun Slings.	Rifle Cartridge Belts.	Rifle Cartridge Belt Suspenders.	Rifle, Ball, Cal. 30.	Rifle, Blank, Cal. 30.	Guard, Cal. 30.
Headquarters Coast Artillery Corps														
1st Co., Coast Artillery Corps					2	63	63	63	62	63	63	2,400		
2nd Co., Coast Artillery Corps				25	2	60	24	5	17	35	60	700	1,200	120
3rd Co., Coast Artillery Corps	1	1	1		2	50	50	50	50	50	45	1,239	654	145
4th Co., Coast Artillery Corps					2	60	58	60	60	58	55	1,320	820	252
5th Co., Coast Artillery Corps					2	62	62	63	62	62	60	1,200		
6th Co., Coast Artillery Corps														
Total	1	1	1	25	10	295	257	241	251	268	283	6,859	2,674	517

ABSTRACT G—CONTINUED.

Serviceable Property as per Companies' Returns.	ORDNANCE AND ORDNANCE STORES.														
	CARTRIDGES.														
	Gallery, Cal. 22.	Revolver, Cal. 38.	Gun Chests.	Gallery Targets.	Revolver, Cal. 38.	Revolver Holsters.	Canteens.	Canteen Straps.	Haversacks.	Haversack Hooks.	Tin Cups.	Knives.	Forks.	Spoons.	Meat Cans.
Headquarters Coast Artillery Corps															
1st Co., Coast Artillery Corps	3,500	300	1	2	5	4	63	63	54	62	60	65	65	65	65
2nd Co., Coast Artillery Corps					3	2	66		68		50	50	50	50	12
3rd Co., Coast Artillery Corps	4,500		5		2	2	63	63	51	50	49				
4th Co., Coast Artillery Corps	1,500				2	2	50	47	60	75	63	60	68	60	60
5th Co., Coast Artillery Corps	9,000	250			3	3	66	58	66	62	70	38	47	59	75
6th Co., Coast Artillery Corps															
Total	18,500	550	6	2	15	13	192	231	299	249	292	213	230	234	212

ABSTRACT G—CONTINUED.

Serviceable Property as per Companies' Returns.	ORDNANCE AND ORDNANCE STORES.															
	Saber, Officers'.	Saber Belt, Officer's.	Saber Belt Slings.	Blanket Roll Straps.	Arm Chest.	Screw Drivers.	Spurs, pairs.	Cartridges.	Fuses.	Shells.	Deflection Boards.	Plotting Boards.	Wind Indicators.	Range Boards.	Sand Drivers.	Field Range.
Headquarters Coast Artillery Corps	1															
1st Co., Coast Artillery Corps	3	3		50	6	12					1	1	1	1	1	1
2nd Co., Coast Artillery Corps	3	3	3		6											
3rd Co., Coast Artillery Corps	3	3	3								1	1	1	1	1	
4th Co., Coast Artillery Corps	3	3	3													
5th Co., Coast Artillery Corps	3	3		66			7	5	5	5						
6th Co., Coast Artillery Corps																
Total	16	15	9	116	12	12	7	5	5	5	2	2	2	2	2	1

ABSTRACT I.—TOTAL SERVICEABLE PROPERTY, ALL DEPARTMENTS.

Total Serviceable Property.	QUARTERMASTER'S SUPPLIES.													
	TABLEWARE AND COOKING UTENSILS.			CLOTHING.										
	Table Forks.	Table Knives.	Teaspoons.	Full Dress Coats, Old Style.	Bandages, Abdominal.	Belts, Waist.	Blankets, Woolen.	Coats, Cotton Khaki.	Coats, Olive Drab.	Breeches, Khaki.	Breeches, Olive Drab.	Trousers, Khaki.	Trousers, Olive Drab.	Blouses, Blue.
Military Supply Depot	------	------	------	34	------	------	66	453	142	731	124	------	94	81
1st Regiment	131	134	107	------	------	------	651	795	621	1,246	561	59	108	52
2nd Regiment	315	298	274	1	------	5	637	838	693	952	638	191	127	52
3rd Regiment	392	391	352	2	53	2	637	925	569	992	503	326	181	8
Coast Artillery Corps	61	71	74	------	------	------	288	340	224	289	235	77	59	25
Total Serviceable	919	894	807	37	53	7	2,279	3,351	1,486	3,970	2,066	653	569	2,215

ABSTRACT I—CONTINUED.

Total Serviceable Property.	QUARTERMASTER'S SUPPLIES.														
	Clothing.														
									Chevrons, Cloth, Pairs.						
	Trousers, Blue.	Caps, Olive Drab.	Caps, Khaki.	Caps, Dress.	Cap Ornaments.	Ornamental Collar Stripes.	Collar Bronze Ornaments.	Bronze Buttons, Collar.	Sergeants.	Corporals.	Caps, Old Style.	Saddlers.	N. C. T. Colors and First Sergeant.	Service.	Signal.
Military Supply Depot	------	204	123	------	------	2,587	5,010	4,500	12	12	104	16	20	------	------
1st Regiment	496	602	12	446	284	------	------	------	77	83	18	------	2	1	2
2nd Regiment	542	698	------	479	210	------	------	------	72	76	29	4	1	------	------
3rd Regiment	617	575	------	359	300	------	------	------	5	56	64	15	------	2	------
Coast Artillery Corps	260	318	------	167	162	------	------	------	15	18	2	------	5	------	------
Total Serviceable	1,915	2,392	135	1,451	956	2,587	5,010	4,500	181	245	317	35	28	3	2

ABSTRACT I—CONTINUED.

Total Serviceable Property.	QUARTERMASTER'S SUPPLIES.														
	CLOTHING.														
	Chevrons for Field Uniforms, Pairs.							Chevrons, Gold Lace, Pairs.							
	N. C. S. Colors and 1st Sergeants.	Sergeants.	Corporals.	Corporals, Lance.	Cooks.	Foreman.	Service.	Corporal, Lance.	Stripes.	Service.	Gauntlets.	Facings, Set.	Gloves, Berlin, Pairs.	Hats, Campaign.	Hat Cords.
Military Supply Depot	81	183	245	72	82	4	4	84	126	107		2	120	370	460
1st Regiment	6	39	36		8								417	625	519
2nd Regiment		10	10		4								60	478	273
3rd Regiment	1	11	1	4							5		151	572	519
Coast Artillery Corps	1	8	12		2								72	229	200
Total Serviceable	89	251	313	76	96	4	4	84	126	107	5	2	820	2,274	1,971

ABSTRACT I—CONTINUED.

Total Serviceable Property.	QUARTERMASTER'S SUPPLIES.													
	Clothing.													
									Shirts.					
	Hat Numbers.	Hat Ornaments.	Helmets, felt, Untrimmed.	Helmet Trimmings, Bands	Leggings, Pairs.	Mittens, Canvas, Pairs.	Mittens, Woolen, Pairs.	Ponchos.	Chambray.	Flannel, Heavy.	Flannel, Light.	Gingham.	Muslin.	Cooking Outfit, Co.
Military Supply Depot			43		489			222	886	313	34	62		5
1st Regiment					709			629	161	181	410			4
2nd Regiment		62			254			527	418	216	218	68		6
3rd Regiment	96				804	48		558	626	333	114	14	30	7
Coast Artillery Corps				37	309		172	98	294		17		1	2
Total Serviceable	96	62	43	37	3,065	48	172	2,034	2,385	1,093	793	144	31	24

ABSTRACT I—CONTINUED.

Total Serviceable Property.	QUARTERMASTER'S SUPPLIES.													
	CLOTHING.									EQUIPAGE.				
						Trouser Stripes, Pairs.								
	First Aid Pockets.	First Aid Pouches.	Housewives.	Overcoats, Blue.	Overcoats, Olive Drab.	Musicians.	N. C. S. and H. C.	Sergeants.	Corporals.	Club Axes.	Axes.	Axe Helves.	Axe Slings.	Barrack Bags.
Military Supply Depot	263		253	60	799					13	25	25	25	25
1st Regiment	454	455	572	43		3	1	17	18		10	4	8	3
2nd Regiment	638	439	615	23				5	8	1	23	23	18	
3rd Regiment	479	470	586	173		4		21	20	1	22	11	16	12
Coast Artillery Corps	234	228	175					6	6					
Total Serviceable	2,068	1,642	2,201	299	799	7	1	49	52	15	80	63	67	40

ABSTRACT I—CONTINUED.

Total Serviceable Property.	QUARTERMASTER'S SUPPLIES.																
	EQUIPAGE.																
				Books, Regimental.			Books, Company.							Drums, Etc.		
	Bed Sacks.	Bed Sheets.		Fund.	Letters Sent.	Order.	Council.	Letters Received.	Order.	Index Received.	Letters Sent.	Index Sent.	Desks, Field.	Drums.	Heads, Snare.	Sticks, Pairs.
Military Supply Depot	36	1						5	4	4	6	2	10	2		
1st Regiment	5	15	1													
2nd Regiment	6						2	2	3			7	7	1	1	1
3rd Regiment	227	16	2			1		2					9	3		
Coast Artillery Corps		54		1	1			1			1	1	4			
Total Serviceable	274	86	3	1	1	1	2	10	7	4	7	10	30	6	1	1

ABSTRACT I—CONTINUED.

Total Serviceable Property.	QUARTERMASTER'S SUPPLIES.															
	EQUIPAGE.															
	Flags, Etc.												Commissary Chest.	Mattresses.	Mattress Covers.	Mess Pans.
	Colors.							Cases for Silk.	Field Hospital.	Staves for Guidon Artillery.	Standards.	Staffs.				
	Silver Bands for Color Staff.	Belt and Sling.	Camp.	Cases.	National.	Regimental.	Cord for Silk.									
Military Supply Depot	3	3	3	3	3	2	2	2		6	4	3		8	1	14
1st Regiment		2		2	2	1			1							
2nd Regiment		1			1											74
3rd Regiment	1		2		2	1			1						53	299
Coast Artillery				2	1						1	2	81			58
Total Serviceable	4	6	5	7	9	4	2	2	2	6	5	5	81	8	54	445

ABSTRACT I—CONTINUED.

Total Serviceable Property.	QUARTERMASTER'S SUPPLIES.														
	EQUIPAGE.														
	Music Pouches.	Stamps, Marking.	Stencil, Alphabet, sets.	Stencil, Numbers, sets.	Stencil Plates, set, complete.	Shelter Tents, Halves.	Trumpets, with E. M. P.	Trumpet Cords and Tassels.	Trumpet Crooks.	Trumpet Mouthpieces.	Whistles.	Officer's Wall Tents.	Officer's Wall Tent Flies.	Officers' Wall Tent Poles.	Storage Tents.
Military Supply Depot	75	500	1,272	216	511	1,743	6,146	4	4	4	-----	10	10	10	1
1st Regiment	-----	-----	-----	-----	-----	535	16	18	-----	12	1	-----	-----	-----	-----
2nd Regiment	-----	-----	1	1	-----	565	14	16	-----	11	1	-----	-----	-----	-----
3rd Regiment	28	-----	-----	-----	-----	437	18	14	-----	10	1	-----	-----	-----	-----
Coast Artillery Corps	-----	-----	-----	-----	-----	224	2	7	-----	2	-----	-----	-----	-----	-----
Total Serviceable	103	500	1,273	217	511	3,504	6,196	59	4	39	3	10	10	10	1

ABSTRACT I—CONTINUED.

Total Serviceable Property.	QUARTERMASTER'S SUPPLIES.															
	EQUIPAGE.															
	Storage Tent Flies.	Storage Tent Poles.	Conical Tents.	Conical Tent Poles.	Tripods, Conical Tenrs.	Spades, S. H.	Shovels, S. H.	Shovels, L. H.	Shelter Tent Pins.	Field Range.	2-ft. Folding Rule.	Hand Axe.	Pick Mattocks with Carrier.	Intrenching Shovels.	Wire Cutters.	Collar Ornaments.
Millitary Supply Depot	1	1	20	20	20	25	25	25								
1st Regiment									570	6	5	6	34	40	126	10
2nd Regiment																
3rd Regiment																
Coast Artillery Corps																
Total Serviceable	1	1	20	20	20	25	25	25	570	6	5	6	34	40	126	10

ABSTRACT I—CONTINUED.

Total Serviceable Property.	QUARTERMASTER'S SUPPLIES.															
	EQUIPAGE.				MUSICAL INSTRUMENTS AND SUPPLIES.											
	Barracks Cleaning Rod	Web Belt.	Blanket Bag Strap.	Sight Covers.	Cymbals, Pairs.	Drums, Bass.	Drums, Snare.	Flutes.	Piccolos.	Triangles.	Trombones.	Altos.	Cases.	Clarinets.	Lyres.	Mouthpieces.
Military Supply Depot							3	2	1		7	10	3	3	3	46
1st Regiment	3	1	1	26	1	1		2	1	3						
2nd Regiment					1	1	2			1	2	2	7		3	2
3rd Regiment					2	1	5	1	2	2	4	20	35	3	2	3
Coast Artillery Corps																
Total Serviceable	3	1	1	26	4	3	10	5	4	6	13	32	45	6	8	51

ABSTRACT I—CONTINUED.

Total Serviceable Property.	QUARTERMASTER'S SUPPLIES.														
	Musical Instruments and Supplies.														
	Music Stands.	Trumpet Cords.	Reeds.	Springs.	Trumpets.	Regulation, Army.	Regulation, Militia.	Regulation, National Guard.	Drill Regulation, Infantry.	Drill Regulation, Coast Artillery.	Drill Regulation, Field Artillery.	Field Service Regulation.	Firing Regulation, Small Arms.	Manual of Guard Duty.	Manual Pay Department.
Military Supply Depot		54			9										
1st Regiment	1					15	14	21	45	10	12	23	39	17	12
2nd Regiment	3					24	8	21	37			22	28	32	
3rd Regiment	3	1	1	1	1	9	9	26	33			19	30	16	3
Coast Artillery Corps						7	7	6	7	47		2	7	7	
Total Serviceable	7	55	1	1	10	55	38	74	122	57	12	66	104	72	15

ABSTRACT I—CONTINUED.

Total Serviceable Property.	QUARTERMASTER'S SUPPLIES.														
	Manual Q. M. Department.	Manual Subsistence Dept.	Manual Private.	Map Reading.	Bayonet Service.	Drum Major Baton.	E flat Bass.	B flat Baritone.	Saxaphone.	Helicon.	Altos.	Oboes.	Trumpets.	Cornets.	Clarinets, B flat.
Military Supply Depot															
1st Regiment	9	15	41	21	5	7	56	52	51	50	54	51	2	2	3
2nd Regiment		1		1											
3rd Regiment	3	1	4	4	2	17	18	4	3	1	6	15	5	1	3
Coast Artillery Corps		1	1	2	2	1	6	3	3	2	1	1	1	1	1
Total Serviceable	12	18	46	28	9	25	80	59	57	53	61	67	8	4	7

ABSTRBCT I—CONTINUED.

Total Serviceable Property.	QUARTERMASTER'S SUPPLIES.															
	Clarinets, E flat.	First Aid Pouches.	Shovels.	Picks.	Axes.	Rules.	Pliers.	Hand Axes, and Carriers.	Pick Mattocks and Carriers.	Intrenching Shovels.	Wire Cutters.	Rule.	Pans.	Potato Mashers.	Spoons, Large.	Pans, Small.
Military Supply Depot																
1st Regiment	1	58	36	6	3	1	1	12	4	20	24	4	2	3	1	1
2nd Regiment																
3rd Regiment	10	4	4	8	2	18	6									
Coast Artillery Corps	1	1	1	1	1	1	1									
Total Serviceable	12	63	41	15	6	20	8	12	4	20	24	4	2	3	1	1

ABSTRACT I—CONTINUED.

Total Serviceable Property.	QUARTERMASTER'S SUPPLIES.							ORDNANCE AND ORDNANCE STORES.						
	Ice Hooks.	Coffee Pots.	Dippers.	Meat Choppers.	Sifters.	Pots.	Pickers and Covers.	Rifles, Gallery, Cal. 22.	Rifles, Cal. 30.	Bayonets.	Bayonet Scabbards.	Gun Slings.	Rifle Cartridge Belts.	Rifle Cartridge Belt Suspenders.
Military Supply Depot														
1st Regiment	1	3	2	1	2	2	6	20	507	505	505	505	505	506
2nd Regiment								20	611	616	604	600	604	602
3rd Regiment								22	584	581	581	530	587	586
Coast Artillery Corps								8	235	233	236	234	233	223
Total Serviceable	1	3	2	1	2	2	6	70	1,937	1,935	1,926	1,635	1,929	1,917

ABSTRACT I—CONTINUED.

Total Serviceable Property.	ORDNANCE AND ORDNANCE STORES.													
	CARTRIDGES.													
	Rifle Balls, Cal. 30.	Rifle, Blank, Cal. 30.	Guard, Cal. 30.	Gallery, Cal. 22.	Revolver, Cal. 38.	Gun Caps.	Frost Sight Covers.	Target Outfit.	Ball Cartridges.	Revolver, Cal. 38.	Revolver Holsters.	Clips.	Canteens.	Canteen Straps.
Military Supply Depot														
1st Regiment	11,892	8,127	2,880	22,000	4,475	23	16	51		40	41	70	560	483
2nd Regiment	8,532	8,843	2,830	27,300						34	34		622	304
3rd Regiment	9,280	6,120	3,430	23,800	43				1,000	43	43		542	258
Coast Artillery Corps	4,950	1,470	3,971	18,500	550	6	2			12	11		126	231
Total Serviceable	34,654	24,560	13,111	91,600	5,068	29	18	51	1,000	129	129	70	1,850	1,276

ABSTRACT I—CONTINUED.

Total Serviceable Property.	ORDNANCE AND ORDNANCE STORES.												
	Haversacks.	Haversack Hooks.	Tin Cups.	Knives.	Forks.	Spoons.	Meat Cans.	Saber, Officer's.	Saber Belt, Officer's.	Saber Belt Slings.	Blanket Roll Straps.	Arm Chest.	Screw Drivers.
Military Supply Depot													
1st Regiment	615	652	603	624	577	576	574	32	31	15	492	55	37
2nd Regiment	640	364	608	395	395	511	606	32	31	18	265	46	21
3rd Regiment	533	339	532	363	362	376	369	39	38	12	114	43	23
Coast Artillery Corps	231	249	242	163	180	184	200	13	12	6	116	6	12
Total Serviceable	2,019	1,604	1,985	1,545	1,514	1,647	1,649	116	112	51	987	150	93

ABSTRACT I—CONTINUED.

Total Serviceable Property.	ORDNANCE AND ORDNANCE STORES.															
	Handspikes, Trail.	Curb Bridle.	Non-Com. Sword.	Saddles, complete.	Bridles.	Saddle Blankets.	Spurs, Pairs.	Cartridges.	Fuses.	Shells.	Non-Com. Swords.	Carriers.	Box Metal Foling Holders.	Barracks Cleaning Rod.	Correspondence Book.	Descriptive Book Property.
Military Supply Depot																
1st Regiment				17	12	2	8				4	4	1	12		
2nd Regiment	6			1	1										1	1
3rd Regiment		1	5	12	10		8									
Coast Artillery Corps							7	5	5	5						
Total Serviceable	6	1	5	30	23	2	23	5	5	5	4	4	1	12	1	1

ABSTRACT I—CONTINUED.

Total Serviceable Property.	Sick Report.	Descriptive Book.	Manual Army Book.	Drill Report.	U. S. Magazine Rifle.	Company Order Book.	Map Reading.	Minor Tactics.	Bayonet Exercise.	First Sergeant Books.	Rule.	Pairs Pliers.	Pick Mattocks.	Holders.	Shovels.	Shovel Holders.
	ORDNANCE AND ORDNANCE STORES.															
Military Supply Depot																
1st Regiment																
2nd Regiment	2	2	1	1	3	3	3	1	1	1	2	2	4	5	4	5
3rd Regiment											14					
Coast Artillery Corps																
Total Serviceable	2	2	1	1	3	3	3	1	1	1	16	2	4	5	4	5

ABSTRACT I—CONTIFUED.

Total Serviceable Property.	ORDNANCE AND ORDNANCE STORES.								MEDICAL PROPERTY AND MEDICINES.							
	Rifle Cleaning Rod.	Winner's Target.	Sight Covers.	2-Ft. Rule.	Hand Axes.	Pick Mattocks and Carriers.	Intrenching Shovels.	Wire Cutters.	Cartridge Belt.	2-Ft. Folding Rule.	Hand Axes with Carriers.	Pick Mattock with Carriers.	Intrenching Shovels.	Wire Cutters.	Canteen Haversack Straps.	Canteen Straps, Web.
Millitary Supply Depot																
1st Regiment																
2nd Regiment	13	1	11	1	4	5	15	3	2							
3rd Regiment										1	4	5	15	3	10	52
Coast Artillery Corps																
Total Serviceable	13	1	11	1	4	5	15	3	2	1	4	5	15	3	10	52

ABSTRACT I—CONTINUED.

Total Serviceable Property.	MEDICAL PROPERTY AND MEDICINES.															
	Old Web Revolvers.	Tan Belts.	Poles.	Pins.	Field Desk.	Regulation Chests.	Medical and Surgical Chests.	Reg. Chest Sterilizer.	Miss. Chest, Small.	Tool Chest.	Miscellaneous Chest.	Dressing Chest.	Furniture Rolls.	Bedding Rolls.	Tent Poles.	Reg. Chest Medicine.
Military Supply Depot																
1st Regiment																
2nd Regiment																
3rd Regiment	3	46	54	270	1	1	1	1	1	1	1	1	2	2	12	1
Coast Artillery Corps																
Total Serviceable	3	46	54	270	1	1	1	1	1	1	1	1	2	2	12	1

ABSTRACT I—CONTINUED.

Total Serviceable Property.	MEDICAL PROPERTY AND MEDICINES.															
	Hospital Tent and Poles.	Hospital Tent Flies.	Brooms.	Spades.	Commode.	Poles.	Picks.	Filters.	Acetylene Gas Light Outfit.	Dry Carbide Boxes.	Deflection Board.	Plotting Board.	Wind Indicator.	Range Board.	Sand Driver.	Field Range.
Military Supply Depot																
1st Regiment																
2nd Regiment																
3rd Regiment	3	3	3	2	1	2	1	1	1	1	1	1	1	1	1	1
Coast Artillery																
Total Serviceable	3	3	3	2	1	2	1	1	1	1	1	1	1	1	1	1

Report of Inspector General

STATE OF NORTH CAROLINA,
OFFICE OF INSPECTOR GENERAL,
WAYNESVILLE, N. C., December 1, 1910.

GENERAL R. L. LEINSTER,
Adjutant General, N. C. N. G.,
Raleigh, N. C.

SIR:—In compliance with the law and regulations governing the North Carolina National Guard, I have the honor to submit my report of the inspection of the Guard for the year ending December 1, 1910.

In obedience to General Orders No. 1, dated Adjutant General's Office, Raleigh, N. C., January 11, 1910, the inspection of the National Guard of North Carolina for the year 1910 was made during the months of February, March and April, at the stations and on the dates indicated in said orders.

I proceeded with the inspection, beginning with Company B, Third Infantry, Raleigh, North Carolina, February 11th, finishing with Company H, First Infantry, Waynesville, North Carolina, April 2d. Lieut. C. M. Butler, Seventeenth Infantry, U. S. A., accompanied me, making the inspection for the United States, as required under the provisions of the law governing the militia of the State.

Detailed reports have already been forwarded to your Department. The following shows results of inspection, giving number present and absent.

SUMMARY OF ATTENDANCE OF FIRST INFANTRY.

Subdivisions.	Present.		Absent.		Present and Absent.		Aggregate.
	Officers.	Men.	Officers.	Men.	Officers.	Men.	
Field, staff, and Noncom. staff	13	6	3	2	16	8	24
Hospital Corps							
Field Music							
Band		24		2		26	26
Company A	1	34	1	6	2	40	42
Company B	3	46		9	3	55	58
Company C	3	42		4	3	46	49
Company D	3	44		5	3	49	52
Company E	3	47		2	3	49	52
Company F	3	41		2	3	43	46
Company G	3	44		6	3	50	53
Company H	3	43		3	3	46	49
Company I	2	45		1	2	46	48
Company K	2	37		6	2	43	45
Company L	3	49		9	3	58	61
Company M	3	39		14	3	53	56
Total	45	541	4	71	49	612	671

SUMMARY OF ATTENDANCE OF SECOND INFANTRY.

Subdivisions.	Present.		Absent.		Present and Absent.		Aggregate.
	Officers.	Men.	Officers.	Men.	Officers.	Men.	
Field, staff, and Noncom. staff	13	5	3	3	16	8	24
Hospital Corps							
Field Music							
Band		19		1		20	20
Company A	2	36	1	4	3	40	43
Company B	3	45		3	3	48	51
Company C	3	38		11	3	49	52
Company D	3	27		15	3	42	45
Company E	3	53		5	3	58	61
Company F	3	47		3	3	50	53
Company G	2	37	1	4	3	41	44
Company H	2	46	1	4	3	50	53
Company I	3	38		8	3	46	49
Company K	3	42		1	3	43	46
Company L	3	47		3	3	50	53
Company M	3	33		12	3	45	48
Total	46	513	6	77	52	590	642

SUMMARY OF ATTENDANCE OF THIRD INFANTRY.

Subdivisions.	Present.		Absent.		Present and Absent.		Aggregate.
	Officers.	Men.	Officers.	Men.	Officers.	Men.	
Field, staff, and Noncom. staff	13	5	3	3	16	8	24
Hospital Corps							
Field Music							
Band		21		3		24	24
Company A	3	36		7	3	43	46
Company B	3	52		8	3	60	63
Company C	3	45		5	3	50	53
Company D	3	44		7	3	51	54
Company E	2	38	1	8	3	46	49
Company F	3	50			3	50	53
Company G	3	34		10	3	44	47
Company H	3	42		6	3	48	51
Company I	3	27		17	3	44	47
Company K	3	39		3	3	42	45
Company L	3	39		2	3	41	44
Company M	3	43		5	3	48	51
Total	48	515	4	84	52	599	651

SUMMARY OF ATTENDANCE OF COAST ARTILLERY COMPANY.

Subdivisions.	Present.		Absent.		Present and Absent.		Aggregate.
	Officers.	Men.	Officers.	Men.	Officers.	Men.	
Field, staff, and Noncom. staff	4	-------	1	-------	5	-------	5
Hospital Corps	-------	-------	-------	-------	-------	-------	-------
Field Music	-------	-------	-------	-------	-------	-------	-------
Band	-------	-------	-------	-------	-------	-------	-------
Company 1	3	35	-------	5	3	40	43
Company 2	3	35	-------	8	3	43	46
Company 3	3	34	-------	15	3	49	52
Company 4	2	42	1	16	3	58	61
Total	15	146	2	44	17	190	207

SUMMARY OF ATTENDANCE OF HOSPITAL CORPS AND MEDICAL DEPARTMENT.

Subdivisions.	Present.		Absent.		Present and Absent.		Aggregate.
	Officers.	Men.	Officers.	Men.	Officers.	Men.	
Field, staff, and Noncom. staff	6	-------	3	-------	9	-------	11
Hosp. Corps, 1st Regt.	1	10	-------	1	1	11	12
Hosp. Corps, 3rd Regt.	1	10	-------	2	1	12	13
Total	8	20	3	3	11	23	36

Report of Surgeon General

State of North Carolina,
Surgeon General's Office,
Asheville.

The Adjutant General, State of North Carolina,
Raleigh, N. C.

Sir:—I have the honor to submit to you this my annual report for 1910.

The year has been one full of interest to the Medical Department, and it gives me pleasure to state that the Corps has shown a livelier interest in the performance of the duties assigned to it than ever before in the history of the North Carolina National Guard. In medico-military matters history is making all the time, and if the Medical Corps of the Guard with its small opportunities and necessary disadvantages can keep even in sight of the Medical Corps of the U. S. Army, which has "set the pace," it is to be congratulated. The Medical Department of the State and Nation are getting closer together, and if the bill now pending in Congress giving even a small yearly pay to the personnel of the Organized Militia becomes a law, it would be of inestimable benefit in this direction, making both the enlisted and commissioned keener to join and more anxious to remain in the service of the State.

During the summer the three Regiments and Coast Artillery went into camp as usual, the First and Second Regiments of Infantry at Camp Glenn, near Morehead City; the Third Regiment of Infantry at Chickamauga with the regular army; and the Coast Artillery at Fort Caswell with a battalion of U. S. Coast Artillery. There were the ordinary petty ailments, but no unusual sickness at any time at any of the encampments.

An active crusade against hookworm was waged by this Department with the hearty co-operation of the Hookworm Department of the State Board of Health, Dr. John A. Ferrell, Assistant Secretary for hookworm, in charge. As noted in last year's report of the Southern recruits examined at Fort Slocum and Jackson Barracks, over 80 per cent were found infected. In view of the disease being largely confined to the South, and with the desire to aid in the eradication of this disease in this State, and further, to secure data fixing the responsibility of different sections of the State for the prevalence of the disease, it was decided to examine the troops at each encampment. It was arranged between the Assistant Secretary for Hookworm (of the Board of Health) and this Department that the latter would collect specimens, forward the same, and the examinations be made at the Laboratory of the Board of Health, and reported back to this Department. The work was new and unpleasant, both to the men and the medical officers on duty, but it gives me great pleasure to state that the work was cheerfully undertaken, and in view of the experience on the part of the larger number of the Corps in such investigation the results were most encouraging, and valuable help rendered the infected soldier by establishing the existence of the worm and pointing the way for ridding himself of the disease. Major Glenn, Captain Witherspoon and Lieutenant Clemenger were at Chickamauga Park with the First Regiment of Infantry; Major Winston, Captain Boyette and Lieutenant Newell with the Third, and Captain Pridgen and Lieutenant Tayloe with the Second at Camp Glenn. I commend these officers for the part taken by each in this trying work. The burden fell heavily upon Captain Pridgen, who by reason of unfortunate circumstances and unforeseen conditions was without aid until the last two days of camp, being in charge of, and responsible for the entire medical and surgical work of the regiment, in addition to this superimposed hookworm investigation. The work could not have fallen upon a more responsive, readier, or more capable officer, and I commend his work most heartily. This Department is deeply appreciative of the invaluable aid of Dr. John A. Ferrell, in charge of the Hookworm Department of the Board of Health, without whose help the work could not have been done at all, this Department not being prepared to take care of the large amount of laboratory work required, nor was it in possession of funds for such a crusade.

The returns of the Third Regiment are regarded as untrustworthy. The specimens were obtained conscientiously and with no little difficulty, as much persuasion and patient explanations were necessary to gain the consent of the men to co-operate in the collections. Most unfortunately, owing to the newness of, and inexperience in the procedure, several hundred of the specimens reached the laboratory in a dried state and the results were of no account in working up a tabulated statement of the degree of infection in the regiment. I venture, however, to express the opinion that the percentage of infection among these troops, coming for the most part from the lower lying portions of the State, and the conditions not being unlike those obtaining in the Second Regiment, the percentage would have been nearly the same. The First Regiment, coming for the most part from the Piedmont and mountain sections, as would be expected, showed a lower percentage of infection.

It is interesting to note as one ascends from the low country the percentage of infection perceptibly decreases. There is little doubt but that this infection, which plays an important role in the economics of the Southern States, will succumb before the solid phalanx of determined effort now being made to eradicate it from the State.

The percentage of infection among the troops is as follows:

	Per Cent.	
First Regiment	.368	
Second Regiment	.577	
Third Regiment	.161	Untrustworthy on account of the condition of specimens received at the laboratory.
Coast Artillery	.291	

Letters were sent to each of the Company Commanders with the names of the infected members of his Company so that they might be officially apprised of the condition and seek relief, the means for which are simple, safe and speedy and inexpensive.

Major Glenn's report of the encampment at Chickamauga is both interesting and instructive; but for lack of space this valuable communication does not appear in full. I greatly regret that the complete account of such thorough work and opportunities enjoyed as evidenced in Major Glenn's report can not reach the eye of every officer of the Medical Corps and Guard.

Letter from Major Glenn follows with extracts from his report of the First Regiment Hospital Corps at the encampment at Chickamauga Park, Ga.

September 3, 1910.

COL. S. WESTRAY BATTLE,
Asheville, N. C.

DEAR COL. BATTLE:—Enclosed please find long delayed report of the encampment at Camp of Instruction, Chickamauga Park, Ga. This report has been complete, with the exception of one or two alterations, for three or four weeks, but it seemed almost impossible since that time to find time to complete and mail it to you.

I am sending a copy of the Sanitary Regulations and Sanitary Inspection at the Camp of Instruction, not so much as a part of my report, but for your information, that you may better judge the completeness of our instructions and also what is required in sanitation by any army at the present time.

Hoping that you will find this report entirely satisfactory, I beg to remain,

Yours respectfully,
EUGENE B. GLENN,
Major, M. C., N. C. N. G.

August 31, 1910.

COL. S. WESTRAY BATTLE,
Surgeon General, Asheville, N. C.

SIR:—I have the honor of respectfully submitting the following report in entirety of the First Regiment Hospital Corps, officers and men, at the recent encampment at Camp of Instruction, Chickamauga Park, Ga.

* * * * * * * *

The food was abundant, of good quality, and well prepared. The drinking water was obtained from a well which was located east of the camp grounds on a ridge above. I was informed that the well was four hundred feet deep. The water was pumped out by an engine and distributed through pipes to the company kitchens and bath rooms. There was plenty of water, but of poor quality, the water being polluted by colon bacilli. The water was boiled by the respective companies before drinking.

Bathing facilities were excellent at the bath houses located at the end of the company streets, in which were located shower baths.

There were incinerators located at the lower end of the company streets, one incinerator for every two companies. A detail was kept at each incinerator and the sanitary conditions in and around the incinerators were kept first class. The night urinal cans were collected and emptied in the incinerators every morning and the cans were burned out by the scavenger, after first treating the inside of cans with crude oil and straw. The incinerators were burned out every morning by the scavenger. The incinerator for the officers was located east and to the left of Officers' Row, and was cared for by the scavenger each morning, as described above in the case of the regimental incinerators. * * *

I desire to make special mention of the valuable assistance rendered by Lieut. F. J. Clemenger in the collection of specimens from the men in the regiment for examination for hookworm disease. The large percentage collected is due principally to his persistent and untiring efforts. There were 535 men in the regiment and there were 453 specimens for hookworm examinations collected, being about 81 per cent. A man from each company was detailed to stay at the incinerators for the purpose of collecting the specimens and filling out the history blanks. Each night the specimens collected during the day were carefully packed and sent by a detail to Chattanooga, from which point they were expressed to Dr. J. A. Ferrell, at the State Laboratory of Hygiene, where they were examined for evidences of hookworm disease by him and his assistants. The following is the positive percentage, by county, town and company, of the 372 specimens examined by Dr. J. A. Ferrell, Assistant Secretary for the eradication of hookworm disease. * * *

The Hospital Corps received instructions daily from an army officer at the Field Hospital, from 9 to 10:30 a. m., and the scheme for work of the Medical Department was as follows:

First day, making camp, tent pitching, and location of Field Hospital.

Second day, pitching Field Hospital, its administration, including the distribution of its equipment, personnel and preparations for the reception of patients, and ambulance drill.

Third day, establishing dressing stations, patients collected and transferred by travois, litter, and horse back, to dressing stations and transferred by ambulance back to Field Hospital.

Fourth day, demonstration of the equipment pertaining to the Field Hospital, the instructions in the use of water filters, sterilizers, and hospital sanitation. Application of first aid on the firing line, establishing aid stations and collecting patients by single bearers, two bearers, and improvised litters.

Eighth day, the establishment of complete line of assistance from the firing line of the Field Hospital and the evacuation of the Field Hospital for the Base Hospital.

Ninth day, participated in morning maneuvers with the regiment, and at 8 o'clock that evening went into bivouac with all the troops over night on Snodgrass Hill, where all the troops were engaged. Returning next morning, we broke to entrain for our home stations.

The Major and Lieutenant Surgeons embarked for Asheville, N. C., on the first section of special troop train at 2:30 p. m., reaching the objective point at 6:30 a. m. on the 21st day of July, 1910. There were no casualties enroute. Captain Witherspoon and Hospital Corps followed on the second section of special troop train, and there were no casualties reported on their return journey.

RECOMMENDATIONS.

First. That the men be required to pass a physical examination at the time of their enlistment, or at their first encampment thereafter.

Second. That the attention of the proper authorities be called to the injuries produced on the instep and heel by the canvas puttee leggings, which were responsible for a great many reporting at sick call for treatment. Leggings with the strap passing underneath the arch of the foot produce no such conditions.

Third. I also recommend that all the hospital supplies and all medicines unfit for use be condemned and that requisition be made for a fresh supply. I consider the present supply unfit for use, due to long service and age, believing that their retirement would be for the best interest of the service.

Respectfully,

EUGENE B. GLENN,
Major Surgeon, First Regiment, N. C. N. G.

Captain Witherspoon, in his report from Fort Caswell, makes the following recommendations. For want of space the report is not published in full, but in it he bears testimony to the untiring efforts and most efficient work of Lieutenant Clemenger in charge of hookworm investigation.

CHARLOTTE, August 31, 1910.

COL. S. WESTRAY BATTLE,
Surgeon General, Asheville, N. C.

SIR:—I have the honor to render the following report of the encampment at Fort Caswell, N. C., of the First, Second, Third, Fourth, and Fifth companies, C. A. C., N. G., and C. A. C., U. S. A., from August 5 to 15, 1910. * * *

I would make the following recommendations:

First. That all enlisted men and officers be examined before going to camp, and all those discovered with chronic and acute maladies be prohibited from attending encampments.

Second. That the enlisted men be offered some inducement to serve their enlistments—it is discouraging to have practically a new roster of men with each encampment.

Third. That the regulation shoe be issued the men, thus relieving the medical corps of much unnecessary work, and the men inconveniences and suffering; that lighter clothing be issued the men, as the olive drab is entirely too heavy for the season of the year at which encampments are held.

Fourth. That the encampments be ordered earlier and last for a period of fourteen days.

Fifth. The medical equipment, in all departments, is incomplete and inadequate by reason of ordinary wear and tear, and was condemned by medical officers at Fort Caswell and Chickamauga as not complying with the standard for field service, and it was recommended that new supplies be issued in exchange.

In connection with the above recommendations I would call your attention to the hardship that falls upon the Charlotte Detachment Hospital Corps in attending two encampments in one month, and I respectfully recommend that a new detachment be organized, or that the Charlotte Detachment be recruited to a sufficient strength if we are expected to furnish medical attendance in the future at two encampments, as we have in the last two years.

Very respectfully,

B. J. WITHERSPOON,
Captain, Medical Corps, N. C. N. G.

This Department approves the recommendations.

Foot troubles amongst our troops are too frequent to be passed over without comment. Footgear is the most important article of the soldier's uniform. Both Napoleon and Wellington are said to have declared that they made war with legs and not with arms. Efficiency is out of the question without physical comfort, and the latter depends as much, or more so, on a suitable shoe than any one article or part of the uniform. The Chief of the Division of Militia Affairs states in speaking of the issue of the uniform marching shoe by the general government of the Organized Militia, that in some States orders prescribe that the uniform shoe should be worn as an essential part of the equipment on all occasions when the uniform is worn, and that shoes in such cases are required to be kept in the armory locker in connection with and as an integral part of the uniform kept there. The issue of the shoe to the Organized Militia is one of the beneficent steps taken to aid the citizen soldier in getting close to the regular, and it is earnestly recommended that the Guard may be thus equipped. But it is one thing to be supplied with the marching shoe and quite another to get the right sort of shoe. A recent examination of the feet of enlisted men at an army post showed that 75 per cent of them were wearing ill-fitting shoes. The Army shoe is of first class material and workmanship, said to be the best in the world, but the shoe should be tried on the foot of the soldier, the fit being inspected to obtain the best results in comfort and efficiency of the man.

Following up the remarks in my last year's report upon anti-typhoid vaccination, the slogan in military medicine is, Forward! Immunizing against typhoid fever is going on in all the armies of the world. Last year I expressed the belief that typhoid fever, that scourge of the military camp, had had its day, and the mortality therefrom would be, in the near future, all but a negligible factor. This is all but *à fait accompli.* The innocuousness of the procedure has been established. The War Departments of many nations are requiring it as a routine measure. Of the 11,338 persons in our Army who have voluntarily submitted to the treatment there have been three cases recorded as typhoid with considerable doubt as to the correctness of the diagnosis in two cases; no deaths.

I hereby recommend the treatment or procedure to our guardsmen, officer and man. And along this line I append a letter from Lieutenant Clemenger in response to a request for expert opinion on the subject. Lieutenant Clemenger is one of our foremost bacteriologists with the scientific bent and training which is making so much for preventive medicine.

COL. S. W. BATTLE,
Surgeon General, N. C. N. G., Asheville, N. C.

SIR:—I have the honor to acknowledge the receipt of your communication relative to the advisability of vaccinating State troops against typhoid fever.

Consensus of opinion among those military authorities who have up to this time inoculated regular army troops, both in this country and in the armies of foreign nations, seems to be that it is a procedure worthy of most serious consideration by those in authority over organizations of any character where field conditions are to be met with.

The procedure seems on the whole to be harmless, and other than a mild toxic reaction consisting of headache, malaïse and chills, with an occasional rise of temperature, there has so far been found to be no deleterious effects. The technique of administration seems to offer the only barrier in the way of successful administration during the camp life of the State Guard. The interval of time between the inoculations has been determined by Colonel Leishman, a pioneer in the crusade against typhoid, to be about ten days between each administration, in his experience, which if absolutely necessary would prevent the utilization of this protective measure in any unit in camp for so short a time.

The utilization of this time interval has not been found necessary, however, in the experience of other men. In fact, the practice as carried out in hospital work by Sir Alworth Wright is to give only two doses, keeping the interval about the same.

It can be well seen that if a determination in advance of leaving for camp of those who desired to submit to this measure, that the first dose be given on the first day in camp, and the last dose on the day of breaking camp. In my opinion, though we might not be able to establish so high a state of immunity, by modification of the plan followed out in the regular army, yet it would be highly justifiable to put this procedure in practice as an experimental measure, and with the help of the line officers collect such data as might be available.

I have in my possession the three strains of the typhoid organisms used while an assistant in the laboratory of Sir Alworth Wright, and they would be available for use in the preparation of vaccines, which would be gladly undertaken in the course of medical duties as a surgeon in the National Guard.

There would be no expense attached to this work which the State would have to pay, and other than the temporary incapacitation here and there of an officer or man from the mild symptoms of reaction, little disturbance of the military regime of the soldiers while in camp would take place.

Considering the past history of wars, and especially our late war with Spain, where more soldiers died from typhoid fever than were actually killed in performance of military duty, by ten times, a procedure not offering the possibility of serious injury to the enlisted men would be justifiable if we could even by a small percentage lessen the incidence of typhoid fever in war.

Very respectfully, F. J. CLEMENGER, M.D.,
First Lieutenant, N. C. N. G.

Respecting conditions at Camp Glenn I have to renew my recommendations of last year: that the water supply which was abundant for one full regiment be increased by putting down more driven wells to meet the requirements of a brigade encampment; that the water be subjected to examination by the Laboratory of Hygiene before each yearly encampment. This was done last summer with a satisfactory report from the Laboratory. I again recommend, if it has not already been done, that a hydrant be placed nearer the site of the hospital.

A pavilion hospital was promised, but thus far I have received no advice that steps were being taken to construct it. It is badly needed, and one answering every purpose would be inexpensive. I earnestly commend this matter to your favorable consideration, and would be pleased to present sketches and make suggestions for the erection of a house for the sick, which in my opinion is of vital importance and should be ready for use in the encampment of 1911.

For the better care of meats and perishable supplies, the present commissary building, or whatever it may be designated, should be extended. This would cost little and the present conditions are impossible in the light of present day needs and sanitation.

RECOMMENDATIONS.

Sodding and grading, as well as road making, would add greatly to the attractions of the camp; these measures coming well with the province of sanitation. Something done each year on a general scheme for a finished camp would bring surprising results in comfort of the soldier by lessening the breeding place of the mosquito, replacing the heavy sand with sod and securing firm, clean, company streets. The camp grounds should be enclosed to prevent the ingress of hogs and cattle. Much complaint has been made by the medical officers at camp that hogs roam at will, upsetting the slop containers and adding greatly to the difficulties of keeping a sanitary camp. Besides no camp can be kept clean or attractive or in any manner improved shared with the hog.

Relating to the Medical Department there should be a reorganization, but thus far I have not been able to formulate a scheme which would work smoothly under conceivable conditions. That the Department is short of commissioned and enlisted personnel I am sure, and after a conference with Captain Thomason, M. C., Assistant to the Bureau of Militia Affairs, U. S. A., I am convinced that there should be organized a Field Hospital and Ambulance Company, and officers commissioned, and men enlisted to carry out such a plan. It will be my duty and pleasure to seek in the very near future a conference with you on this question so vital to the interest of the Medical Department of the Guard, and ask your co-operation in carrying out some plan of the kind before the summer encampments begin.

Finally I respectfully recommend that His Excellency, the Governor, be requested to reissue commissions to the Medical Corps to more nearly conform to the regulations now existing in the U. S. Army. The designation Surgeon, Assistant Surgeon has been done away with and Major, Captain and Lieutenant, Medical Corps, has been adopted. For example—Major Glenn's commission would read, Major E. B. Glenn, Medical Corps, N. C. N. G., in the new commission, if such meets the approval of yourself and the Governor.

I was more than pleased by the interest evinced by the Medical Department of the Bureau of Militia Affairs, and it is my desire to turn this visit to helpful account in our own Department.

Very respectfully,

S. WESTRAY BATTLE,

Surgeon General.

Report of Paymaster General

STATE OF NORTH CAROLINA,
OFFICER OF PAYMASTER GENERAL,
FAYETTEVILLE, N. C., December 1, 1910.

THE ADJUTANT GENERAL, STATE OF NORTH CAROLINA,
Raleigh, N. C.

SIR:—I have the honor of submitting herewith the report of this Department for the fiscal year ending November 30, 1910.

RECEIPTS.

Balance on hand last report, November 30, 1909		$8,689.51
Jan. 13.	On account of 1909 appropriation	7,500.00
May	On account of 1910 appropriation	5,000.00
June	On account of 1910 appropriation	5,000.00
July	On account of 1910 appropriation	5,000.00
	From disbanded company	217.52
	Total	$31,407.03

DISBURSEMENTS.

COMPANIES, BANDS AND DIVISIONS.

First Infantry companies	$2,875.00	
Second Infantry companies	3,000.00	
Third Infantry companies	3,000.00	
First Infantry Band	250.00	
Second Infantry Band	250.00	
Third Infantry Band	250.00	
Division Naval Brigade	1,375.00	
Coast Artillery	1,125.00	
Field Artillery	125.00	
		$12,250.00

BRIGADE AND REGIMENTAL HEADQUARTERS, AND COMPANIES, DIVISIONS, AND CORPS COMMANDERS.

Brigade Commander, First Brigade	$150.00	
Commander First Infantry	150.00	
Commander Second Infantry	150.00	
Commander Artillery Corps	75.00	
Commander Third Infantry	150.00	
Commander Naval Brigade	150.00	
		825.00

ADJUTANT GENERAL'S DEPARTMENT.

Miss Annie Travis	$300.00	
Lieut. Col. R. L. Leinster, A. A. G	351.00	
Maj. Gordon Smith, Acting A. A. G	10.00	
Gen. T. R. Robertson, Chief of Ordnance	300.00	
		$961.00

QUARTERMASTER GENERAL'S DEPARTMENT.

Gen. Francis A. Macon, salary	$499.92	
Miss Magdalene Landis, stenographer	480.00	
		979.92

PAYMASTER GENERAL'S DEPARTMENT.

Col. J. G. Hollingsworth, salary in full	$374.94	
Col. S. W. Cooper, salary three months	124.98	
		499.92

SURGEON GENERAL'S DEPARTMENT.

Charlotte Hospital Corps	$75.00	
Clinton Hospital Corps	37.50	
Reidsville Hospital Corps	75.00	
		187.50

ENCAMPMENT EXPENSES.

Transportation	$940.70	
Drug bills	143.92	
Company photos	10.00	
		1,094.62

GENERAL FUNDS AND MISCELLANEOUS.

Gen. T. R. Robertson, salary	$319.92	
Transportation and subsistence for troops, October 14, 1910	563.25	
Special work, R. E. Lumsden	6.50	
W. H. Powell, two pipes	.50	
R. T. Daniel, exchange on money	25.45	
Bill, Gastor W. Roberts	13.75	
Bill, Gen. Joseph A. Storch	20.00	
Bill, J. L. Currin	25.65	
Insurance on supplies at Henderson	65.00	
Payment to Disbursing Officer at Camp Perry, Ohio	73.33	
Transportation of Gen. B. S. Royster, P. J. Macon and W. C. Rodman to St. Louis and return	285.00	
		1,398.35

PAY FOR ENLISTED MEN.

First Infantry	$2,198.75	
Second Infantry	2,078.25	
Third Infantry	2,403.00	
Battery A	137.75	
Coast Artillery	959.00	
Naval Brigade	293.75	
Third Infantry Band	123.00	
		$8,193.50
		$26,389.81
Balance on hand December 1, 1910		5,017.22
		$31,407.03

Respectfully, S. W. COOPER,
Paymaster General, N. C. N. G.

Report of Commissary General

STATE OF NORTH CAROLINA,
OFFICE OF SUBSISTENCE DEPARTMENT,
FRANKLINTON, N. C., December 21, 1910.

R. L. LEINSTER, ADJUTANT GENERAL,
Raleigh, N. C.

SIR:—I have the honor to submit herewith the annual report and recommendations of this Department.

In compliance with General Orders Nos. 13, 15, May 19, June 11, 1910, I communicated with the Commissaries of the Second and Third Infantry, N. C. N. G., pertaining to the number of men to be subsisted and rations preferred for their respective Regiments at the approaching encampment. Upon receipt of their replies, I asked and received bids from leading wholesale houses of Baltimore, Richmond, Norfolk, Wilmington, New Bern and Raleigh, also from bakeries, ice plants and butchers. After obtaining bids, comparing quality and net delivery prices at Camp Glenn, I placed orders with the lowest bidders in accordance with instructions from the War Department.

The supplies for each Regiment were ordered to arrive at Camp Glenn two days preceding the Regiments, invoices and bills of ladings were mailed to me.

(Quality, price and prompt delivery being equal, this Department will give the nearest market to Camp preference in all purchases.)

On arriving at Camp Glenn, 24 hours preceding each Regiment, I found all supplies unloaded by the railroad company at Morehead City, as the storage facilities at Camp Glenn were inadequate to accomodate both Quartermaster and Commissary supplies, consequently, I had considerable work in having the goods reloaded and shipped back to Camp Glenn. However, I succeeded in getting the same delivered in time to be issued to the men, except one issue of coffee to the Second Regiment, which was delayed two hours by the railroad company. In this connection, I would suggest that the railroad company be required to leave all supplies at Camp Glenn instead of taking to Morehead City.

Rations were issued on the regular approved ration return form, prescribed by the War Department: 25 cents per day for field, 40 cents for travel.

The order requiring rations to be issued to a Company Commission Officer is a splendid one and should be enforced.

Upon inspection of the kitchens and mess hall, I found the enlisted men perfectly satisfied with the quality of rations, but the quantity was hardly sufficient. Considering the advance of provisions, etc., I would suggest that the field allowance be increased to 35 cents a day.

I congratulate the Third Regiment on having the Commissariat that they have; always at his post and looking after the subsistence of his men.

The morning of the arrival of the Second Regiment, General Macon called at my tent, accompanied by Company Commissaries, requesting that I issue mornings' rations, as the Regimental Commissariat was quartered at the Atlantic Hotel and not in Camp. I proceeded to do so until his arrival. Would recommend that officers of the Subsistence Department be quartered in Camp.

I wish to commend Company F, Second Infantry, as being the only Company that used the army issue of tin tableware, their mess hall and kitchen being kept in first class condition. This Company also had enlisted cooks.

I organized a cooking school, which I found very interesting and instructive to the cooks and Commissary Sergeants.

I would recommend that regulations regarding enlisted cooks be fully enforced, as it is useless for this Department to instruct non-enlisted cooks. In this connection I would suggest that enlisted cooks together with Commissary Sergeants and *as many men as possible* attend this school. We will have demonstrations of quick cooking on the field.

I recommend the purchase of one regimental bakery wagon and ovens. We need this very much and could use it at encampments, making necessary bread, together with the valuable instruction to the cooks. This bakery wagon would soon pay for itself, thus saving the State the manufacturers' profits and exorbitant express charges.

I earnestly recommend that a commissary building be erected at once, at Camp Glenn, equipped with refrigerator, ice cellar, counters, desk, scales, etc. I find the present structure entirely inadequate to accommodate both the Quartermaster and Commissary stores.

I recommend that an order be issued requiring each Company to clean their range and cooking utensils and check same before leaving Camp, and to be inspected by the Commissary Department. This order would stop the losing of cooking utensils, which has been so common in the past. Also have them ready for emergencies.

In conclusion, I wish to say that this is my first year's experience in this Department. I am sorry to say, I found the Subsistence Department as I did, the Small Arms Practice and Rifle Range, six years ago hardly in existence, a mere side line of the Quartermaster's Department.

"My shoulder is to the wheel" and I beg all officers and enlisted men in the Guard to assist in establishing a Commissary Department equal to that of any State.

Should war be declared with any great nation, this Department would be called upon at a moment's notice to subsist thousands of men. All of this responsibility comes under the Commissary Department, and without assistance from some experienced officers attached to my staff it would be a difficult position. I regret to say that none of my assistants were ordered out to assist me and to *get experience,* at the last encampment, but hope that in the future it may be possible for them to attend.

Frederick The Great said, "The art of conquering is lost without the art of subsistence." Wellington prided himself on being a first class Commissariat. Lincoln said, "The Subsistence Department of the Union Army was like a well regulated stomach, worked so smoothly that they were not conscious of having it."

I wish to thank all officers and enlisted men and especially Sergeant Waddington, U. S. A., for courtesies shown in building up this branch.

Very respectfully,

W. L. McGHEE,

Colonel and Commissary General.

Report of the Chief of Ordnance

STATE OF NORTH CAROLINA,
ORDNANCE DEPARTMENT,
RALEIGH, December 1, 1910.

THE ADJUTANT GENERAL OF NORTH CAROLINA,
Raleigh, N. C.

SIR:—I have the honor herewith to submit the annual report of this Department for the period commencing December 1, 1909, and ending November 30, 1910, to which are attached detailed statements of all ordnance received and issued, marked respectively Exhibit "A" and Exhibit "B." In the special capacity of commanding officer of the Military Supply Depot I have issued also to the Guard such Quartermaster supplies as were required from time to time, and have rendered an account of the same to the Quartermaster General. The State has now on hand and available for issue military stores of all kinds, and in sufficient quantities to meet present needs. Our warehouse facilities are ample for storage purposes and the military property of the State in my charge is well housed and protected.

In obedience to General Orders I was on duty at the State Rifle Range last July while the Second Infantry and Third Infantry were engaged in target practice. The high scores of both officers and men showed great improvement in marksmanship, and indicated that much time had been spent on the home ranges, both in the gallery and in the field.

The State Range is in very good condition, but some additional work is necessary to remedy a few defects, which should receive attention before the next annual small arms practice at that point.

I have the honor to recommend that the present storage house be converted into a pit shed, and placed midway of the line of targets. I further recommend that a range house be built for storage purposes near the 500 yards firing point, and accessible at all times without interfering with actual work on the range. I further recommend that a better system of telephone communication between the firing points and the pit be installed.

Very respectfully,

THOMAS R. ROBERTSON,
Chief of Ordnance.

EXHIBIT A.

ORDNANCE STORES RECEIVED FROM DEC. 1, 1909, TO NOV. 30, 1910.

Rifles, new magazine, cal. 30, star gauged	15
Rifles, new magazine, cal. 30, star gauged, with telescopic musket sight	3
Rifles, new magazine, cal. 30, star gauged, with Maxim silencers,	8
Rifles, gallery practice, cal. 22	8
Ball cartridges for new magazine rifles, cal. 30	184,800
Blank cartridges for new magazine rifles, cal. 30	10,000
Ball cartridges for gallery practice rifles, cal. 22	115,000
Ball cartridges, revolver, cal. 38	34,000
Aiken Iron Standard treadle targets, complete	14
Rifle range streamers and halyards	10
Marking disks and staves, short range	30
Marking disks and staves, mid-range	34
Flags, danger, for rifle range	5
Flags, ricochet, for rifle range	5
Targets, paper, A	300
Targets, paper, B	300
Targets, paper, C	300
Targets, paper, N	25
Targets, paper, X	1,200
Targets, paper, Y	200
Targets, paper, Z	200
Targets, gallery practice, iron	8
Pasters, target	150,000
Cartridge holders	130
Telescopic musket sights and pouches	3
Rifle marksman's pins, bronze	300
Rifle sharpshooter's badges, bronze	10
Expert rifleman's badges, bronze	10
Pistol marksman's pins, bronze	30
Pistol sharpshooter's badges, bronze	15
Pistol expert's badges, bronze	6
Blanket roll straps, tan, sets	1,500
Canteens, O. D	400
Canteen straps, web	600
Haversacks	200

Haversack snap hooks	600
Meat cans	200
Tin cups	500
Belgian aiming devices	164
Time interval recorders for Coast Artillery	12
Intrenching rules	40
Wire cutters	120
Hand axes and carriers	170
Pick mattocks and carriers	260
Intrenching shovels and carriers	756
Field artillery oil, gallons	10
Field artillery grease, pounds	65
Field artillery blacking, boxes	2
Metal fouling solutions for small arms, bottles	360
Saddle cloths and insignia, general officers' sets	1
Officers' sabers	12
Officers' saber belts, russet	12

EXHIBIT B.—ORDNANCE STORES ISSUED DECEMBER 1, 1909, TO NOVEMBER 30, 1910.

ORGANIZATION.	Springfield Rifles, Cal. 30.	Bayonets, New.	Scabbards, New.	Gun Slings.	Waist Belts, Rifle, Web.	Suspenders, Sets.	Revolvers, Cal. 38.	Holsters.	Revolver Field Belts.	Springfield Rifles, Star Guaged.	Gallery Practice Rifles, Cal. 22.	Telescopic Musket Sights and Cases.	Belgian Aiming Devices.	Ball Cartridges, Cal. 22.	Ball Cartridges, Cal. 30.	Blank Cartridges, Cal. 30.	Ball Cartridges, Cal. 38.	Cartridge Holders.	Officers' Sabers.	Officers' Belts, Russet.	Saddles.	Briddles.	Bridle Bits.	Spurs, Pairs.	Blanket-roll Straps, Sets.
FIRST INFANTRY:																									
Field, Staff and Band							2	3	4												2				28
Company A				2					3	1				1,000	1,200		300								50
Company B	1					2	1						2	1,000			200		2	2	1				55
Company C														6,000	1,200		100								22
Company D																									
Company E									5					1,000	1,200		100								50
Company F		1							2	1				2,00	1,200										50
Company G														1,00					2	1					
Company H	1			1					3					1,0[illegible]	1,200										50
Company I										1				6,00	2,00	500									53
Company K								1		1				2,00	1,00										50
Company L	6	8	7	8	7	7								8,00	2,00	500	500		1	1					50
Company M														1,00		500									50

SECOND INFANTRY:																									
Field, Staff and Band					1				2	1							100				2				4
Company A				5			3	3						1,000											
Company B								2						1,630	1,200										
Company C														2,000					3	3					
Company D										1			2	3,000				10							
Company E	1	3	3	3	2	2				2				1,000	1,200										53
Company F									3						901	500									
Company G														1,000											
Company H	1			1						1				4,000	1,200										
Company I							1	1						1,000											
Company K							2	2						1,000											
Company L	8	8	8	8	8	8				1					1,200										52
Company M									5																
THIRD INFANTRY:																									
Field, Staff and Band	2			2			3	3	2	2					60				3	2	6	4		3	28
Company A				3					3	1				1,000											
Company B		1								2			2	4,000				15							
Company C	9	12	12	9	11	11								3,000											
Company D														1,000											
Company E														1,000											
Company F				10						1				1,000											
Company G		1	1	1	1					1				1,000	1,200										

EXHIBIT B—CONTINUED.

ORGANIZATION.	Springfield Rifles. Cal. 30.	Bayonets, New.	Scabbards, New.	Gun Slings.	Waist Belts, Rifle, Web.	Suspenders, Sets.	Revolvers, Cal. 38.	Holsters.	Revolver Field Belts.	Springfield Rifles, Star Guaged.	Gallery Practice Rifles, Cal. 22.	Telescopic Musket Sights and Cases.	Belgian Aiming Devices.	Ball Cartridges, Cal. 22.	Ball Cartridges, Cal. 30.	Blank Cartridges, Cal. 30.	Ball Cartridges, Cal. 38.	Cartridge Holders.	Officers' Sabers.	Officers' Belts, Russet.	Saddles.	Briddles.	Bridle Bits.	Spurs, Pairs.	Blanket-roll Straps, Sets.
THIRD INFANTRY—*Con.*																									
Company H		1	1		1									1,000	1,200										
Company I									3					1,000											
Company K														1,000											
Company L					3		3	3						2,000	1,200	1,500			3	2					
Company M									2					1,000	1,200		240								
COAST ARTILLERY:																									
Field and Staff							4	4	1								180								
First Company	13	13	13	13	13	13		1	2		2			6,00	1,200		500		3	3					
Second Company					5				3		2			5,00				20							
Third Company														1,00											
Fourth Company	10	10	10	10	10	10			3		2			10,00	1,200			20							50
Fifth Company	63	63	63	63	63	63			6		2			11,00	1,200			20							66

FIELD ARTILLERY:																									
Battalion A																	500								
General Staff	3			4			9	9	2	1					160		760				2		1	1	
Brigade Staff							1	1	1															1	
HOSPITAL CORPS:																									
First Infantry							1	1	1																
Second Infantry																									
Third Infantry																									

EXHIBIT B—CONTINUED.

ORGANIZATION.	Pouches for First Aid Packets.	Canteens.	Canteen Straps, Web.	Haversacks.	Haversack Hooks.	Canteen, Haversack Straps, Tan.	Meat Cans.	Knives.	Forks.	Spoons.	Tin Cups.	Aiken Iron Targets, Complete.	Target Pasters.	Field Paper Targets.	Gallery Targets, Iron.	Gallery Paper Targets.	Intrenching Rules.	Wire Cutters.	Hand Axes and Carriers.	Pick Mattocks and Carriers.	Intrenching Shovels and Carriers.	Field Artillery Oil, Gallons.	Field Artillery Grease, Lbs.	Harness Soap, Boxes.	Leather Blacking Ingredients, Boxes.
[illegible]:																									
Field, Staff and Band	28	8		1		4	12	25	16	26	18	1	10,000	22											
Comp'y A	48	2	5				1	25	22	10	6					10	1	3	4	5	15				
Comp'y B	58	5	55	2		5	5	3	6	5	2	1	5,000	23	1	10	1	3	4	6	18				
Comp'y C	48				120							1		13	1	10	1	3	4	6	18				
Comp'y D	45															10	1	3	4	6	18				
Comp'y E	50	17	50	10	60			25	10	15	14					10	1	3	4	5	15				
Comp'y F	50	14	14		120		1				4					10	1	3	4	6	18				
Comp'y G	50										28					10	1	3	4	5	15				
Comp'y H	50	42	20	7				19	10	11	10					10	1	3	4	5	15				
Comp'y I	50	3	10		100		3	33	27	5	7	1		20	1	10	1	3	4	6	18				
Comp'y K	50	6		2	100		1			2						10	1	3	4	6	18				
Comp'y L	58	24		6	116		5	12	7	6		1	5,000	22		10	1	3	4	6	18				
Comp'y M	50															10	1	3	4	5	15				

SECOND INFANTRY:																									
Field, Staff and Band	23	10	10	4		4	5	11	5	5	5	2	18,000	40											
Company A	50															10	1	3	4	6	18				
Company B	50	1	5	3			2	4			18						1	3	4	5	15				
Company C	50		50	45	145												1	3	4	6	18				
Company D	45															10	1	3	4	5	15				
Company E	58	6	6	2							6					10	1	3	4	6	18				
Company F	53		15		120			41	31	3	36						1	3	4	5	15				
Company G	50																1	3	4	6	18				
Company H	61	1	66							10				33			1	3	4	7	21				
Company I	50	1	1														1	3	4	5	15				
Company K	50																1	3	4	6	18				
Company L	58	11	11	16	16		10	10	17	8	10	1	10,000	22			1	3	4	7	21				
Company M	45		10													10	1	3	4	5	21				
THIRD INFANTRY:																									
Field, Staff and Band	31	31	28	30		3	31	31	31	31	30														
Company A	50				20			5	5							10	1	3	4	6	18				
Company B	58		20									3		12	1		1	3	4	6	18				
Company C	50	6	6	13			9				21						1	3	4	5	15				
Company D	50																1	3	4	5	15				
Company E	48																1	3	4	5	15				
Company F	50											1	5,000	30		10	1	3	4	5	15				
Company G	45			1				6				1	5,000	30		10	1	3	4	5	15				

EXHIBIT B—CONTINUED.

ORGANIZATION.	Pouches for First Aid Packets.	Canteens.	Canteen Straps, Web.	Haversacks.	Haversack Hooks.	Canteen, Haversack Straps, Tan.	Meat Cans.	Knives.	Forks.	Spoons.	Tin Cups.	Aiken Iron Targets, Complete.	Target Pasters.	Field Paper Targets.	Gallery Targets, Iron.	Gallery Paper Targets.	Intrenching Rules.	Wire Cutters.	Hand Axes and Carriers.	Pick Mattocks and Carriers.	Intrenching Shovels and Carriers.	Field Artillery Oil, Gallons.	Field Artillery Grease, Lbs.	Harness Soap, Boxes.	Leather Blacking Ingredients, Boxes.
[illegible]D INFANTRY—*Con.*																									
Company H	50	16	7	22			2	1	1	3	25						1	3	4	6	18				
Company I	58		58													10	1	3	4	7	21				
Company K	50																1	3	4	5	15				
Company L	50	50	50									1	5,000	22		10	1	3	4	6	18				
Company M	50	5	63					16	36	19	5					10	1	3	4	5	15				
COAST ARTILLERY:																									
Field and Staff		1	1				1	1	1	1															
First Company	12	11	65		126	6	65	10	10	10	10				1										
Second Company	50														1										
Third Company	63															20									
Fourth Company	58	9	9	8	60		11	31	36	21	30				1										
Fifth Company	66	7	7					10	10	15															

FIELD ARTILLERY:																									
Battalion A		2		1		3	1	3	2	2	3											10	70	5	2
General Staff	2																								
Brigade Staff																									
HOSPITAL CORPS:																									
First Infantry	12																								
Second Infantry																									
Third Infantry	12																								

8

Report of Brigadier General

HEADQUARTERS OF FIRST BRIGADE,
NORTH CAROLINA NATIONAL GUARD,
OXFORD, December 31, 1911.

THE ADJUTANT GENERAL OF NORTH CAROLINA,
Raleigh, N. C.

SIR:—I have the honor to submit my report as Commanding Officer of the First Brigade for the year 1910.

The Brigade is composed of the same organizations as set out in my report for the year 1909, with the following exceptions: The First Battery Field Artillery has been transferred to the Coast Artillery Corps and designated as the Fifth Company, Coast Artillery Corps, and Company B, First Infantry, located at Charlotte, has been mustered out of the service for inefficiency.

The organizations of the Brigade encamped, during the year, for field instruction and rifle practice, as follows: First Infantry at the Joint Maneuvers, Chickamauga Park, Ga., July 11-20th, inclusive; Third Infantry for field instruction and rifle practice, at Camp Glenn, Morehead City, N. C., July 6-13th, inclusive; and Second Infantry for field instruction and rifle practice, at Camp Glenn, Morehead City, N. C., July 19-26th, inclusive.

The report of the work done by the First Infantry at Chickamanga Park was very gratifying. This Regiment, in addition to participating in the maneuvers, received special instructions in camp sanitation, guard duty, preparing camp and in cooking and preparing field rations.

The work of the Second and Third Infantries, at Camp Glenn, in field instruction and rifle practice, was progressive and the results were very satisfactory. Great improvement was shown in rifle practice, guard duty and camp sanitation. I was gratified to note these improvements and I was much pleased at the improvement in the discipline of the enlisted men.

The Second Infantry qualified three expert riflemen, two sharpshooters, one hundred and forty-seven marksmen, forty-five first class, eighty second class, and one hundred and fifty third class.

The Third Infantry qualified three sharpshooters, one hundred and fourteen marksmen, forty-six first class, ninety-one second class, and one hundred and fifty-three third class.

The totals of both Regiments were as follows: three experts, five sharpshooters, two hundred and sixty-one marksmen, ninety-one first class, one hundred and seventy-one second class, and three hundred and three third class.

The above figures do not include those who qualified in the fourth class.

During the tour of duty of the Second and Third Infantries at Camp Glenn I made a careful inspection of tentage and other Quartermaster's and Ordnance supplies, and condemned a large quantity of tentage and other stores, detailed reports of these inspections having been forwarded to your Department.

I beg to make the following recommendations:

1. That suitable buildings be erected at Camp Glenn for storing and properly protecting Quartermaster, Ordnance and Commissary supplies.

2. That water supply and sewerage be provided for the Hospital Corps, and that additional tentage be purchased for this Department.

3. That sufficient additional tentage be purchased so that a Brigade Encampment may be held.

4. That Regimental, Battalion and Company Commanders pay more attention to instructions with respect to guard duty and camp sanitation.

Captain Marcus B. Stokes, 10th Infantry, U. S. A., was on duty at Camp Glenn with both of the Regiments and his services were of the highest value to the officers and enlisted men.

To the members of my staff, to your Department and to the officers of the Guard I tender my thanks for valuable suggestions and many courtesies. Respectfully,

B. S. ROYSTER,

Brigadier General, Commanding First Brigade, North Carolina National Guard.

Report of Commanding Officer First Infantry

HEADQUARTERS FIRST INFANTRY, N. C. N. G.,
SHELBY, N. C., December 10, 1910.

THE ADJUTANT GENERAL, N. C. N. G.,
Raleigh, N. C.

SIR:—Below will be found my annual report of the First Regiment, N. C. N. G., for the year 1910. Pursuant to orders from the Adjutant General, the First Regiment proceeded to the maneuver camp at Chickamauga Park, Ga., arriving there July 13th and remaining until the 20th. We were brigaded with the Second and Fifth Georgia Regiments under command of Brigadier General Anderson. The course of instruction was gradual, beginning with squad, and covering company, battalion and regimental movements, and finally brigade formations. While in camp, the health of the Regiment was good, much improvement was made, and a great amount of information was gained. The United States officers assigned to our Regiment, both commissioned and non-commissioned, were of invaluable service to the Regiment, and the instructions they gave made a lasting impression on both officers and men. The Regiment was complimented by the officers in charge of the camp for the clean camp they kept and for the full turnout of men on drill and their general sobriety and behavior while in camp. Below will be found the attendance at the maneuver camp:

Field and Staff	16
Hospital Corps	11
Band and Noncoms.	30
Company A	46 men, 3 officers.
Company B	51 men, 3 officers.
Company C	41 men, 3 officers.
Company E	48 men, 3 officers.
Company F	43 men, 3 officers.
Company G	45 men, 3 officers.
Company H	43 men, 3 officers.
Company I	48 men, 3 officers.

Company K .... 40 men, 3 officers.
Company L .... 46 men, 3 officers.
Company M .... 40 men, 3 officers.

Company D, stationed at Charlotte, was disbanded and mustered out of the service during the year. I beg leave to suggest that a new company be organized to fill the vacancy in the Regiment at as early a date as is convenient and I feel sure that there are men in Charlotte who can organize a good company there. During the inspection, made in company with the Inspector General and Lieutenant Butler, U. S. A., I am pleased to state that I found the property kept in much better condition than heretofore. Some improvement in drill was noticed, but not so much as I had expected to see. All the company officers had installed their gallery targets and seemed to be getting good results from them. I wish to recommend that the expense allowance of the colonels be increased to $300.00 per year on the express condition that they visit each company at its home station at least once a year, and that each captain be allowed $100.00 per year for expenses. The death of our old Colonel while filling the position of Adjutant General carried universal sorrow to the hearts of the men of the regiment and we feel that his place will be hard to fill. That his successor may measure up to the high standard that he has set is my earnest wish and desire, and I hereby volunteer my aid and assistance in whatever way he may call on me.

Very respectfully,

J. T. GARDNER,
Colonel Commanding First North Carolina Infantry.

Report of Commanding Officer Second Infantry

HEADQUARTERS SECOND INFANTRY, N. C. N. G.,
WASHINGTON, N. C., December 31, 1910.

THE ADJUTANT GENERAL, N. C. N. G.,
Raleigh, N. C.

SIR:—I have the honor to submit my annual report for the year.

There has occurred no unusual circumstances to record.

The condition of the Regiment is healthy—though, as always, in the militia, some defects exist.

The equipment is better than in years, and it is believed that company commanders, as well as the enlisted men, are awakening to the necessity of caring for uniforms more than heretofore.

On July 19th Companies A, B, C, D, E, F, G, H, I, K, L, Band and Kinston Hospital Corps Detachment, arrived at Camp Glenn for rifle practice and drill. The arrangement of train schedules necessitated in one or more instances departure from home station on the 18th. While it is appreciated that patriotism should warrant service without pay in extreme cases, it would appear that, as a matter of principle, the pay should cover the entire period of duty. It is without doubt true that a sufficient saving could be made in other directions in connection with encampment periods which would secure this for the coming years. The charge can not be brought against the Guard that it is actuated by mercenary motives merely, if the years in which they served without pay and at personal expenditure, are taken into consideration.

While the chief work of the tour of duty at Camp Glenn was rifle practice, the schedule was arranged to include field movements by companies and battalions. The results in each were very satisfactory. The amount of work performed was about double that of the previous year with the same amount of cheerfulness on the part of participants. The routine of work was such that the company on detail at the pit today holds rifle practice tomorrow, and next day either guard duty or drill. In no case was any undue hardship inflicted, and better results were obtained by keeping all hands busy.

The strength of the Regiment by June report was 50 officers and 616 enlisted. Present at Camp, 50 officers and 513 enlisted. Company M did not report at Camp.

Of those present at Camp .... officers and .... enlisted reported on the range, the Regiment qualifying 3 expert riflemen, 2 sharpshooters, 147 marksmen. Compared with the result of the previous year, when 2 sharpshooters, 53 marksmen were qualified, the result is very gratifying. It is not deemed needful to give the result in detail, as this has already been done in General Orders.

There was some delay in issue of subsistence the first day or so—though in no wise the fault of the Regimental Commissary. It is pertinent here to emphasize the recommendation made before that this issue be made exclusively by the proper regimental officer. Surely, unless he is required to perform the duties of his office in its entirety on such occasions he can not reasonably be expected to become sufficiently well trained therein to secure the best service should he be thrown upon his own resources in an actual campaign.

The Medical Staff performed their duties well and ably. On account of urgent duties at home, Major H. I. Clark did not report at Camp at all; therefore, the entire work fell upon Captain C. L. Pridgen, until the arrival some days later of Lieutenant A. K. Tayloe. The sanitary conditions of the Camp, while they were not all that could be desired, showed some improvement over previous years. This appears to be a hard lesson for the militia to learn, although a *most* important one. Some day it is feared the negligence will be brought home very forcibly—indeed, it is believed that a longer period of encampment would exact its toll in serious illness.

Upon invitation of the committee in charge of the celebration of the 200th anniversary of the settlement of the city of New Bern, all the Companies, except F and H, participated in the parade. The courtesy of the Norfolk & Southern Railroad in granting this stop-over privilege is to be commended, as was also that of the citizens of the city for their invitation.

Some of the men were overcome by heat, one seriously, necessitating leaving him at the hospital upon departure of his Company. For medical attention given him while there, acknowledgment is made to Dr. Norfleet M. Gibbs, of that city.

The Companies of the Regiment were inspected twice during the year. First at their home stations by the Inspector General, accompanied by Lieut. C. M. Butler, U. S. A., and at Camp Glenn by Captain M. B. Stokes, U. S. A., who reported in the dual capacity of inspector and instructor, and his assistance was of much value.

Sergeant Jno. Waddington, U. S. A., upon completing his tour at the home stations, reported for duty also. It is hoped that a similar detail may be secured each year of an enlisted man of the regular army, thus affording to the enlisted militiaman the same benefits the officer enjoys through contact with one whose business is soldiering.

In the death of General Armfield the Guard suffered a severe loss, but whatever of consolation there may be, is in the knowledge of the fact that the Guard is better today by reason of his effort. His example will always be an inspiration to those who were associated with him.

Respectfully,

H. C. BRAGAW,

Colonel Second Infantry, N. C. N. G.

Report of Commanding Officer Third Infantry

STATE OF NORTH CAROLINA,
HEADQUARTERS THIRD INFANTRY, N. C. N. G.,
REIDSVILLE, N. C., December 1, 1910.

TO THE ADJUTANT GENERAL OF NORTH CAROLINA,
Raleigh, N. C.

SIR:—I have the honor of submitting the following report of Third Infantry for the fiscal year ending November 30th, 1910.

The present strength of the Regiment is as follows:

Commissioned officers	51
Enlisted men	680
Total	731

The Regiment was inspected by Col. Thomas Stringfield, Inspector General, and Lieutenant C. M. Butler, of the Seventeenth Infantry, U. S. A., beginning Febraury 15th and ending March 15th, 1910. All of the organizations passed creditable inspections, and none were disbanded during the year.

ENCAMPMENT.

Pursuant to General Orders No. 13, issued from the Adjutant General's office May 19, 1910, we proceeded to camp at Camp Glenn, Morehead City, N. C., leaving our home stations July the 6th and arriving at camp on the morning of the 7th.

CALLS FOR DUTY.

The following calls were observed during the encampment:

First call for Reveille	5:00 a. m.
Reveille	[illegible] a. .
Assembly	: a. .
Fatigue	: a. .
Sick Call	: a. .
Mess	: a. .
Drill	: a. .

Assembly	6:45 a. m.
Recall	9:00 a. m.
Guard mounting, first call	9:00 a. m.
Adjutant's Call	9:15 a. m.
Noncommissioned Officers' School	11:00 a. m.
Mess	12:00 m.
Officers' School	1:00 p. m.
Drill, first call	4:00 p. m.
Assembly	4:30 p. m.
Recall	5:30 p. m.
Parade, first call	6:00 p. m.
Assembly	6:20 p. m.
Mess	7:30 p. m.
Tattoo	9:00 p. m.
Call to quarters	10:45 p. m.
Taps	11:00 p. m.

We found the camp in very good condition, with tents pitched. The Colonel's and Staff's quarters were located at one corner of the camp, instead of the center, as they should have been.

DUTY PERFORMED.

Each day, for the first three days, one battalion was ordered on the firing line at the range. One battalion furnished a company for guard duty, markers, scorers, and all other special details. The remaining battalion performed the regular morning and afternoon drills, these duties alternating each day. All battalions participated in the parades and reviews. Lieutenant Colonel R. L. Leinster was detailed as statistical officer; Lieutenant Colonel Thomas R. Orrell was detailed as chief range officer, and Major A. K. Powers, as assistant.

ATTENDANCE.

The following organizations reported for duty as follows:

Organization.	Commissioned Officers Present.	Commissioned Officers Absent.	Enlisted Present.	Enlisted Absent.
Field and staff	15		8	
Band			26	2
Company A	3		38	9
Company B	2	1	47	6
Company C	3		43	18
Company D	3		39	10
Company E	3		41	12
Company F	2	1	52	
Company G	3		29	11
Company H	3		44	2
Company I	3		37	7
Company L	3		40	
Company M	3		39	4
Reidsville Hospital Corps	3		10	4
Total	49	2	493	83

Company K, of Weldon, was excused from attending Camp by the Commander in Chief, on account of their farms being in bad condition and they would have sacrificed a great deal by attending.

TARGET PRACTICE.

There has been a great improvement in the target firing during the past year, it being much better than any previous year, and undoubtedly it is due to gallery practice in the armories.

The Regiment qualified 124 marksmen and 3 sharpshooters, against 53 marksmen for last year.

CAMP INSPECTIONS.

Brigade Commander General B. S. Royster and Staff attended, and General Royster three times inspected the encampment.

Captain M. B. Stokes, of Tenth United States Infantry, besides giving general instructions, inspected the camp one day and took notes of the workings of the camp at all times. The benefits derived from his being with us were very beneficial indeed; he corrected all errors noted and gave us valuable instructions wherever needed.

TRAIN SERVICE.

In many respects the train service was very unsatisfactory, and I made a special report to General Armfield in regard to it just after returning from camp.

RIOT CALLS.

There has been no occasion for any of the troops to be called out on account of riots, and as our National Guard becomes more like that of the regular army these outbreaks will become fewer each year.

REMARKS.

During the past year the Regiment has been supplied with all necessary clothing and other supplies. The enlisted men are becoming more and more interested each year, and the changes are not so many as they were before. There has been a general improvement in the Regiment in all respects during the year.

While there was some drinking at our last encampment, it was not among the enlisted men. I hope to see the time when we can have an encampment without any drunkenness, and as I see it, the only way for us to have it, is for those who are in the habit of drinking to abstain from it while at camp, and then we would have better service and a better report from the outside world. In an encampment we are one body, and when one person, especially an officer, does an unbecoming thing the whole Regiment has to suffer for it. I make these suggestions for our good and because I think they are needed. We are in the service of the State and the United States, and therefore are at all times liable to criticism.

It is a sad thought to think that we shall never again meet our beloved, honored, and faithful General Armfield at our encampments. He has left us when we needed him most; his death has caused an aching void in the hearts of every Guardsman in the State. I have many evidences of his personal friendship and will miss his counsel and friendship more than I can express. His traits of character were that of a true soldier, diffident and gentle as a woman, fearless and brave as a lion, and in his heart there was no place for guile or deceit. As the Commander of the Third Infantry, and voicing their sentiments, we cherish his memory with a love that fails not and hope when the battles of life are over that we may meet in a brighter and better world.

To the Commander in Chief, to all superior and subordinate officers, and to the enlisted men of the Regiment I would express my heartfelt thanks for the services that they have rendered, and to those who have not discharged their duty they will have an opportunity to do so during the coming year.

Respectfully submitted,

J. N. CRAIG,
Colonel Third Infantry, N. C. N. G.

Report of Commander Coast Artillery Corps

HEADQUARTERS COAST ARTILLERY CORPS,
NORTH CAROLINA NATIONAL GUARD,
SALISBURY, N. C., December 15, 1910.

THE ADJUTANT GENERAL,
Raleigh, N. C.

SIR:—I have the honor to submit annual report of the Coast Artillery Corps as follows:

The strength of the Corps at the end of the military year is as follows:

	Officers.	*Men.*
Field, Staff and Noncommissioned Staff	5	16
First Company	3	55
Second Company	3	57
Third Company	3	50
Fourth Company	3	60
Fifth Company	3	55
Total	20	293

Battery A, Field Artillery, was transferred to this command by Special Orders No. 56, May 16, 1910, being designated the Fifth Company, and was assigned by the Commanding Officer, Artillery District of the Cape Fear, to Battery Swift (8-in. B. L. Rifles).

At the joint coast defense exercises in this district, held at Fort Caswell August 5th to 15th, all of the above organizations served in the batteries to which they were assigned by the District Commander. Copy of report on these exercises is inclosed herewith and made a part hereof.

ORGANIZATION.

The organization of the field and staff, noncommissioned staff and the several companies is in conformity with that of the Coast Artillery Corps, U. S. Army. The minimum company of Coast Artillery Reserves is 63 enlisted men, however, and prior to the exercises of 1911 the undersigned will endeavor to have the companies which are below that number at present recruited to at least that strength. Smaller companies or companies depleted by the inability of the enlisted men to attend the annual exercises works greatly to the detriment of the company's progress in artillery drill, instances having been noted in some districts of companies reporting for duty with such a small number of men as to be unable to man the fire control station and one gun in the battery to which they were assigned.

ARMS.

The companies are armed with the United States Magazine Rifle, cal. 30, a fine weapon. It seems to be a fact, however, that we, like others of the National Guard, have not as yet solved the question of the proper care and use of the rifle.

UNIFORM.

The uniform question is no longer a bugbear to the members of the organization. During the year an issue of excellent quality olive drab clothing, flannel shirts, caps and canvas strap puttee leggins having been made. With the blue dress uniform (obsolete pattern) which is now on hand in the companies, this gives them three complete uniforms, which with proper care will last for years. It is a fact that the Guardsman's uniform suffers much less from use than from abuse, and some system of making the enlisted man responsible for his uniform and its condition should be devised, a system based on his responsibility for its money value and one which provides for its own carrying out.

GALLERY TARGET OUTFITS.

During the year gallery target outfits have been issued to each of the companies, and while the reports show some improvement in the firing it is observed that no regular systematic course of instruction is being followed. These outfits if properly used should be great factors in the improvement in a company's shooting and should prove a stimulus in attendance and interest.

ARMORY EQUIPMENT.

Out of the appropriation by Congress for the fiscal year ending June 30th, last, the Ordnance Department was able to furnish to each of my companies except the Fifth, the following fire control apparatus which has been installed in the armories:

1 Plotting Board.
1 Deflection Board.
1 Gunner's Quadrant.

It is hoped that provision will be made for the early issue of base end instruments and telephone sets to complete this equipment.

INSTRUCTION.

The four companies which have received their armory equipment have had the benefit of some instruction in the use thereof. Up to this time, however, the instruction has been of an elementary nature and will continue to be so until the complete equipment is installed and instructors detailed from the Coast Artillery Corps, as provided in Circular No. 21, W. D., 1908.

RECOMMENDATIONS.

It is recommended that the strength of this organization be increased by one company.

That the troops of this command be issued the brown canvas or blue denim uniform for wear at the guns.

That a camp of instruction for commissioned officers of this command be requested by the Adjutant General, to take place during the current fiscal year, preferably in June, and to be held, of course, at Fort Caswell.

CONCLUSION.

The undersigned can not conclude this report without reference to his personal grief and the great loss to the National Guard of the State in the death of General Joseph F. Armfield, the Adjutant General. He knew the needs of the Guard as few men can know it, and the solution of some of its troubles as effected by him in his eighteen months' administration stands as a lasting monument to his knowledge of its imperfections.

To those of us who followed him to Cuba in 1898 he needs no eulogy; he was the ideal soldier, and every man, of whatever rank, loved and had faith in the silent man who rode at the regiment's head.

Thanking you for the kindly interest you have always shown in our organization, and expressing a hope that we may so perform all of our duties as to warrant a continuance of that interest, I am, sir, Very respectfully,

MAX L. BARKER,

Major Coast Artillery Corps, Commanding.

Report of Commander of Naval Militia

NAVAL BRIGADE, NORTH CAROLINA,
U. S. S. ELFRIDA,
NEW BERN, N. C., December 19, 1910.

SIR:—I have the honor to hand you herewith my report for year ending December 30, 1910.

This has been a year of very great progress in the Naval Militia. Having had the interest of your Department ever with us, there has been created a new spirit and interest for naval duty among the Divisions, and they have built until nearly all of them have reached the maximum strength permitted under the law.

During the year the Navy Department loaned to the State the torpedo boat *Dupont* and it was assigned to the First Battalion, the expense of this ship, in bringing her to the home port, being assumed by the city of New Bern and the county of Craven. It is a matter of very great pride to the Brigade that Commander Bradham and his crew brought the *Dupont* from the Charleston, S. C., yard to this port in record time and without an accident. A report of this submitted by Commander Bradham, is hereby attached, marked "Appendix A."

Upon advice of your Department, a request was filed with the Navy Department for a detail of a regular officer from the Navy to attend our summer exercises on the *Elfrida* and *Dupont* in the capacity of adviser and instructor. Lieut. C. H. Shaw, U. S. N., was detailed for this duty and reported on July 1st, and remained with us until August 15th. The Brigade was fortunate indeed to have with them upon their cruises so amiable an officer and gentleman, so able an instructor for the officers and men.

The summer exercises were entered into by the officers and men with a great deal of enthusiasm, each Division cruising on the U. S. S. *Elfrida,* with the exception of the Fifth Division, which cruised on the *Dupont,* handling her entirely within themselves under the able assistance of the regular ship keepers. Watch, divisional and deck duty was performed by the officers of the Divisions, the ships being under the immediate command of either myself or Mr. Bradham, of the First Battalion. The routine ship duties of the Regular Navy were performed by the men.

Target practice with small arms and the one pounders was indulged in by all the Divisions. On account of the late arrival of the ammunition for the three pounders, the Second Division was the only one holding record target practice, eleven (11) hits being recorded at 1,600 yards range out of twelve shots, which is a remarkable showing for the gun pointers, especially from the fact that they had no previous practice or drill in handling this gun.

I have to recommend that legislation be secured for the Brigade, so that they may be certain of holding their annual exercise each year. An appropriation should be made by the State to its Navy, for the maintenance of its ships, for the purpose of paying the transportation and subsistence and expense of the summer exercise, whether held as the Navy may direct on the battleship fleet or by individual Divisions on its own ships.

I desire to extend to you thanks of the officers and men of the Brigade for your very kind interest in the organization.

Respectfully,

TOM C. DANIELS,

Captain Commanding, N. C. N. M.

GEN. R. L. LEINSTER, Raleigh, North Carolina.

NEW BERN, N. C., June 29, 1910.

SIR:—(1) The following report of special detail of officers and crew assigned to take over, man and sail the U. S. T. B. *Dupont*, Charleston, S. C., to home station, New Bern, is respectfully submitted:

(2) CREW:

C. D. Bradham, Commander, commanding.
W. G. Dixon, Lieutenant, Navigator.
R. Barcliff, Lieutenant, Engineer Officer.
M. McDaniel, Quartermaster.
A. Lempke, Quartermaster.
L. Parsons, machinist.
E. Brinson, machinist.
S. Halvorsen, machinist.
J. Smith, fireman.
J. Hill, fireman.
Kilpatrick, fireman.
K. Bryan, oiler.
H. Ross, oiler.
S. Smith, oiler.
Larbut, cook.
Roberson, cook.
Halton, water tender.
E. Mashburn, water tender.
C. Mashburn, coal passer.
Newkirk, coal passer.
T. Smith, M. of A.

A total of 3 officers and 19 men, all told.

(3) ITINERARY:

1910.

June 15. Left New Bern *via* A. C. L. R. R., 9:30 a. m.
June 15. Arrived Charleston via A. C. L. R. R., 11:30 p. m.; met by Navy Yard tug.
June 15. Arrived Navy Yard, quartered aboard U. S. S. *Atlanta*.
June 16. Reported to commanding officer, Torpedo Division; assigned to *Dupont*, 7:30 a. m.
June 16. Trial trip down bay, 3:30-5:30 p. m.
June 17. Taking aboard stores and equipment.
June 17. Trial trip down bay, 3 p. m.; compensating compasses.
June 18. Taking on stores, 7:30 a. m. to 1:30 p. m.
June 18. Cast away, Navy Yard dock, 3:05 p. m.
June 18. Passed Sea Buoy, Charleston Light. Ship bearing S.W. x W., three miles distant, from which departure was taken. 4:35 p. m.
June 19. Frying Pan Lightship abeam, 2:10 a. m. Course, N.E.½E.
June 18. Cape Romain whistling buoy abeam, 6:10.

June 19. Passed Ocracoke Bar, 3:05 p. m.
June 19. Tied up Blades dock, New Bern, 9 p. m.

(4) CREW EXERCISED:

Making out station billets; shaking down.

June 16. Getting up steam; getting under way; inspection of boilers, engines, living compartments, condition of bilges, bilge suctions, storerooms, bunkers, deck gear and ground tackle; testing electric plant, etc. Cruising down bay; docking.

June 17. Checking invoices of stores and equipment; breaking below; getting up steam; casting away; steam steering; cruising; compensating compasses; swinging ship; docking.

June 18. Receiving, checking up stores; breaking below; getting up steam; getting under way; making ready for sea; lookout duty; location of buoys and day marks.

June 19. Steaming; use of charts; location of day marks; steering; lead and log. Docking at New Bern. Crew disembarked.

(5) EFFICIENCY.—The crew, excepting cook, stood watch in turn, showing a knowledge of every department. The steam engineering department showed highest efficiency, maintaining average steaming record with comparative ease and minimum consumption of coal and water. The regular ship's keepers stood watch, instructed our men in details of ship's routine, were willing and highly efficient in general.

(6) DISCIPLINE was excellent. Orders were obeyed promptly and cheerfully. Shore liberty was granted freely, yet without any abuse or tardiness. Every man seemed to take a pride in his station, and was quiet, dignified and unassuming.

(7) The *Dupont* is probably the best ship of the Navy in her class, 175 feet long, 17 feet 6 inches beam, 7 feet draft, speed 32 knots, under forced draft, coal consumption 1 ton to the knot. Equipped with three boilers and two engines, twin screws, horse-power rated about 4,200. Armament: Three 18-inch torpedo tubes and 3 1-pound rapid-fire guns. The general condition is good; was recently overhauled by force on board preparatory for summer cruise and everything was put in the best possible condition. The starboard engine is excellent and port engine very good. The general condition of living quarters, bilges, bilge suctions, storerooms, bunkers, pumps, blowers, condensers, steam and feed lines, deck work (hatches, gaskets, stanchions, etc.), steam steering gear, evaporators and pumps, and boilers is good. Equipment is good; ordnance, navigation, electric, engineer, carpenter and sailmaker departments are in good condition. Mess gear good; wardroom, china, glass and silver complete. Fitted with searchlight, Ardois signal and electric lights. The report of A. M. R. Allen, Midshipman, U. S. N., who has been in command for past year, is appended as part of this report and shows general condition of *Dupont*.

The behavior of the *Dupont* while at sea and during entire trip was all that could be desired. The commanding officer of the Reserve Torpedo Division, Capt. C. A. Blakeley, and the officers of his department, as well as the entire wardroom officers of the U. S. S. *Atlanta*, where crew messed and were quartered during stay at Navy Yard, were very considerate and did everything possible to instruct crew in handling a torpedo boat and manifested very kind interest in our preparations for sailing.

(8) Attached hereto is—

(*a*) Report of Midshipman A. M. R. Allen on general condition of *Dupont*.

(*b*) Copy of order, C. A. Blakeley, commanding Reserve Torpedo Divisions, officially turning over *Dupont* to Commonwealth of North Carolina.

(*c*) Copy of receipt given Navy Department for transfer of U. S. S. *Dupont*.

(*d*) Copy of invoices of equipment.

Respectfully submitted, C. D. BRADHAM,
Commander, N. C. Naval Militia.

CAPT. T. C. DANIELS,
Commanding N. C. Naval Militia,
New Bern, N. C.

RETURN OF STRENGTH, LAND FORCES

	Number of Regiments of Cavalry, Field Artillery, or Infantry, or companies of Coast Artillery.	Actual Strength, December 31. Commissioned.	Actual Strength, December 31. Enlisted.	Number of Companies of all Organizations.	Commissioned Officers. Brigadier Generals.	Colonels.	Lieutenant Colonels.	Majors.	Surgeons.	Assistant Surgeons.	Adjutants.	Quartermasters.	Commissaries.	Coast Artillery Engineer.	Inspectors of Small-Arms Practice. Brigade.	Inspectors of Small-Arms Practice. Regimental.	Chaplains.	Captains.	First Lieutenants.	Second Lieutenants.	Total.	Enlisted Men, According to Grades. Noncommissioned Officers.	Musicians.	Private.	Total.
----	-------	1	-------	------	1	------	------	------	------	------	------	------	------	------	------	------	------	------	------	------	1	------	------	------	------
----	-------	5	-------	------	1	1	------	3	------	------	------	------	------	------	------	------	------	------	------	------	5	------	------	------	------
----	-------	4	-------	------	------	1	1	2	------	------	------	------	------	------	------	------	------	------	------	------	4	------	------	------	------
----	-------	4	-------	------	------	1	1	2	------	------	------	------	------	------	------	------	------	------	------	------	4	------	------	------	------
----	-------	5	1	------	1	------	1	2	------	------	------	------	------	------	------	------	------	1	------	------	5	1	------	------	1
----	-------	4	-------	------	------	1	1	2	------	------	------	------	------	------	------	------	------	------	------	------	4	------	------	------	------
----	-------	12	-------	------	------	1	1	4	------	6	------	------	------	------	------	------	------	------	------	------	12	------	------	------	------
----	-------	------	36	------	------	------	------	------	------	------	------	------	------	------	------	------	------	------	------	------	------	14	------	22	36
----	-------	4	-------	------	------	1	1	2	------	------	------	------	------	------	------	------	------	------	------	------	4	------	------	------	------
----	-------	4	-------	------	------	1	1	2	------	------	------	------	------	------	------	------	------	------	------	------	4	------	------	------	------
----	-------	6	1	------	------	1	1	3	------	------	------	------	------	------	1	------	------	------	------	------	6	1	------	------	1
----	5	20	302	5	------	------	------	1	------	------	1	1	------	1	------	------	------	5	6	5	20	56	8	238	302
----	3	153	1,932	35	------	3	3	9	------	------	12	3	12	------	------	3	3	35	35	35	153	446	55	1,431	1,932
----	8	222	2,268	40	3	11	11	32	3	6	13	4	12	1	1	3	3	41	41	40	222	548	63	1,687	2,263

FIRST REGIMENT OF INFANTRY.

Headquarters: Shelby, N. C. Commissioned Officers, 16; Enlisted Men, 3.

Designation.	Commissioned Officers.	Actual Enlisted Strength.	Station.
Company A	3	49	Hickory.
Company B	3	60	Gastonia.
Company C	3	49	Winston-Salem.
Company D			Charlotte.
Company E	3	52	Statesville.
Company F	3	59	Asheville.
Company G	3	53	Shelby.
Company H	3	47	Waynesville.
Company I	3	46	Mt. Airy.
Company K	3	44	Asheville.
Company L	3	61	Concord.
Company M	3	54	High Point.
Band		28	

SECOND REGIMENT OF INFANTRY.

Headquarters: Washington, N. C. Commissioned Officers, 16; Enlisted Men, 8.

Designation.	Commissioned Officers.	Actual Enlisted Strength.	Station.
Company A	3	43	Tarboro.
Company B	3	54	Kinston.
Company C	3	50	Rocky Mount.
Company D	3	58	Goldsboro.
Company E	3	61	Goldsboro.
Company F	3	53	Fayetteville.
Company G	3	66	Washington.
Company H	3	54	Clinton.
Company I	3	45	Edenton.
Company K	3	45	Wilson.
Company L	3	61	Lumber Bridge.
Company M	3	47	Wadesboro.
Band		26	

COAST ARTILLERY CORPS, 3.

Designation.	Commissioned Officers.	Actual Enlisted Strength.	Station.
First Company	3	60	New Bern.
Second Company	3	65	Wilmington.
Third Company	3	52	Greensboro.
Fourth Company	3	63	Salisbury.
Fifth Company	3	62	Charlotte.

HOSPITAL CORPS, 3.

Designation.	Commissioned Officers.	Actual Enlisted Strength.	Station.
First Company		12	Charlotte.
Second Company		12	Kinston.
Third Company		12	Reidsville.

ped
as
cre
con
tor
sail
(
(
Du
(
sio
lin
(
Du
(

CA

RETURN OF PUBLICATIONS ISSUED UNDER SECTION 17, ACT OF JANUARY 21, 1903.

	Army Register.	Army Regulations.	Army Ration, Issue and Conversion Tables.	Coast Artillery Drill Regulations, paper.	Hospital Corps Drill Regulations.	Infantry Drill Regulations.	Manual of Guard Duty.	Manual for Army Cooks.	Manual of Arms, Magazine Rifle.	Manual for Court-Martial.	Manual for the Pay Department.	Manual for Quartermasters Serving in the Field.	Manual for Subsistence Department.	Digest of Opinions, Judge-Advocate General.	Soldier's Handbook.	Field Service Regulations.	Small-Arms Firing Regulations.	Manual, Army, Baker's.	Manual, Q. M. Department.	Manual Infantry, Private.	Engineer's Field Manual.
On hand last report	2	60	3	50	12	300	300	72	350	6	1		10	1	350	200	300			360	
Received since last report	3	12			10	50				12	3	3	25	1		200	175	2	10		2
Total to be accounted for	5	72	3	50	22	350	300	72	350	18	4	3	35	2	350	400	475	2	10	360	2
Remaining on hand	5	72	3	50	22	350	300	72	350	18	4	3	35	2	350	400	475	2	10	360	2

Amount appropriated annually by the State for the support of the Organized Militia, $30,000.00.

Number of males available for military duty, but unorganized, 300.000.

REPORT OF SMALL-ARMS FIRING FOR THE YEAR 1910.

Organization.	Rifle Firing. — Classification and Figure of Merit. Average Strength, Present and Absent, Commissioned and Enlisted, for the Entire Period of Firing.	Per Cent of Average Strength Qualified.	Expert Riflemen.	Sharpshooters.	Marksmen.	First Class Men.	Second Class Men.	Third Class Men.	Fourth Class Men.	Figure of Merit.	Total Firing, Rifle.	Total Firing, Pistol.	Figure of Merit Previous Year.
THIRD REGIMENT:													
Field and Staff	18	100			6	5	4	2	1	66.39	18	10	47.43
Company A	41	100			5		9	14	13	26.90	41	2	35.67
Company B	49	100		2	15	8	12	12		63.67	49	3	34.09
Company C	47	100			12	7	11	15	2	53.76	47	2	29.92
Company D	42	100			12	1	7	13	9	42.00	42	2	35.13
Company E	45	100			14	2	5	14	10	43.33	45	2	30.23
Company F	54	100			11	8	15	15	5	48.24	54	2	31.35
Company G	39	100			9	6	5	13	6	44.51	39	2	34.38
Company H	46	100			2	1	7	14	22	17.10	46	1	23.38
Company I	40	100			7	3	3	16	11	31.15	40	2	28.71
Company K*													46.35
Company L	44	100			7	3	8	17	9	34.18	44	3	35.07
Company M	40	100		1	14	2	5	8	10	51.00	40	2	30.76
	505			3	114	46	91	153	98	42.53	505	33	32.32

*Excused by Governor.

Organization.	Average Strength, Present and Absent, Commissioned and Enlisted, for the Entire Period of Firing.	Per Cent of Average Strength Qualified.	Expert Riflemen.	Sharpshooters.	Marksmen.	First Class Men.	Second Class Men.	Third Class Men.	Fourth Class Men.	Figure of Merit.	Total Firing, Rifle.	Total Firing Pistol.	Figure of Merit Previous Year.
	RIFLE FIRING. Classification and Figure of Merit.												
Second Regiment:													
Field and Staff	19	100			9	2	4	4		67.89	19	12	42.33
Company A	50	100			9	4	2	18	17	31.14	50		28.97
Company B	44	100			17	4	3	9	11	51.16	44	3	42.81
Company C	42	100			11	7	5	8	11	44.68	42	3	36.06
Company D	51	100	1	2	34	1	5	8		84.41	51	2	47.87
Company E	52	100	1		10	4	8	20	9	40.56	52	3	36.86
Company F	47	100			8	7	6	15	11	38.00	47	3	34.89
Company G	47	100			6	1	8	12	20	25.74	47	3	27.82
Company H	45	100	1		12	4	7	15	6	50.16	45	3	34.52
Company I	43	100			10		11	17	5	40.12	43	3	19.30
Company K	43	100			3	1	12	14	13	26.23	43	3	29.59
Company L	47	100			18	10	9	10		63.83	47	3	49.27
Company M*													27.24
	530		3	2	147	45	80	150	103	46.37	530	42	34.55
	1,035		3	5	261	91	171	303	201	44.44	1,035	75	33.45

*Excused by Governor.

General Orders

STATE OF NORTH CAROLINA,
GENERAL HEADQUARTERS,
ADJUTANT GENERAL'S DEPARTMENT,

GENERAL ORDERS No. 1. RALEIGH, N. C., January 11, 1910.

The annual inspection of organizations of the North Carolina National Guard will be made at their respective home stations by the United States Inspector and the State Inspector, as follows:

Station	Month	Day	Organization
Raleigh	February	15	Company B, 3d Infantry, and Band.
Lumber Bridge	February	16	Company L, 2d Infantry.
Fayetteville	February	17	Company F, 2d Infantry.
Wilson	February	18	Company K, 2d Infantry.
Wilmington	February	19	2d Coast Artillery Company.
Clinton	February	21	Company H, 2d Infantry.
Rocky Mount	February	22	Company C, 2d Infantry.
Goldsboro	February	23 and 24	Companies D and E, 2d Infantry.
Kinston	February	25	Company B and Band, 2d Infantry.
New Bern	February	26	1st Coast Artillery Company.
Edenton	February	28	Company I, 2d Infantry.
Washington	March	1	Company G, 2d Infantry and Hdqrs. 2d Infantry.
Tarboro	March	2	Company A, 2d Infantry.
Weldon	March	3	Company K, 2d Infantry.
Warrenton	March	4	Company H, 3d Infantry.
Oxford	March	5	Company E, 3d Infantry.
Henderson	March	7	Company C, 3d Infantry.
Louisburg	March	8	Company D, 3d Infantry.
Franklinton	March	9	Company F, 3d Infantry.
Durham	March	10	Company M, 3d Infantry.
Burlington	March	11	Company I, 3d Infantry.
Lexington	March	12	Company A, 3d Infantry.
Reidsville	March	14	Company G, 3d Infantry, Reg. Hdqrs. and Hospital Corps.
Thomasville	March	15	Company L, 3d Infantry.
Winston-Salem	March	16	Company C, 1st Infantry.
Mount Airy	March	17	Company I, 1st Infantry.
Greensboro	March	18	3d Coast Artillery Company.
Salisbury	March	19	4th Coast Artillery Company.
High Point	March	21	Company M, 1st Infantry.

Concord	March 22	Company L, 1st Infantry.
Charlotte	March 23-24	Company D, 1st Infantry, Battery A, Field Artillery and Hospital Corps.
Wadesboro	March 25	Company M, 2d Infantry.
Shelby	March 26	Company G, 1st Infantry.
Dallas	March 28	Company B, 1st Infantry and Hdqrs. 1st Infantry.
Statesville	March 29	Company E, 1st Infantry.
Hickory	March 30	Company A, 1st Infantry.
Asheville	March 31 and April 1	Companies F and K, and Band.
Waynesville	April 2	Company H, 1st Infantry.

Commanding officers will parade their commands for inspection on the dates named at such hour as may be fixed by the inspectors.

All officers having Government property in charge will arrange the same to be conveniently inspected. Any property lost and not heretofore reported and duly accounted for, also unserviceable or wornout property, will be brought to the attention of the inspectors, and such action taken relative to the same as directed.

Troops will parade in such uniform and equipment as the inspectors indicate. All uniforms should be cleaned to permit the wearing of either. All equipment will be arranged so as to turn out in full field equipment, if so ordered.

All field, staff, and noncommissioned staff officers stationed at or nearest companies being inspected will present themselves at the time, uniformed as directed by the inspectors, for inspection.

By order of the Commander in Chief: J. F. ARMFIELD,
Adjutant General.

STATE OF NORTH CAROLINA,
ADJUTANT GENERAL'S DEPARTMENT,

GENERAL ORDERS No. 2. RALEIGH, January 27, 1910.

I. Company and detachment commanders will have enlisted men of their commands perform gallery practice as often as possible during the months of February, March and April, 1910.

II. Preliminary to firing, commanding officers will see that the range is safe and kept so, and all firing done under the supervision of a commissioned officer.

III. The soldier should be taught the nomenclature of the rifle, sighting, position, and aiming, before the actual firing at target begins.

IV. *Scores.* Gallery practice will be conducted in scores of five shots, the number of such scores to be fired at a practice to be determined by the company commander.

V. No report of the results of the firing will be required, but a record of it should be kept in the company for the instruction and guidance of the soldier.

VI. Gallery practice is held at ranges of fifty and seventy-five feet. A suitable and safe backstop will be provided and sufficient light on the target. Either the iron or paper target X can be used.

VII. *Test of proficiency in gallery practice.* The soldier having fired the required instruction practice, will, after such additional practice as the company commander deems necessary, be required to fire the proficiency test, which is as prescribed in the following table:

GALLERY PRACTICE TEST, SLOW FIRE.

Range (feet)	Targets.	Position.	Time Limit.	Scores.	Percentage Required to Qualify.
50	X	Standing	A maximum of 1 minute to each shot; time counted from execution of "ready" to delivery of shot.	2	80
50	X	Kneeling		2	80
75	X	Sitting		2	80
75	X	Prone		2	80

VIII. Should the soldier not make the required percentage for proficiency, he will be required to repeat the preliminary drills.

IX. A report, giving list of names and scores of those qualifying in the proficiency test, will be made each month to the regimental inspector small-arms practice through regimental commander.

By order of the Commander in Chief: J. F. ARMFIELD,
Adjutant General.

STATE OF NORTH CAROLINA,
ADJUTANT GENERAL'S DEPARTMENT,

GENERAL ORDERS No. 3. RALEIGH, February 8, 1910.

I. Relative to the inspection of the organizations of the N. C. N. G. by the United States and State inspectors, as provided for in General Orders No, 1, A. G. O., January 10, the following is added:

II. All Government property in possession of company or detachment commanders or other responsible officers will be arranged previous to inspection in groups, piles, etc., in the same sequence as the articles appear on the property returns, in order to facilitate the verifying process. All serviceable and unserviceable property will be separated and placed in different piles.

III. The inspection of personnel (commissioned as well as enlisted) will be held in full field equipment and service uniform.

By order of the Commander in Chief: J. F. ARMFIELD,
Adjutant General.

STATE OF NORTH CAROLINA,
ADJUTANT GENERAL'S DEPARTMENT,

GENERAL ORDERS NO. 4. RALEIGH, February 14, 1910.

So much of General Orders No. 1, C. S., relative to the inspections of the Coast Artillery Corps companies, First Battery Field Artillery, the Hospital Corps detachments, by the U. S. Inspecting Officer is rescinded, and these organizations will be inspected by that officer as follows:

Fourth Company Coast Artillery Corps, Salisbury, April 4th.
Third Company Coast Artillery Corps, Greensboro, April 5th.
First Company Coast Artillery Corps, New Bern, April 6th.
Second Company Coast Artillery Corps, Wilmington, April 7th.
Battery A, Field Artillery, Charlotte, April 8th.
Charlotte Hospital Corps Detachment, April 8th.
Reidsville Hospital Corps Detachment, April 9th.

The State Inspector will inspect these organizations as prescribed in General Orders No. 1.

By order of the Commander in Chief: J. F. ARMFIELD,
Adjutant General.

STATE OF NORTH CAROLINA,
ADJUTANT GENERAL'S DEPARTMENT,

GENERAL ORDERS NO. 5. RALEIGH, February 25, 1910.

The following questions are hereby submitted to the officers of the North Carolina National Guard, to be returned to this office with written answers to same, not later than April 1, 1910, as prescribed in General Orders No. 4, A. G. O., February 24, 1910.

In case there is not sufficient space below the questions to permit of the answer being written out in full, officers will use the blank space on sheet, numbering the answers to correspond with the number of the question answered.

All questions herein refer to the 4-inch map of Fort Leavenworth and vicinity, which accompanies text-book "Studies in Minor Tactics."

By order of the Commander in Chief: J. F. ARMFIELD,
Adjutant General.

1. (*a*) On this map what features are represented in blue?..........
....

(*b*) What ones in black?...
....

(*c*) What is shown in brown?..
....

2. Draw the conventional signs found on the 4-inch Leavenworth map for the following:

Improved road ....
Unimproved road ....

Trail ....

Railroad ....

Railroad running through a cut............................

Railroad running on an embankment.........................

Woods ....

Orchard ....

Vineyard (see north of 30)...................................

Hedge along a road...

Wagon bridge ....

Stream ....

Stream flowing through deep cut (see branches of Corral Creek north and east of the U. S. Penitentiary)................................

Barbed-wire fence ....

3. (*a*) Of the three ways of representing a scale, which one is used on this map?..

(*b*) From the scale on this map determine how many inches equal one mile. Explain your solution..................................

....

(*c*) Having found how many inches equal one mile, determine what the R. F. is. Explain your solution...............................

....

4. Draw a graphical scale for this map, each division to represent one-fourth of a mile. Explain your method...........................

....

5. Lay the map on a table so that it will be oriented. Explain in your own words how you did this.......................................

....

6. In what direction is 47 from 17; 19 from 17; 21 from 17; Atchison Hill from Sentinel Hill?..

....

7. Follow this route of march on the map:

48 (at southwest corner of map), 46, Barnes' Road, 44, 42, 28, Zimmerman Road, 56, 60, 62, Metropolitan Avenue, Grant Avenue to A, Pope Avenue, C, Hancock Avenue, D, E, 12, 14 (Atchison Cross), G, H (Frenchman), 17, 45, Kickapoo, 43, 19, 15, 11, Sheridan's Drive, D, 8, Prison Lane to U. S. Penitentiary.

NOTE.—If you can get any kind of a map of the country where you are living (see page 40, Sherrill's book), write out a route of march similar to the above, and some time when it is convenient to walk, ride or drive out over the roads, see if you can, by using your map, follow the route you indicated. This is a problem of great use in actual service.

8. What is the distance in yards from 17 to 47?....................

What is the distance in miles from 15 to 19?........................

9. What is the difference in height between the top of Sentinel Hill and the fork of the roads at G?..

10. Where the contours are very close together, how is the slope of the ground? ....

Is the country flat or hilly in the vicinity of the Polo grounds?.......

If the Missouri River rises 10 feet, what happens to the point of land on which the Polo grounds are situated?.............................

....

11. Draw the profile of the road from 62 to 64.

12. Draw the profile of Prison Lane from 8 to 72.

13. Company A is at 4, guarding the Rock Island bridge which crosses the Missouri River at Fort Leavenworth. Company B is at the western end of the Terminal bridge (bottom of map). Both companies are ordered to march to 17 by the shortest route, so as to arrive there at 8 a. m.

What route does Company A take, and what is the distance it marches?

....

14. If it marches three miles an hour, how long does it take to make the march, and at what hour should it start? Explain your solution.

....

....

15. What route does Company B take, and what is the distance it marches? ....

16. How much sooner does Company B have to start than Company A?

....

17. Where is Company B when Company A starts?................

18. At 7 a. m. a message is sent from 17 to Company B. The messenger walks three miles per hour. Where does he meet the company? Explain your solution...

....

19. If a mounted messenger had been sent and he marched seven miles per hour, where would he have met the company? Explain your solution.

....

....

20. Where is the most level stretch of road that Company B marches over? ....

Where is the steepest stretch?...................................

Where is the highest point on this road?..........................

21. Company B had out an advance guard.

In marching from H to 17, where would the left flankers probably march, the enemy being expected from the west?......................

22. Could an enemy's scout on Crook Point see 17?...............

When would he probably first see Company A?....................

23. If the captain of Company A learned from a farmer when he reached 11 (in the woods about 1,000 yards east of 15), that the enemy had a lookout on Crook Point, how could he conduct his company to 17 without being seen?..

24. Can the bridge over Salt Creek, 550 yards west of 15, be seen by the scout on Crook Point?..

25. If you were in command of the two companies at 17, and you desired to establish an outpost where it could observe the bridge over Salt Creek, west of 15, and another outpost where it could observe the bridge over Plum Creek, south of 47, where would you post the outposts?

....

....

....

....

STATE OF NORTH CAROLINA,
OFFICE OF ADJUTANT GENERAL,

GENERAL ORDERS No. 5A. RALEIGH, March 2, 1910.

A silver cup, designated the Dupont Trophy, has been presented to this Department by the Dupont Company, for indoor shooting competition by organizations of the North Carolina National Guard. The competition will be held under the following conditions:

One team from each of the different companies;

Teams to consist of five officers and men;

Number of shots for each man, 7 standing and 7 prone;

Two sighting shots will be allowed each man off shoulder, no sighting shots prone;

Distance, 50 feet;

Kind of target used, X;

Competition to be held annually prior to the 1st of May, the trophy to be awarded to the team making highest aggregate score;

The trophy to remain in competition indefinitely.

The first competition will be held at home station of companies on April 11, 1910, under the supervision of the company commander, who will forward not later than the 12th of April, 1910, a certified record of the score made by the team, giving each man's name and score, together with the target used, attached.

By order of the Commander in Chief: J. F. ARMFIELD,
Adjutant General.

STATE OF NORTH CAROLINA,
ADJUTANT GENERAL'S DEPARTMENT,

GENERAL ORDERS No. 6. RALEIGH, April 2, 1910.

Before a general court-martial, which convened at Wilmington, N. C., pursuant to Special Orders No. 1, A. G. O., January 11, 1910, and of which Commander C. D. Bradham, Naval Militia, was president, and J. C. B. Ehringhaus, Fifth Division, Naval Militia, was Judge Advocate, was arranged and tried, Ensign George Thomas Williamson, First Division Naval Militia.

CHARGE I. *Disobedience of orders in violation of the Twenty-first Article of War.*

SPECIFICATION: In that Ensign George T. Williamson, Ensign, First Division of the Naval Brigade of North Carolina National Guard, having received lawful command from his superior officer, Lieutenant Cuthbert Martin, commanding First Division of the Naval Brigade of North Carolina National Guard, to report at the Division Armory, at eight o'clock p. m., August twelfth, 1909 (for the annual inspection of said First Division of the Naval Brigade of the North Carolina National Guard, did willfully disobey the same.

CHARGE II. *Absence from annual inspection in violation of the Thirty-third Article of War.*

SPECIFICATION: In that Ensign George T. Williamson, First Division, Naval Brigade of North Carolina National Guard, not being prevented by sickness or other necessity, did fail to repair, at the fixed time, to the place appointed by the commanding officer for the annual inspection of his Division.

CHARGE III. *Conduct to the prejudice of good order and military discipline in violation of the Sixty-second Article of War.*

SPECIFICATION 1: In that Ensign George T. Williamson, First Division Naval Brigade of North Carolina National Guard, having received a lawful order from Lieutenant Cuthbert Martin, First Division, Naval Brigade of the North Carolina National Guard, said Lieutenant Cuthbert Martin being in the execution of his office, to repair to the Division Armory for annual inspection of said Division of the aforesaid Brigade at eight o'clock on the evening of August twelfth, 1909, did willfully disobey the same.

SPECIFICATION 2: In that Ensign George T. Williamson, First Division, Naval Brigade of North Carolina National Guard, having been duly and lawfully fined pursuant to the rules and regulations duly prescribed by said First Division, Naval Brigade of North Carolina National Guard, under and by virtue of the laws of North Carolina, section forty-nine hundred and seventeen, Revisal of 1905, and having been duly and lawfully ordered to pay said fine and the same having been legally demanded of him, has refused and does refuse to pay said fine, without lawful excuse.

SPECIFICATION 3: In that Ensign George T. Williamson, First Division, Naval Brigade of North Carolina National Guard, it being his duty as Ensign of said First Division, Naval Brigade of North Carolina National Guard, to attend his command at the time of the annual inspection thereof, did fail and neglect to perform said duty. This at Wilmington, N. C., on the twelfth day of August, 1909.

SPECIFICATION 4: In that Ensign George T. Williamson, First Division, Naval Brigade of North Carolina National Guard, did fail to repair to the Division Armory of his command when ordered by his superior officer so to do, and refused and neglected to render any lawful excuse for such refusal to perform and neglect of duty.

This at Wilmington, N. C., on the twenty-first day of October, 1909.

To which charges and specifications the accused pleaded as follows:

To the first specification of the first charge, "Not guilty."

To the first charge, "Not guilty."

To the first specification, second charge, "Not guilty."

To the second specification of the second charge, "Not guilty."

To the first specification of the third charge, "Not guilty."

To the second specification of the third charge, "Not guilty."

To the third specification of the third charge, "Not guilty."

To the fourth specification of the third charge, "Not guilty."

To the third charge, "Not guilty."

FINDINGS.

The specifications of the first charge, proved in part. And that the accused, Ensign George T. Williamson, is of the first charge guilty in less degree than charged.

The specification of the second charge is proved.

And of the second charge, guilty.

The first specification of the third charge is proved in part.

The second specification of the third charge is proved.

The third specification of the third charge is proved.

The fourth specification of the third charge is proved in part.

And of the third charge guilty in less degree than charged.

SENTENCE.

To pay a fine of five dollars and to be publicly reprimanded, and if the fine is not paid by said Ensign Williamson within ten days after order or reprimand is promulgated, to be dismissed from the service.

THE EXECUTIVE DEPARTMENT,
RALEIGH, N. C., April 2, 1910.

The verdict of guilty of the first charge is disapproved.

The verdict of guilty of the second charge is approved.

The verdict of guilty of the third charge is approved upon second and third specifications, and disapproved as to first and fourth specications.

In view of the extenuating circumstances disclosed by the testimony, I commute the sentence of the court to a fine of five dollars.

W. W. KITCHIN.

By order of the Commander in Chief: J. F. ARMFIELD,
Adjutant General.

STATE OF NORTH CAROLINA,
ADJUTANT GENERAL'S DEPARTMENT,

GENERAL ORDERS No. 7. RALEIGH, April 11, 1910.

For the information of those concerned, officers are advised that all except a very few papers, containing answers to questions submitted to them in General Orders, No. 5, A. G. O., February 25, 1910, have been received at this office, and will be graded and such grades entered on the officers' efficiency record.

Answers to questions are very good, and indicate study and an intelligent conception of the matter submitted to them, and speaks well for future progress.

By order of the Commander in Chief: J. F. ARMFIELD,
Adjutant General.

STATE OF NORTH CAROLINA,
ADJUTANT GENERAL'S DEPARTMENT,

GENERAL ORDERS No. 8. RALEIGH, April 16, 1910.

The winning team for the Dupont trophy contest is Company L, Second Infantry, station Lumber Bridge. The following is the team and score:

Capt. J. B. MALLOY, standing	5-5-5-4-4-5-5
Private J. T. MCRAINEY, standing	5-5-5-5-5-5-4
Private T. A. HALL, standing	4-5-4-4-5-4-4
Private J. D. JACKSON, standing	5-5-5-4-5-5-5
Private G. H. BEARD, standing	5-5-4-4-5-5-5
Capt. J. B. MALLOY, prone	5-5-5-5-5-5-5
Private J. T. MCRAINEY, prone	5-4-5-5-5-5-5
Private T. A. HALL, prone	5-5-5-4-4-5-5
Private J. D. JACKSON, prone	4-5-5-5-4-5-5
Private G. H. BEARD, prone	5-5-5-4-4-5-5
Total score	332

By order of the Commander in Chief: J. F. ARMFIELD,
Adjutant General.

STATE OF NORTH CAROLINA,
ADJUTANT GENERAL'S DEPARTMENT,

GENERAL ORDERS No. 9. RALEIGH, April 27, 1910.

The following will constitute the field service uniform, arms and equipment of the North Carolina National Guard, and will be worn and carried in months as follows:

During the months of May, June, July and August:

Khaki breeches,
Khaki blouse,
Campaign hat (in post, khaki cap),
Leggins,
Tan shoes (light marching).

During the months of September, October, November, December, January, February and March:

Olive drab breeches,
Olive drab blouse,
Campaign hat (in post, olive drab cap),
Leggins,
Tan shoes (light marching).

Blanket roll as follows:

1 shelter half,
1 set shelter poles,
1 guy rope,
5 shelter pins,
1 poncho,
1 blanket,
1 pair socks,
1 comb,
1 toothbrush,
1 piece of soap,
1 set blanket-roll straps,
1 housewife,
1 towel.

Arms as follows:

1 rifle, cal. 30,
1 field belt with suspenders (and when ordered to active duty, 90 rounds ball cartridges, cal. 30, carried),
1 bayonet and scabbard,
1 first-aid packet and pouch,
1 canteen,
1 haversack,
1 knife,
1 fork,
1 spoon,
1 tin cup,
1 meat can.

Entrenching tools as follows will be carried by the Infantry:

1 2-ft. folding rule per company,
4 hand-axes per company, with carrier,
1 pick-mattock per squad, with carrier,
3 shovels, entrenching, with carrier,
3 wire-cutters per company.

Musicians and noncommissioned staff will wear haversacks and canteen with strap.

Officers will wear olive drab or khaki uniforms as in the months prescribed above.

MOUNTED OFFICERS.

Personal equipment: Blanket, canteen, meat can, knife, fork, spoon, tin cup, saber belt, spurs, field-glass, watch, compass, note-book and pencils (including red and blue).

Arms: Saber and revolver.

DISMOUNTED OFFICERS.

Personal equipment: Blanket, canteen and strap, tin cup, meat can, knife, fork, spoon, haversack and strap, saber belt, field-glass, watch, compass, note-book and pencils (including red and blue).

Arms: Saber and revolver.

By order of the Commander in Chief: J. F. ARMFIELD,
Adjutant General.

STATE OF NORTH CAROLINA,
ADJUTANT GENERAL'S DEPARTMENT.

GENERAL ORDERS No. 10. RALEIGH, April 27, 1910.

To carry out section 4903 of the laws governing the North Carolina National Guard, that "every person accepting an office in the National Guard shall, as early as practicable and when ordered by the Commander in Chief, appear before an examining board to be appointed by the Commander in Chief, which board shall examine said officer as to his military and other qualifications," examining boards will be organized from time to time at different posts to meet this requirement.

By order of the Commander in Chief: J. F. ARMFIELD,
Adjutant General.

STATE OF NORTH CAROLINA,
ADJUTANT GENERAL'S DEPARTMENT,

GENERAL ORDERS No. 11. RALEIGH, May ...., 1910.

The following extracts from report of inspections of organizations of the North Carolina National Guard is published for the information of those concerned. Responsible officers are charged to take careful note of all deficiencies as outlined, and take the necessary action at once to remedy these deficiencies.

By order of the Commander in Chief: J. F. ARMFIELD,
Adjutant General.

FIRST INFANTRY.

COMPANY "A."

The captain resigning just before the inspection, and the first lieutenant not being present, left the company in command of second lieutenant, who did all he could to make the company show to advantage. The property was only fairly well kept, and in fair condition. The personnel appears to be very good, and with more attention paid by the commissioned officers, would develop into a number one organization.

COMPANY "B."

This company, which has been in service only a short time, is very well drilled and made a most satisfactory showing; the property is well cared for and in good condition. The efficiency of the officers justifies the hope that the company will be made one of the best in the Guard.

COMPANY "C."

This company continues to improve both in discipline and in drill. The property was in good condition and well cared for. The company is well officered, and a most commendable military spirit pervades.

COMPANY "D."

This company is being neglected. The captain does not devote the necessary time and attention to its management, nor to the study of drill regulations. The property is not well cared for, and a great deal lost. A part of the property looked as if it had been purposely torn. Unless there are changes made and great improvement in condition, in a short time, the company should be mustered out of service.

(Mustered out of service.)

COMPANY "E."

There has been very much improvement in this company in the past year, both as to drill and discipline. The company has moved into a new armory, which is a great improvement over the old one; the property in the quartermaster's room was in excellent condition, but the lockers were too much crowded. Apparently there is much more interest taken in company affairs by officers and men.

COMPANY "F."

The company's captain resigned a short time before inspection, leaving the organization in a very bad condition; much property left out of the armory and a great deal lost. Guns and equipment were left in dirty condition. Maj. W. G. Smith, retired, was placed in command, and in the short space of a few weeks looked up a good deal of property and had same returned to armory, and had guns and equipment in excellent condition for inspection. The organization, as turned over to the new captain, was in very good condition. I believe, under the present officers, the company bids fair to be one of the best in the Guard.

COMPANY "G."

The company has improved very much in general appearance, personnel, drill and discipline over last year, the property was well arranged and in good condition, but there was too much loss of property. The recruits had not been drilled in the nomenclature of rifle; officers are active and efficient.

COMPANY "H."

Appearance, personnel, drill and discipline very much improved over last year; the property is well cared for and in good condition; the property loss is very small in this company. It speaks well for the organization.

COMPANY "I."

This company has made improvement over last year in discipline and drill; the property was very well cared for and in good condition. The officers are interested and painstaking and should in a very short time have the company up to the highest standard of discipline and efficiency.

COMPANY "K."

This company has made marked improvement over last year in personnel, general appearance, discipline and drill. The property is in much better condition, and shows more care taken of it. The captain is taking constant interest in the organization. The captain should appoint two musicians.

COMPANY "L."

This company has made much improvement over former inspections; the drill and discipline was very satisfactory and demonstrated the fact that this is one of the best and most efficient companies in the Guard. The officers are all uniformed and there is great interest in the organization. The property is well cared for and in excellent condition.

COMPANY "M."

In general appearance, personnel, drill and discipline this company has made marked improvement over former inspections. Property in good condition and well arranged in store room, but is not looked after as closely as should be. There is too much loss of property. Officers active and efficient, and a most commendable military spirit pervades.

BAND.

This band is in excellent condition. Property well cared for and in good condition; lockers neat and clean; property room in good condition; a good organization.

SECOND INFANTRY.

COMPANY "A."

This company shows improvement in personnel and general appearance over last inspection; the property is in good condition, but there is too much loss of property. There is much room for improvement in drill and discipline; men did not know nomenclature of rifle; noncommissioned officers not well instructed; captain thinks there will be very much improvement in another year.

COMPANY "B."

This company has greatly improved in personnel and general appearance. The great loss of property, was informed, was due to former officers who did not keep property in the armory. Captain very energetic, but men lack individual instruction.

COMPANY "C."

The company has only been in service for a short time, is very well drilled and made a most satisfactory appearance at inspection. The men are fairly well acquainted with nomenclature of the rifle; did not comply with G. O. No. 3; the property is in good condition and well cared for. The officers are active and efficient.

COMPANY "D."

This company is not up to its usual standard of efficiency; all the property has not been kept in the armory as required, and was not arranged as systematically as at former inspections; the quartermaster's room should be made larger, and the leaks in the armory should be repaired to prevent damage to property.

COMPANY "E."

This company has made improvements; the property was in excellent condition and well cared for. The property room was neat and everything so arranged as to facilitate the inspection of property. Noncommissioned officers and men well instructed in the nomenclature of the rifle, and the military spirit is very strong in this company.

COMPANY "F."

Captain does not obey the regulations in keeping the property in the armory. There was an inexcusable shortage of property. Very little, if any, attempt had been made to have property arranged for inspection as ordered. Unless there is more attention paid to the care of property, and the men not allowed to carry property off, I doubt the advisability of continuing this company in the service.

COMPANY "G."

In personnel, drill and discipline, this company continues most satisfactory, but there is too much loss of property; property crowded in lockers and not properly arranged in store room for inspection. The company is well officered, and an excellent military spirit is maintained. The captain was absent.

COMPANY "H."

At inspection the company showed to excellent advantage, both as to physical appearance and knowledge of duties. Noncommissioned officers were well instructed. The property was in very good condition and well taken care of. The company is well officered and in excellent condition.

COMPANY "I."

This company has not improved as it should. Only about one-half of the men knew the different parts of the rifle; drill and discipline poor; company could not execute squads right correctly. Did not comply with G. O. No. 3. The property was in good condition and well cared for.

COMPANY "K."

Through recent changes in the officers of the company, and the resignation of the captain, it was not in position to make as good showing as it did last year. The showing made at inspection was very satisfactory, as the men drilled well and the discipline was very good. The company does not comply with paragraph 28, Organized Militia Regulations; did not comply with G. O. No. 3.

COMPANY "L."

This company has made improvement over last year in discipline and drill, as well as the care of property; the property is well cared for and in good condition. The company did not comply with G. O. No. 3; all the property is kept in the armory; did not separate serviceable and unserviceable property; improvement noted as having been made in the quartermaster's store room.

COMPANY "M."

This company is being neglected. The captain does not give the necessary time and attention to its management nor study of the regulations; property is not kept in armory; there is great loss of property, and the property is not properly looked after. The citizens of the town and county do not give the company their moral or any other kind of support. Unless there is great improvement in a short while, I recommend, to the interest of the service, that this company be mustered out of the service.

BAND.

This band has made improvement in general appearance, but they do not take care of their property. The bin in which the property is kept was dirty and in disorder; did not look like it had been cleaned in a year; no system about anything; makes very good music.

THIRD INFANTRY.

COMPANY "A."

This company has made improvement over last year in drill and discipline. The property is in good condition and well cared for. The company complied with G. O. No. 3, and it also complies with paragraph 28, Organized Militia Regulations, in that it has its full quota of noncommissioned officers.

COMPANY "B."

The company shows improvement over last year; all property in good condition and well cared for; guns not cleaned; complied with G. O. No. 3, and complies with paragraph 28, Organized Militia Regulations, in that it has a full quota of noncommissioned officers and men. The company has improved in discipline and drill.

COMPANY "C."

This company has not improved; in fact it is going down hill. The property is not kept in the armory, and a good deal is lost. The men were not familiar with their guns; discipline and drill only fair; did not comply with G. O. No. 3, and does not comply with paragraph 28, Organized Militia Regulations, in that there are only five corporals. Unless there is great improvement in the conditions the company should be mustered out of service.

COMPANY "D."

This company is getting along very well, but is not improving as much as it should; the property is fairly well cared for, but all of it is not kept in the armory all the time; did not comply with G. O. No. 3; men did not know nomenclature of rifle very well. Drill and discipline only fair.

COMPANY "E."

This company is getting along very well; the property is very well cared for and in good condition; very few of men know the nomenclature of the rifle; did not comply with G. O. No. 3; drill and discipline only fair; noncommissioned officers were not properly instructed.

COMPANY "F."

This company is getting along very fair and making satisfactory improvement in discipline and drill; the property is well cared for, and there is very little loss of property; the company is well officered, and the men make a very good military appearance.

COMPANY "G."

This company has made improvement; the personnel, drill, discipline, care of property and general efficiency continues more satisfactory; the officers and men show constant interest in the organization, and the company makes a creditable military appearance.

COMPANY "H."

This company has made substantial improvement over last year, and bids fair to make a good organization if it keeps up the improvement. Property is not all kept in armory as required by regulations, and that accounts for a loss of property; did not comply with G. O. No. 3.

COMPANY "I."

This company has not improved as it should; the property is not all kept in the armory, as required by the regulations; as a consequence there is a great loss of the same. The attendance was poor, but it was a very bad night for inspection. The property in the armory was well arranged.

COMPANY "K."

This company has made marked improvement in drill and discipline. The property is well cared for, and in good condition. The organization is well officered, and the men make a soldierly appearance. Much interest is shown in the company by the citizens of the town.

COMPANY "L."

This was the first appearance of this company for inspection, having been organized since last inspection, and the showing the company made was most commendable and satisfactory. The property is well cared for.

COMPANY "M."

This company has made improvement in drill and discipline. The lockers were overcrowded, and the quartermaster's room was dirty and disorderly. There is ample room for the storing of all property, and it should be systematically arranged. The men were well acquainted with the nomenclature of the rifle.

BAND.

This band continues in a most satisfactory manner; property is kept in much better shape than last year and better cared for. The organization has built new lockers and is better prepared to care for the property. This is a very good band.

COAST ARTILLERY CORPS.

FIRST COMPANY.

This organization is getting along very well. The general appearance, personnel and discipline very good. The men did not know nomenclature of rifle, and did not comply with G. O. No. 3. The general efficiency of this company appears very good.

SECOND COMPANY.

In general appearance, drill and discipline this company makes an excellent appearance. The lockers were dirty and in disorder. There was such an accumulation of old property that there was not room for it. The company does not comply with paragraph 32, Organized Militia Regulations.

THIRD COMPANY.

This company has not made improvements it should in the past year. The men did not know the nomenclature of the rifle, and drill and discipline were only fair. The armory was not as neat as it should be, and the lockers were in disorder.

FOURTH COMPANY.

This company is getting along fairly well. The noncommissioned officers lack proper instruction, and the men did not know the nomenclature of rifle. Property was in good shape and well arranged for inspection, but there was too much loss of property.

FIELD ARTILLERY.

BATTERY A.

There has been improvement in the care of property, and all of the property is in much better shape than last year, but I am of the opinion that unless the appropriation can be greatly increased that it will never amount to much as a Battery. I think it would be best to change this organization into an infantry company or a Coast Artillery Corps company, for as it is now it is no use to the State or the United States Government.

STATE OF NORTH CAROLINA,
ADJUTANT GENERAL'S DEPARTMENT,

GENERAL ORDERS No. 12. RALEIGH, May 11, 1910.

Inspections of organizations of the North Carolina Naval Militia will be made at their respective home stations by Lieutenant Colonel H. D. Harper, Assistant Inspector General, as follows:

Oriental Division, June 29th.
New Bern Division, June 30th.
Windsor Division, July 1st.
Plymouth Division, July 2d.
Elizabeth City Division, July 3d.

The commanding officers will parade their commands for inspection on the dates named, at such hour as may be fixed by the inspector.

All officers having Government property in charge will arrange the same to be conveniently inspected. Any property lost and not heretofore reported and duly accounted for, also unserviceable or worn-out property, will be brought to the attention of the inspector and such action taken relative to the same as directed. Troops will parade in such uniform and equipment as the inspector may indicate. All equipment will be arranged so as to turn out in full equipment, if so ordered. All field, staff and warrant officers stationed at or nearest division being inspected, will present themselves at the time, armed and uniformed as directed by the inspector for inspection.

By order of the Commander in Chief: J. F. ARMFIELD,
Adjutant General.

STATE OF NORTH CAROLINA,
ADJUTANT GENERAL'S DEPARTMENT,

GENERAL ORDERS No. 13. RALEIGH, May 19, 1910.

I. Organizations of the North Carolina National Guard will encamp for instruction, in 1910, as follows:

The First Infantry at the joint maneuvers, Chickamauga Park, Ga., July 11-20, inclusive;

The Coast Artillery Corps, joint seacoast defense exercises, Fort Caswell, August 5-15, inclusive;

Third Infantry for field instruction and rifle practice, Camp Glenn, Morehead City, July 6-13, inclusive;

Second Infantry, for field instruction and rifle practice, Camp Glenn, Morehead City, July 19-26, inclusive.

II. The Quartermaster General will furnish the necessary transportation to organizations for the different movements, and for troops attending joint camps with the Regular Army, under direction of the Chief

Quartermaster, Department of the Gulf. Each organization commander will be advised by the Quartermaster General of the schedule of movement of his command.

III. The Surgeon General will designate the necessary medical attendance.

IV. The Commissary General will furnish subsistence to the Second and Third Infantry not to exceed the allowance prescribed by the War Department.

V. Attention of commanding officers is called to par. 185 of the Militia Regulations, as amended by Circular 2, Division of Militia Affairs, War Department, January 27, 1910, relating to the necessity for at least three months prior service or equivalent in instrutcion.

VI. The minimum strength of each organization attending these encampments should be not less than four full sets of 4s (32 men, *i. e.*, 28 privates and 4 corporals), and the approximate number of sergeants (6). No company will be be considered as warranting the expenditure of Federal funds for transportation, subsistence, and pay, that has a strength less than that indicated above.

VII. Troops will wear service uniform and carry the full field equipment as prescribed in G. O. No. 9, A. G. O., current series.

VIII. No ball cartridges will be carried by companies or individual soldiers. Good order and the strictest discipline will be maintained by all responsible officers en route to and from and during encampment.

By order of the Commander in Chief: J. F. ARMFIELD,
Adjutant General.

STATE OF NORTH CAROLINA,
ADJUTANT GENERAL'S DEPARTMENT,

GENERAL ORDERS No. 14. RALEIGH, June 4, 1910.

Organizations of the North Carolina Naval Militia will cruise aboard the *Elfrida* for instructions as follows:

Windsor Division, July 1-8th.
Oriental Division, July 11-17th.
Plymouth Division, July 25-31st.
Elizabeth City Division, August 1-7th.
New Bern Division, August 8-14th.

The commanding officer of the naval militia will cause such instruction to be given as is most needed by the men of each division. Strict discipline will be maintained aboard ship and shore at all times.

On completion of cruise a report in full of same will be rendered by the commanding officer of the naval militia to this department.

By order of the Commander in Chief: J. F. ARMFIELD,
Adjutant General.

STATE OF NORTH CAROLINA,
ADJUTANT GENERAL'S DEPARTMENT,

GENERAL ORDERS No. 15. RALEIGH, June 11, 1910.

I. In connection with the encampment of the Third and Second Infantry, as provided in General Orders No. 13, A. G. O., May 19, 1910, regimental commanders will cause each enlisted man and officer to practice firing on the range. Special Course C will be fired. Officers, when the rifle firing is completed, will fire a revolver course for qualification as marksmen and sharpshooters. In addition to rifle firing, regimental commanders will cause a course of instruction, including field exercises, to be performed each day, that will be progressive in nature and such as will best promote the efficiency of the troops; and adopt necessary measures for the care and safe-keeping of all Government property and to insure at all times good order and discipline.

II. Regimental commanders will provide for the inspection of all organizations of their command, while in camp, by an officer of the United States Army designated by the Secretary of War for that purpose.

III. The Quartermaster General will prepare the camp by erecting the necessary tentage, having the water supply, latrines and bath houses in working order; provide the necessary fuel for cooking and issue to each company commander a cooking range and appurtenances for a company unit, on arrival of the company in camp, the same to be carried back by the company to home station and kept with the property of the company as a part of the field equipment.

IV. The Commissary General will have submitted to him, in ample time for purchase, a list of articles of subsistence stores desired by each regimental commander for his regiment. He will purchase and furnish the same not to exceed in price the prescribed Government allowance. He will observe the requirements of the War Department in submitting receipts and vouchers for purchases and disbursements. He will proceed to Camp Glenn two days previous to the arrival of the troops and be prepared to issue subsistence stores on arrival of the same.

V. Regimental commissaries will draw and issue rations to their respective regiments on regular approved ration returns in the prescribed manner, not to exceed 25 cents for field rations and 40 cents for travel rations. All issue of rations to a company will be made to a commissioned officer of the same, who must be present at all issues made to his company.

VI. The regimental quartermasters will precede their organizations to camp one day. On arrival at camp they will draw and receipt for all necessary camp equipage for their respective regiments, and will immediately after camp return all property, accounting in the regular manner for any lost or destroyed property.

VII. The Chief of Ordnance will provide the necessary ammunition, targets and range equipment and have the range ready for firing on arrival of troops and have all necessary supplies furnished as needed during the time of encampment, so as not to delay the firing.

VIII. Officers will receive pay for services in connection with this encampment for only the time for which they are present and performing duty, and during the time specified for the encampment, for any time other than dates of encampment, only on orders from the proper authority.

IX. Regimental commanders will, on the completion of the tour of duty of their respective regiments, make a written report of same, embracing a complete record of all firing and of all service performed by the command.

By order of the Commander in Chief: J. F. ARMFIELD,
Adjutant General.

STATE OF NORTH CAROLINA,
ADJUTANT GENERAL'S DEPARTMENT,

GENERAL ORDERS No. 16. RALEIGH, August 8, 1910.

The following officers, noncommissioned officers and privates of the North Carolina National Guard qualified in the grades indicated during target practice at Camp Glenn, July, 1910:

GENERAL STAFF.

Brig. Gen. J. F. Armfield........................Marksman.
Brig. Gen. F. A. Macon........................Marksman.
Lieut. Col. R. L. Leinster........................Marksman.
Maj. Thos. R. Orrell........................Expert Rifleman.
Maj. Thos. R. Orrell........................Revolver Expert.

THIRD INFANTRY.

REGIMENTAL FIELD AND STAFF.

Col. J. N. Craig........................Marksman.
Lieut. Col. S. W. Minor........................Marksman.
Maj. C. L. McGhee........................Marksman.
Capt. A. T. McCullen........................Marksman.
Capt. C. J. Smith........................Marksman.
Capt. R. W. Morphis........................Marksman.

COMPANY A.

Lieut. R. F. Chitty........................Marksman.
Lieut. J. W. Bean........................Marksman.
Sergt. K. D. Davis........................Marksman.

Corpl. J. C. Farabee........................Marksman.
Corpl. B. R. Yarborough......................Marksman.

COMPANY B.

Capt. W. F. Moody..........................Marksman.
Lieut. E. B. Parrish.........................Sharpshooter.
Sergt. H. C. Simmons........................Marksman.
Sergt. B. S. Parker..........................Marksman.
Sergt. R. T. Holderfield......................Marksman.
Corpl. H. N. Parrish.........................Sharpshooter.
Corpl. B. G. Cates...........................Marksman.
Corpl. A. P. Arnold..........................Marksman.
Private Lee Layton..........................Marksman.
Private W. F. Danieley......................Marksman.
Private E. Ruth ....Marksman.
Private Will Nowell.........................Marksman.
Private D. C. Hardy.........................Marksman.
Private R. G. Justice........................Marksman.
Private R. E. Lee...........................Marksman.
Private T. H. Stapleford......................Marksman.
Private L. P. Pool..........................Marksman.

COMPANY C.

Capt. W. H. Wester, Jr......................Marksman.
Sergt. F. C. Wyckoff........................Marksman.
Sergt. A. B. Wester.........................Marksman.
Corpl. C. B. Crabtree........................Marksman.
Corpl. T. H. Alford.........................Marksman.
Private H. B. Marrow........................Marksman.
Private A. E. Murphy........................Marksman.
Private J. M. Grissom.......................Marksman.
Private Robt. Dunn ....Marksman.
Private W. T. Johnston......................Marksman.
Private C. E. Hayes.........................Marksman.
Private W. T. Greenway.....................Marksman.

COMPANY D.

Capt. C. H. Banks...........................Marksman.
Sergt. S. G. Boddie.........................Marksman.
Sergt. E. S. Merritt.........................Marksman.
Corpl. R. H. Jones..........................Marksman.
Private C. E. Gilliam........................Marksman.
Private R. Z. Gupton........................Marksman.
Private R. L. Furman........................Marksman.
Private J. J. Lancaster......................Marksman.
Private A. C. Jones.........................Marksman.

11

Private Ed. Lancaster ....Marksman.
Private G. E. Booth..........................Marksman.
Private E. C. Gupton.........................Marksman.

COMPANY E.

Capt. T. G. Stem.............................Marksman.
Lieut. E. E. Fuller..........................Marksman.
Lieut. E. L. Parham..........................Marksman.
Sergt. J. O. Faucett.........................Marksman.
Sergt. J. L. White...........................Marksman.
Sergt. H. B. Averette........................Marksman.
Sergt. R. D. Howard..........................Marksman.
Corpl. I. B. Wilson..........................Marksman.
Corpl. L. E. Byrum...........................Marksman.
Private D. K. Taylor.........................Marksman.
Private L. B. Knott..........................Marksman.
Private Lee Gooch ....Marksman.
Private N. H. Blackwell......................Marksman.
Private J. W. Mangum.........................Marksman.

COMPANY F.

Capt. I. H. Kearney..........................Marksman.
Sergt. W. A. Cook............................Marksman.
Sergt. E. M. Edwards.........................Marksman.
Private J. E. Faulkner.......................Marksman.
Private R. W. Woodlief.......................Marksman.
Private B. H. May............................Marksman.
Private O. M. Boaz...........................Marksman.
Private J. B. Pearce.........................Marksman.
Private W. G. Wilder.........................Marksman.
Private J. R. Cook...........................Marksman.
Private C. C. Kearney........................Marksman.

COMPANY G.

Capt. R. G. Gladstone........................Marksman.
Sergt. Claude Jones..........................Marksman.
Sergt. Robt. Ray ....Marksman.
Corpl. W. A. Smith...........................Marksman.
Private J. T. Beaver.........................Marksman.
Private J. B. Martin.........................Marksman.
Private J. R. Gunn...........................Marksman.
Private J. A. Moorefield.....................Marksman.
Private C. W. Huffines.......................Marksman.

COMPANY H.

Sergt. P. M. Burton..........................Marksman.
Private J. M. Booth..........................Marksman.

COMPANY I.

Lieut. J. D. Apple..........................Marksman.
Corpl. I. B. Meachan.........................Marksman.
Private T. McAdams ....Marksman.
Private G. W. Foster........................Marksman.
Private B. Huffines ....Marksman.
Private A. Y. Watson........................Marksman.
Private C. Pickard ....Marksman.

COMPANY L.

Sergt. H. S. Williams........................Marksman.
Corpl. R. O. Little..........................Marksman.
Corpl. J. M. White...........................Marksman.
Corpl. E. O. Harris..........................Marksman.
Private J. T. Fowler.........................Marksman.
Private R. T. Marlow........................Marksman.
Cook A. E. Perry............................Marksman.

COMPANY M.

Capt. S. C. Chambers........................Marksman.
Lieut. C. F. Bennett..........................Marksman.
Sergt. T. B. Edwards........................Sharpshooter.
Sergt. E. R. Highfill.........................Marksman.
Corpl. C. M. Powell..........................Marksman.
Corpl. S. G. Marshall........................Marksman.
Private L. A. Jacobs.........................Marksman.
Private C. W. Thomas.......................Marksman.
Private J. R. Whitaker.......................Marksman.
Private G. L. O'Brien........................Marksman.
Private J. L. Hayes..........................Marksman.
Private E. F. Kerr...........................Marksman.
Private J. G. Hackney.......................Marksman.
Private Henry Berry ....Marksman.
Private J. I. Harper..........................Marksman.

REVOLVER COURSE.

Lieut. Col. S. W. Minor......................Marksman.
Capt. I. H. Kearney..........................Marksman.
Lieut. J. W. Bean.............................Marksman.
Lieut. Gordon Smith ....Marksman.
Lieut. R. F. Chitty............................Marksman.
Lieut. S. E. Winston..........................Marksman.
Lieut. A. A. Russell..........................Marksman.
Lieut. B. D. Ashlin...........................Marksman.
Lieut. J. H. Mobley...........................Marksman.
Sergt. Maj. W. A. Holding...................Marksman.

SECOND INFANTRY.

Regimental Field and Staff.

Maj. T. S. Pace............................Marksman.
Maj. W. C. Rodman..........................Marksman.
Maj. C. B. Elliott.........................Marksman.
Capt. H. H. Murray.........................Marksman.
Capt. S. Cohen ....Marksman.
Lieut. W. L. Barlowe, Jr...................Marksman.
Color Sergt. N. R. Morgan..................Marksman.
Color Sergt. D. C. Parker..................Marksman.
Bat. Sergt. Maj. R. T. Warren..............Marksman.

REVOLVER COURSE.

Col. H. C. Bragaw..........................Marksman.
Maj. T. S. Pace............................Sharpshooter.
Maj. C. B. Elliott.........................Marksman.
Capt. H. H. Murray.........................Marksman.
Capt. S. Cohen ....Marksman.
Lieut. S. P. Clark.........................Marksman.
Lieut. W. L. Barlowe, Jr...................Marksman.
Sergt. Maj. E. H. Lewis....................Marksman.
Color Sergt. D. C. Parker..................Marksman.

Company A.

Sergt. D. B. Carlisle......................Marksman.
Sergt. W. H. Hackney.......................Marksman.
Sergt. J. P. Mayo..........................Marksman.
Corpl. W. H. Brown.........................Marksman.
Private B. F. Lane.........................Marksman.
Private Zeno Price.........................Marksman.
Private B. Johnson ....Marksman.
Private W. G. Craft........................Marksman.
Private T. Pender ....Marksman.

Company B.

Capt. A. L. C. Hill........................Marksman.
Lieut. J. I. Brown.........................Marksman.
Lieut. J. O. H. Taylor.....................Marksman.
Sergt. G. V. Gray..........................Marksman.
Sergt. J. A. Jackson.......................Marksman.
Sergt. C. A. Tyndal........................Marksman.
Corpl. James A. Faulkner...................Marksman.
Corpl. W. A. Faulkner......................Marksman.
Corpl. ——— Sutton ....Marksman.
Corpl. W. M. Hall..........................Marksman.
Artificer C. B. Hight......................Marksman.

Cook P. W. Wallace........................Marksman.
Private R. H. Malpass......................Marksman.
Private W. O. Faulkner.....................Marksman.
Private G. F. Marshburn....................Marksman.
Private Frank Hughes......................Marksman.
Private Garland Sparrow....................Marksman.

REVOLVER COURSE.

Capt. A. L. C. Hill.........................Marksman.
Lieut. J. I. Brown..........................Marksman.
Lieut. J. O. H. Taylor......................Marksman.

COMPANY C.

Capt. J. S. Lewis...........................Marksman.
Lieut. L. C. Covington......................Marksman.
Lieut. H. L. Daughtry......................Marksman.
Sergt. W. O. Hight.........................Marksman.
Sergt. J. D. Winstead......................Marksman.
Sergt. H. F. Morton........................Marksman.
Private H. L. Best.........................Marksman.
Private G. W. Bartholomew..................Marksman.
Private W. R. Braswell.....................Marksman.
Musician Z. Motzno........................Marksman.
Musician W. S. Laney......................Marksman.

REVOLVER COURSE.

Capt. J. S. Lewis...........................Marksman.
Lieut. H. L. Daughtry......................Marksman.

COMPANY D.

Capt. E. A. Simpkins.......................Marksman.
Lieut. S. E. Malone........................Expert Rifleman.
Lieut. G. C. Derr...........................Marksman.
Sergt. G. L. Pittman.......................Marksman.
Sergt. C. S. Peele..........................Marksman.
Sergt. C. E. Aycock........................Marksman.
Sergt. Geo. H. Parker......................Marksman.
Sergt. W. S. Dewey.........................Marksman.
Corpl. A. L. Sasser.........................Sharpshooter.
Corpl. B. W. Cox...........................Marksman.
Corpl. J. R. Overman.......................Marksman.
Corpl. J. H. Wrenn.........................Marksman.
Private T. F. Rackley.......................Marksman.
Private W. A. Murdock.....................Marksman.
Private B. E. Barnes.......................Marksman.
Private M. Lynch..........................Marksman.

Private G. F. Whitfield.......................Marksman.
Private J. H. Capps...........................Marksman.
Private E. F. Wells...........................Marksman.
Private N. M. Stafford........................Marksman.
Private J. E. Parker..........................Marksman.
Private M. Hinnant ....Marksman.
Private A. M. Tyner...........................Marksman.
Private C. L. Phillips........................Marksman.
Private J. S. Benson..........................Marksman.
Private J. T. West............................Marksman.
Private H. Atkinson ....Marksman.
Private ——— Williford ....Marksman.
Private F. Hinnant............................Marksman.
Private Clarence Thompson ....Marksman.
Private J. H. Casey...........................Marksman.
Private C. C. Carr............................Marksman.
Private S. G. Rackley.........................Marksman.
Private B. F. Waters..........................Marksman.
Musician E. R. Hales..........................Sharpshooter.
Cook R. E. Pearce.............................Marksman.
Artificer J. W. Wright........................Marksman.

REVOLVER COURSE.

Lieut. S. E. Malone...........................Revolver Expert.
Lieut. G. C. Derr.............................Marksman.

COMPANY E.

Capt. E. C. Prince............................Expert Rifleman.
Lieut A. O. Clement...........................Marksman.
Lieut. Ben. Witherington ....Marksman.
Sergt. W. A. Dickins..........................Marksman.
Sergt. B. F. Adams............................Marksman.
Sergt. O. C. Jones............................Marksman.
Corpl. W. H. Adams............................Marksman.
Corpl. L. R. Creech...........................Marksman.
Private Walter Anderson.......................Marksman.
Private J. B. Dunn............................Marksman.
Cook W. M. Norman.............................Marksman.

REVOLVER COURSE.

Capt. E. C. Prince............................Marksman.
Lieut. A. O. Clement..........................Marksman.

COMPANY F.

Capt. E. R. MacKethan.........................Marksman.
Lieut. Paul Watson ....Marksman.

Sergt. F. N. Bennett..........................Marksman.
Sergt. R. J. Lamm..........................Marksman.
Corpl. N. S. McNeil..........................Marksman.
Private N. A. Lindsey..........................Marksman.
Private Lee Pittman..........................Marksman.
Private E. A. Matthews..........................Marksman.

COMPANY G.

Capt. R. B. Crowell..........................Marksman.
Sergt. R. R. Handy..........................Marksman.
Sergt. Grover Hodges..........................Marksman.
Private J. E. Williams..........................Marksman.
Private C. M. Hooten..........................Marksman.
Private J. E. Tetterton..........................Marksman.

REVOLVER COURSE.

Capt. R. B. Crowell..........................Marksman.

COMPANY H.

Capt. C. M. Faircloth..........................Marksman.
Sergt. W. O. Small..........................Expert Rifleman.
Sergt. W. R. Herring..........................Marksman.
Sergt. ——— Cooper..........................Marksman.
Corpl. O. R. Bizzell..........................Marksman.
Corpl. G. McPhail..........................Marksman.
Private W. J. House..........................Marksman.
Private W. M. Rackley..........................Marksman.
Private M. J. Hargrove..........................Marksman.
Private H. T. Wynne..........................Marksman.
Private E. T. Kennedy..........................Marksman.
Private S. Strickland..........................Marksman.
Cook W. H. Boyett..........................Marksman.

REVOLVER COURSE.

Capt. C. M. Faircloth..........................Marksman.

COMPANY I.

Capt. W. S. Privott..........................Marksman.
Lieut. W. A. Barrow..........................Marksman.
Sergt. E. L. Gray..........................Marksman.
Sergt. G. H. Thompson..........................Marksman.
Sergt. Frank White..........................Marksman.
Sergt. W. B. Rea..........................Marksman.
Private Frank Davenport..........................Marksman.
Private John Darden..........................Marksman.

Private C. H. Collins........................Marksman.
Cook R. K. Hall..............................Marksman.

REVOLVER COURSE.

Capt. W. S. Privott.........................Marksman.
Lieut. W. A. Barrow.........................Marksman.

COMPANY K.

Private G. D. Strickland....................Marksman.
Private Maek Davis ....Marksman.
Private ——— Webb ....Marksman.

COMPANY L.

Capt. J. B. Malloy..........................Marksman.
Lieut. D. A. Barlow.........................Marksman.
Sergt. L. M. Currie.........................Marksman.
Sergt. C. L. Beard..........................Marksman.
Sergt. Collier Cobb ....Marksman.
Corpl. W. E. Graham.........................Marksman.
Private O. S. McArthur......................Marksman.
Private A. M. Hall..........................Marksman.
Private A. P. Everett.......................Marksman.
Private W. H. Freeman.......................Marksman.
Private E. A. McGilvary.....................Marksman.
Private D. A. Perry.........................Marksman.
Private J. G. Council.......................Marksman.
Private J. T. McRaney.......................Marksman.
Private G. H. Beard.........................Marksman.
Private R. D. Jackson.......................Marksman.
Private T. D. Jackson.......................Marksman.
Private J. M. McMillan......................Marksman.

REVOLVER COURSE.

Capt. J. B. Malloy..........................Marksman.

By order of the Commander in Chief: J. F. ARMFIELD,
Adjutant General.

STATE OF NORTH CAROLINA.
ADJUTANT GENERAL'S DEPARTMENT,

GENERAL ORDERS No. 17. RALEIGH, September 14, 1910.

For the purpose of examining officers designated by the Governor for a commission in the North Carolina National Guard, as provided in section 4903, G. O. No. 6, this office, April 8, 1909, the following boards are established:

Lieut. Col. White G. Smith,
Maj. L. W. Young,
Capt. Chas. I. Bard.

Maj. J. J. Bernard,
Capt. W. F. Moody,
First Lieut. Z. P. Smith.

Maj. R. L. Flannigan,
Capt. J. E. Deitz,
Lieut. Charles Turner.

Col. H. C. Bragaw,
Maj. W. C. Rodman,
Capt. R. B. Cowell.

Capt. W. R. Robertson,
Capt. F. L. Black,
Capt. W. M. Robey.

Maj. T. S. Pace,
Capt. H. H. Murray,
Capt. C. F. Batts.

Col. J. L. Ludlow,
Lieut. Col. J. C. Bessent,
Capt. J. G. Wooten.

Capt. E. R. McKeithan,
Capt. J. B. Malloy,
Lieut. A. R. Williams.

Maj. Max L. Barker,
Capt. Chas. E. Smith,
Capt. Walter R. Cox.

Col. A. C. Davis,
Lieut. Col. J. W. Bizzell,
Capt. S. Cohen.

Capt. E. D. Kuykendall,
Capt. S. Glenn Brown,
First Lieut. R. W. Brewer.

Lieut. Col. J. Van Metts,
Lieut. Col. Thos. R. Orrell,
Capt. E. A. Metts.

Col. J. N. Craig,
Capt. R. G. Gladstone,
Capt. R. W. Morphis.

Col. J. T. Gardner,
Capt. A. L. Bulwinkle,
Capt. O. M. Gardner.

Lieut. Col. S. W. Minor,
Capt. S. C. Chambers,
First Lieut. Chas. F. Bennett.

Maj. C. L. McGhee,
Capt. I. H. Kearney,
Capt. C. H. Banks.

By order of the Commander in Chief:

J. F. ARMFIELD,
Adjutant General.

STATE OF NORTH CAROLINA,
ADJUTANT GENERAL'S DEPARTMENT,

GENERAL ORDERS No. 18. RALEIGH, September 6, 1910.

Announcement is made of the death of Col. JAMES G. HOLLINGSWORTH, Paymaster General of the North Carolina National Guard, which occurred at 8 o'clock yesterday evening in Richmond, Va.

Colonel HOLLINGSWORTH enlisted in Company A, Second Regiment, Fayetteville, in 1887; commissioned First Lieutenant and served in that capacity throughout the Spanish-American War; mustered out of the United States service November 16, 1898; commissioned Captain of Company A, First Infantry, National Guard of North Carolina, June 5, 1910; Major and Brigade Quartermaster, August 18, 1904; promoted to Colonel and Paymaster General April 3, 1909, in which position he was serving at his death.

As a young man of upright character and splendid ability, he was esteemed and respected by all who knew him. He was an efficient officer and served faithfully and well. The interment will be in Fayetteville, and the commanding officer at that post will provide an appropriate funeral escort. All officers of the North Carolina National Guard will wear the prescribed badge of military mourning for thirty days.

By order of the Commander in Chief:

J. F. ARMFIELD,
Adjutant General.

STATE OF NORTH CAROLINA,
ADJUTANT GENERAL'S DEPARTMENT,

GENERAL ORDERS No. 19. RALEIGH, October 19, 1910.

With profound sorrow and deepest grief, announcement is made of the death of Brigadier General JOSEPH FRANKLIN ARMFIELD, late Adjutant General of North Carolina, at his home in Statesville at 7:40 o'clock p. m., October 12, 1910. All officers of the North Carolina National Guard will wear the prescribed badge of military mourning for thirty days.

General ARMFIELD as a young man entered the service of the State as a private in Company "K," Third Regiment, the company being locally known as "Iredell Blues." He was soon appointed First Sergeant and served in that capacity until May 9, 1885, when he was elected and commissioned First Lieutenant; one year later, May 10, 1886, he was elected and commissioned Captain of the company (this company being later transferred as Company "A," Fourth Regiment), which office he held until December 1, 1892, when he was elected Colonel of the Fourth Regiment.

In 1898, when war was declared against the Kingdom of Spain, Colonel ARMFIELD and every company of his regiment volunteered for service in the war, and his regiment formed the nucleus around which was organized the First North Carolina Volunteer Infantry, which regiment was mustered into the service of the United States at Raleigh, May 5, 1898, with Colonel ARMFIELD commanding. As Colonel of the First North Carolina Volunteers, he served in the Spanish-American War, reflecting credit on his State and the Nation by moulding his regiment into one of the best military organizations in the volunteer army, and being chosen by Gen. Fitzhugh Lee to lead the first troops through the Cuban capital. For about three months of the service with the United States forces in Cuba, Colonel ARMFIELD served as commanding officer of the First Brigade, Second Division, Seventh Army Corps, the brigade being composed of the First North Carolina Volunteer Infantry, Second Illinois Volunteer Infantry and the One Hundred and Sixty-first Indiana Volunteer Infantry. When the troops were ordered back to the States for muster out, Colonel ARMFIELD with his regiment was mustered out at Savannah, Ga., April 22, 1899.

After the Spanish-American War, when the First Regiment was reorganized, he was elected and commissioned Colonel, February 12, 1902, which office he held until March 10, 1903, when he was promoted Brigadier General of the First Brigade, and served until March 2, 1909, when he received the highest military office within the gift of his State, being appointed Adjutant General by Governor Kitchin. General ARMFIELD'S military service from private to Adjutant General covered a period of about thirty years.

Though a born field soldier, yet he possessed rare executive ability, and during his seventeen months administration as Adjutant General he displayed such rare ability as to place the military establishment in better state of efficiency and discipline than ever before.

In the death of General ARMFIELD the State lost its foremost soldier of this generation and one of its best citizens—the National Guard its best beloved and most gifted leader. As a soldier he was prompt, dutiful, obedient, firm without tyranny, gallant and brave, ever watchful of the best interests and traditions of the service. As a citizen he was pure, upright, progressive in his ideals and loyal to his State; a man without guile, he wore the white flower of a blameless life. In his old home, surrounded by loved ones, friends and comrades, with the faith of a Christian and the dignity of a general, he answered the final reveille and his knightly spirit passed over the river to rest with the fearless and brave who have gone before.

His martial form was followed to its last resting place by the battalions he had commanded in life and a riderless horse in mute tribute of sorrow. Taps have been sounded over his low green tent and brave eyes are dim with tears, but we who loved and followed him in life and revere his memory in death, let us remember his virtues and how he strove for our uplift and benefit, and inspired by his high example and integrity, renew our faith and allegiance to the flag under which we serve and the country in which we live, striving to carry on the work which he had so well started, to successful culmination. The State and the Nation are richer by his having lived, he left an impress for good that will last as long as time, and as we think of him we think of the poet's lines:

"The knightliest of a knightly race,
Who since the days of old,
Have kept the lamps of chivalry
Alight in hearts of gold."

By order of the Commander in Chief:

R. L. LEINSTER,
Lieutenant Colonel and Asst. Adjutant General.

STATE OF NORTH CAROLINA,
ADJUTANT GENERAL'S DEPARTMENT,

GENERAL ORDERS No. 20. RALEIGH, November 21, 1910.

Paragraph No. 1, General Orders No. 13, dated A. G. O., Raleigh, N. C., May 19, 1910, is amended to read as follows:

The Fourth Company Coast Artillery, located at Salisbury, N. C., will be paid for services from August 4, to August 16, 1910, inclusive. The extra time specified was necessary for this organization to reach Fort Caswell, N. C., in time for joint exercises and to reach home station on return trip from joint seacoast defense exercises.

By order of the Commander in Chief: R. L. LEINSTER,
Adjutant General.

STATE OF NORTH CAROLINA,
ADJUTANT GENERAL'S DEPARTMENT,

GENERAL ORDERS No. 21. RALEIGH, November 22, 1910.

Commissions have been issued the following named officers of the personal and general staffs, North Carolina National Guard:

Name.	Date.	Rank.	Vice.
R. L. Leinster	Nov. 1, 1910	Brig. Gen., Adj. Gen.	Armfield, deceased.
Albion Dunn	Aug. 4, 1910	Col. and Aide de Camp	Fleming, deceased.
Sol. W. Cooper	Sept. 8, 1910	Col. and Paymaster Gen.	Hollingsworth, deceased.
Gordon Smith	Nov. 18, 1910	Maj. and Asst. Adj. Gen.	Leinster, promoted.
S. Glenn Brown	Nov. 17, 1910	Maj. and Asst. Adj. Gen.	Leinster, promoted.

Maj. Gordon Smith is assigned to duty in the Adjutant General's office, Raleigh, N. C., and will report for duty to the Adjutant General as early as practicable.

Major S. Glenn Brown is herewith detailed for duty as Assistant Adjutant General of the First Brigade, and will report for duty to Brigadier General B. S. Royster, Oxford, N. C., at the earliest practicable date.

By order of the Commander in Chief: R. L. LEINSTER,
Adjutant General.

STATE OF NORTH CAROLINA,
ADJUTANT GENERAL'S DEPARTMENT.

GENERAL ORDERS No. 22. RALEIGH, December 19, 1910.

I. Section 349a, Regulations North Carolina National Guard, is hereby further amended to read as follows:

When property is issued by a commissioned officer to an enlisted man a receipt should be taken therefor at the time the issue is made, and when an enlisted man turns in property the officer should give a receipt for same.

II. This amendment will be pasted in the proper place in Article XXXI.

By order of the Commander in Chief: R. L. LEINSTER,
Adjutant General.

Register of the National Guard of North Carolina

COMMANDER IN CHIEF,

GOVERNOR WILLIAM WALTON KITCHIN.

BRIGADIER GENERAL R. L. LEINSTER, ADJUTANT GENERAL.

PERSONAL STAFF OF THE COMMANDER IN CHIEF.

Name.	Office.	Rank.	Date of Rank.	Residence.
Alex. J. Feild	Private Secretary	Colonel	Jan. 29, 1909	Raleigh.
Charles E. Johnson	Aide de Camp	Colonel	Jan. 29, 1909	Raleigh.
Henry A. Grady	Naval Aid	Colonel	Jan. 29, 1909	Clinton.
H. Montague	Aide de Camp	Colonel	Jan. 29, 1909	Winston-Salem.
Finlay L. Williamson	Aide de Camp	Colonel	Jan. 29, 1909	Burlington.
C. B. Armstrong	Aide de Camp	Colonel	Jan. 29, 1909	Gastonia.
C. M. Carr	Aide de Camp	Colonel	Jan. 29, 1909	Durham.
Albion Dunn	Naval Aid	Colonel	Aug. 4, 1910	Greenville.

GENERAL STAFF.

ADJUTANT GENERAL'S DEPARTMENT.

Name.	Office.	Rank.	Date of Rank.	Residence.
R. L. Leinster	Adjutant General	Brig. Gen.	Nov. 1, 1910	Raleigh.
Alfred Williams	Asst. Adjt. Gen.	Colonel	Jan. 24, 1901	Raleigh.
Gordon Smith	Asst. Adjt. Gen.	Major	Nov. 18, 1910	Raleigh.
S. G. Brown	Asst. Adjt. Gen.	Major	Nov. 17, 1910	Greensboro.
A. A. Hicks	Asst. Adjt. Gen.	Major	April 1, 1909	Oxford.
E. A. Daniel, Jr.	Asst. Adjt. Gen.	Major	April 1, 1909	Washington.
W. A. Foil	Asst. Adjt. Gen.	Major	April 1. 1909	Concord.

QUARTERMASTER GENERAL'S DEPARTMENT.

Name.	Office.	Rank.	Date of Rank.	Residence.
Francis A. Macon	Q. M. General	Brig. Gen.	Feb. 1905	Henderson.
Wyndham E. Gary	Asst. Q. M. Gen.	Lieut. Col.	June 10, 1903	Henderson.
H. S. Leard	Asst. Q. M. Gen.	Major	May 20, 1910	Raleigh.
Mark W. Williams	Asst. Q. M. Gen.	Major	April 3, 1909	Charlotte.
J. S. Poythress	Asst. Q. M. Gen.	Major	May 20, 1910	Henderson.
J. W. Dalton	Asst. Q. M. Gen.	Major	April 3, 1909	Winston-Salem.
J. L. Currin	Asst. Q. M. Gen.	Captain	Aug. 1, 1905	Henderson.

INSPECTOR GENERAL'S DEPARTMENT.

Name.	Office.	Rank.	Date of Rank.	Residence.
Thos. Stringfield	Inspector Gen.	Colonel	Jan. 2, 1907	Waynesville.
Henry D. Harper	Asst. Insp. Gen.	Lieut. Col.	April 1 1909	Kinston.
H. B. Parker	Asst. Insp. Gen.	Major	April 1, 1909	Goldsboro.
J. D. Gwynn	Asst. Insp. Gen.	Major	April 1, 1909	Reidsville.
J. P. Meadows	Asst. Insp. Gen.	Major	April 1, 1909	Roxboro.
Wm. Badham	Asst. Insp. Gen.	Major	April 1, 1909	Edenton.
J. C. Michie	Asst. Insp. Gen.	Major	April 1, 1909	Durham.

COMMISSARY DEPARTMENT.

Name.	Office.	Rank.	Date of Rank.	Residence.
Wyatt L. McGhee	Com. General	Colonel	Jan. 12, 1905	Franklinton.
R. H. Reinhardt	Asst. Com. Gen.	Major	April 15, 1909	Lincolnton.
I. W. Little	Asst. Com. Gen.	Major	April 15, 1909	Wilmington.
C. A. Hunt	Asst. Com. Gen.	Major	April 15, 1909	Lexington.
Roger Gant	Asst. Com. Gen.	Major	April 15, 1909	Oxford.

ENGINEER'S DEPARTMENT.

Name.	Office.	Rank.	Date of Rank.	Residence.
Jacob L. Ludlow	Chief of Engineers	Colonel	Jan. 12, 1905	Winston-Salem.
R. S. Neal	Asst. Chief Eng.	Lieut. Col.	April 1, 1909	Washington.
Quint E. Smith	Asst. Chief Eng.	Major	Feb. 1, 1908	Concord.
Robt. M. Coburn	Asst. Chief Eng.	Major	April 1, 1909	Raleigh.
J. C. Mintz	Asst. Chief Eng.	Major	April 1, 1909	Shallotte.
Thos. B. Whitted	Asst. Chief Eng.	Major	April 15, 1909	Charlotte.

PAY DEPARTMENT.

Name.	Office.	Rank.	Date of Rank.	Residence.
S. W. Cooper	Paymaster Gen.	Colonel	Sept. 8, 1910	Fayetteville.
Wentworth W. Peirce	Asst. P. M. Gen.	Lieut. Col.	April 3, 1909	Goldsboro.
Raleigh T. Daniel	Asst. P. M. Gen.	Major	Feb. 24, 1905	Weldon.
R. G. Allsbrook	Asst. P. M. Gen.	Major	April 3, 1909	Tarboro.
Edward L. Conn	Asst. P. M. Gen.	Major	April 3, 1909	Raleigh.
E. G. Sherrill	Asst. P. M. Gen.	Major	April 3, 1909	Greensboro.
M. L. Cannon	Asst. P. M. Gen.	Major	July 1, 1909	Concord.

ORDNANCE DEPARTMENT.

Name.	Office.	Rank.	Date of Rank.	Residence.
Thos. R. Robertson	Chief of Ordnance	Colonel	Mar. 26, 1903	Raleigh.
J. W. Bizzell	Ordnance Officer	Lieut. Col.	April 20, 1910	Goldsboro.
J. B. Thomas	Ordnance Officer	Major	April 3, 1909	Louisburg.
A. K. Powers	Ordnance Officer	Major	April 3, 1909	Burgaw.
J. C. Mills	Ordnance Officer	Major	April 3, 1909	Rutherfordton.
J. M. Campbell	Ordnance Officer	Major	April 3, 1909	Asheville.
J. Leigh Skinner	Ordnance Officer	Major	April 3, 1909	Raleigh.
L. B. Bristol	Ordnance Officer	Major	July 19, 1909	Statesville.
Thos. Orrell	Ordnance Officer	Major	June 30, 1910	Wilmington.

JUDGE ADVOCATE GENERAL'S DEPARTMENT.

Name.	Office.	Rank.	Date of Rank.	Residence.
A. C. Davis	Judge Adv. Gen.	Colonel	April 3, 1909	Goldsboro.
V. C. Bullard	Asst. Judge Advocate General.	Lieut. Col.	April 3, 1909	Fayetteville.
T. A. Lyon	Asst. Judge Advocate General.	Major	April 3, 1909	Elizabethtown.
J. D. Proctor	Asst. Judge Advocate General.	Major	April 3, 1909	Lumberton.
A. P. Godwin	Asst. Judge Advocate General.	Major	April 3, 1909	Gatesville.
Elijah Moffitt	Asst. Judge Advocate General.	Major	April 3, 1909	Ashboro.

MEDICAL DEPARTMENT.

Name.	Office.	Rank.	Date of Rank.	Residence.
S. Westray Battle	Surgeon General	Colonel	July 1, 1909	Asheville.
Philip J. Macon		Lieut. Col.	July 1, 1909	Warrenton.
E. B. Glenn		Major	Feb. 24, 1905	Asheville.
A. R. Winston		Major	Mar. 24, 1905	Franklinton.
J. V. McGougan		Major	July 1, 1909	Fayetteville.
H. I. Clark		Major	Feb. 21, 1910	Scotland Neck.
B. J. Witherspoon		Captain	May 12, 1906	Charlotte.
E. C. Boyette		Captain	Nov. 22, 1906	Charlotte.
M. B. Abernethy		Captain	May 18, 1908	Reidsville.
Claud L. Pridgen		Captain	Mar. 26, 1910	Kinston.
J. Lewis Hanes		1st Lieut.	Feb. 19, 1907	Winston-Salem.
H. A. Newell		1st Lieut.	April 21, 1910	Louisburg.
F. J. Clemenger		1st Lieut.	June 30, 1910	Asheville.
A. K. Tayloe		1st Lieut.	July 15, 1910	Washington.

FIRST BRIGADE.

Name.	Office.	Rank.	Date of Rank.	Residence.
B. S. Royster	Brig. Commander	Brig. Gen.	April 1, 1909	Oxford.
S. G. Brown	Asst. Adjt. Gen.	Major	Nov. 17, 1910	Greensboro.
J. W. Dalton	Chief Q. M.	Major	April 3, 1909	Winston-Salem.
Roger Gant	Chief Commissary	Major	April 15, 1909	Oxford.
Jno. C. Michie	Inspector	Major	April 15, 1909	Durham.
J. B. Thomas	Ordnance Officer	Major	April 15, 1909	Louisburg.
R. T. Daniel	Paymaster	Major	Feb. 24, 1905	Weldon.
J. D. Proctor	Judge Advocate	Major	April 3, 1909	Lumberton.
J. Leigh Skinner	Inspector S. A. P.	Major	April 23, 1909	Raleigh.
H. I. Clark	Surgeon	Major	Feb. 21, 1910	Scotland Neck.
Henry T. Osborne	Aide de camp	1st Lieut.	Jan. 9, 1911	Oxford.
Arthur C. House	Aide de camp	1st Lieut.	Jan. 27, 1911	Weldon.

FIELD AND STAFF.

Name.	Office.	Rank.	Date of Commission.	Residence.
J. T. Gardner	Colonel	Colonel	Jan. 30, 1905	Shelby.
J. C. Bessent	Lieut. Col.	Lieut. Col.	Oct. 7, 1907	Winston-Salem.
R. L. Flannigan	Major	Major	July 20, 1899	Statesville.
D. D. Parks	Major	Major	Aug. 12, 1907	Mount Airy.
L. W. Young	Major	Major	Dec. 7, 1907	Asheville.
W. R. Minter	Chaplain	Captain	July 1, 1907	Lincolnton.
W. R. Robertson	Adjutant	Captain	June 1, 1904	Charlotte.
J. F. Roberts	Commissary	Captain	May 15, 1905	Shelby.
J. D. Lineberger	Quartermaster	Captain	Nov. 15, 1905	Shelby.
A. W. Freeman	Bat. Adjutant	1st Lieut.	Dec. 12, 1899	Waynesville.
Joe Hill	Bat. Adjutant	1st Lieut.	Aug. 2, 1901	Concord.
H. A. Millis	Bat. Adjutant	1st Lieut.	June 25, 1909	High Point.
P. W. Eshelman	Bat. Com. and Quartermaster.	2d Lieut.	June 16, 1905	High Point.
J. F. Witt	Bat. Com. and Quartermaster.	2d Lieut.	June 25, 1909	Mount Airy.
R. H. Morrison	Bat. Com. and Quartermaster.	2d Lieut.	June 1, 1908	Stanley.

COMPANIES.

Name and Station of Company.	Name of Officer.	Rank.	Date of Rank.
A	G. W. Payne	Captain	April 8, 1910
Hickory Rifles,	W. C. Keever	1st Lieut.	April 8, 1910
Hickory.	G. L. Huffman	2d Lieut.	April 8, 1910
B	A. L. Bulwinkle	Captain	Feb. 20, 1909
Gastonia.	J. M. W. Summey	1st Lieut.	Feb. 20, 1909
	W. S. Barfield	2d Lieut.	Feb. 20, 1909
C	J. G. Wooten	Captain	Jan. 17, 1908
Forsyth Riflemen,	J. A. Stith	1st Lieut.	Nov. 14, 1904
Winston.	Wm. A. Holder	2d Lieut.	Jan. 4, 1909
D	John A. Parker	Captain	April 5, 1909
Hornet's Nest Riflemen,	Brent S. Drane	1st Lieut.	Mar. 6, 1911
Charlotte.	R. M. Johnston	2nd Lieut.	Mar. 6, 1911
E	J. E. Deitz	Captain	Jan. 27, 1902
Iredell Blues,	C. H. Turner	1st Lieut.	Oct. 3, 1900
Statesville.	Neal Garrison	2d Lieut.	May 4, 1906
F	J. H. Koon	Captain	May 27, 1910
Blue Ridge Rifles,	York Coleman	1st Lieut.	May 27, 1910
Asheville.	Carl H. Felmet	2d Lieut.	Mar. 5, 1910
G	O. Max Gardner	Captain	June 13, 1907
Cleveland Guards,	J. F. Jenkins	1st Lieut.	June 13, 1907
Shelby.	Chas. P. Roberts	2d Lieut.	April 23, 1910
H	J. H. Howell	Captain	April 28, 1910
Richland Rifles,	J. B. Hoyle	1st Lieut.	Oct. 19, 1903
Waynesville.	Geo. F. Plott	2d Lieut.	April 28, 1910
I	W. A. Jackson	Captain	Oct. 7, 1906
Blue Ridge Guards,	Hiram Stanley	1st Lieut.	Mar. 29, 1910
Mount Airy.	J. H. Gwyn	2d Lieut.	Mar. 29, 1910

FIRST INFANTRY—COMPANIES—CONTINUED.

Name and Station of Company.	Name of Officer.	Rank.	Date of Rank.
K	C. L. Bard	Captain	Nov. 11, 1905
Asheville Light Infantry,	D. E. Penland	1st Lieut.	June 6, 1910
Asheville.	H. E. Johnson	2d Lieut.	June 6, 1910
L	Louis A. Brown	Captain	Mar. 19, 1908
Cabarrus Black Boys,	F. Y. McConnell	1st Lieut.	Oct. 19, 1909
Concord.	Robt. C. Thompson	2d Lieut.	Oct. 19, 1909
M	E. P. Carpenter	Captain	Feb. 9, 1909
High Point Rifles,	J. J. Griffith	1st Lieut.	Jan. 26, 1911
High Point.	M. B. Shiplett	2d Lieut.	Jan. 26, 1911

SECOND INFANTRY.

FIELD AND STAFF.

Name.	Office.	Rank.	Date of Commission.	Residence.
H. C. Bragaw	Colonel	Colonel	Dec. 4, 1902	Washington.
J. Van B. Metts	Lieut. Colonel	Lieut. Col.	Feb. 22, 1907	Wilmington.
C. B. Elliott	Major	Major	Dec. 4, 1902	Edenton.
T. S. Pace	Major	Major	Dec. 4, 1902	Wilson.
W. C. Rodman	Major	Major	Mar. 26, 1908	Washington.
Hugh H. Murray	Adjutant	Captain	June 22, 1909	Wilson.
Nathaniel Harding	Chaplain	Captain	Aug. 16, 1884	Washington.
S. Cohen	Insp. S. A. P.	Captain	Mar. 31, 1903	Goldsboro.
J. N. Pearce	Quartermaster	Captain	May 4, 1905	Wilson.
F. L. Black	Commissary	Captain	April 21, 1908	Charlotte.
W. L. Barlow	Bat. Adjutant	1st Lieut.	July 7, 1910	Tarboro.
Donald J. Murray	Bat. Adjutant	1st Lieut.	Jan. 26, 1909	Wilson.
R. Graham White	Bat. Adjutant	1st Lieut.	April 5, 1909	Edenton.
J. T. Lumley	Bat. Com. and Quartermaster.	2d Lieut.	July 7, 1910	Goldsboro.
S. P. Clark	Bat. Com. and Quartermaster.	2d Lieut.	June 26, 1909	Wilson.
W. H. Herring	Bat. Com. and Quartermaster.	2d Lieut.	April 14, 1909	Clinton.

COMPANIES.

Name and Station of Company.	Name of Officer.	Rank.	Date of Rank.
A	Paul Jones	Captain	Feb. 9, 1906
Edgecombe Guards,	J. A. Jenkins	1st Lieut.	July 4, 1906
Tarboro.	F. M. Carlisle	2d Lieut.	July 11, 1910
B	A. L. C. Hill	Captain	April 14, 1909
Kinston Rifles,	J. I. Brown	1st Lieut.	Sept. 24, 1908
Kinston.	J. O. H. Taylor	2d Lieut.	April 24, 1909
C	J. S. Lewis	Captain	Feb. 18, 1909
Rocky Mount,	H. L. Dougherty	1st Lieut.	Jan. 9, 1911
	A. E. Dixon	2d Lieut.	Aug. 9, 1911
D Goldsboro Rifles, (First Organization), Goldsboro.	E. A. Simkins	Captain	Jan. 28, 1909
	S. E. Malone	1st Lieut.	Jan. 28, 1909
	G. C. Derr	2d Lieut.	Jan. 28, 1909
E Goldsboro Rifles, (Second Organization), Goldsboro.	A. O. Clement	Captain	Jan. 9, 1911
	B. F. Adams	1st Lieut.	Feb. 21, 1911
	O. C. Jones	2d Lieut.	Jan. 9, 1911
F Fayetteville Light Infantry, Fayetteville.	Paul Watson	Captain	Feb. 4, 1911
	A. R. Williams	1st Lieut.	Dec. 14, 1908
	A. G. Murchison	2d Lieut.	Feb. 4, 1911
G Washington Light Infantry, Washington.	R. B. Cowell	Captain	Jan. 9, 1911
	B. B. Ross	1st Lieut.	Jan. 9, 1911
	C. W. Mc. Devitt	2d Lieut.	June 19, 1910
H	C. M. Faircloth	Captain	Feb. 3, 1905
Sampson Light Infantry,	G. K. Hobbs	1st Lieut.	July 1, 1910
Clinton.	N. F. Whitfield	2d Lieut.	July 1, 1910
I	W. S. Privott	Captain	June 1, 1909
Edenton Light Infantry,	W. A. Barrow	1st Lieut.	June 24, 1909
Edenton.	Jno. G. Wood, Jr.	2d Lieut.	Oct. 12, 1909

SECOND INFANTRY—COMPANIES—CONTINUED.

Name and Station of Company.	Name of Officer.	Rank.	Date of Rank.
K	C. F. Batts	Captain	April 17, 1910
Wilson Light Infantry,	W. H. Suggs	1st Lieut.	April 17, 1910
Wilson.	W. G. Barnes	2d Lieut.	April 17, 1910
L Lumber Bridge Light	J. B. Malloy	Captain	Oct. 13, 1906
Infantry,	D. A. Barlow	1st Lieut.	Oct. 13, 1906
Lumber Bridge.	J. L. Shaw	2d Lieut.	June 22, 1909
M	Adam Lockhart	Captain	June 7, 1910
Pee Dee Guards,	Seber Lockhart	1st Lieut.	June 7, 1910
Wadesboro.	H. B. Covington	2d Lieut.	June 7 1910

THIRD INFANTRY

FIELD AND STAFF.

Name.	Office.	Rank.	Date of Commission.	Residence.
J. N. Craig	Colonel	Colonel	Dec. 4, 1902	Reidsville.
S. W. Minor	Lieut. Colonel	Lieut. Col.	Mar. 28, 1903	Durham.
C. L. McGhee	Major	Major	Dec. 4, 1902	Franklinton.
J. J. Bernard	Major	Major	Dec. 4, 1902	Raleigh.
R. M. Albright	Major	Major	Dec. 4, 1902	Raleigh.
A. McCullen	Chaplain	Captain	Dec. 1, 1898	Washington.
Don. E. Scott	Adjutant	Captain	Feb. 5, 1910	Graham.
R. W. Morphis	Commissary	Captain	July 30, 1903	Reidsville.
Baxter Durham	Quartermaster	Captain	Feb. 24, 1910	Raleigh.
C. J. Smith	Insp. S. A. P.	Captain	Jan. 16, 1909	Henderson.
S. E. Winston	Bat. Adjutant	1st Lieut.	Jan. 10, 1903	Youngsville.
W. R. Miller	Bat. Adjutant	1st Lieut.	July 6, 1906	Raleigh.
Henry J. Hervey	Bat. Adjutant	1st Lieut.	Feb. 14, 1911	Raleigh.
R. T. Burton	Bat. Com. and Quartermaster.	2d Lieut.	July 6, 1910	Reidsville.
W. C. Harris	Bat. Com. and Quartermaster.	2d Lieut.	May 11, 1910	Raleigh.
S. L. Rotter	Bat. Com. and Quartermaster.	2d Lieut.	Mar. 14, 1908	Raleigh.

COMPANIES.

Name and Station of Company.	Name of Officer.	Rank.	Date of Rank.
A	W. H. Phillips	Captain	June 29, 1907
Lexington Rifles,	R. F. Chitty	1st Lieut.	Feb. 14, 1910
Lexington.			
B	W. F. Moody	Captain	May 15, 1904
Raleigh Light Infantry,	Z. P. Smith	1st Lieut.	July 26, 1907
Raleigh.	E. B. Parrish	2d Lieut.	Aug. 13, 1908
C	W. H. Hester, Jr.	Captain	April 20, 1910
Vance Guards,	Richard J. Jones	1st Lieut.	April 27, 1910
Henderson.	Bennett P. Rose	2d Lieut.	April 27, 1910
D	C. H. Banks	Captain	April 24, 1909
Louisburg Rifles,	J. A. Turner	1st Lieut.	April 24, 1909
Louisburg.	J. R. Perry	2d Lieut.	April 24, 1909
E	Thaddeus G. Stem	Captain	May 11, 1910
Granville Grays,	E. E. Fuller	1st Lieut.	May 11, 1910
Oxford.	E. L. Parham	2d Lieut.	June 4, 1910
F	I. H. Kearney	Captain	Feb. 21, 1905
Franklin Guards,	E. A. Long	1st Lieut.	Feb. 21, 1905
Franklinton.	E. M. Edwards	2d Lieut.	Mar. 3, 1905
G	R. G. Gladstone	Captain	Nov. 9, 1897
Reidsville Rifles,	W. B. Millner	1st Lieut.	June 20, 1906
Reidsville.	J. H. Mobley	2d Lieut.	Dec. 7, 1907
H	F. P. Wiggins	Captain	Jan. 25, 1911
Warren Guards,	W. H. Burroughs	1st Lieut.	Jan. 25, 1911
Warrenton.	J. C. Price	2d Lieut.	Jan. 25, 1911
I	J. C. Freeman	Captain	April 2, 1906
Holt Guards,	J. D. Apple	1st Lieut.	April 21, 1906
Burlington.	A. A. Russell	2d Lieut.	Feb. 14, 1910

THIRD INFANTRY—COMPANIES—CONTINUED.

Name and Station of Company.	Name of Officer.	Rank.	Date of Rank.
K	----------	Captain	Dec. 4, 1908
Weldon Light Infantry,	Jno. G. Ellis	1st Lieut.	June 16, 1910
Weldon.	H. B. Harris	2d Lieut.	Nov. 30, 1908
L	W. O. Burgin	Captain	April 5, 1909
Thomasville Blues,	Zed. Griffith	1st Lieut.	April 5, 1909
Thomasville.	C. H. Newby	2d Lieut.	April 5, 1909
M	S. C. Chambers	Captain	Mar. 16, 1909
Durham Light Infantry,	Chas. F. Bennett	1st Lieut.	Jan. 9, 1909
Durham.	B. D. Ashlin	2d Lieut.	Mar. 16, 1908

COAST ARTILLERY CORPS.

FIELD AND STAFF.

Name.	Office.	Rank.	Date of Commission.	Residence.
Max L. Barker	Major	Major	Jan. 12, 1909	Salisbury.
L. M. Dodamead	Adjutant	Captain	Jan. 14, 1909	High Point.
W. D. Marrow	Art. Engineer	Captain	Jan. 14, 1909	Greensboro.
Walter R. Cox	Quartermaster	Captain	Sept. 26, 1909	Salisbury.
C. L. Shaver	Ordnance Officer	1st Lieut.	July 5, 1910	Salisbury.

Name and Station of Company.	Name.	Rank.	Date of Commission.
First Company, Coast Artillery. New Bern.	J. H. Weddell	Captain	Nov. 12, 1908
	Ralph H. Smith	1st Lieut.	Jan. 1, 1909
	Wm. R. Pate	2d Lieut.	Jan. 1, 1909
Second Company, Wilmington.	Edwin A. Metts	Captain	May 29, 1909
	P. L. Cantwell	1st Lieut.	Mar. 9, 1909
	J. B. Lynch	2d Lieut.	Mar. 9, 1909
Third Company, Greensboro.	E. D. Kuykendall	Captain	Mar. 4, 1908
	R. W. Brewer	1st Lieut.	Mar. 23, 1909
	C. D. Smith	2d Lieut.	Mar. 23, 1909
Fourth Company, Salisbury.	Chas. E. Smith	Captain	April 23, 1909
	Alfred O. Lombard	1st Lieut.	June 2, 1910
	M. F. Hatcher	2d Lieut.	July 22, 1910
Fifth Company. Charlotte.	W. M. Robey	Captain	June 7, 1910
	C. B. Ross	1st Lieut.	May 4, 1909
	Jno. R. Neal	2d Lieut.	May 4, 1909

NAVAL BRIGADE.

COMMANDER AND STAFF.

Name.	Office.	Rank.	Date of Rank.	Residence.
Thomas C. Daniels	Commanding	Captain	Mar. 30, 1904	New Bern.
F. H. Shipp	Chief of Staff	Lieut. Com.	July 5, 1909	New Bern.
E. Ellis Williams	Chief Engineer	Lieut. Com.	Mar. 24, 1906	New Bern.
R. DuVal Jones	Surgeon	Lieut. Com.	Feb. 22, 1907	New Bern.
C. W. Hollowell	Paymaster	Lieut. Com.	Feb. 9, 1910	Elizabeth City.
A. T. Willis	Signal Officer	Lieutenant	Nov. 14, 1908	New Bern.
C. F. Smith	Chaplain	Lieutenant	July 6, 1908	Elizabeth City.
W. J. Jackson	Aid	Lieut., J. G.	June 1, 1907	Plymouth.
M. H. Allen	Aid	Lieut.	July 15, 1910	New Bern.

FIRST BATTALION.

Name.	Office.	Rank.	Date of Rank.	Residence.
C. D. Bradham	Commanding	Commander	May 11, 1904	New Bern.
W. G. Dixon	Navigator	Lieutenant	July 5, 1909	Oriental.
R. Barcliff	Engineer Officer	Lieutenant	July 5, 1909	Oriental.
J. F. Patterson	Surgeon	Lieutenant	Feb. 20, 1908	New Bern.
J. S. Claypoole	Paymaster	Lieutenant	Feb. 9, 1910	New Bern.
W. E. Smith	Asst. Engineer	Lieut., J. G.	July 20, 1904	New Bern.
J. E. Bunting	Gunnery Officer and Adjutant.	Lieut., J. G.	July 5, 1909	Wilmington.

Division and Name.	Rank.	Date of Rank.	Residence.
SECOND DIVISION:			
C. J. McSorley	Lieutenant	May 24, 1904	New Bern.
R. H. Dowdy	Lieutenant, J. G.	Aug. 6, 1907	New Bern.
Nelson P. Angel	Ensign	May 5, 1909	New Bern.
SIXTH DIVISION:			
A. F. Midyett	Lieutenant	Aug. 19, 1910	Oriental.
A. B. Morris	Lieutenant, J. G.	Dec. 5, 1910	Oriental.
B. B. O'Neil	Ensign	Dec. 5, 1910	Oriental.

SECOND BATTALION.

Name.	Office.	Rank.	Date of Rank.	Residence.
J. L. Phelps	Commanding	Commander	Feb. 15, 1908	Creswell.
J. T. Smithwick	Executive Officer	Lieut. Com.	May 11, 1904	Windsor.
----------	Navigator	Lieutenant	----------	
Brad. Sanders	Engineer Officer	Lieutenant	July 5, 1909	Elizabeth City.
A. W. Disosway	Surgeon	Lieutenant	Feb. 20, 1908	Plymouth.
Clarence Latham	Paymaster	Lieutenant	June 4, 1908	Plymouth.
J. C. B. Ehringhaus	Gunnery Officer	Lieut., J. G.	Oct. 13, 1910	Elizabeth City.

Division and Name.	Rank.	Date of Rank.	Residence.
THIRD DIVISION:			
W. M. Sutton	Lieutenant	July 5, 1906	Windsor.
F. M. Dunston	Lieutenant, J. G.	Sept. 17, 1909	Windsor.
J. W. Johnson	Ensign	June 19, 1908	Windsor.
FOURTH DIVISION:			
W. R. Hampton	Lieutenant	July 15, 1910	Plymouth.
J. S Norman	Lieutenant, J. G.	Mar. 30, 1910	Plymouth.
William R. Hardison	Ensign	Mar. 4, 1910	Plymouth.
FIFTH DIVISION:			
W. A. Worth	Lieutenant	June 15, 1907	Elizabeth City.
A. L. Sanders	Lieutenant, J. G.	Dec. 28, 1910	Elizabeth City.
J. K. Wilson	Ensign	Dec. 28, 1910	Elizabeth City.
SEVENTH DIVISION:			
W. B. Hudson	Lieutenant	Aug. 15, 1910	Hertford.
H. T. Shannonhouse	Lieutenant, J. G.	Aug. 15, 1910	Hertford.
R. T. Brinn	Ensign	Nov. 25, 1910	Hertford.

RETIRED OFFICERS

	Retired Rank.	
A. L. Smith	Brigadier-General	Charlotte
F. A. Olds	Brigadier-General	Raleigh
W. A. Bobbitt	Brigadier-General	Kinston
W. B. Rodman	Brigadier-General	Charlotte
W. C. Jones	Brigadier-General	Wilmington
Jno. F. Bruton	Brigadier-General	Wilson
Walker Taylor	Brigadier-General	Wilmington
Robt. S. Young	Brigadier-General	Concord
Jno. A. Pollock	Brigadier-General	Kinston
T. J. Winston	Colonel	Durham
Leo D. Heartt	Lieutenant-Colonel	Raleigh
P. T. Jones	Lientenant-Colonel	Henderson
W. F. Robertson	Lieutenant-Colonel	Wilmington
Chas. S. Jordan	Lieutenant-Colonel	Asheville
A. H. Harris	Lieutenant-Colonel	Wilmington
White G. Smith	Lieutenant-Colonel	Asheville
H. M. Chase	Lieutenant-Commander	Wilmington
B. F. Payne	Major	Raleigh
E. R. MacKethan	Major	Fayetteville
Robt. S. Stuart	Major	Asheville
A. J. Ellington	Major	Reidsville
Jas. F. Jordan	Captain	Raleigh
J. K. Tew	Captain	Clinton

ANNUAL REPORT

OF THE

ADJUTANT GENERAL

OF THE

STATE OF NORTH CAROLINA

FOR THE

YEAR 1911

EDWARDS & BROUGHTON PRINTING CO.
STATE PRINTERS
1912

CONTENTS

	PAGE
North Carolina National Guard	7
Report of drills, target practice and field instruction	16
Report of Quartermaster General	23
Report of Inspector General	33
Report of Surgeon General	37
Report of Paymaster General	45
Report of Commissary General	48
Report of Brigade Commander	51
Report of Commanding Officer First Infantry	53
Report of Commanding Officer Second Infantry	55
Report of Commanding Officer Third Infantry	57
Report of Commanding Officer Coast Artillery Corps	60
Report of Commanding Officer Naval Brigade	64
Cruise of the Naval Brigade	65
General Orders	73
Circulars	117
Report of Chief of Ordnance	145
Roster of active officers	147
Roster of retired officers	161
Return of strength	*folder*

ANNUAL REPORT

OF THE

ADJUTANT GENERAL

State of North Carolina,
Adjutant General's Department,
Raleigh, N. C., December 31, 1911.

To His Excellency, Honorable William Walton Kitchin, Governor and Commander in Chief.

Sir:—I have the honor to submit herewith annual report of the Military Department for the year ending December 31, 1911.

Since last annual report was submitted the following changes have been made in the land and naval forces:

A company of infantry mustered in at Charlotte, March 6th, and assigned as Company D, First Infantry.

A company of infantry mustered in at Dunn, March 28th, and assigned as Company M, Second Infantry.

A company of infantry mustered in at Asheboro, November 9th, and assigned as Company K, Third Infantry.

A division of naval militia mustered in at Washington, November 27th, and assigned as Sixth Division.

These organizations were to fill existing vacancies.

The following additional organizations of sanitary troops have been mustered into the service of the State:

Ambulance Company, No. 1, stationed at Raleigh, June 28th.

First Field Hospital, stationed at Asheville, July 19th.

These two organizations of sanitary troops were mustered in in order to comply with Section 111 of the Militia Law and to conform to the organizations provided for the United States Army and the Organized Militia, and in accordance with Section 4882 of the Military Code of North Carolina. In this connection, I wish to express my appreciation to Col. S. Westray Battle, Surgeon General N. C. N. G., and to Capt. Henry D. Thomason, Medical Corps U. S. A., for many wise suggestions and kind assistance in the reorganization of our Medical Department. Our Surgeon General has given unstintedly of his time and means to place the Medical Department in a high state of efficiency.

The following organizations, having fallen below the standard of efficiency required, have been disbanded and mustered out of the service of the State:

Company K, Third Infantry, stationed at Weldon, June 7th.

Company M, Second Infantry, stationed at Wadesboro, March 11th.

Sixth Division, Naval Brigade, stationed at Oriental, October 5th.

Detachment, Hospital Corps, stationed at Charlotte, October 23d.

The annual return of strength of the Guard is as follows:

LAND FORCES:		
Commissioned officers	237	
Enlisted men	2,277	
		2,514
NAVAL FORCES:		
Commissioned officers	40	
Enlisted men	324	
		364
Total all arms		2,878
Aggregate strength exceeding previous year		51

The Organized Militia of North Carolina now consists of one Brigade of three regiments of Infantry, each regiment having its full complement of field, staff and line officers; a Coast Artillery Corps of five companies with full complement of field and staff officers; one Field Hospital; one Ambulance Company; two Hospital Corps detachments, with full complement of medical officers for our entire Organized Militia. The Naval Militia consists of six divisions, organized into two battalions, which constitute the Naval Brigade. This branch of the service has the full complement of commissioned officers.

I am pleased to report that there has been continued and marked improvement in the general efficiency of the troops of the State, as will be shown by the reports of the Inspector General's Department and the Small-arms Practice Department. This statement is also borne out by the reports of the regimental and corps commanders. The interest in the service manifested by officers and enlisted men is most gratifying, and upon the continuance of this interest and application depends the future progress of the North Carolina National Guard toward higher efficiency. Under the law the commanding officers of the line are to a large extent responsible for the discipline and training of the troops and the further improvement of the State's military force rests largely on these officers; it is important that they be given every opportunity for training and instruction both in theory and practice. To this end there has been established a correspondence school in this office which covers a five months' course and each officer of the Guard is given the opportunity of taking the course prescribed. Capt. A. J. Dougherty, 30th U. S. Infantry, is conducting this school and it is a pleasure to report that our officers have taken hold of the lessons and problems with interest and zeal, and their answers to the problems indicate that they understand military map reading and the handling of troops in the field.

Our National Guard service has now progressed to that point where it may be said that there is no room for drones in the commissioned personnel. A man desiring to assume the responsibilities of a commissioned officer should have both the capacity and inclination to perfect himself in military science by study and application, else he can not hope to discharge his official duties creditably and will only retard the organization to which he may be attached. A single drone or incompetent may block successful administration throughout an entire command.

There have been fewer resignations of officers and applications for the discharge of enlisted men than usual and it is hoped that our competent and well-trained officers and enlisted men will remain in the service as long as is practicable. To the end that our commissioned officers may be given an opportunity to perfect and improve themselves in the military profession, it is contemplated to prescribe in orders early in the new year for a camp of instruction for infantry officers and officers of the Medical Corps, and for the officers of the Coast Artillery to attend a course of lectures and instruction at Fort Caswell, N. C. The correspondence school for infantry officers and officers of the Medical Corps will lead up to the instruction to be given at the officers' camp in May.

The Legislature of 1911 enacted into law your recommendation that the salary of the Adjutant General be increased to Two Thousand Dollars ($2,000.00) per annum. This Legislature also provided for an allowance of Fifty Dollars ($50.00) per year each for company commanders and company Q. M. Sergeants, which provision has already shown its efficacy in bringing about improved conditions of the care of company property.

There has been constructed several local rifle ranges during the year. A five hundred yard Government range has been established at Asheville and is equipped with three Aiken treadle targets. Interest in rifle practice continues unabated, as is shown by the improvement in marksmanship over previous years and published in the annual report of small-arms practice. A total of four hundred and fifty-four marksmen, two sharpshooters and twenty expert riflemen were qualified on the range at Camp Glenn. This does not include other marksmen who qualified on local ranges near home station. This exceeds the number of high grade marksmen shown in any previous report.

The State was represented in the National Matches at Camp Perry, Ohio, by a rifle team which, while not making as high a score as hoped for, yet made by far the highest score and took the highest stand of any of the teams which our State has had at the National Matches. The State bad no team in the National Matches of 1909 and 1910. Our team this year, for this reason, was somewhat handicapped for lack of experience and sufficient training on the Camp Perry range. The 1911 team made eight hundred and forty-one more points over the same ranges than the 1908 team, which shows very great improvement in marksmanship.

Rifle and pistol practice and competition was held by company teams consisting of one commissioned officer and nine enlisted men from each company of the several regiments of infantry and Coast Artillery Corps on the following dates and places:

Company teams, Third Infantry, on the range at Raleigh, April 18-20, inclusive.

Company teams, Second Infantry, on the range at Goldsboro, April 25-27, inclusive.

Company teams, First Infantry, on the range at Gastonia, May 3-5, inclusive.

The DuPont Trophy was the chief trophy contested for at these competitive shoots. This trophy was won first by the team from Company B, Third Infantry, Raleigh, N. C. Company L team, Second Infantry, Lumber Bridge, led the teams of the Second Infantry. Company K team, First Infantry, led the teams of the First Infantry. There were quite a number of local prizes offered by the citizens of the towns at which the competitive shoots were held, consisting of cash prizes and trophies.

Brig. Gen. B. S. Royster, commanding First Brigade, offered a gold medal, to be known as the Royster Medal, to the individual who made the highest total score; this prize was won by Sergeant J. H. Brown, Company K, First Infantry, Asheville.

Col. W. L. McGhee, Commissary General, offered a medal, to be known as the McGhee Medal, to the individual who made the second highest total score; this medal was won by Corporal J. W. Wade, Company D, Second Infantry, Goldsboro.

Capt. W. F. Moody, commanding Company B, Third Infantry, one of the most capable and enthusiastic riflemen in the Guard, whose team won the DuPont Trophy, offered to put up the trophy again to be contested for by the leading company teams of each regiment. This competition was held on the range at Raleigh June 5-7. Company L team, Second Infantry, Lumber Bridge, winning the trophy in this competition.

Company B, Third Infantry, Raleigh, made the highest classification and figure of merit in marksmanship for the year. Company D, Second Infantry, Goldsboro, made the second highest classification and figure of merit. Company D, First Infantry, Charlotte, made the third highest classification and figure of merit.

The First Infantry qualified eight expert riflemen and two hundred and ten marksmen. The Second Infantry qualified six expert riflemen and one hundred and fifty-five marksmen. The Third Infantry qualified six expert riflemen, two sharpshooters and eighty-nine marksmen.

Twenty-two of our officers attended the manœuvers of the Regular Army near San Antonio, Texas, for periods of two weeks each exclusive of time consumed in travel. The officers who attended these manœuvers report that they were well cared for by the Regulars and that much valuable information was gained which will be helpful to them in handling troops in the field.

Upon the request of this department for a Regular Army officer to be detailed for duty with the Organized Militia of this State as Inspector-instructor, Capt. A. J. Dougherty, 30th U. S. Infantry, was detailed. Captain Dougherty reported for duty July 1st, and since that date has been on duty with our troops. Captain Dougherty is well qualified for his duties as Inspector-instructor, being a graduate of the United States Army Service School, at Fort Leavenworth, Kansas, and of the War College, Washington, D. C. He is a capable, enthusiastic, hard-working officer, and our military establishment, I am sure, will feel the good effects of his intelligent work among us.

The officers of the Coast Artillery Corps attended a course of instruction under the supervision of the commanding officer at Fort Caswell June 12-18. All the officers who attended this course of lectures and instruction report that much was learned for their benefit as Coast Artillery officers.

During the year regimental and corps organizations encamped as follows:

Third Infantry at Camp Glenn, July 10-17.

Second Infantry at Camp Glenn, July 20-27.

First Infantry at Camp Glenn, August 3-10.

Coast Artillery Corps at Fort Caswell, August 7-18.

Each regiment at Camp Glenn fired the marksman's record course, "Special Course C," and carried out a program of field instruction, including a manœuver problem requiring one day's work, which was entered into with zest and enthusiasm by officers and enlisted men and successfully carried out.

The Coast Artillery Corps maintained their splendid reputation at record target practice with the 12-inch mortars and 8-inch rifles at Fort Caswell. Two organizations—the 4th Company, Salisbury, and 5th Company, Charlotte, making a hundred per cent hits.

The Naval Brigade made their annual cruise, July 19-August 16, by divisions on the U. S. S. *Elfrida,* the U. S. Torpedo Boat *Foote* being out of repair. The routine ship duties and target practice with one and three pounders were successfully carried out by those divisions which were not prohibited by weather conditions and unavoidable circumstances. Officers' and petty officers' schools were conducted each day. Lieutenant Dutton, U. S. N., was detailed by the Navy Department to accompany the cruises as instructor. His work was beneficial and appreciated by officers and men. I give herewith copy of Lieutenant Dutton's official report to the Navy Department:

U. S. S. *Elfrida* and U. S. S. *Foote*, North Carolina Naval Militia, Lieut. Benjamin Dutton, Jr., United States Navy:

The summer cruise of the naval milita of North Carolina was originally planned to last from July 19 to August 16. This time was to be divided into three periods of about one week each, and during each period two of the six divisions which compose the organization were to cruise, one on the *Elfrida* and one on the *Foote*. This plan was carried out with some modifications.

Such small watch, quarter and station bills as may be made out for the *Elfrida* were well done, with some knowledge of the customs of the service, and were well carried out.

The officers and men were for the most part willing and anxious to do their duty smartly and in the proper manner. But neither the officers nor the men have any but the smallest knowledge of the work. The officers are elected to their positions and apparently for no special fitness. I found officers who did not know the rules of the road, nor the simplest details of piloting, and practically nothing of gunnery. The chief boatswain's mate furnished by the Navy Department as a shipkeeper is their chief reliance in navigating. Steps should be taken, as a matter affecting the safety of lives and property, to make those holding commissions in the organization pass an examination on the rules of the road and piloting. One officer in the organization, a commander, informed me that he knew nothing of ships, adding that he was a fine infantry man. The trouble is that these people look upon their organization more in a military than in a naval light, and they will continue to do so until they are made to pass an examination and awaken an interest in things naval.

The men are capable and willing enough, but not instructed. The discipline was good at all times, considering the nature of the organization.

I attempted to have two instruction periods in the forenoon for the men, with one in the afternoon for the officers, but this was not carried out well except with the New Bern division, under the command of Commander C. D.

Bradham. With this division considerable real work was done, and the cruise was completed with a target practice, carried out in strict conformity to the rules, which was a credit to the division in every way.

It is my opinion that the units of this organization are so widely scattered that it can never be made into an efficient naval reserve. As it is now the men of the New Bern division have the ship nearly the entire year. The other divisions are practically military companies who have the privilege of going on a cruise for a week once a year. They are not seafaring men by profession and certainly can not learn to be in a week under officers who know little more about it than themselves. Perhaps if the *Elfrida* could be sent to the homes of the different divisions in rotation, and stay in each port for a month, their interest would be awakened and something learned.

The organization contains good material and could be made of value as a naval reserve. But the present system is wrong and will have to be changed if good results are to be obtained. Officers must be obtained who have some knowledge of naval work, or some way must be found to give the present officers more instruction than can be given in one week. The present organization is not recruited from people who have had any experience on vessels outside of the Naval Militia ships, and a great deal of instruction would be necessary, since it would have to begin with first principles. A cruise of at least ten days should be required each year of each division, and shore liberty should not be given on more than two days. I understand that the division at Windsor has not made a cruise in several years, and the Oriental division refused to cruise this year. Such divisions are not worthy of any support from the Navy Department, and their equipment should be withdrawn.

This report, in the main unfavorable, is written with full knowledge of the fact that there is no pay or other incentive for the Naval Militia to work hard and give up their time to the organization. Credit is due them for what has been accomplished and for a keen desire to learn. My treatment among them was always the most courteous and considerate. But the fact remains that at present the organization is far more military than naval, and with the divisions scattered as they are and recruited largely from landsmen, it will be very difficult to make it otherwise.

The U. S. S. *Foote* should be withdrawn. They do not like her, and her machinery is in bad condition. It is most too much to expect men not accustomed to ship life to live in her crowded, uncomfortable quarters and have any desire left for work.

The following companies have been called on during the year in the aid of civil authority:

Companies B and E, Third Infantry; Companies K and M, Second Infantry; Company H, First Infantry.

The Correspondence School, which is being conducted from this office under the charge of Capt. A. J. Dougherty, U. S. A., covers a five-months' course commencing with November of this year to April, 1912. The course includes one map problem each month for field officers and company commanders and one lesson each month for post or company school, to be conducted by the commissioned officer of the company.

In these lessons three drills are outlined and explained. The lessons and problems are progressive and will prove beneficial to those officers who study them.

During the year considerable repairs and improvements were made on the buildings and grounds at Camp Glenn. The storage house in the rifle pit was moved from the west to the east end of the pit, making same more accessible. A new warehouse building was constructed near the five hundred yard firing point which has proven most convenient for storing ammunition and supplies. Twenty-five score tables were made for use of scorers during record target practice. A new commissary supply building, containing an apartment of sufficient size to hold a carload of ice, was built. A new mess pavilion for sanitary troops, considerable repairs to the old buildings and driveways of crushed stone and walkways of granolithic were made in convenient places in and around camp, which have added much to the comfort and convenience of troops. This work was under the immediate supervision of Major J. S. Poythress, of the Quartermaster's Department.

During the year two ambulance wagons have been acquired for the Ambulance Company and full equipment for the Field Hospital. New pyramidal tents sufficient for one regiment, twenty officers' wall tents, four hospital tents, one storage tent, a supply of clothing and field equipment, twenty-two hundred pairs of russet marching shoes have been received.

Our National Guard has been adjudged by the War Deparement as equipped for field service.

I recommend that the concrete butt in the rifle pit at Camp Glenn be painted green or colored green with some material so as not to cause such a strong reflection on the eyes of the men who work the targets; that the house now occupied by Sergeant Guthrie at Camp Glenn be shingled and repaired; that the waterworks be overhauled and repaired; that the work of making driveways of crushed stone and walkways of granolithic or some other material be continued; that some intelligent effort be made to get grass to growing on the camp site; that no more regimental mess halls be built, but that in future, build the regulation mess hall for company units in the field; that some steps be taken to require the owners of the fish factories near Camp Glenn to cease operations during the encampment period or while troops are in camp, and to disinfect their premises and take every precaution to minimize the odor arising from the factories. I recommend that a sufficient sum be allowed to the Naval Brigade to pay the subsistence and pay of the enlisted men and officers of the Brigade for a cruise of at least ten days each year. I further recommend that the supply department be reorganized, to the end that this office can get ready and accurate information as to the amount and condition of supplies on hand and where located, and that organization commanders and accountable officers can be furnished with accurate information as to their account with the State.

Realizing the lack of information by the general public on matters pertaining to the military department of our Government and that the perpetuity of our Government rests on the patriotism of our young men, I again recommend that some suitable text-book setting forth the aims and purposes of our military establishment be taught in the public schools.

I take this occasion to express my thanks to your Excellency for uniform support and wise counsel in everything which tended toward improvement and higher efficiency in the military and naval service of the State.

In closing, I wish to express publicly my appreciation to the officers and enlisted men of the North Carolina National Guard for their hearty coöperation during the year, and to Major Gordon Smith, A. A. G., and to Miss Ethel Wynne, clerk in this office, for efficient and faithful service in carrying on the work of this department.

Very respectfully,

R. L. LEINSTER,

The Adjutant General.

REPORT OF DRILLS, TARGET PRACTICE, AND FIELD INSTRUCTION OF THE ORGANIZED MILITIA OF THE STATE OF NORTH CAROLINA.

Organization	Company, Troop, Battery, or Detachment	Camp of Instruction		Rendezvous for Target Practice		Rendezvous for Drill		Date of Inspection	
		Number of Consecutive Days	Average Number Present	Number of Times	Average Number Present	Number of Times	Average Number Present	By State Inspector	By United States Inspector. (Sec. 14, M. L.)
First Infantry	A	8	46	10	22	24	35	Mar. 23	Mar. 23
	B	8	56	16	18	29	35	Mar. 28	Mar. 28
	C	8	44	10	20	25	44	Mar. 14	Mar. 14
	D	8	53	10	18	27	48	*	*
	E	8	50	8	22	38	44	Mar. 22	Mar. 22
	F	8	48	12	20	55	38	Mar. 24	Mar. 24
	G	8	49	10	16	24	41	Mar. 20	Mar. 20
	H	8	49	12	18	27	40	Mar. 27	Mar. 27
	I	8	46	10	16	28	36	Mar. 15	Mar. 15
	K	8	43	12	20	27	35	Mar. 24	Mar. 24
	L	8	43	10	18	26	48	Mar. 16	Mar. 16
	M	8	50	10	18	24	44	Mar. 17	Mar. 17
	Band	8	24	----	----	24	24	Mar. 25	Mar. 25

*Company D, new organization. Had not been equipped when inspection was held. Mustered into service March 6, 1911.

REPORT OF DRILLS, TARGET PRACTICE, ETC.—CONTINUED.

Organization	Company, Troop, Battery, or Detachment	Camp of Instruction		Rendezvous for Target Practice		Rendezvous for Drill		Date of Inspection	
		Number of Consecutive Days	Average Number Present	Number of Times	Average Number Present	Number of Times	Average Number Present	By State Inspector	By United States Inspector. (Sec. 14, M. L.)
Second Infantry	A	8	43	8	35	24	36	Feb. 28	Feb. 28
	B	8	44	9	36	40	38	Feb. 24	Feb. 24
	C	8	49	8	35	24	38	Feb. 21	Feb. 21
	D	8	49	12	40	24	44	Feb. 22	Feb. 22
	E	8	54	12	41	26	47	Feb. 23	Feb. 23
	F	8	49	10	36	28	39	Feb. 17	Feb. 17
	G	8	47	8	35	24	37	Feb. 27	Feb. 27
	H	8	50	12	45	24	44	Feb. 20	Feb. 20
	I	8	46	4	40	24	49	Feb. 25	Feb. 25
	K	8	44	6	38	24	35	Feb. 18	Feb. 18
	L	8	55	5	40	24	46	Feb. 16	Feb. 16
	M	8	46	6	40	20	37	*	*
	Band	8	22	----	----	48	20	Feb. 24	Feb. 24

*Company M, new organization. Mustered in March 28, 1911.

REPORT OF DRILLS, TARGET PRACTICE, ETC.—CONTINUED.

Organization	Company, Troop, Battery, or Detachment	Camp of Instruction		Rendezvous for Target Practice		Rendezvous for Drill		Date of Inspection	
		Number of Consecutive Days	Average Number Present	Number of Times	Average Number Present	Number of Times	Average Number Present	By State Inspector	By United States Inspector. (Sec. 14, M. L.)
Third Infantry	A	8	40	3	38	24	37	Mar. 10	Mar. 10
	B	8	50	18	30	24	47	Feb. 15	Feb. 15
	C	8	50	5	25	26	36	Mar. 4	Mar. 4
	D	8	47	4	28	36	44	Mar. 6	Mar. 6
	E	8	44	4	29	30	41	Mar. 3	Mar. 3
	F	8	52	8	35	32	46	Mar. 7	Mar. 7
	G	8	38	12	30	24	35	Mar. 11	Mar. 11
	H	8	43	3	35	24	35	Mar. 2	Mar. 2
	I	8	46	3	40	27	40	Mar. 9	Mar. 9
	K							Mar. 1	Mar. 1
	L	8	44	3	40	24	41	Mar. 13	Mar. 13
	M	8	44	5	35	24	37	Mar. 8	Mar. 8
	Band	8	22			40	22	Feb. 15	Feb. 15

*Company K, stationed at Weldon, N. C. Mustered out for inefficiency June 7, 1911.

REPORT OF DRILLS, TARGET PRACTICE, ETC.—CONTINUED.

Organization	Company, Troop, Battery, or Detachment	Camp of Instruction		Rendezvous for Target Practice		Rendezvous for Drill		Date of Inspection	
		Number of Consecutive Days	Average Number Present	Number of Times	Average Number Present	Number of Times	Average Number Present	By State Inspector	By United States Inspector. (Sec. 14, M. L.)
Coast Artillery Corps	First	12	42	----	----	24	39	Apr. 6	Apr. 6
	Second	12	40	----	----	38	46	Apr. 7	Apr. 7
	Third	12	52	----	----	24	40	Apr. 5	Apr. 5
	Fourth	12	62	----	----	29	42	Apr. 4	Apr. 4
	Fifth	12	45	----	----	38	40	Apr. 3	Apr. 3
First Field Hospital*	1	8	33	----	----	15	33	----	----
Ambulance Co.†	1	8	38	----	----	18	34	----	----

*New organization. Mustered in July 19th, 1911, after annual inspection.
†New organization. Mustered in June 28th, 1911, after annual inspection.

RIFLE FIRING.

Organization	Average Strength, Present and Absent, Commissioned and Enlisted, for the Entire Period of Firing	Per Cent of Average Strength Qualified	Expert Riflemen	Sharpshooters	Marksmen	First Class Men	Second Class Men	Third Class Men	Fourth Class Men	Figure of Merit	Total Firing, Rifle	Total Firing, Pistol	*Figure of Merit Previous Year
	Classification and Figure of Merit												
FIRST INFANTRY:													
Field and Staff	18	77.00			8	1	2	3	4	66.72	18		
Company A	46	78.27	1		14	2	6	14	9	55.21	46		
Company B	56	66.07			16	2	4	15	19	44.64	46		
Company C	44	77.04			16	4	5	9	10	60.00	44		
Company D	53	71.88	2		20	2	4	12	13	61.69	53		
Company E	50	88.00			21	4	3	16	6	63.90	50		
Company F	48	64.58	1		15	0	5	11	16	50.71	48		
Company G	49	68.56			17	2	5	10	15	53.58	49		
Company H	49	78.77	1		19	5	8	8	8	70.00	49		
Company I	46	71.30	1		21	3	3	11	7	71.95	46		
Company K	43	74.41	2		18	1	3	10	9	69.06	43		
Company L	43	72.08			10	5	4	12	12	45.23	43		
Company M	50	80.00			15	4	9	12	10	54.80	50		
Totals			8		210	35	61	143	138	58.74	595	60	

*The First Regiment participated in joint maneuvers at Chicamauga Park, Ga., July 11th to 20th, 1910, and did not engage in rifle practice in 1910, except some of the companies on local ranges.

RIFLE FIRING—CONTINUED.

Organization	Average Strength, Present and Absent, Commissioned and Enlisted, for the Entire Period of Firing	Per Cent of Average Strength Qualified	Expert Riflemen	Sharpshooters	Marksmen	First Class Men	Second Class Men	Third Class Men	Fourth Class Men	Figure of Merit	Total Firing, Rifle	Total Firing, Pistol	*Figure of Merit Previous Year
	Classification and Figure of Merit												
SECOND INFANTRY:													
Field and Staff	20	80.00			5	3	2	6	4	50.50	20		
Company A	43	60.46			8	2	4	12	17	34.18	43		66.00
Company B	44	75.00			14	3	9	7	11	58.90	44		75.00
Company C	49	73.47	1		12	2	10	11	13	50.20	49		73.81
Company D	49	89.79	3		20	7	5	9	5	80.91	49		84.41
Company E	54	64.81	1		11	2	10	11	19	43.24	54		82.69
Company F	49	65.30			10	7	1	14	17	40.10	49		76.60
Company G	47	72.36			8	7	4	15	13	39.87	47		57.45
Company H	50	98.00			21	4	6	18	1	68.00	50		86.67
Company I	46	58.69			9	3	3	12	19	37.30	46		88.37
Company K	44	72.72			13	3	3	13	12	48.40	44		69.77
Company L	55	69.09	1		12	1	3	21	17	38.72	55		65.96
Company M	46	65.21			12	5	4	9	16	46.95	46		
Totals			6		155	49	64	158	164	53.90	596	62	

*Company M was excused by Governor from attending encampment of 1910.

RIFLE FIRING—CONTINUED.

Organization	Average Strength, Present and Absent, Commissioned and Enlisted, for the Entire Period of Firing	Per Cent of Average Strength Qualified	Expert Riflemen	Sharpshooters	Marksmen	First Class Men	Second Class Men	Third Class Men	Fourth Class Men	Figure of Merit	Total Firing, Rifle	Total Firing, Pistol	*Figure of Merit Previous Year
	CLASSIFICATION AND FIGURE OF MERIT												
THIRD INFANTRY:													
Field and Staff	17	94.12			5	2	3	6	1	57.94	17		
Company A	40	77.50			5	5	9	12	9	39.25	40		26.59
Company B	50	92.00	3	2	19	7	6	9	4	85.80	50		63.67
Company C	50	70.00			3	5	4	23	15	23.60	50		51.60
Company D	47	85.53			11	7	12	10	7	55.30	47		41.79
Company E	44	70.45			8	8	3	12	13	44.79	44		43.11
Company F	52	69.22			13	8	7	8	16	51.05	52		48.15
Company G	38	68.41	2		7	8	2	7	12	53.81	38		44.36
Company H	43	58.13			1	5	7	12	18	23.13	43		16.63
Company I	46	65.21	1		3		7	20	15	24.63	46		30.88
Company K*													50.75
Company L	41	90.24			7	7	9	14	4	48.29	44		50.75
Company M	44	63.63			7	1	9	11	16	35.45	44		42.34
Totals			6	2	89	63	78	144	130	44.31	515	58	

*Company K disbanded June 7th, 1911.

RETURN OF STRENGTH, LAND FORCES.

Designation	Commissioned Officers	Actual Enlisted Strength	Authorized Maximum Enlisted Strength	Station
HEADQUARTERS:				
First Infantry	15	3	8	Shelby.
Second Infantry	16	8	8	Washington.
Third Infantry	16	8	8	Reidsville.

Designation	Commissioned Officers	Actual Enlisted Strength	Authorized Maximum Enlisted Strength	Station
FIRST INFANTRY:				
Company A	3	43	65	Hickory.
Company B	3	49	65	Gastonia.
Company C	3	47	65	Winston-Salem.
Company D	3	59	65	Charlotte.
Company E	3	51	65	Statesville.
Company F	3	53	65	Asheville.
Company G	3	48	65	Shelby.
Company H	3	53	65	Waynesville.
Company I	3	43	65	Mt. Airy.
Company K	3	44	65	Asheville.
Company L	3	46	65	Concord.
Company M	3	57	65	High Point.
Band		26	28	Asheville.

COAST ARTILLERY CORPS.

Designation	Commissioned Officers	Actual Enlisted Strength	Authorized Maximum Enlisted Strength	Station
First Company	3	40	65	Newbern.
Second Company	3	56	65	Wilmington.
Third Company	3	51	65	Greensboro.
Fourth Company	3	67	65	Salisbury.
Fifth Company	3	60	65	Charlotte.

Designation	Commissioned Officers	Actual Enlisted Strength	Authorized Maximum Enlisted Strength	Station
SECOND INFANTRY:				
Company A	3	40	65	Tarboro.
Company B	3	48	65	Kinston.
Company C	3	50	65	Rocky Mount.
Company D	3	54	65	Goldsboro.
Company E	3	54	65	Goldsboro.
Company F	3	50	65	Fayetteville.
Company G	3	44	65	Washington.
Company H	3	48	65	Clinton.
Company I	3	54	65	Edenton.
Company K	3	46	65	Wilson.
Company L	3	55	65	Lumber Bridge.
Company M	3	44	65	Dunn.
Band		28	28	Kinston.

NAVAL BRIGADE.

Commissioned Officers	40
Enlisted Men	324
Total	364

Designation	Commissioned Officers	Actual Enlisted Strength	Authorized Maximum Enlisted Strength	Station
THIRD INFANTRY:				
Company A	3	48	65	Lexington.
Company B	3	50	65	Raleigh.
Company C	3	56	65	Henderson.
Company D	3	54	65	Louisburg.
Company E	3	58	65	Oxford.
Company F	3	67	65	Franklinton.
Company G	3	40	65	Reidsville.
Company H	3	47	65	Warrenton.
Company I	3	51	65	Burlington.
Company K	3	49	65	Asheboro.
Company L	3	57	65	Thomasville.
Company M	3	40	65	Durham.
Band		28	28	Raleigh.

HOSPITAL CORPS.

Designation	Commissioned Officers	Actual Enlisted Strength	Authorized Maximum Enlisted Strength	Station
First Field Hospital	3	33	45	Asheville.
Ambulance Company No. 1	3	43	55	Raleigh.
Hospital Corps Detachment		12	12	Reidsville.
Hospital Corps Detachment		12	13	Kinston.

	Number of Regiments of Cavalry, Field Artillery, or Infantry, or Companies of Coast Artillery	Actual Strength, December 31		Authorized Maximum Strength, as Fixed by Laws of the State, Territory, or District of Columbia		Number of Companieso f all Organizations	COMMISSIONED O								
		Commissioned	Enlisted	Commissioned	Enlisted		Brigadier Generals	Aides-de-Camp (not including Aids to Governor)	Colonels	Lieutenant Colonels	Majors	Adjutants	Quartermasters	Commissaries	Coast Artillery Engineers
		3													
s															
Department		5					1		1		3				
s Department		4							1	1	2				
eneral's Dep't		4							1	1	2				
epartment		5	1				1			1	3				
tment		4	1						1		3				
		19							1	1	6				
			100			2									
		4							1		3				
		6							1	1	3				
ent		7	1						1	1	3				
rps	5	20	277	20	325	5					1	1	1		1
	3	156	1,897	156	2,463	36	1	2	3	3	9	12	3	12	
	8	237	2,277	176	2,788	43	3	2	11	9	38	13	4	12	1

Report of Quartermaster General

STATE OF NORTH CAROLINA,
OFFICE OF QUARTERMASTER GENERAL,
HENDERSON, N. C., December 31, 1911.

THE ADJUTANT GENERAL, *Raleigh, N. C.*

SIR:—I have the honor to submit the annual report of the operations of the Quartermaster's Department for the year ending November 30, 1911.

For convenience the report is divided into the following:

Abstract A, serviceable property, First Regiment.

Abstract B, serviceable property, Second Regiment.

Abstract C, serviceable property, Third Regiment.

Abstract D, unserviceable property, First Regiment.

Abstract E, unserviceable property, Second Regiment.

Abstract F, unserviceable property, Third Regiment.

Abstract G, serviceable property, Coast Artillery Corps.

Abstract H, unserviceable property, Coast Artillery Corps.

Abstract I, statement of all property, both serviceable and unserviceable, for the three regiments and the Military Supply Depot, and the Coast Artillery Corps.

Abstrict J, Schedule of Encampment Movement.

TRANSPORTATION.

The transportation facilities and accommodations were not satisfactory in a few instances which were reported to me. This was notably true respecting the Louisburg, Warrenton, Gastonia, and perhaps one or two other companies. The reason for the unsatisfactory accommodations was due either to a lack of diligence or an oversight on the part of the car inspector.

These companies deserve the highest commendation for the excellent spirit and soldierly manner which was shown by their deportment under most trying circumstances. It is safe to say that better service will be given hereafter.

The trouble this year was due, perhaps, to the fact that the movement was unusually large and, also, by reason of the inability of the Atlantic Coast Line Company to provide any part of the equipment. The cars for the use of the troops located on this road were furnished, upon my request, by the Norfolk Southern Company. I desire to thank Mr. Croxton for this, as well as many other courtesies.

Major Leard, Captain Conn, and Mr. LeGrande and Mr. Jones, as representatives of their respective companies, were exceedingly accommodating, and I am sure left nothing in their power undone to secure for us safe, satisfactory and efficient transportation service. The schedules under which the movements were handled is forwarded herewith.

CAMP GLENN.

Our troubles at the camp site this summer caused the greatest possible annoyance and anxiety, and that there was evidence of unavoidable inconvenience was not surprising. The wells which had furnished abundance of water for the past encampments failed us almost entirely, the pumps were out of repair, the water pipes had corroded and ruptured in the ground, and several of the hydrants were down and unserviceable. Through the efforts of Major Poythress, whose trials and tribulations were many, the water line was repaired, a well bored, so that provision was made before the encampment to supply water upon the arrival of the troops.

MAIL SERVICE.

It seems quite impossible to secure the proper delivery of mail during encampments. The Y. M. C. A. Representatives are exceedingly accommodating and do all in their power to get and deliver the camp mail, but I am convinced that without the coöperation of the postal authorities a satisfactory mail service is unattainable; therefore, I respectfully recommend that this matter be taken up with the Post Office Department for adjustment.

IMPROVEMENTS.

With the completion of a Commissary house, the laying of pavements and streets this year, I feel that it is now possible to make one regiment fairly comfortable at the camp site. The recent appointment of a capable caretaker will prove to be a most important step towards the improvement of the camp site. He is a young man of ability, highly enthused over his work and fully capable of handling the whole proposition. With this man in charge there will be no need for the detail of others to attend to the preparations for future encampments. I respectfully recommend that I be authorized to secure for him a horse, cart, and such other things that he may need for immediate employment in the preparation of the grounds, etc.

I desire to thank the officers of the Guard for their helpful coöperation which has been evidenced in many ways and under various and trying circumstances during the year. They have at all times responded when called upon without one single exception. I desire also to commend my assistants, Lt. Col. W. E. Gary, Maj. J. S. Poythress, and Maj. H. S. Leard, for their very efficient services.

Respectfully submitted,

FRANCIS A. MACON,

Quartermaster General, Brigadier General, N. C. N. G.

Abstract J

STATE OF NORTH CAROLINA,
OFFICE OF QUARTERMASTER GENERAL,
HENDERSON, June 28, 1911.

CIRCULAR No. 1.

Pursuant to Paragraph III, General Orders No. 8, Adjutant General's Department, May 22, 1911, the following is published for the information and guidance of all concerned:

SCHEDULE.

THIRD INFANTRY—COL. J. N. CRAIG, COMMANDING.

TO CAMP GLENN.

CO. A—LEXINGTON.

Lv. Lexington July 9, Southern train No. 46, at 5:19 p. m.
Ar. Goldsboro July 10, Special, at 12:30 a. m.
Lv. Goldsboro, Norfolk-Southern Special, at 12:45 a. m.
Ar. Morehead City, Special, 4:45 a. m., July 10.

CO. B AND BAND—RALEIGH.

Lv. Raleigh 9:30 p. m., July 9, Norfolk-Southern Special. (After arrival S. A. L. Special.).
Ar. at Morehead 5 a. m., July 10.

CO. C—HENDERSON.

Lv. Henderson July 9, S. A. L. Special, 7:10 p. m.
Ar. Raleigh, S. A. L. Special, 9 p. m.
Ar. Morehead, Norfolk-Southern Special, 5 a. m., July 10.

CO. D—LOUISBURG.

Lv. Louisburg July 9, S. A. L., 6 p. m.
Ar. Franklinton, S. A. L. train No. 330, 6:30 p. m.
Lv. Franklinton, S. A. L. Special, 7:50 p. m.
Ar. Raleigh, S. A. L. Special, 9 p. m.
Lv. Raleigh, Norfolk-Southern Special, 9:30 p. m.
Ar. Morehead City, Special, 5 a. m., July 10.

CO. E—OXFORD.

Lv. Oxford July 9, S. A. L. train No. 442, 6:05 p. m.
Ar. Henderson, S. A. L. 442, 6:50 p. m.
Lv. Henderson, S. A. L. Special, 7:10 p. m.
Ar. Raleigh, S. A. L. Special, 9 p. m.
Lv. Raleigh, Norfolk-Southern Special, 9:30 p. m.
Ar. Morehead City, 5 a. m., July 10.

Co. F—Franklinton.

Lv. Franklinton July 9, S. A. L. Special, 7:50 p. m.
Ar. Raleigh, S. A. L. Special, 9 p. m.
Lv. Raleigh, Norfolk-Southern Special, 9:30 p. m.
Ar. Morehead, Norfolk-Southern Special, 5 a. m, July 10.

Co. G—Reidsville.

Lv. Reidsville (Company and Hospital Corps) July 9, Southern train No. 35, 5:22 p. m.
Ar. Goldsboro July 10, Special, 12:30 a. m.
Lv. Goldsboro, Norfolk-Southern Special, 12:45 a. m.
Ar. Morehead City, Special, 4:45 a. m., July 10.

Co. H—Warrenton.

Lv. Warrenton, Warrenton R. R. Special, 5:50 p. m., July 9.
Lv. Warren Plains July 9, S. A. L. Special, 6:15 p. m.
Ar. Henderson, S. A. L. Special, 7:05 p. m.
Lv. Henderson, S. A. L. Special, 7:10 p. m.
Ar. Raleigh 9 p. m.
Lv. Raleigh, Norfolk-Southern, 9:30 p. m.
Ar. Morehead 5 a. m., July 10.

Co. I—Burlington.

Lv. Burlington July 9, Southern Special, 8:10 p. m.
Ar. Goldsboro July 10, Special, at 12:30 a. m.
Lv. Goldsboro July 10, Special, at 12:45 a. m.
Ar. Morehead, Special, July 10, at 4.45 a. m.

Co. L—Thomasville.

Lv. Thomasville July 9, Southern train No. 46, at 5:40 p. m.
Ar. Goldsboro, Special, at 12:30 a. m., July 10.
Lv. Goldsboro, Special, at 12:45 a. m., July 10.
Ar. Morehead City, Special, at 4:45 a. m., July 10.

Co. M—Durham.

Lv. Durham, Southern Special, at 9:30 p. m.
Ar. Goldsboro, Special, at 12:30 a. m., July 10.
Lv. Goldsboro, Special, at 12:45 a. m.
Ar. Morehead City, Special, at 4:45 a. m.

Southern Railway Equipment for Third Infantry.

Reidsville Company and Hospital Corps—two coaches and one baggage car.
Lexington Company and Thomasville Company—one coach for each company and one baggage car to be used jointly.
Burlington Company and Durham Company—one coach for each company and one baggage car to be used jointly.
Pullman on Greensboro Special.

NORFOLK-SOUTHERN EQUIPMENT FOR THIRD INFANTRY.

One coach and one combination coach and baggage car for Company B and Band.

S. A. L. EQUIPMENT FOR THIRD INFANTRY.

One Pullman from Warren Plains.
One coach from Warren Plains.
One baggage car from Warren Plains.
One coach from Oxford.
One baggage car from Oxford.
One coach from Henderson.
One baggage car from Louisburg.
One coach from Louisburg.
One coach from Franklinton.

The Warrenton Company will use baggage car provided from that point, same to be delivered to the Warrenton Railroad the morning of the 9th of July; coach will also be delivered to the Warrenton Railroad at Warren Plains the morning of the 9th.

Oxford and Henderson companies will use the same baggage car, same to start from Oxford. The Louisburg and Franklinton companies will use same baggage car, same to start from Louisburg.

SECOND INFANTRY—COL. H. C. BRAGAW, COMMANDING.

TO CAMP GLENN.

CO. A—TARBORO.

Lv. Tarboro July 19, train No. 91, 7:40 p. m.
Ar. Rocky Mount, 8:20 p. m.
Ar. Wilson, 9:20.
Ar. Morehead 6:30 a. m., July 20, 1911.

CO. B, BAND AND HOSPITAL CORPS—KINSTON.

Company and Hospital Corps, Lv. Kinston 3 a. m., July 20.
Ar. Morehead 6:15 a. m., July 20.

CO. C—ROCKY MOUNT.

Lv. Rocky Mount, A. C. L. No. 91, 8:23 p. m.
Ar. Wilson, 9:20.
Ar. Morehead, 6:30 a. m., July 20.

COS. D AND E—GOLDSBORO.

Lv. Goldsboro, regular train, No. 16, at 10:15 p. m.
Special from New Bern, Ar. Morehead City 3 a. m., July 20.

CO. F—FAYETTEVILLE.

Lv. Fayetteville July 19, train No. 42, Raleigh & Southport, 5:10 p. m., one coach and one baggage car. Equipment furnished by initial line.

Ar. Raleigh 8:20 p. m.

Lv. Raleigh, Norfolk-Southern, No. 6, 9:15 p. m.
Ar. Wilson 11:30 p. m.
Ar. Morehead 6:30 a. m., July 20, 1911.

Co. G—WASHINGTON.

Lv. Washington July 20, Norfolk-Southern No. 5, 2:30 a. m., one coach, baggage loaded with Edenton.
Ar. Chocowinity, Special, 2:40 a. m.
Lv. Chocowinity, 3:50 a. m.
Ar. Morehead, 6:30 a. m., July 20.

Co. H—CLINTON.

Lv. Clinton, A. C. L. train No. 40, at 3 p. m., July 19.
Ar. Goldsboro, 10:05 p. m.
Lv. Goldsboro, No. 16, 10:15 p. m., Norfolk-Southern.
Ar. Morehead, 3 a. m., July 20.

Co. I—EDENTON.

Lv. Edenton, Norfolk-Southern Special No. 5, 12:05 a. m., July 20; one coach and baggage car, furnished by Norfolk-Southern.
Ar. Washington 2:20 a. m.
Lv. Washington at 2:30 a. m.
Ar. Morehead 6:30 a. m.

Co. K—WILSON.

Lv. Wilson, Norfolk-Southern Special, July 20, 12:40 a. m.; one coach, baggage loaded with Fayetteville equipment, furnished by Norfolk-Southern.
Ar. Chocowinity 3:40 a. m.
Lv. Chocowinity 3:50 a. m.
Ar. Morehead 6:30 a. m.

Co. L—LUMBER BRIDGE.

Lv. Lumber Bridge, A. C. L. No. 66, 9:50 p. m., July 19.
Ar. Morehead 6:30 a. m., July 20.

Co. M—DUNN.

Lv. Dunn, A. C. L., July 19, No. 86, 11:18 p. m.
Ar. Wilson 12:38.
Ar. Morehead 6:30 a. m., July 20.

FIRST INFANTRY—COL. J. T. GARDNER, COMMANDING.

TO CAMP GLENN.

Co. A—HICKORY.

Lv. Hickory, Southern Special, 5:25 p. m., August 2.
Lv. Goldsboro, Norfolk-Southern, at 3:30 a. m.
Ar. Morehead City 7:30 a. m., August 3.

Co. B—Gastonia.

Lv. Gastonia on Southern train No. 12 at 4:55 p. m., connecting with Special at Greensboro. Special to leave Greensboro at 10:15 p. m., August 2.

Ar. Goldsboro 3:15 a. m., August 3.

Lv. Goldsboro 3:30 a. m.

Ar. Morehead 7:30 a. m., August 3.

Co. C—Winston.

Lv. Winston, Southern regular train 238 at 8:10 p. m., connecting with special at Greensboro. Special train to leave Greensboro at 10:15 p. m., August 2.

Ar. Goldsboro 3:15 a. m., August 3.

Lv. Goldsboro, Norfolk-Southern, 3:30 a. m.

Ar. Morehead 7:30 a. m., August 3.

Co. D and Hospital Corps—Charlotte.

Lv. Charlotte, S. A. L. Special train, 8 p. m., August 2.

Ar. Raleigh, S. A. L. Special, 2:35 a. m., August 3. To be delivered to Norfolk-Southern immediately upon arrival at Raleigh, to be operated special to Morehead.

Lv. Raleigh on Special Norfolk-Southern, 2:40 a. m.

Ar. Morehead 8:40 a. m., August 3.

Co. E—Statesville.

Lv. Statesville, Southern Special, at 6:55 p. m., August 2.

Lv. Goldsboro, Norfolk-Southern Special, at 3:30 a. m.

Ar. Morehead 7:30 a. m., August 3.

Co. F—Asheville.

Two Companies and Band Lv. Asheville 2:30 p. m., August 2.

Lv. Goldsboro, Norfolk-Southern Special, 3:30 a. m.

Ar. Morehead 7:30 a. m., August 3.

Co. G—Shelby.

Lv. Shelby, S. A. L. train No. 132, 4:50 p. m., August 2.

Ar. Charlotte, S. A. L., 7:25 p. m., August 2.

To be delivered to Norfolk-Southern immediately upon arrival at Raleigh, to be operated on special to Morehead.

Lv. Raleigh 2:40 a. m.

Ar. Morehead 8:40 a. m., August 3.

Co. H—Waynesville.

Lv. Waynesville, Southern train, 12:05 p. m., August 2.

Lv. Goldsboro, Norfolk-Southern, at 3:30 a. m.

Ar. Morehead 7:30 a. m., August 3.

Co. I—MOUNT AIRY.

Lv. Mount Airy on Southern train 336, 1:30 p. m., August 2, 1911, connecting with Special at Greensboro, special train to leave Greensboro at 10:15 p. m., August 2.
Ar. Goldsboro 3:15 a. m., August 3.
Lv. Goldsboro, Norfolk-Southern, 3:30 a. m.
Ar. Morehead City 7:30 a. m., August 3.

Co. K—ASHEVILLE.

Same as Co. F and Band.

Co. L—CONCORD.

Lv. Concord on Southern train No. 12 at 6:43 p. m., connecting with Special at Greensboro. Special leaves Greensboro 10:15 p. m., August 2.
Ar. Goldsboro 3:15 a. m., August 3.
Lv. Goldsboro, Norfolk-Southern, at 3:30 a. m.
Ar. Morehead 7:30, August 3.

Co. M.—HIGH POINT.

Lv. High Point, Southern Special train, 9:28 p. m., August 2.
Lv. Goldsboro, Norfolk-Southern, 3:30 a. m.
Ar. Morehead City 7:30 a. m., August 3.

SOUTHERN RAILWAY EQUIPMENT FOR FIRST INFANTRY.

Waynesville Company—one coach and one baggage car.

Asheville—two companies and band—three coaches and one baggage car. One Pullman.

Hickory Company—one coach, baggage of this company to be handled in baggage car with Waynesville Company.

Statesville Company—one coach and one baggage car.

Gastonia Company—one coach and one baggage car.

Concord Company—one coach, baggage of this company to be handled in baggage car with Gastonia Company.

High Point Company—one coach, baggage of this company to be loaded in baggage car from Statesville.

Mt. Airy Company—one coach and one baggage car.

Winston Company—one coach, baggage of this company to be loaded in baggage car from Mount Airy.

S. A. L. EQUIPMENT FOR FIRST INFANTRY.

From Shelby—one coach and one baggage car.

From Charlotte—one Pullman sleeper and one coach. The above equipment to be delivered to the Norfolk-Southern immediately upon arrival at Raleigh to be operated on schedule to Morehead City.

COAST ARTILLERY CORPS—MAJ. MAX L. BARKER, COMMANDING.

TO FORT CASWELL, N. C.

1ST COMPANY—NEW BERN.

Lv. New Bern A. C. L., 9:30 a. m.
Ar. Wilmington 12:50 p. m.

2D COMPANY—WILMINGTON.

Lv. Wilmington on Government boat for Fort Caswell.

Ar. at a time to be arranged between the Fort Caswell officials and the commanding officers of 2d Co., Coast Artillery Corps.

3D COMPANY—GREENSBORO.

Lv. Greensboro Southern train No. 112, 12:45 a. m., August 7.

Ar. Wilmington 9:45 a. m., August 7.

4TH COMPANY—SALISBURY.

Lv. Salisbury, Southern train No. 12 at 8 p. m., August 7.

Ar. Wilmington, 9:45 a. m. August 8.

5TH COMPANY—CHARLOTTE.

Lv. Charlotte, S. A. L. train No. 40, at 5 a. m., August 7.

Ar. Wilmington 12:20 p. m., August 7.

Companies will leave Wilmington on Harper Boat Line the days of arrival at 2:30 p. m.

The return schedule for the Morehead movement will be published by the Quartermaster General at Camp Glenn, and for the Fort Caswell movement, it will be arranged by Major Max. L. Barker, commanding Coast Artillery Corps North Carolina, for the Quartermaster General North Carolina, so that the troops will arrive home from Fort Caswell at or before midnight, August 18.

Pay Rolls in duplicate are forwarded herewith to the Commanding Officers of the Infantry Organizations. These rolls will be prepared in accordance with directions printed thereon, and delivered to the Disbursing Officer at Camp Glenn. Transportation requests are forwarded direct to the Company Commanders, and for the Regimental Field and Staff Officers to the Regimental and Battalion Commanders. FRANCIS A. MACON,

Brigadier General, Quartermaster General, N. C.
United States Disbursing Officer.

Report of Inspector General

STATE OF NORTH CAROLINA,
OFFICE OF INSPECTOR GENERAL,
WAYNESVILLE, N. C., December 1, 1911.

GENERAL R. L. LEINSTER, *Adjutant General, N. C. N. G., Raleigh, N. C.*

SIR:—As directed by General Order No. 1' dated Raleigh, N. C., January 14, 1911, I have the honor to report the results of the annual inspection of the three regiments of Infantry, three Bands and three companies of the C. A. C. of the North Carolina National Guard, for the year ending December 1, 1911. The first and second companies, C. A. C., being inspected by Lieut. Col. H. D. Harper.

The inspection beginning in Raleigh with Company B and Band, Third Infantry, and the Adjutant General's Department on February 14 and 15, 1911, and finishing with Third Company, C. A. C., at Greensboro, April 5, 1911. Lieut. M. A. Wells, Seventeenth Infantry, U. S. A., accompanied me, making the inspection of Second and Third Regiments, and Capt. Rex Van Den Corput relieving him and making inspection of the First Regiment and the C. A. C. companies.

Detailed reports have already been forwarded your department. It also shows property loss for the years 1910 and 1911, a comparison of which might be beneficial to a good many company commanders.

The following shows results of inspection, giving number present and absent.

Very respectfully,

THOS. STRINGFIELD,
Colonel and Inspector General, N. C. N. G.

SUMMARY OF ATTENDANCE OF THE DEPARTMENTS.

Subdivisions	Officers Present	Officers Absent	Officers Present and Absent	Aggregate	Remarks
Adjutant General's Department	3	3	6	6	The different staff departments turn out very poorly; not fifty per cent were out for inspection.
Quartermaster General's Department	3	3	6	6	
Inspector General's Department	3	4	7	7	
Commissary Department	1	5	6	6	
Engineering Department	1	5	6	6	
Pay Department	2	5	7	7	
Ordnance Department	3	5	8	8	
Judge Advocate General's Department	0	6	6	6	
Medical Department	7	6	13	13	
First Brigade Department	4	6	10	10	
Total	27	48	75	75	

SUMMARY OF ATTENDANCE OF THE FIRST REGIMENT.

Subdivisions	Present		Absent		Present and Absent		Aggregate	Money Value of Property not Accounted for 1911	Money Value of Property not Accounted for 1910
	Officers	Men	Officers	Men	Officers	Men			
Field, Staff, and N. C. Staff	16	5	------	2	16	7	23	$--------	$--------
Hospital Corps	------	------	------	------	------	------	------	--------	--------
Field Music	------	------	------	------	------	------	------	--------	--------
Band	------	24	------	1	------	25	25	--------	--------
Company A	3	37	------	11	3	48	51	37.16	96.23
Company B	2	43	------	5	2	48	50	57.95	6.57
Company C	3	42	------	2	3	44	47	58.81	27.01
Company D	Not	inspe	cted i	n 1911	------	------	------	--------	177.60
Company E	3	43	------	5	3	48	51	41.53	136.53
Company F	2	37	1	8	3	45	48	100.82	171.20
Company G	3	44	------	6	3	50	53	88.76	111.65
Company H	3	46	------	3	3	49	52	51.34	3.32
Company I	3	37	------	3	3	40	43	15.27	52.03
Company K	3	34	------	11	3	45	48	118.85	56.98
Company L	3	41	------	6	3	47	50	19.80	20.70
Company M	3	45	------	7	3	52	55	70.50	106.63
Total	------	------	------	------	------	------	------	$ 660.79	$ 966.45

SUMMARY OF ATTENDANCE OF THE SECOND REGIMENT.

Subdivisions	Present		Absent		Present and Absent		Aggregate	Money Value of Property not Accounted for 1911	Money Value of Property not Accounted for 1910
	Officers	Men	Officers	Men	Officers	Men			
Field, Staff, and N. C. Staff	10	4	6	3	16	7	23	$	$
Hospital Corps									
Field Music									
Band		28				28	28		
Company A	3	37		3	3	40	43	73.13	114.85
Company B	3	47		4	3	51	54	48.35	226.18
Company C	3	43		9	3	52	55	70.16	8.84
Company D	3	47		3	3	50	53	33.62	89.57
Company E	3	54			3	54	57	45.50	35.77
Company F	3	41		8	3	49	52	61.00	197.00
Company G	2	37		5	2	42	44	77.52	142.36
Company H	2	43	1	3	3	46	49	2.67	4.74
Company I	2	41	1	2	3	43	46	82.89	38.05
Company K	3	38		7	3	45	48	286.81	64.40
Company L	3	43		7	3	50	53	78.83	21.16
Company M	Disbanded 1911								227.06
Total								$ 860.48	$1,169.98

SUMMARY OF ATTENDANCE OF THE THIRD REGIMENT.

Subdivisions	Present		Absent		Present and Absent		Aggregate	Money Value of Property not Accounted for 91	Money Value of Property not Accounted for 190
	Officers	Men	Officers	Men	Officers	Men			
Field, Staff, and N. C. Staff	11	7	5		16	7	23	$	$
Hospital Corps									
Field Music									
Band		24		4		28	28		
Company A	3	41		1	3	42	45	36.64	41.12
Company B	2	42	1	21	3	63	66	16.65	97.40
Company C	2	40	1	16	3	56	59	180.24	136.74
Company D	3	44		8	3	52	55	42.56	63.71
Company E	3	35		12	3	47	50	127.17	52.05
Company F	3	45		2	3	47	50	9.58	3.36
Company G	3	36		5	3	41	44	88.09	46.35
Company H	3	26		18	3	44	47	122.97	121.40
Company I	3	39		6	3	45	48	22.31	237.24
Company K	2	24		2	2	26	28	71.77	5.11
Company L	3	34		6	3	40	43	51.99	3.48
Company M	3	34		5	3	39	42	175.57	40.28
Total								$ 945.54	$ 848.24

SUMMARY OF ATTENDANCE OF THE COAST ARTILLERY CORPS.

Subdivisions	Present		Absent		Present and Absent		Aggregate
	Officers	Men	Officers	Men	Officers	Men	
Field, Staff, and N. C. Staff	4		1		5		5
Hospital Corps							
Field Music							
Band							
First Company	3	35		8	3	43	46
Second Company	3	59		3	3	62	65
Third Company	3	29		14	3	43	46
Fourth Company	3	42			3	42	45
Fifth Company	2	42	1	5	3	47	50
Total	18	207	2	30	20	237	257

Report of Surgeon General

STATE OF NORTH CAROLINA,
SURGEON GENERAL'S OFFICE,
ASHEVILLE, December 31, 1911.

TO THE ADJUTANT GENERAL OF THE STATE OF NORTH CAROLINA.

SIR:—I have the honor to submit herewith my annual report for the year 1911.

A great step forward has been taken in a reorganization of the Medical Department, and as this report will come under the eye of the commissioned and most of the enlisted personnel of the several departments, it seems appropriate that I should make note of what constitutes the Medical Department as it stands today, for the benefit of those who may read your report to His Excellency, the Governor of North Carolina. In this connection I desire to convey to you the expressions of appreciation for your hearty coöperation in my efforts to organize an efficient Medical Department, which will be ready to reflect credit upon itself and the State whenever it may be needed in time of war, and to show preparedness in time of peace in keeping step with the other organizations which go to make up the National Guard of North Carolina. For without such ready response and help there can be no organization and no esprit. I also desire to thank Capt. H. D. Thomason, Medical Corps, U. S. Army, Assistant to the Chief, Division of Militia Affairs, War Department, Washington, D. C., for his unfailing sympathy and readiness to help in promoting the efficiency of this Department. Every Medical Department of the Organized Militia owes Captain Thomason a debt of gratitude for his loyal support and assistance.

General Orders, No. 10, from your Department, issued at Raleigh, June 2, 1911, prescribe that the entire personnel of the Medical Department and all other persons assigned to duty therewith, shall be known as Sanitary Troops. The Department consists of a Medical Corps, a Medical Reserve Corps and a Hospital Corps. When not in field service all enlisted personnel of the Sanitary Troops are attached (on paper) to the units, Field Hospital and Ambulance Companies. When in the field various Detachments from these units are to be assigned to duty with the different commands. In obedience to orders as above issued the organization of Field Hospital, No. 1, at Asheville was placed in the hands of Maj. F. J. Clemenger and a working unit of two commissioned and thirty-three enlisted men were mustered in. The organization of Ambulance Company, No. 1, two commissioned and forty-three enlisted men, with Capt. W. C. Horton in command, was in like manner carried out at Raleigh, N. C. Hitherto the Hospital Corps consisted of three detachments, at Charlotte, Reidsville and Kinston, serving respectively with the First, Third and Second Regiments. Owing to conditions it was deemed undesirable to continue the detachment at Charlotte, which detachment has been mustered out and its properties sent to the State Arsenal at Raleigh. The detached organizations at Reidsville and Kinston, the two remaining detachments of the Hospital Corps, will keep up their organizations at these respective points prepared for service in the field wherever the interests of the service require.

With the approval of the Department, a third Detachment of five Hospital Corps men will be stationed at Salisbury to serve with the Coast Artillery. Prior to the organization of the Medical Department, and owing to the lack of enlisted men in the Hospital Corps, the Coast Artillery has been without dependable attendance during the summer exercises at Fort Caswell. While this can not occur in the future it is deemed wise to recommend that a small Detachment of the Corps be organized and stationed with Major Barker, commanding at Salisbury.

Paragraph 33, Field Service Regulations 1910, directs that for duty in the field Sanitary Troops are divided into: First, those assigned to regiment and other combatant units; second, those formed into independent Sanitary units, such as Ambulance Companies and Field Hospitals.

Quoting from Circular No. 19 from the Division of Militia Affairs, it will be observed as late as November 9, 1910, that "Recent investigation by the Division of Militia Affairs demonstrates that, with rare exceptions, no Ambulance Companies or Field Hospitals have been provided for in the organization of the Organized Militia of the States and Territories. In case of mobilization, therefore, in military divisions, there would be an almost complete deficiency of sanitary units which normally should be provided therefor."

Since that time, in a very interesting and instructive paper, Captain Thomason, Medical Corps, Assistant to the Chief, Division of Militia Affairs, states that there has been organized in the Militia 12 Ambulance Companies and 11 Field Hospitals; 20 of each being organized or in process of organization, and that counting the 20 as organized, that the Militia is still short 41 Field Hospitals and 41 Ambulance Companies. I commend this contribution of Captain Thomason, read before the Association of Military Surgeons at its meeting in Milwaukee, September 26 to 29, 1911, and published in the *Military Surgeon* in November, to the commissioned and enlisted personnel of the Medical Department. Captain Thomason handles the subject of the Sanitary Troops in a most masterly manner and clearly sets forth and comprehensively what is being done for Organized Militia by the General Government and what the various States are doing for themselves in the way of its Sanitary service. So, then, we have reason to feel encouraged if not satisfied with our status, and from what I learn from without, the National Guard of North Carolina is one of the very best organizations in the Organized Militia of the United States, and stands ready to take its place with credit in the front of the "first line of defense of the nation" should the call come.

The annual encampment of the Infantry regiments took place as usual at Camp Glenn and the entire body of the Sanitary Troops had the opportunity to participate therein. These exercises were most beneficial, interesting, and instructive. The Detachments from Reidsville and Kinston were on duty and did credit to themselves and were helpful to the new organizations. The Field Hospital and Ambulance Company, composed of as fine a lot of young men as could be found, exhibited zeal and energy, and under the instruction of Sergeant White, from the Hospital Corps of the Medical Department of the Regular Army, derived great benefit from instruction. Sergeant Sullivan, of the Reidsville Detachment of the Hospital Corps, who has had the advantage of excellent medico-military training in the Regular Army, upon request of this Department was detailed also to assist in instructing the new units and was most helpful. Both Sergeants White and Sullivan are soldiers every inch, and I can not speak in praise too high of their soldiery qualities and the useful knowledge imparted to the new organizations. Sergeant White's intimate knowledge of the Manual of the Medical Department of the army, the organization of the Department, general duties, etc., and his technique in education and training combine to make him a most valuable man and his detail for duty with the Organized Militia a most important one. It is to be hoped that this Department can have the benefit of Sergeant White's services from time to time. Sergeant Sullivan's services, too, might be used to good advantage in like manner, especially for service in the field.

There was no unusual sickness at camp and very little of any sort except a case of smallpox in one of the Washington Companies. The following extract from Captain Pridgen's report gives the history of the case:

KINSTON, N. C.

COLONEL S. WESTRAY BATTLE, *Surgeon General, Asheville, N. C.*

SIR:—I have the honor to report that I assembled the Kinston Detachment of the Hospital Corps as per orders and proceeded to Camp Glenn. The train was inspected and found in good condition with the exception of one or two drinking cups missing.

Before the hospital quarters had been erected at Camp Glenn a suspect was brought in from a Washington company, who we found to have smallpox. He was immediately quarantined in a separate tent and a guard placed over him. He was given proper attention. We tried to return the case to Washington, from whence it came, in the same car, the railroad authorities agreeing, but the county authorities of Beaufort refused to accept him. This was immediately brought to your attention, and after consultation with you and Major McGougan, it was decided to keep the case under quarantine at camp. This was done, and the tentage, etc., was burned after the stay of the next regiment by order of General Macon. A guard was detailed to stay with the case between camps. The camp was inspected each day and found in better condition than heretofore. There was comparatively little sickness among the men. The few minor operations again demonstrated the fact that we need better quarters for a hospital. The entire Washington company was vaccinated and the equipment and tentage of the Washington company was fumigated. My detachment of the Hospital Corps was taken to the field for manœuvres and did its duty well. We followed the firing line with the first-aid station in our rear in command of Major McGougan. The wounded were taken from the trenches, given first-aid and removed by litter to the first-aid station, from there the Raleigh Ambulance Company, under Lieutenant Horton, coveyed them to the dressing station at the first cross-roads in our rear. After the battle we were ordered to the dressing station, where Major McGougan gave a talk on first-aid. Most of our outfit was left behind for the next regiment, as the field hospital was to be on hand and had not received its equipment. There was no sickness in the detachment, and no case was left on hand when camp broke, save the smallpox case.

This covers the main points of our service, and I have the honor to be,

Very respectfully, CLAUD L. PRIDGEN,
Captain, M. C., N. C. N. G.,
Commanding Kinston Detachment of the Hospital Corps.

Following are extracts from the reports of Maj. F. J. Clemenger, commanding Field Hospital, No. 1, First Lieutenant W. Meyers Hunter, on duty with the Coast Artillery, and Capt. W. C. Horton, Commanding Ambulance Company, No. 1:

COLONEL S. WESTRAY BATTLE, *Surgeon General, N. C. N. G.*

SIR:—Relative to the Field Hospital attendance at the annual encampment of the First Regiment, I beg to state that organization left Asheville with the units of the regiment from this section, and on reaching Morehead City immediately went into camp in the quarters formerly occupied by the other sanitary troops preceding us.

Considering the fact that our organization was less than a month old, I feel that our work while there was encouraging and we may have every reason to expect some good work in the future.

No systematic attempt was made to administer typhoid inoculations, as a satisfactory plan for completion of the immunization had not been worked out, but I would suggest that a committee of three or more medical officers be assigned this subject for special consideration, and see if it can not be arranged in some way to give the troops the benefit of this valuable procedure.

Under the direction of Major Glenn, Chief Medical Officer of the camp, First Lieutenant A. F. Reeves and First Lieutenant Edwin F. Fenner were assigned to duty with the Field Hospital, and rendered valuable assistance in the training of the men and in conducting the routine of the camp.

Much valuable instruction was received from Sergeant White, who had been assigned to special duty from the Regular Army, and Sergeant Sullivan of the Reidsville Hospital Corps.

Breaking camp, we embarked with the troops and reached home without mishap. Might I here state that the car furnished for the Field Hospital was neither lighted nor iced by the railway company for the return journey.

No prevailing disease occurred during the encampment, and the men were seemingly very well prepared for the trip.

Very respectfully, F. J. CLEMENGER,
Major, Medical Corps, Commanding Field Hospital No. 1.

COLONEL S. WESTRAY BATTLE, *Surgeon General, N. C. N. G.*

SIR:—With six men of the Hospital Corps I arrived at Fort Caswell at 5 p. m., August 7th. The health of the five companies on the whole was good, the last days furnishing most of our work, as the men were forced to hard drills and duties in the excessive heat, resulting in slight prostrations and minor complaints, necessitating "light duty." The only treatments of importance were two cases, one of appendicitis and one badly contused foot, with apparently good recoveries. The appendix case reported was sent home in good condition on crutches.

The personal and camp hygiene could not have been improved upon. The incinerator, in my mind, is a positive solution of the excreta proposition, and is hereby endorsed.

The habits and conduct of the men were unusually good. I think in part this can be attributed to their association with the well disciplined regulars, who teach them minor points by contact that our own officers could not by verbal instruction.

Major Winston was the most competent and congenial man I ever had the pleasure of working with or under. I hope to meet him again in our work. Our Adjutant General honored us with a visit.

Major Winston and I both delivered a short lecture to the State and post officers on subjects relating to personal and camp hygiene. While not a lecturer, I believe much good can come of lectures on sanitation and military tactics.

The Hospital Corps was subjected to more of the military duties of camp life than ever before. Our detachment was in charge of a sergeant on dress parades and reviews, while Major Winston and I discarded the scalpel for the sabre and served on Major Barker's staff.

I think the encampment can be put on record as a most profitable one for all. The pleasure seeking element were conspicuous by their absence. I would, however, suggest more time for recreation and pleasure, as we had absolutely none, as none of us left the camp once.

Yours respectfully, W. MEYERS HUNTER,
First Lieutenant, Medical Corps.

RALEIGH, N. C.

COLONEL S. WESTRAY BATTLE, *Surgeon General, N. C. N. G., Asheville, N. C.*

SIR:—I have the honor to submit the following brief report of Ambulance Company No. 1, in camp. Strength of the company in camp:

Sergeants, first class	2
Sergeants	7
Privates	26
Lieutenants	2
	37

Ambulance Company went into camp July 20, 1911. Messed with Hospital Corps of Kinston; arrangements bad, but best we could do under circumstances. Two drills per day under the splendid leadership of Sergeants White and Sullivan; appeared with infantry for inspection July 24th. Were in the manœuver, stationed with the defense, July 25th; some real instructive practice. Rendered assistance to Hospital Corps in care of the sick.

The commissioned officers of the Ambulance Company inspected camp twice daily.

Very respectfully, W. C. HORTON,
Captain, Medical Corps, N. C. N. G.

Splendid work has been done this year in inoculation for typhoid fever. In regard to the benefit derived from the treatment aimed at the eradication of the hookworm, sufficient time has not yet elapsed to gauge the amount of good done, and it is much more difficult to arrive at any conclusion as to the benefit derived from such treatment in the National Guard than it is in the Regular Army where the men are constantly under observation. There can be but little doubt that our work in this direction has resulted in a decided improvement in the general health of the infected men of the Guard; hence an improvement in efficiency.

The matter of inoculation against typhoid in the Organized Militia presents many difficulties, but it is the conviction of this Department that the work should be carried on vigorously, notwithstanding the disadvantages which come from the men not being in camp long enough to take the full treatment recognized as best for the prevention of this dread disease, hitherto the scourge of the military camp. Many guardsmen have availed themselves of the treatment during the year; the typhoid prophylactic having been supplied to this Department from the Adjutant General's office, which was in turn supplied by the War Department upon requisition. It is my opinion, in view of the three treatments required at intervals of ten days, that the first inoculation should take place during an encampment and those taking the treatment should be supplied with two doses of the prophylactic so that the two inoculations completing the treatment might be conducted at home. The prophylactic for this purpose should be supplied in ampullæ or flasks containing a single dose; whereas for inoculating a number at a time the larger flasks would be more convenient. The innocuousness of the treatment and the freedom from any sort of complications commend itself to general use in civil as well as military life, and next to diphtheria antitoxin perhaps no discovery of modern times has proven so valuable and will continue to be such a boon to humanity.

For those of the sanitary personnel of the Organized Militia who were fortunate enough to have the duty, the Manœuver Camps at San Antonio and Leon Springs, Texas, during the summer furnished unusual opportunities to observe and take part in every phase of work on the field, field hospital and ambulance company instruction, experience in making and breaking camp, marching, bivouacing, locating aid and dressing stations and field hospitals, selecting routes of evacuation from aid stations to the rear, including map reading and topography. It is to be regretted that more of the Sanitary personnel of the Organized Militia could not have had this experience. Two officers of the Medical Corps of North Carolina National Guard enjoyed the privilege of this duty. With upwards of twelve thousand troops in camp through the immunizing influences of the trphoid proyhylactic that disease was—*mirabile dictu*—not to be found on the sick reports. In the annals of military history there is nothing to compare to this record.

I regret that the Medical Corps could not be represented at the Field Service School for Medical officers at Fort Leavenworth, Kansas. The War Department, through the Division of Militia Affairs, permitted six medical officers of the Organized Militia of the United States to attend this school for six weeks beginning April first. Major Glenn was designated and detailed for this duty from the North Carolina National Guard, but upon the establishment of the mobilization camps near the Mexican border his detail was changed to the Manœuver Camps. Though we may not be successful, this Department will endeavor each year to have one of its officers at this school.

Pursuant to your approval, I am making arrangements for a Correspondence School for the Corps, having received favorable answers from a sufficient number of the commissioned personnel to warrant making a request for an instructor in the Regular Army. I have been much gratified with the cheerful and enthusiastic response to my inquiries as to whether such a course of instruction would be acceptable.

The Corps is also keen to attend the camp of instruction for infantry officers to be held in May, in Raleigh, and I entertain the hope that the entire Medical Corps may participate and receive instruction as it is understood that a Medical officer of the Regular Army will also be in attendance for this purpose.

RECOMMENDATIONS.

About Camp Glenn there are many things needing attention. For the most part I renew my recommendations of last year, though I note an improvement at each encampment.

May the good work of cementing the company walks and macadamizing the company streets go on to completion.

It was observed that the wire screens about the commissary were left to rust out and were absolutely useless for the purpose intended.

The mess hall should be longer and a sanitary pantry should be arranged for with each kitchen.

A field bakery in my opinion would prove economical and would furnish better bread.

As a sanitary measure faucets should be attached to the drinking cans.

My attention was called to the desirability of having a guard for duty about the mess hall. Colonel McGee deserves high praise for organizing a regimental cooking school. I commend this school to your favorable consideration. I found the school much interested in the work. Colonel McGee assembled the school and together we went over the importance and value, on the human economy, of good food properly prepared. I heartily endorse this school for each regiment.

Again I have to call the attention of the Department to the matter of water supply. During the encampment for a time there was an alarming scarcity of water. At present the water plant consists of one well 200 feet deep and 14 driven wells from 14 to 25 feet deep. There should be more driven wells and I urgently recommend that another deep well be sunk that sufficient water of good quality may be available at any and all times, especially should this be done in order to provide for a brigade encampment.

I have to renew my recommendations regarding the footgear of the soldier. Very respectfully,

S. WESTRAY BATTLE,
Surgeon General.

Report of Paymaster General

STATE OF NORTH CAROLINA,
OFFICE OF PAYMASTER GENERAL.
FAYETTEVILLE, N. C., December 1, 1911.

THE ADJUTANT GENERAL, STATE OF NORTH CAROLINA,
Raleigh, N. C.

SIR:—I have the honor of submitting herewith the report of this department for the fiscal year ending November 30, 1911:

RECEIPTS.

Balance on hand last report, November 30, 1910	$5,017.22
Jan. 6. On account State appropriation	6,000.00
16. N. & W. Railroad Co., rebate	.20
24. On account State appropriation	2,000.00
Feb. 10. On account State appropriation	2,000.00
Mar. 9. From Co. C, First Regiment—fire loss	31.26
May 5. On account State appropriation	5,000.00
June 3. On account State appropriation	10,000.00
Sept. 9. On account State appropriation	2,500.00
12. On account State appropriation	5,000.00
Nov. 18. On account State appropriation	5,000.00
Total	$42,548.68

DISBURSEMENTS.

COMPANIES, BANDS AND DIVISIONS.

First Infantry	$3,559.00	
Second Infantry	3,660.00	
Third Infantry	3,475.00	
First Infantry Band	250.00	
Second Infantry Band	275.00	
Third Infantry Band	275.00	
Division Naval Brigade	1,500.00	
Coast Artillery	1,375.00	
Field Artillery	125.00	
		$14,494.00

BRIGADE AND REGIMENTAL HEADQUARTERS, COMPANIES, DIVISIONS AND CORPS COMMANDERS.

First Brigade Commander	$150.00
Commander First Infantry	150.00
Commander Second Infantry	150.00
Commander Third Infantry	150.00

Commander Naval Brigade	150.00	
Commander Artillery Corps	75.00	
		825.00

ADJUTANT GENERAL'S DEPARTMENT.

Miss Annie Travis, stenographer	$95.00	
Miss Ethel Wynne, stenographer	425.00	
Miss Nellie Hinsdale, stenographer	9.00	
Major Gordan Smith	300.00	
General Thomas R. Robertson, C. of O	360.00	
		1,189.00

QUARTERMASTER GENERAL'S DEPARTMENT.

General Francis A. Macon, salary	$499.92	
Miss Magdalene Landis, salary	495.00	
		994.92

SURGEON GENERAL'S DEPARTMENT.

Charlotte Hospital Corps	$75.00	
Kinston Hospital Corps	75.00	
Reidsville Hospital Corps	75.00	
		225.00

PAYMASTER GENERAL'S DEPARTMENT.

Colonel S. W. Cooper, salary	$499.92	
		499.92

GENERAL FUNDS AND MISCELLANEOUS.

General Thos. R. Robertson, Chief of O.	$360.00	
Transportation	13.84	
Special stenographic work	9.00	
General F. A. Macon, funds for N. G.	243.69	
W. E. Gary, nurse for smallpox	30.00	
Guns & Man Publishing Co.	2.75	
Charlotte Transfer Co., drayage	1.50	
Jno. Wadington, work and transportation	75.00	
Subsistence for troops	62.75	
H. J. McBuie, work on P. M. G. books	12.00	
Western Union Telegraph Co., service	26.73	
Drugs and supplies	89.73	
C. L. Shade, miscellaneous	25.50	
General F. A. Macon, express on money	5.25	
Expense rifle team (Camp Perry, Ohio)	73.23	
Dues National Guard Association U. S.	25.00	
Expense delegate N. G. Association	82.00	
Raleigh Telephone Company	25.25	
		1,163.22

PAY FOR ENLISTED MEN.

First Infantry	$2,218.25	
Second Infantry	2,280.00	
Third Infantry	2,157.25	
Coast Artillery	791.75	

Naval Brigade	430.75	
Infantry Bands	413.75	
		8,291.75
Total		$27,682.81
November 30, 1911, by balance		14,865.87
		$42,548.68

RECEIPTS.

Received from the Norfolk & Southern Railroad Company for the improvement of Camp Glenn	$2,500.00

DISBURSEMENTS.

On account of the improvement of Camp Glenn	$1,500.03	
November 30, 1911, balance	999.97	
	$2,500.00	$2,500.00

PAYMASTER GENERAL DR.

To balance, State funds	$14,865.87
To balance, N. & W. funds (Camp Glenn)	999.97
	$15,865.84

Respectfully,

S. W. COOPER,
Paymaster General, N. C. N. G.

Report of Commissary General

STATE OF NORTH CAROLINA,
OFFICE OF SUBSISTENCE DEPARTMENT.
FRANKLINTON, N. C., December 31, 1911.

R. L. LEINSTER, *Adjutant General,*
Raleigh, N. C.

SIR:—I have the honor to submit herewith the annual report and recommendations of the Subsistence Department:

In compliance with Special Order No. 77, June 14, 1911, I reported for duty at Camp Glenn in connection with the Third Infantry in July and the First Infantry in August. On arrival of each regiment I saw, in person, that the sanitary conditions of the mess halls, water supply, ice cans, rations, cooking utensils, fuel, etc., were in good condition and ready for use. After the Commissary Department of these regiments had been arranged satisfactorily for the subsistence of the troops, I proceeded to organize an Army Sanitary and Commissary Cooking School, first procuring of the Commanding officer of each regiment an order requiring the enlisted cooks and Commissary Sergeants to report to this school at 4 p. m. each day and answer roll call for instructions. After the first day nearly every soldier connected with the Commissary Department answered roll call, those who did not were marched in by a Corporal's guard. I then proceeded to instruct the Commissary Department of the First Brigade in culinary art and the science of drawing and preparing rations for their respective commands. I also used in connection a plan I had previously received from Major Mueller, Commissary First Brigade Pennsylvania N. G., who is considered by Army officers the best authority in the Commissary Department in the United States. I also had valuable information from General Wood and Captain Halbrook, Commissary U. S. A., in charge cooking school at the Texas Manœuver Camps. After the first day the students became deeply interested and worked hard to learn the army ration issue, "Conversion Tables" and how to cook and prepare field, haversack and emergency rations. Many of the enlisted cooks and Commissary Sergeants manifest a desire to learn the art of cooking, they show intelligence and aptitude and should be sent to the Army Cooking School.

The Regimental Commissaries seemed to understand their work, the art of issuing, but were handicapped in buying supplies as they had to buy in small quantities, and, of course, at retail prices twenty-five cents per day allowance per man did not buy much. The War Department and other States require the Commissary General to advertise these orders for stores subject to the lowest cash bidder, then the Commissary General is required to buy the Goverment allowance per day for the enlisted men at wholesale, carload prices and freight rate, less trade and cash discounts, and issue same daily or in bulk to the Regimental Commissaries, whose duty is to issue to the Company Commissary on requisition signed by one of his company commissioned officers. This plan of buying and distributing is adopted by the Government and other States, and North Carolina should follow suit and then our enlisted men will have more rations and will be better satisfied and will stop kicking. The above plan was carried out in 1910 and not a single enlisted man complained about his rations at that encampment.

Napoleon and great warriors of all nations realized that well fed enlisted men were essential to their success in battle.

Our Commissary Department has previously been run by the staff of other departments and it should be handled by the Commissary General, as the other States are doing, and then he could take some interest and pride in the work. It reminds us of the condition of our target practice and Rifle Range about six years ago but now the United States Government and Virginia report that we have an up to date Rifle Range and target practice. Why not put our shoulders to the wheel and have a Commissary Department equal to any of our sister States, and then when war comes our Commissary Department will not be incompetent as it was at the breaking out of the Spanish-American War.

RECOMMENDATIONS.

That the Regimental Mess Hall at Camp Glenn be built one-third longer, let down on the ground with concrete floor avoiding fire risk from cook ranges.

That one kitchen be removed from each end of the hall to each side at the center to make more cooking room.

That the kitchens and pantries be provided with wire screen doors, locks and water heaters.

That the ice water cans be provided with faucets.

That servants be stopped from sleeping in the mess halls.

That we have a guard for the mess halls night and day.

That we have a portable fireless cook range and a bakery oven so as to have fresh, hot bread. The express that we are now paying on cold loaf bread will pay for this bakery oven the first year.

That we feed the enlisted man better, half pay him and he will serve out several enlistments instead of only one.

That a company commissioned officer be compelled to figure out and sign every requisition for rations for his company at all the future encampments.

That our Commander in Chief request the War Department to continue our present Army Officers and Adjutant General with the Guard indefinitely.

Speaking from about twenty-five years' observation and continuous service I can safely say that the above officers are doing more to prepare the Guard for actual service than any heretofore.

I am proud to know that our Guard is going forward in every department and is better prepared for war than ever.

Very respectfully,

W. L. McGhee,
Colonel and Commissary General N. C.

Report of Brigadier General

HEADQUARTERS OF FIRST BRIGADE,
NORTH CAROLINA NATIONAL GUARD,
OXFORD, December 30, 1911.

THE ADJUTANT GENERAL, STATE OF NORTH CAROLINA,
Raleigh, N. C.

SIR:—I have the honor to submit my annual report of the First Brigade for the year 1911.

STRENGTH OF BRIGADE.

First Infantry, 52 officers, 625 men; Second Infantry, 52 officers, 621 men; Third Infantry, 52 officers, 645 men; Brigade, field and staff, 3; a grand total of 2,050.

GENERAL CONDITION.

In view of the fact that the Brigade was not ordered to camp as a whole, I did not have the opportunity of informing myself as to its efficiency in field movements and other work incident to a Brigade camp. Each of the regiments was in camp for eight days during the months of July and August, at Camp Glenn, and I was present a part of the time during each period of encampment.

I was gratified to note that there has devoloped in each of the regiments a greater interest in target practice and that the work on the range is prosecuted by officers and men in a much more intelligent manner than heretofore. The officers appear to have awakened to the necessity of giving to the men careful and accurate instruction in the use of their rifles and the men manifested, what seemed to me, a real desire to learn.

The work on the range this year was more satisfactory than ever before and I believe great good will result therefrom.

I inspected the quarters and equipment of each of the regiments while they were in camp, and in most respects found conditions satisfactory. A very large percentage of the men do not take proper care of their clothing, and after a few days in camp their appearance is far from cleanly. I was pleased to note that one of the regiments made the necessary arrangements for washing and scrubbing the uniforms and other clothing of the men, and this added much to the health, comfort and appearance of the regiment.

I commend this practice to every company commander of the Guard, and while the troops are in camp the commanding officer should see that means are provided for this work.

Each of the regiments had one day's experience in manœuvers and the problems were executed very creditably.

The limited time in camp made it impossible to take up the many phases of the work in which officers and men need instruction, but every available hour was made use of and I am confident that all concerned are better equipped for service than heretofore.

The drills and ceremonies showed marked improvements over former years and nearly all of the officers and men seemed to realize that "work" was the watchword of the camps.

The discipline, while lax in a few instances, was, altogether, better than usual, and I regard this as encouraging.

Capt. M. B. Stokes, 10th Infantry, U. S. A., and Capt. A. J. Dougherty, 30th Infantry, U. S. A., were retailed for duty with the troops during the camps and each of them rendered services of great value to the officers and men. They entered enthusiastically into the work and they were busy all the time. I acknowledge my indebtedness to them for many valuable suggestions and instructions.

RECOMMENDATIONS.

First. That the necessary supplies and equipment be provided for an encampment of the Brigade during the coming year.

Second. That the period of encampment be longer, so that there may be time for target practice and at least three days devoted to manœuver work.

Third. That better facilities be provided for the work of the Hospital Corps.

CONCLUSION.

I feel that the people of the State are beginning to appreciate the National Guard, and if the officers and men manifest the proper interest in its uplift and betterment we shall soon have an organization in keeping with our needs and one which will be a pride to the State.

I tender my thanks to you for the interest you have at all times taken in the work of my department and for the intelligent and businesslike management you have given to your office.

My aides, Lieutenants Henry T. Osborne and Arthur C. House, were on duty with me during the camps, and to them I am indebted for faithful and efficient service.

Respectfully submitted,

B. S. ROYSTER,

Brigadier General, Commanding First Brigade, N. C. N. G.

Report of Commanding Officer First Infantry

HEADQUARTERS FIRST INFANTRY, N. C. N. G.,
SHELBY, N. C., December 4, 1911.

THE ADJUTANT GENERAL, N. C. N. G.,
Raleigh, N. C.

SIR:—I herewith beg to submit my annual report for the year 1911. No disorders of any kind have occurred within the bounds of my regiment this year.

Pursuant to orders from the A. G. O., the First Regiment went into camp at Morehead City, August 2-10, for instruction in rifle practice and field movements. Captains Stokes and Dougherty, U. S. A., were in camp and on our arrival assisted the regiment in every way possible to make our stay in camp profitable and instructive. Captain Stokes instructed the Adjutant and regimental clerks how to get out orders in proper form, make out Morning reports, Sick reports, and other necessary paper work, and also met the officers of the regiment once a day for instructing them in the drills and movements of the troops the next day. This proved very beneficial and all showed daily improvement. Captain Dougherty took charge of the range and by dint of hard work and proper instruction, assisted by Lt. Col. Bizzell, Major Powers and Captain Morrison, I. S. A. P. of the regiment, developed more marksmen and experts than any other regiment of the State, also several experts, over 200 in all, this being an improvement of over 400 per cent on the record made by the regiment at its last shoot on the range. Every officer and man worked with a will and each tried to excel the other, both in drill and rifle practice and in the field maneuvers.

The drill began with the company the first day, then battalion drill, regimental parade, and on the last day a march and sham battle. With the exception of one morning, all officers and men reported for duty at the pit or drill field on time. The order in camp was the best I have ever had or seen in all my thirty-six years' service. For this I wish to thank each officer and man individually. It makes me feel proud to command such a regiment. Capt. J. F. Roberts, Regimental Commissary, issued the rations and all had a sufficient supply for their needs. Colonel McGhee gave the cooks instruction each day which they reported were of great benefit. Major Bernard was very prompt in getting up the reports of the shooting each day, and posting the names and scores of each man before night. This promptness on his part was appreciated by both officers and men. There were present in camp 46 officers and 583 enlisted men, 5 officers and 63 enlisted men being absent. The total strength of the regiment today is 51 officers and 646 enlisted men, or a total of 697.

The troops should have at least ten days in camp, exclusive of coming and going, to get best results. The health of the regiment was excellent, for which I wish to thank Major Glenn and his assistants as they certainly looked after the sanitation of the camp. The regiment is in the best condition that it has been in since 1898, and from what I saw of the Regulars in San Antonio in April, the First could take the field in twenty-four hours' notice and make a creditable showing in any kind of service. It is my earnest desire that each officer will read this to his command and then resolve that they will do better another year.

Respectfully submitted,

J. T. GARDNER,

Colonel First N. C. Infantry, Commanding.

Report of Commanding Officer Second Infantry

HEADQUARTERS SECOND INFANTRY, N. C. N. G.
WASHINGTON, December 12, 1911.

THE ADJUTANT GENERAL,
Raleigh, N. C.

SIR:—I have the honor to submit my report for the year.

With the exception of annual encampment, July 20-27, there is little to note.

The Regiment reported at Camp with 48 officers and 589 enlisted out of a total of 52 officers and 646 enlisted. This does not include the strength of Ambulance Co. No. 1—2 officers and 36 enlisted, nor Detachment Sanitary Troops—4 officers and 12 enlisted.

The scope of the work was the same as last year, battalions alternating in target firing, field instruction and camp guard.

Results of firing having been already published from your office, it is deemed unnecessary to cumber this report with a repetition.

The plan of requiring Regimental Commissary to exercise in full the duties of his office, including purchase of supplies, confirms my opinion formerly expressed, that this is the best solution of the subsistence problem. This Department was ably managed. It is respectfully submitted at the same time that this same practice be adopted with regard to the Medical Department; that is, to place entire responsibility upon and allow full credit to the officers who would be in charge in the field.

The necessity for giving more careful attention to sewer connections and waste pipes in mess halls is particularly emphasized.

It is recommended that all fruit and soft drink stand privileges to outside parties be withheld and regimental exchanges be established, under control of the Commissary, for the benefit of the enlisted men.

Some comments made by the U. S. Army Inspector are incorporated herein for greater emphasis:

Cos. C, E and K did not bring equipment to camp.
Co. K, no canteens.
Cos. K, H and M, no shelter tents.
Cos. A, H, K, L and M, no entrenching tools.

The following officers showed *exceptional ability:*

Captain F. L. Black, Commissary.
Captain A. L. C. Hill, Co. B.

The following officers showed *ability above the average:*

Captain H. H. Murray, Adjutant.
Captain C. L. Pridgen, Assistant Surgeon.
Captain Paul Jones, Co. A.
Captain C. M. Faircloth, Co. H.
Captain J. B. Malloy, Co. L.

The following deserve especial commendation for promptness with which their companies responded to all duty:

Captain A. O. Clement, Co. E.
Captain W. S. Privotte, Co. I.

Publication of these comments is made in hope that the publicity given may stimulate others in their effort.

In closing permit me to suggest that in the future such criticisms as those embodied in the report of the Commissary General last year be purged therefrom, especially in view of the *facts* as existed. The conduct of Regimental Staff is subject to criticism of none but their immediate Commander and the Commander-in-Chief. Captain Black's administration of his office has always been to the entire satisfaction of the commanding officer and of the enlisted men of the Regiment.

Respectfully,

H. C. BRAGAW,
Colonel Second Infantry, N. C. N. G.

Report of Commanding Officer Third Infantry

HEADQUARTERS THIRD INFANTRY, N. C. N. G.
REIDSVILLE, N. C., December 22, 1911.

TO THE ADJUTANT GENERAL N. C. N. G.,
Raleigh, N. C.

SIR:—I have the honor of submitting the following report for the year ending November 30, 1911:

There has nothing unusual taken place in the regiment during the year, everything has passed in a very quiet and peaceful way. I think good feeling generally prevails throughout, and all parties have tried to discharge their duties. One company has been disbanded during the year, Company K. Since Company K was disbanded we have only eleven companies and band. Recently a company has been organized at Asheboro, N. C., which will give the regiment the full number of companies again.

ENCAMPMENT.

Our annual encampment was held at Morehead City July 10th to 17th, all companies being present except Company K. Total number of officers present, 59; enlisted men, 505. There seemed to be a general good feeling during the encampment, both among officers and enlisted men, all willing to perform their duties in a cheerful and soldierly manner. The duties performed were about the same that we had last year, except our manœuvers were more complete the last year.

The following calls were observed:

First call	5:00 a.m.
Reveille	5:10 a.m.
Assembly	5:15 a.m.
Mess	5:30 a.m.
Police	6:00 a.m.
Sick call	6:30 a.m.
DRILL.	
First call	7:05 a.m.
Assembly	7:15 a.m.
Recall	8:15 a.m.
GUARD MOUNT.	
First call	8:45 a.m.
Assembly	8:55 a.m.
Adjutant's call	9:00 a.m.
First Sergeant's call	11:50 a.m.

Mess	12:00 noon.
Officers' call	1:30 p.m.
DRILL.	
First call	3:20 p.m.
Assembly	3:30 p.m.
Recall	5:00 p.m.
PARADE.	
First call	5:35 p.m.
Assembly	5:45 p.m.
Adjutant's call	6:00 p.m.
Mess	7:00 p.m.
Tattoo	9:45 p.m.
Taps	10:00 p.m.

One day was devoted specially to field manœuvers, the regiment being divided, Lt. Col. S. W. Minor being in command of the attack and Major J. J. Bernard in command of the defense. We were very much gratified to have with us again Capt. M. B. Stokes, who made a general inspection of the camp and its workings. We feel indebted to him for the painstaking and careful way in which he instructed us and feel we derived a great benefit by having him with us.

We also had Captain A. J. Dougherty, U. S. A., and we found in him a splendid worker and helper at all times and under all circumstances; his officers' school each day was specially instructive. We are glad to have him with us and feel that he will be a great helper to the guard. The Brigade Commander, General B. S. Royster, and his staff was with us in camp, and General Royster inspected the regiment one day. The Adjutant General was also with us and observed the general workings of the camp. We had hoped to have the Governor visit us, but owing to sickness in his family he was prevented from being with us.

TRAIN SERVICE.

The train service was much better this year than usual. I had fewer complaints than ever before; and with the exception of the trains leaving camp on our return home there would have been no complaints. The first section was to leave at 7:30 p. m. and the second section at 8:30 p. m., but both sections were more than an hour late in starting, consequently some of the companies did not make connections next morning and were delayed several hours in getting home.

RECOMMENDATIONS.

I would respectfully recommend that at our next encampment we have more field manœuvers, extended order drills, regimental and battalion drills. We need the target practice but we can get that, to some extent, in our armories, and the field movements we can only get at our encampments, so occasionally I think we should make the drilling the main work of our encampments.

I wish to thank the Commander in Chief, the Adjutant General, the Brigade Commander, the officers specially attached to the regiment for duty, for their many kindnesses and services rendered.

To the commissioned officers and enlisted men of the regiment, I wish to express my hearty thanks, without any exceptions to any one, for the hearty and cheerful manner in which they all discharged their duties.

Hoping that when we meet again we will be feeling better, by having been recognized and rewarded more fully by the government for our services. Very respectfully submitted,

J. N. CRAIG,
Colonel Third Infantry, N. C. N. G.

Report of Commander Coast Artillery Corps

HEADQUARTERS COAST ARTILLERY CORPS, N. C. N. G.
SALISBURY, December 15, 1911.

THE ADJUTANT GENERAL,
Raleigh, N. C.

SIR:—I have the honor to submit report of the operations of the Coast Artillery Corps for the year 1911, as required by law:

The strength of the Corps at the end of the fiscal year is as follows:

	Officers.	*Men.*
Field and Staff	5	
First Company	3	37
Second Company	3	52
Third Company	3	55
Fourth Company	2	70
Fifth Company	3	60
Totals	19	274

It will be seen that one company is at present below the minimum, but the company commander has recently discharged some of his inactive enlisted men and is now recruiting to the authorized strength.

During the year the Corps has lost two officers, one, Captain Weddell, by retirement after fifteen years' service, and the other, First Lieutenant Lombard, by resignation. The changes in the enlisted strength of the several companies have not been as numerous as heretofore, and we have carried to camp a larger percentage of experienced men than formerly.

PERSONNEL.

It can be said that the personnel of the organization as a whole is above the average in this or other States, and much stress has been laid on recruiting the very best possible class of men for this service. Coast Artillery, while not necessarily requiring a better class, does require a different class of men. It is a service which puts a premium on advanced education, and men possessing this advantage are to be sought in recruiting.

UNIFORM.

With the exception of complaint of misfits and a shortage in Khaki in one company, the uniform question is very satisfactory. It is a fact that with more changes of Khaki issued to our companies we would be better supplied in the uniform line than the U. S. Coast Artillery. It was observed during the recent joint coast defense exercises that our troops were fully uniformed with olive drab while the Regulars were not; that we had been issued the new pattern blue denim fatigue uniform while they were using the obsolete brown canvas, and that our men used the olive drab cap with the Khaki uniform while they used the Khaki cap. This matter was first spoken of by an officer of the garrison and it is very gratifying.

ARMS.

No change has been made in the small arm, the troops of this command being armed with the U. S. Magazine Rifle, cal. 30.

ARMORY EQUIPMENT.

Stop watches, for use as time interval recorders, have been added to the armory equipment during the current year. It is expected that the equipment will be very materially added to during the year 1912. Before it will be possible to do very effective work on the indoor plotting apparatus it will be necessary to be furnished with observing instruments and telephone sets.

INSTRUCTION.

Instruction made much progress during the year. Under General Order No. 7, A. G. O., eleven officers of the Corps attended a course of instruction at Fort Caswell from June 12th to 18th. Detailed report of this tour was furnished your office immediately upon its termination. The companies comprising the organization participated in the joint coast defense exercises at Fort Caswell August 7th to 18th, and every officer who attended the course in June found that he was much better equipped to handle his company and his duties by reason of having attended.

JOINT EXERCISES.

During the joint exercises the program, as published in General Orders No. 25, Headquarters Artillery District of the Cape Fear, was carried out in its entirety. Owing to fair weather conditions the instruction and target practice were kept abreast of the schedule and we were left two days for duties not included in the original program. This period was devoted to simulated war conditions and battle practice and the results obtained more than repaid us for the additional energy expended. During the exercises it was our pleasure to have with us for two days Capt. Edward Carpenter, C. A. C., in charge of

Coast Artillery matters in the Militia Division, and the Adjutant General of North Carolina, who spent two days in camp. If our efforts succeeded in making a favorable impression on these two officers we are much gratified.

INSPECTIONS.

The troops of this command were inspected in April by Capt. Rex Van D. Corput, C. A. C., and Col. Thomas Stringfield, Inspector General. The Commanding Officer has visited three of the five companies during the year, and a visit to each of the companies is planned for January of the coming year. The Ordnance property in the armories of the companies was inspected in September by First Lieut. Charles T. Harris, Ordance Department. Some minor defect was found in the gun arm of the plotting board in use by the Fourth Company, and it has since been ordered returned to the Frankford Arsenal for correction.

TARGET PRACTICE.

While the results as a whole of the target practice at Fort Caswell did not quite come up to the practice of 1910; some very creditable work at the guns was done, the firing of the Fourth Company, Salisbury, and the Fifth Company, Charlotte, leading.

CONCLUSION.

In conclusion I desire to commend the Coast Artillery troops for their excellent behavior en route and in camp, and for the very excellent spirit which prevails in the organizations. I desire, also, to thank you for your interest in the Corps and to assure you that we are striving to merit an increase of that interest.

It is a matter of general regret that our good friend, Colonel H. H. Ludlow, will be no longer with us at Fort Caswell, he having been assigned a new station since our last exercises. He has been in command at Fort Caswell ever since our organization and has never allowed his interest in our welfare to wane. Even while in command of the Department he maintained an interest in us which we highly appreciate.

RECOMMENDATIONS.

I desire to renew my recommendations of the past two years that the strength of this organization be increased by one, and if possible, two companies.

That the Officers' School of Instruction at Fort Caswell be held June 10th to 15th.

That the company commanders of the Coast Artillery Corps be furnished with the lesson papers being sent out by your office to similar officers of Infantry. Very respectfully,

MAX. L. BARKER,
Major Coast Artillery Corps, Commanding.

Report of Commander of Naval Militia

NAVAL BRIGADE, NORTH CAROLINA,
U. S. S. ELFRIDA,
NEW BERN, N. C., December 31, 1911.

TO THE ADJUTANT GENERAL,
Raleigh, N. C.

SIR:—I have the honor to submit herewith my report of the Naval Brigade for the year 1911:

None of the Divisions of the Brigade have been called to the aid of civil authorities.

The practical work of the Brigade during the year was set forth in my report of the summer exercises and would ask that you include the same as a part of this report.

In compliance with recommendations made in the report on summer exercises, the Sixth Division at Oriental was disbanded and a new Division was mustered in at Washington, N. C., to take its place.

Great improvement, both in detail and enthusiasm for the service, has been manifested in the Brigade.

It is recommended that Division Commanders and Quartermasters receive pay same as the Commanding Officer and Quartermasters of the other branches of the State's forces. That the additional two Divisions permitted by law be organized and mustered into the Brigade. That the men be allowed ten days cruise instead of eight. That a system of examinations for Commissioned Officers be adopted. That the Commanding Officer of the Brigade be elected by the line officers of the Brigade instead of appointed by the Governor. That on account of the very high rent paid by the Second Division for its armory and the fact that the arsenals of the General Storekeeper and Ordnance Officer of the Brigade and the storage rooms for the two vessels, are located in said armory, that an allowance of ten dollars ($10.00) per month be authorized to him, to assist in meeting his armory rental.

TOM C. DANIELS.

Cruise of the Naval Brigade

U. S. S. ELFRIDA, NEW BERN, N. C., September 23, 1911.

TO THE ADJUTANT GENERAL, *Raleigh, N. C.*

SIR:—1. In compliance with paragraph 5, General Orders No. 13, A. G. O., N. C., 1911, I have the honor to make the following report.

2. At the request of the Commanding Officer of the Fifth and Seventh Divisions, they were permitted to change their time of cruising, exchanging dates with each other.

The torpedo boat *Foote* not being in condition to prove serviceable for the cruising of the Sixth Division, at the request of the Commanding Officer of that division, their dates were changed to August 19th to 27th.

3. The general scope of the work for the separate cruises was mapped out in accordance with the plans laid down by the Navy Department, which was to embrace principally target practice of record on both the one and three-pounders. The detail or routine of duty prescribed for both ships was:

5:00 a.m.	Call cooks.
5:30 a.m.	Secure and stow hammocks.
6:00 a.m.	Coffee.
6:15 a.m.	Wash down and clean brightwork.
7:00 a.m.	Swimming exercises.
7:15 a.m.	Breakfast.
8:00 a.m.	Boat drills.
9:00 a.m.	Muster.
9:30 a.m.	Scrub decks.
10:00 a.m.	Sub-calibre target practice with one-pounder.
12:00 m.	Dinner.
1:00 p.m.	Sighting drills and target practice with three-pounders.
4:00 p.m.	Wash down.
4:30 p.m.	Signal practice.
	Officers' school.
5:00 p.m.	Liberty party.
6:00 p.m.	Supper.
7:00 p.m.	Liberty party and swing hammocks.
9:00 p.m.	Lights out.
11:00 p.m.	Last liberty boat.

4. The work of the men not on duty was devoted to constructing rafts and erecting target screens under the supervision of the Ordnance Officer and the Naval Officer detailed by the Department as instructor.

5. The work of the men was carried on with a great deal of enthusiasm and interest, and a great deal of good and instruction was gained by them.

6. Upon my arrival at Hertford, N. C., on July 19th, to take command of the cruise of the Third and Seventh Divisions, I received a wire from the commanding officer of the Third Division stating that his men had not reported in accordance with instructions, but that they could report on the next day with fifteen men (telegram attached, marked Appendix "A"), and as this number was not sufficient to man the ship, I wired Lieutenant Willis,

in command of the U. S. S. *Elfrida*, to sail at once with such members of the Third Division as had reported and to join me in Albemarle Sound that afternoon and let the Seventh Division, which had reported with comparatively full strength on board the *Foote*, be transferred to the *Elfrida* and the cruise of that division carried on, as it would be impracticable to wait another day for the Third Division, who could not report with sufficient men and officers to man the ship. The *Foote* was found to be unserviceable for practical work, and I decided that the best interest of the Brigade and the better instruction of this Division, which was on its first cruise, could be carried out aboard the *Elfrida*.

The officers of the Fifth Division, accompanied by the engineer officers of the Second Battalion, had reported aboard the *Foote* at Hertford for inspection of the ship prior to their cruising upon her, and after a consultation with them, it was decided that with their assistance and the regulars on the *Foote*, that we should proceed with the Seventh Division to Wade's Point Light at the mouth of the Pasquotank River, have the *Elfrida* to meet us there, transfer the Seventh Division to the *Elfrida*, and that the officers of the Fifth Division would take the *Foote* to Elizabeth City and during the interim before their cruising date, such repairs could be made as to permit of their cruising upon the *Foote*. The *Elfrida* came alongside the *Foote* at 9 p. m., the Seventh Division was transferred to the *Elfrida*, and the *Foote* turned over to Lieutenant Sanders of the Fifth Division, who proceeded to Elizabeth City with her.

The cruise of the Seventh Division was carried on as per the routine mapped out, and much enthusiastic work and instruction was gained by this Division.

7. The Fourth Division on the *Elfrida* and the Fifth Division on the *Foote* cruised on their assigned dates. The Fifth Division, on account of the bad condition of the *Foote*, experienced much difficulty, and a greater part of their cruise was taken up with mishaps and they did not arrive at Morehead City until towards the end of the period. Their men being pretty badly worn out by continuous work, at the request of their commanding officer, they were relieved from target work and permitted to make such repairs as were necessary to get the ship back to the home port at New Bern, where the *Elfrida* went for coal and water, prior to the return of the division to their home port. It was deemed to the best interest to transfer the Fifth Division to the *Elfrida* together with the Fourth Division, and return them to their homes.

8. The cruise of the First Battalion was under the command of its commanding officer. The record of the cruises of the Second and Sixth Divisions comprising that battalion are hereto attached, marked Appendix "B" and "C."

The commanding officer of the Sixth Division came to New Bern to see me, and requested that the cruise of his division be delayed from the 9th to the 19th of August, as he had been notified by the big lumber mill at his town, in whose employ were a large percentage of his men, that it would shut down on the 15th for two weeks, and that it would work a hardship on his men to take them away from their work for a week a few days before the mill would shut down, thus compelling them to lose their wages for eight days, when in fact they would be at liberty and were desirous of attending the cruise when the mill closed down, and it would thus enable him to take out approximately his entire division. The *Foote* not being in condition for the cruise of this division, without making extensive repairs at a cost of about two hundred dollars, and rather than work a hardship upon his men, I changed his dates as per his request, and substituted the *Elfrida* as the cruising ship.

Commander Bradham of the First Battalion, finding it impossible to take out this division, Lieutenant Commander Shipp of the Brigade Staff was assigned to this duty (cruise report, Appendix "C"). The commanding officer of the Sixth Division stated that his men would like to cruise to Norfolk, Va., instead of Morehead City. I did not deem it advisable, on account of the depth of water in the canal, to permit this request, as the *Elfrida* draws too much water to safely pass through this canal, and for the further reason that I thought it to the best interest of the division that the outlined plan of the Navy Department for target practice should be carried out foremost of all, and I so advised them ten days prior to his cruising dates. The commanding officer of this division came to New Bern on the day preceding his cruise dates, drew his subsistence money from the Paymaster, and purchased supplies for his cruise, with the full knowledge of the fact that his division would not be permitted to cruise anywhere other than upon the designated point, until after the target work and practice had been completed, and that Commander Shipp had been instructed accordingly, and it seemed to be satisfactory to him. On the 19th, Commander Shipp assumed command of the *Elfrida* and proceeded to Oriental to take out this division. Upon his arrival there he was informed by the commanding officer of the division, who had brought his men down on the dock, ready to go aboard ship, that unless the cruise was to proceed at once to Norfolk, Va., that he would not permit his men to take cruise. Commander Shipp informed him that his instructions were to take his division out for target practice, and when that work had been completed that the division could cruise to Norfolk or any other point that it might be desired within the dates provided for the cruise. Commander Shipp called me over 'phone and informed me of the result of his conversation with Lieutenant Midyett, and asked for further instructions. I told him to tell Mr. Midyett to take his men aboard the *Elfrida*, carry out his target work, and that then they could cruise to Norfolk, taking up such drills enroute as are provided in the general Navy routine. He informed me that the division absolutely refused to cruise. I then instructed him to proceed with the ship to Point of Marsh, Pamlico Sound, and take up target raft, which had been anchored there for the work of this division, and return with it to New Bern. This he proceeded to do, but found that on account of the heavy seas and with short crew he was unable to take up target, so he returned with ship to this port. A week later Lieutenant Willis, with a crew from the Second Division, proceeded with the *Elfrida*, took up target raft and brought same to New Bern.

I instructed Mr. Shipp to have the commanding officer turn over to him his receipted invoices for subsistence expenditures and such money as he should have on hand, out of the appropriation for subsistence of his cruise, and to return same to the Paymaster. The commanding officer of the Sixth Division refused to turn over his statement and funds to Mr. Shipp, stating that he would make his statement and returns to the Paymaster. The Paymaster informed me that he had written to Mr. Midyett for his invoices and the balance of funds in his possession, and that he had been unable to get a reply thereto. Consequently, on the 18th inst., I directed a letter to the commanding officer of the Sixth Division, stating the Paymaster's request and ordering him to file his account at once. To this order he has paid no attention. The Paymaster informs me that there are some bills outstanding against this division, and that he is unable to make his report as directed by you until he received the report from commanding officer of the Sixth Division, so that all accounts can be settled and his returns made.

9. I would therefore recommend:

(1) That you take such action as you deem best to have the commanding officer of this division file his report with the Paymaster.

(2) That the Sixth Division can be of no further service and benefit to the brigade, and that therefore it be disbanded.

The officers of this division absolutely know nothing of infantry drill, and have never been able to acquire any knowledge in that line of work (note report of Inspector General); that they have been continued in the brigade on account of their qualifications for ship duty, and as they have shown that they do not care for any work and instruction along these lines, but desired their cruise to be simply a pleasure jaunt, I deem it for the best interest of the brigade that they be mustered out.

(3) The Third Division and two of its officers have always been much interested in their work, and their failure to participate in this year's cruise was on account of the negligence of their commanding officer, and I deem it for the best interest of the service and this division that his resignation be requested and that an election be held for his successor.

10. Target work was curtailed to some extent on account of the contractors not getting the target raft completed in time for most of the cruises, and consequently the Second Division was the only division that held practice with the three-pounders, and it was deemed best that their work, on account of their good pointers, should be confined entirely to that gun, in order that the record of the brigade for this season's target work should be maintained. The Fourth and Seventh Divisions confined their practice, on account of the non-arrival of the target screens, to the one-pounders. The final record for one-pounder target practice was 4.35 hits per minute, with a final score of 2.6225. The final score for the three-pounder will be found in report of cruise of the First Battalion (Appendix "B").

11. Report of engineer officer of the Second Battalion concerning the *Foote* during the cruise of the Fifth Division is hereto attached (marked Appendix "D").

12. I desire to especially commend Lieutenant Benj. Dutton, Jr., U. S. N., who was detailed by the Navy Department to accompany the cruises, for his enthusiasm and zeal, both as an instructor to the officers' school, which was held on board daily, and to the petty officers and enlisted men. To his work was due the very great enthusiasm and pleasure with which the men of the various divisions returned to their home ports. As an instructor to the officers, of commanding rank, watch, divisional and engineering, he was of invaluable service to the brigade. He was painstaking, minute and thorough, and was only too glad at all times to answer and explain any and all questions. His instructions made the officers more interested in themselves and their work, and they will be much better able to assume the command of their relative rank in performing their duties provided for them in this service.

TOM C. DANIELS.

"B"—CRUISE OF FIRST BATTALION.

HEADQUARTERS FIRST BATTALION,
NEW BERN, N. C., August 18, 1911.

TO CAPT. T. C. DANIELS, *Commanding N. C. N. B., New Bern, N. C.*

SIR:—1. I submit report of cruise of First Battalion. The Sixth Division (Oriental) did not cruise.

2. The Second Division (New Bern) embarked on *Elfrida*, August 9th, under my command. Lieutenant C. J. McSorley, Executive Officer; Lieutenant J. B. Green, Ordnance; Lieutenant G. D. Bowden, Watch, and Lieutenant Commander E. E. Williams, Engineer Officer; Lieutenant B. Dutton, Jr., U. S. N., Instructor—six officers and 23 men, 29 all told.

3. Itinerary:

Aug. 9.	Second Division embarked on *Elfrida*	9:00 a.m.
	Cast aloose from Blades' Dock	10:00 a.m.
	Tied up Meadows' marine railway	10:30 a.m.
	Cast aloose Meadows' railway	2:20 p.m.
	Anchored mouth of Neuse River	9:55 p.m.
	Point of Marsh beacon one mile distant, bearing N. E. ½ E.	
10.	Carrying out target anchors	4:00 a.m.
	Underway for Morehead City	9:25 a.m.
	Tied up railroad dock, Morehead City	1:25 p.m.
11.	Underway from Morehead	7:08 a.m.
	Anchored at target range	11:00 a.m.
	Underway, placing range buoys	12:00 m.
	Last buoy placed	4:00 p.m.
	Swinging ship	4:00 p.m.
	Anchored one-half mile from target	5:30 p.m.
12.	Underway for Morehead	12:20 p.m.
	Tied up at dock, Morehead	4:20 p.m.
13.	Tied up at railroad dock, Morehead City.	
14.	Cast aloose from dock	7:05 a.m.
	Anchored at target range	11:05 a.m.
15.	Underway for target practice	12:00 m.
	Underway from Point of Marsh	5:10 p.m.
	Tied up Blade's dock, New Bern	9:25 p.m.

4. The crew was exercised:

August 9th. Embarking; receiving station billets; shaking down; loading ground tackle for target raft, consisting of four 750-pound anchors, cables and buoys for range; making cables fast and towing target raft; steam engineering; instructions in helm and compass, log and lead; use of sexant, plotting position.

August 10th. Placing target raft; carrying out anchors; general instructions underway; piloting, buoys, ranges and use of charts; washing down, polishing bright work.

August 11th. General instructions underway; scrubbing decks; signals (wigwag and hand semaphore); laying out range; placing range buoys; swimming; swinging ship for determination of deviation of compass; plotting position by three point bearing.

August 12th. Sub-caliber practice; instruction of officers by Lieutenant Dutton in gunnery and ordnance; men instructed in seamanship by Boatswain Lempke and in ordnance by Chief Gunner's Mate Hello: instructions underway; washing down; docking.

August 13th. Shore liberty.

August 14th. Getting underway; instructions underway; use of lead; log and chart; school of officers and men; subcaliber practice; plotting position by three point bearing; boats under oars.

August 15th. Getting underway; steaming on range; target practice three-pounder; firing three strings of ten shots each by gun crews; making fast; disembarking.

5. Division was divided into two deck divisions of two watches each. Fire, collision and abandon ship bills posted on bulletin board.

6. Men did duty as lookouts, anchor and life-buoy watch, scrubbed deck, cleaned bright work, signal work, towing target raft, loading ground tackle and carrying out same. The latter was exceedingly laborious and tedious.

7. Officers received daily instruction by Lieutenant Dutton, in use of instruments of navigation and piloting. Spotting and range finding was good.

8. Target practice score:

Name	Shots	Hits	Time	Hits Per M.	Per Cent	Final Score
Scales	10	6	4.10	2.77	.60	1.66
Moore	10	7	4.17	1.63	.70	1.14
Holton	10	5	2.30	2.00	.50	1.00
Average	10	6	3.39	2.14	.60	1.27

This practice was held in accordance with Naval Militia Publication No. 3, except as modified by Circular Letter No. 12 of March 11th, 1911. Every detail was under the supervision of Lieutenant Dutton, U. S. N., and conformed to regulation target work as far as possible. Caliber, 3-pounder. One gun pointer being allowed for each 25 men of enlisted strength, also the regular complement of sight setters, loaders and plugmen to complete the gun crews. On account of short time allowed for subcaliber practice the gun crews were remarkably efficient; however, two of pointers had seen target practice with this type of gun on last season's cruise, also on *Prairie* cruise, 1909, with 3-inch gun.

Target raft and screens were of regulation pattern, built for the purpose under specifications of Navy Department. Range was of regulation distance, being an equilateral triangle of 1,600 yards. Ship's time on range, 4 min. 44 sec., at ten knots. Lieutenant Green acted as spotter; Lieutenant Dutton as umpire; Lieutenants McSorley and Bowden, divisional officers; C. G. M. Hello, ordnance; M. A. Smith, time keeper; C. B. M. Lempke in charge of repair boat. They were untiring and enthusiastic and their efforts produced the same spirit in the men, as the result of score shows.

9. Discipline: Good.

10. Efficiency: Division showed general improvement on deck and in engine room, and a fair knowledge of seamanship, gunnery and routine. The

officers are generally studious and show a fair knowledge in piloting, rudiments of navigation and duties as watch officers. As a whole, the crew was enthusiastic and performed every duty with cheerfulness.

11. The weather was ideal, the mess good and the cruise instructive. We were fortunate in having Lieutenant Dutton as instructor. He was patient, earnest and diligent.

12. Recommendation: Each gun crew should be allowed three strings of ten shots each, to be fired separate days, the last to count as official score.

Very respectfully, C. D. BRADHAM,
Commander First Battalion, N. C. Naval Brigade.

"C"—FAILURE OF SIXTH DIVISION TO CRUISE.

U. S. S. ELFRIDA, NEW BERN, N. C., August 31, 1911.

TO THE COMMANDING OFFICER N. C. N. M.

SIR:—1. I beg to report that in accord with Brigade Orders No. 17, Commander Bradham being unable to attend cruise, I proceeded with the U. S. S. *Elfrida* to Oriental, August 19th, for the purpose of cruising the Sixth (Oriental) Division, N. C. N. M.

2. On arrival at Oriental I was informed by Lieutenant Midyette that it was his purpose to take the Sixth Division to Norfolk, leaving at 3 p. m. the 19th, returning for target work Tuesday night, the 22d.

3. As my instructions were to take this division to the range, the target work being the principal practice laid down by the Navy Department, I informed him that it would be impossible to make trip until the target work was completed.

4. Captain Daniels was reached over long distance phone and he instructed that the division would have to go on range and qualify men before any trip to Norfolk or other point could be made.

5. Lieutenant Midyett stated that his men would not go on range until the trip to Norfolk promised by him to his men was made.

6. The boat being provisioned by Lieutenant Midyett, he having purchased stores in New Bern the 18th, Captain Daniels instructed that I proceed to the range and secure target (this being the last division to cruise) and bring same to New Bern, but found it impossible to handle this with the ship's crew of six men, so returned with boat to New Bern.

F. H. SHIPP,
Chief of Staff.

"D"—CRUISE OF THE FIFTH DIVISION.

ELIZABETH CITY, N. C., August 15, 1911.

MR. T. C. DANIELS, CAPTAIN N. B., *New Bern, N. C.*

SIR:—I herewith submit my report of the cruise with the Fifth Division on U. S. S. torpedo boat *Foote*. Our first cruise on Sunday, July 23d, to Nags Head. We had a pleasant trip that was very instructive and aided the men to familiarize themselves with the boat.

When out from Nags Head about one hour running, along very smoothly, the forward blower engine fell to pieces, which put that out of commission. The trouble, from my best observation, was caused by the breaking off of one of the bolts which holds the crank brasses.

On our cruise to Morehead, when out from Elizabeth City about two hours, the dynamo engine was put out of commission by breaking off one of the bolts in the cross head, which completely demoralized that engine. With a few other minor accidents the cruise was instructive, especially to the engine crew.

While the boat and machinery was very much out of repair we managed to complete the cruise without having to build a new boat. The regular engine crew (with the exception of the oiler, who seemed to be more of a chronic grumbler,) did all in their power to help and instruct our men. The machinist, water tender and fireman deserve special mention for their service and instructions.

Yours truly,

BRAD SANDERS.

General Orders

STATE OF NORTH CAROLINA,
ADJUTANT GENERAL'S DEPARTMENT,

GENERAL ORDERS NO. 1. RALEIGH, January 14, 1911.

I. The annual inspections of the organizations of the North Carolina National Guard by the officer representing the United States and the Inspector General, North Carolina National Guard, for the current year, will be made on the following dates and places:

Raleigh ....February 14..Headquarters North Carolina National Guard.
Raleigh ....February 15.......Band and Company B, Third Infantry.
Lumber Bridge...February 16......................Co. L, Second Infantry.
Fayetteville .....February 17..Co. F, Second Infantry and Pay Department.
Wilson ....February 18......................Co. K, Second Infantry.
Clinton ....February 20......................Co. H, Second Infantry.
Rocky Mount.....February 21......................Co. C, Second Infantry.
Goldsboro ....February 22 and 23........Cos. D. and E, Second Infantry.
Kinston ....February 24............Co. B and Band, Second Infantry.
Edenton ....February 25......................Co. I, Second Infantry.
Washington .....February 27..Co. G, Second Infantry, and Headquarters Second Infantry.
Tarboro ....February 28......................Co. A, Second Infantry.
Weldon ....March 1..........................Co. K, Third Infantry.
Warrenton ......March 2..........................Co. H, Third Infantry.
Oxford ....March 3.Co. E, Third Infantry, and Brigade Headquarters.
Henderson ......March 4.Co. C, Third Infantry, and Q. M. G. Department.
Louisburg ....March 6..........................Co. D, Third Infantry.
Franklinton .....March 7..........................Co. F, Third Infantry.
Durham ....March 8..........................Co. M, Third Infantry.
Burlington ......March 9..........................Co. I, Third Infantry.
Lexington ......March 10.........................Co. A, Third Infantry.
Reidsville ......March 11.Co. G, Third Infantry, Regimental Headquarters.
Thomasville .....March 13.........................Co. L, Third Infantry.
Winston-Salem ..March 14.........................Co. C, First Infantry.
Mount Airy .....March 15.........................Co. I, First Infantry.
High Point ......March 16.........................Co. M, First Infantry.
Concord ....March 17.........................Co. L, First Infantry.
Wadesboro ......March 18.........................Co. M, Second Infantry.
Shelby ....March 20.Co. G, First Infantry and First Regiment Headquarters.
Gastonia ....March 21.........................Co. B, First Infantry.
Statesville ......March 22.........................Co. E, First Infantry.
Hickory ....March 23.........................Co. A, First Infantry.
Asheville ....March 24 and 25..Cos. F and K, and Band, First Infantry.
Waynesville .....March 27.........................Co. H, First Infantry.

INSPECTION MEDICAL DEPARTMENT.

Charlotte ....March 1, 1911............Hospital Corps, First Regiment.
Reidsville ....March 2, 1911.............Hospital Corps, Third Regiment.
Kinston ....March 3, 1911..........Hospital Corps, Second Regiment.

INSPECTION COAST ARTILLERY CORPS.

Charlotte ....April 3, 1911......................5th Company, C. A. C.
Salisbury ....April 4, 1911........................4th Company, C. A. C.
Greensboro ......April 5, 1911........................3d Company, C. A. C.
Wilmington .....April 6, 1911........................1st Company, C. A. C.
New Bern ......April 7, 1911.......................2d Company, C. A. C.

II. In compliance with instructions of the War Department, separate inspections will be held on the same day by the Inspector General, North Carolina National Guard, and the United States inspecting officer.

III. Commanding officers will be prepared to parade their commands in field equipment at such times as indicated by the inspectors.

IV. The inspection will include all United States and State property available for military service, both in the State Arsenal and in the hands of organizations.

V. During the inspecting of any property in the store-rooms of organizations or at State Arsenal, the responsible or other commissioned officer should be present with a sufficient detail of men to handle the property. In order to expedite this work, this property should be previously sorted and neatly arranged for inspection, and the responsible officer have a list of same and retained copy of annual property return.

VI. All United States property which is reported unserviceable or unsuitable by the United States inspecting officer should be submitted as soon as practicable after inspection to the action of the Surveying Officer, as prescribed by Art. XXXVI, Regulations N. C. National Guard.

VII. When in the judgment of the Inspecting Officer it is deemed necessary, officers and noncommissioned officers will be examined by the inspector as to their general efficiency and knowledge of their respective duties, and where found deficient, incompetent, inattentive, or negligent in the performance of their duties, a special report as to commissioned officers will be forwarded without delay through the Inspector General's Department, in order that where circumstances warrant it, such officers may be examined and reported upon as to the advisability of their continuance in the service. Noncommissioned officers found to be inefficient will be reported by the Inspector to the commanding officer of the organization for his action.

VIII. Company property and record books must be fully written up and presented for inspection.

IX. All field, staff and noncommissioned staff officers will report for inspection in field equipment when inspections are held at home stations, or to the nearest station where inspections are held.

X. The Coast Artillery Corps and the Medical Department will be inspected on dates indicated by officers of the Regular Army of the same branches of the service.

XI. All Government property in the State Arsenal will be inspected by a special inspecting officer of the United States Army, February 23, 1911, and Government property at Camp Glenn, N. C., by the same officer, February 24, 1911.

By order of the Commander in Chief:

R. L. LEINSTER,
Adjutant General.

STATE OF NORTH CAROLINA,
ADJUTANT GENERAL'S DEPARTMENT,

GENERAL ORDERS NO. 2. RALEIGH, February 10, 1911.

Captain E. R. McKethan, Company F, Second Infantry, at his own request, has been retired from active duty in the North Carolina National Guard, and, in accordance with section 4906, Laws Governing the North Carolina National Guard, is given the rank of Major on the retired list.

Captain E. R. McKethan entered the service of the State as private in the Fayetteville Independent Light Infantry in June, 1890, and continued as a member of same, either as pay member while absent from the State or active, until the present. Elected Captain and duly commissioned in the old organization in 1899. He advocated the return of the company to the National Guard, and on July 1, 1901, enlisted with company and appointed First Sergeant of what was then Company A, First Regiment, North Carolina National Guard, and was afterwards promoted through several grades to rank of Captain, the company being transferred and assigned as Company F, Second Infantry, North Carolina National Guard.

In 1898, being at that time in Savannah, Ga., he enrolled with Company C, Savannah Volunteer Guards Battalion, for War with Spain, and afterwards enlisted with Company assigned as Company K, Second Georgia Volunteer Infantry, at Griffin, Ga., and sent at once with regiment to Tampa, Fla., this being the first Southern regiment to reach Tampa. Mustered out as First Sergeant at Savannah, Ga., in November, 1898.

By order of the Commander in Chief:

R. L. LEINSTER,
Adjutant General.

STATE OF NORTH CAROLINA,
ADJUTANT GENERAL'S DEPARTMENT,

GENERAL ORDERS NO. 3. February 23, 1911.

In carrying out General Orders No. 222, War Department, series of 1910, the following modification of the Regulations for the uniform of officers and enlisted men of the North Carolina National Guard is prescribed:

With the special full-dress uniform and mess jacket, the white waistcoat with small gold or gilt regulation buttons and black silk tie will be worn. The buttons in the shirt will always be plain gold buttons.

Socks.—With the blue uniform, black socks will be worn; with the white uniform, white socks and white shoes will be worn.

Aiguillette.—Officers entitled to wear the aiguillette will wear it with all uniforms except the service uniform. It will be secured to the shoulder of the dress coat by a small cloth loop and black button placed just inside the shoulder strap, the aiguillette loops to be supported by the concealed dress-coat buttons. On a general officer's dress coat, it will be looped as to the full-dress coat.

Full-dress saber slings and saber knots will be worn with the dress and white uniforms.

Caps.—The use of the khaki cap will be discontinued and the olive drab cap will be worn in place of it. The dress cap will no longer form part of the uniform. The full-dress cap will be worn with the dress uniform.

Trousers.—The use of service trousers of olive drab and cotton khaki will be discontinued; they will no longer form a part of the uniform.

Spurs.—Whenever boots are worn spurs will be worn. All officers when mounted will wear spurs.

The style of breeches now used will continue to form part of the service uniform.

By order of the Commander in Chief: R. L. LEINSTER,
The Adjutant General.

STATE OF NORTH CAROLINA,
ADJUTANT GENERAL'S DEPARTMENT,

GENERAL ORDERS NO. 4. RALEIGH, March 22, 1911.

I. Rifle and pistol practice and competition will be held by teams, consisting of one commissioned officer and nine enlisted men from each company of the several regiments of infantry, on the following dates and places:

II. Target practice and competitive shooting for teams of the Third Infantry, on the range at Raleigh, N. C., April 18-20, inclusive. For teams of the Second Infantry, on the range at Goldsboro, N. C., April 25-27, inclusive. For teams of the First Infantry, on the range at Gastonia, N. C., May 3-5, inclusive.

III. All teams will be chosen by the company commanders and report to the post adjutant on date and at place designated, not later than 12 o'clock noon.

IV. Target practice will be engaged in first, and the time for the competitive shooting to commence will be announced by the chief range officer.

V. Regimental inspectors of small-arms practice will have all necessary arrangements for target practice to begin at 9 a. m.

VI. The marksman's record course, special course "C," will be followed, as prescribed in S. A. Firing Regulations, both in the practice and competition.

Pistol practice will be engaged in by officers after the competitive rifle shooting is over.

VII. The team making the highest score will be awarded the "Dupont Trophy." The teams in each regiment which make the highest and second highest scores will each be awarded a suitable prize. A prize will be awarded to the individual who makes the highest score.

VIII. During the progress of a match or competition no one except the officers on duty at the range, the competitors and scorekeepers will be permitted within the ropes, without special permission of the officer in charge.

IX. The squads of competitors will be stationed five yards in rear of firing point, where each competitor must remain until called by the score-keeper or range officer to take his position at the firing point.

X. Competitors may fire with the deliberation deemed necessary, provided that the time limit for the total number of shots required be not exceeded. The time will be taken from the firing of the first shot to firing of the last shot at each range. No time credit will be carried back from one range to another.

If an accident to a target, difficulty in operating the same, or other reason over which the competitor has no control, cause delay, such time credit as the range officer may decide will be allowed. All shots fired after the expiration of time limit will be recorded as misses.

No sighting shots will be allowed in the competition.

XI. Team captains will submit lists of names of members of teams, upon arrival in camp, to post adjutant.

XII. Score cards will be prepared, giving name, rank, company, and regiment of competitor, before firing begins.

All ammunition will be issued at firing point.

XIII. All members of teams must be members of the North Carolina National Guard.

Officers and enlisted men will bring cots and necessary field equipment, with the exception of shelter tent and intrenching tools.

XIV. The olive drab uniform, with cap and olive drab shirt and leggings, will be worn while en route to camp and return to home station; khaki breeches, service hat, and olive drab shirt will be worn on the range.

The senior officer present will be held responsible for the conduct of troops while traveling and in camp.

XV. Regimental inspectors of small-arms practice will submit certified report of firing to this office, giving individual and team scores, as early as practicable after the close of encampment.

XVI. The Quartermaster General and disbursing officer will provide all necessary and proper transportation, quarters, and other camp facilities, and be prepared to pay off troops the last day of each encampment.

XVII. Regimental commissaries will furnish subsistence as prescribed by regulations governing the organized militia.

XVIII. All information relative to this camp of instruction for promotion of rifle practice not contained in this order will be furnished in due time from this office.

By order of the Commander in Chief: R. L. LEINSTER,
Adjutant General.

STATE OF NORTH CAROLINA,
ADJUTANT GENERAL'S DEPARTMENT,

GENERAL ORDERS NO. 5. RALEIGH, April 7, 1911.

I. General Orders, No. 4, A. G. O. N. C., C. S., is amended to read as follows:

Teams consisting of one commissioned officer and nine enlisted men from each company of the Coast Artillery Corps will engage in rifle and pistol practice in competition with the company teams of the several regiments of infantry on the following dates and places:

Teams of the First and Second Companies, stationed at New Bern and Wilmington, respectively, on the range at Goldsboro with company teams of the Second Infantry, April 25-27, inclusive.

The team of the Third Company, stationed at Greensboro, N. C., on the range at Raleigh, with company teams of the Third Infantry, April 18-20, inclusive.

The teams of the Fourth and Fifth Companies, stationed at Salisbury and Charlotte, respectively, on the range at Gastonia, with company teams of the First Infantry, May 3-5, inclusive.

II. The teams of the Coast Artillery Corps will be guided by General Orders, No. 4, A. G. O. N. C., C. S.

By order of the Commander in Chief: R. L. LEINSTER,
Adjutant General.

STATE OF NORTH CAROLINA,
ADJUTANT GENERAL'S DEPARTMENT,

GENERAL ORDERS NO. 6. RALEIGH, May 17, 1911.

I. Rifle practice and competition will be held on the range at Raleigh, June 5-7, 1911, inclusive, by teams consisting of one commissioned officer and nine enlisted men from each of the following named organizations:

Company K, First Infantry, Asheville.

Company L, Second Infantry, Lumber Bridge.

Company B, Third Infantry, Raleigh.

II. The marksman's record course, special course "C," will be followed, as prescribed in Provisional Small Arms Firing Manual, 1909.

Target practice will be engaged in first, and the time for the competitive shooting to commence will be announced by the range officer.

The rules and regulations for outdoor competitions, as prescribed in Provisional Small Arms Firing Manual, 1909, will govern, except as herein modified; coaching will be permitted in the matches—the coach being allowed on the firing line with the men competing.

III. No individual shall be eligible to be entered as a member of any team who has not been continuously in the service of the State of North Carolina as a member of the organization he represents for at least sixty days preceding the date of match in which he participates.

Team Captains will submit lists of names, giving rank and date of enlistment of members of the teams, upon arrival in camp, to the executive officer.

IV. The olive drab uniform, with cap and olive drab shirt and leggings, will be worn while en route to camp and return to home station; khaki breeches, service hat and olive drab shirt will be worn on the range.

Pay, transportation, quarters and subsistence will be allowed for enlisted men, and pay, transportation and quarters for officers.

Officers and enlisted men will bring cots and necessary field equipment.

By order of the Commander in Chief: R. L. LEINSTER,
The Adjutant General.

STATE OF NORTH CAROLINA.
ADJUTANT GENERAL'S DEPARTMENT,

GENERAL ORDERS No. 7. RALEIGH, May 18, 1911.

I. The Field, Staff and Company Officers of the Coast Artillery Corps will assemble at Fort Caswell, N. C., June 12 to 18, 1911, for the purpose of attending a course of lectures and instructions under the direction and supervision of the Commanding Officer, Artillery District of Cape Fear.

II. Officers will leave home station in time to report to the Commanding Officer, Fort Caswell, not later than 4 p. m., June 12th.

III. The instruction will be given by the Commissioned Officers of the Regular Forces. The scope of instruction will be in part as follows:

1. Drill with rifle, learning the movements in conformity with regulations, and in detail.
2. Sabre drill.
3. Squad drill.
4. Artillery drill.
5. Administration.

a. Field and staff on duty in their respective offices.

b. The company officers to go on duty with the several companies.

c. Instruction in paper work.

d. The manner of handling the kitchen, the duties performed by the First Sergeant, the Quartermaster Sergeant, and their responsibilities.

e. The manner of cleaning clothes, equipments, barracks, etc.

IV. Bunks, springs, mattresses and pillows will be provided at the Fort; officers will carry other necessary bedding, field equipment and text-books.

V. All officers who can avail themselves of this opportunity will notify the Adjutant General, not later than June 1st.

Officers who comply with this order will receive pay for six days and transportation and quarters. The Quartermaster General will furnish the necessary transportation.

VI. Upon completion of this course of instructions at Fort Caswell, the Commanding Officer, Coast Artillery Corps, will make detailed report to this office of duties performed and instructions received.

By order of the Commander in Chief: R. L. LEINSTER,
The Adjutant General.

STATE OF NORTH CAROLINA,
ADJUTANT GENERAL'S DEPARTMENT,

GENERAL ORDERS No. 8. RALEIGH, May 22, 1911.

I. The several organizations of the North Carolina National Guard will rendezvous for target practice, field instruction, and joint coast defense exercises on the following dates and places:

Third Infantry, at Camp Glenn....................July 10-17.
Second Infantry, at Camp Glenn....................July 20-27.
First Infantry, at Camp Glenn....................August 3-10.
Coast Artillery Corps, at Fort Caswell.............August 7-18.

II. During the respective encampments the troops will be inspected by an officer of the Regular Army as to preparedness for field service. Troops will wear the service uniform and carry field arms, equipments, and kits, as prescribed by paragraphs 242 and 243, Militia Regulations, 1910, except as herein modified—no overcoats, ammunition, haversack rations, emergency rations, or identification tags will be required for the field inspection.

III. The Quartermaster General will provide the necessary transportation, quartermaster's stores, and camp equipage; prepare the camp, having tent floors placed with tents, poles, tripods, and pins in readiness for erection of tents upon arrival of troops; having the water supply, latrines, and bathhouses in fit condition; provide fuel, forage, and necessary wagon transportation, and furnish each organization commander with schedules of the going and return trip, not later than July 1st.

IV. Regimental quartermasters will proceed to Camp one day prior to arrival of troops and make requisition upon the Post Quartermaster for tentage, camp equipage, wagon transportation, fuel and forage, giving receipt for same, and be prepared to issue upon arrival of troops, and upon completion of tour of duty, turn in Government property to Post Quartermaster, invoicing and taking receipt for same.

V. Regimental commissaries will purchase, provide, and issue subsistence for their respective organizations in accordance with laws and regulations governing the Organized Militia, and, to perform this duty, will proceed to place of rendezvous three days previous to arrival of troops, and will be prepared to issue rations.

VI. The Surgeon General will designate the necessary sanitary troops for each regiment and separate corps.

VII. Company commanders are notified that pay, transportation, and subsistence will not be furnished to company organizations that do not carry a minimum strength of thirty-eight enlisted men and one commissioned officer.

VIII. Regimental commanders will provide while in camp for a written examination of all first and second lieutenants who have been commissioned since July 1, 1910. The questions for the examination will be taken from the following text-books and pages, inclusive, indicated:

North Carolina National Guard Regulations:
Pages 60-61, 64-69, 76-77, 83-85, 103-124, 132-141.

Infantry Drill Regulations, U. S. A., 1904:
Pages 1-18, 61-90, 162-164, 170-176, 177-180, 181-202.

Field-service Regulations, 1910:
Pages 64-89, 146-156.

Manual of Guard Duty, 1908:
Pages 1-68, 80-84, 91-95.

Provisional Small-arms Firing Manual, 1909:
Pages 36-54, 104-109.

IX. While traveling, officers and noncommissioned officers will be guided by paragraphs 247, 248, Field-service Regulations, 1910. All officers are enjoined to read Article VII, Regulations, North Carolina National Guard.

X. In the target practice the marksman's record course, Special Course

"C," should be followed, and troops should carry sufficient supply of "Three in One" oil for cleaning rifles and revolvers. Company commanders will inspect rifles each day before troops report at range for target practice.

The field instruction should be progressive, and, when practicable, tactical walks for officers should be conducted and battle exercises engaged in.

Regimental commanders will require the bands of their respective regiments to have rehearsal at least once each day, except Sunday, and hold not less than three concerts in camp on different dates during the period of service.

The senior medical officer present will require the detachment hospital corps to engage in litter drill and other exercises in accordance with Hospital Corps Drill Regulations.

XI. The cost of transportation, pay, and subsistence, etc., for the organizations which encamp at Camp Glenn will be met by Federal funds allotted to the State under section 1661, R. S., as amended, and all troops will be paid for eight days, except such officers and enlisted men as are authorized in this order and in subsequent special orders from this office to receive pay for a longer period.

By order of the Commander in Chief:

R. L. LEINSTER,
Adjutant General.

STATE OF NORTH CAROLINA,
ADJUTANT GENERAL'S DEPARTMENT,

GENERAL ORDERS NO. 9. RALEIGH, May 23, 1911.

I. Annual inspection of the North Carolina Naval Militia for the current year will be made at home stations of organizations by Lieutenant Colonel H. D. Harper, Assistant Inspector General, on the following dates:

Second Division	New Bern	June 29th.
Sixth Division	Oriental	June 30th.
Fifth Division	Elizabeth City	July 1st.
Seventh Division	Hertford	July 3d.
Fourth Division	Plymouth	July 5th.
Third Division	Windsor	July 6th.

II. Commanding officers will be prepared to parade their commands in such uniform and equipment and at such time as designated by the Inspector.

The inspection will include all United States and State property in possession of organizations. During the inspecting of any property in the storerooms of organizations, the responsible or other commissioned officer will be present with a sufficient detail of men to handle the property. In order to expedite the work, all property should be previously sorted and neatly arranged for inspection, and the responsible officer should have a list of same and retained copy of annual property return.

III. When in the judgment of the inspecting officer it is deemed necessary, officers and warrant officers will be examined by the Inspector as to their general efficiency and knowledge of their respective duties, and where found deficient, incompetent, inattentive, or negligent in the performance of their duties, a special report as to the commissioned officers will be forwarded without delay through the Inspector General's Department, in order that, where circumstances warrant it, such officers may be examined and reported upon as to the advisability of their continuance in the service. Warrant officers found to be inefficient will be reported by the Inspector to the commanding officer of the organization for his action.

IV. Company property and record books must be fully written up for inspection.

By order of the Commander in Chief: R. L. LEINSTER,
Adjutant General.

STATE OF NORTH CAROLINA,
ADJUTANT GENERAL'S DEPARTMENT,

GENERAL ORDERS No. 10. RALEIGH, June 2, 1911.

I. In order to comply with the requirements of Section III, Militia Law, approved by Act of Congress, January 21, 1903, the Medical Department, National Guard of North Carolina, will be changed to conform to the organization provided for the United States Army and the Organized Militia of the United States, as prescribed in Regulations and General Orders of the War Department, and Section 4882 of the Military Code of North Carolina.

II. The Medical Department of the National Guard of North Carolina shall consist of one Surgeon General with the rank of Colonel; one assistant Surgeon General, with the rank of Lieutenant Colonel; and of the commissioned and enlisted personnel authorized by law for that Department, for the purposes of State administration. This personnel and all other persons assigned to duty therewith, shall be collectively known as *sanitary troops.*

III. For duty in the field, the sanitary troops shall be divided into, first, those assigned to regiments and other combatant units; second, those assigned to independent sanitary units, as field hospitals and ambulance companies.

IV. The Medical Department of the National Guard of North Carolina, in addition to the officers heretofore mentioned for State administration, shall consist (one) a Medical Corps; (two) a Medical Reserve Corps; (three) a Hospital Corps.

V. The Medical Corps of the National Guard of North Carolina shall consist of medical officers, who shall be commissioned after examination and qualification as to their physical, general and professional knowledge, and aptitude for the service, before a board appointed by the Governor, to consist of not less than three medical officers of the National Guard of North Carolina, and receive the recommendation of said board.

VI. The Medical Reserve Corps shall consist of medical officers commissioned in the grade of First Lieutenant only, upon the recommendation of the Surgeon General of the State. The commissions so given shall confer on the holders thereof when assigned to active duty all the authority, rights and privileges of commissioned officers of like grade in the Medical Corps of the National Guard of North Carolina, *except promotion.* Officers of the Medical Reserve Corps shall have rank in said corps according to the date of their commission therein, and when employed on active duty shall rank next below all of the officers of like grade in the National Guard of North Carolina.

VII. Officers of the Medical Reserve Corps may be assigned to active duty at any time, upon the recommendation of the Surgeon General.

VIII. All commissioned officers of the Medical Corps and of the Medical Reserve Corps must be citizens of the United States and legally qualified practitioners of medicine and surgery in accordance with the laws of the State of North Carolina.

IX. The Hospital Corps shall consist of men enlisted for service in the Medical Department and of men transferred from the line to the Hospital Corps. The number of officers and men in the Medical Department shall at all times be sufficient to provide the sanitary personnel, as required by Regulation in the Army of the United States.

X. All original vacancies in the Medical Corps of the National Guard of North Carolina, created by this reorganization, shall, so far as practicable, be filled by appointment in the grade of First Lieutenant, subject to examination and recommendation by a board of not less than three officers of the Medical Corps appointed by the Governor. Promotion in all grades shall be by seniority, subject in all cases to qualification and recommendation from a board of not less than three officers of the Medical Corps appointed by the Governor after passing a physical and professional examination before such board.

XI. All First Lieutenants of the Medical Corps, after serving for a period of three years as medical officers in the National Guard of the State of North Carolina, or its equivalent, as commissioned medical officers in the Armies of the United States or the Organized Militia, shall be promoted to the grade of Captain after qualifying physically and professionally and receiving the recommendation of a board of not less than three officers of the Medical Corps of the National Guard of North Carolina, appointed by the Governor.

XII. The Surgeon General shall be in control of the Medical Department, subordinate only to the officer commanding the National Guard and the Governor as Commander in Chief. He shall direct the examination of candidates for appointment and promotion in the Medical Corps and in the Hospital Corps and recommend appointments in the Medical Reserve Corps.

XIII. In addition to the Surgeon General and Assistant Surgeon General, as provided in paragraph II of this order, the Medical Corps at present shall consist of six majors, fifteen captains or first lieutenants.

XIV. The Hospital Corps shall consist of ten sergeants, first class, twenty-four sergeants or corporals, and one hundred and twenty-five privates, first class, and privates.

XV. The foregoing commissioned and enlisted personnel to be increased or reduced as the needs of the service require.

XVI. To provide for the medical service in the field, officers and enlisted men of the Medical Department will be assigned as follows:

Brigade Headquarters, one major (chief surgeon); one major (sanitary inspector); one captain or first lieutenant.

XVII. To each regiment of infantry, one major, three captains or first lieutenants. For each independent troop of cavalry, battery of artillery, independent company of signal corps, one captain or first lieutenant; for field hospital, one major, two captains or first lieutenants; for an ambulance company, three captains or first lieutenants.

XVIII. HOSPITAL CORPS. When not in field service, all enlisted personnel of sanitary troops will ordinarily be attached to the sanitary units, namely, field hospitals and ambulance companies, but when in service in the field, the following provisions shall apply:

Brigade Headquarters, one sergeant, first class, three privates, first class, or privates. For field hospital, three sergeants, first class, six sergeants or corporals, twenty-four privates, first class, or privates. For ambulance company, two sergeants, first class; seven sergeants or corporals; thirty-four privates, first class, or privates. To each regiment of three battalions, one sergeant, first class, three sergeants or corporals, twelve privates, first class, or privates. For a battalion of infantry or squadron of cavalry, one sergeant or corporal, three privates, first class, or privates. For a battery of artillery, acting independently, one sergeant or corporal, three privates, first class, or privates.

XIX. In camp, regiments will establish regimental infirmaries and not regimental hospitals; these infirmaries will care for those slightly sick or slightly injured only; all serious cases or those promising absence from duty longer than twenty-four hours must be transferred to the field hospital. Regiments operating independently will, under proper authority, establish regimental hospitals.

DUTIES IN GENERAL.

The Medical Department is charged with the following duties:

(*a*) The initiation of all hygienic measures to insure the good health of troops.

(*b*) The direction and execution of all measures of public health among the inhabitants of occupied territory.

(*c*) The care of sick and wounded on the march, in camp, on the field of battle, and after their removal therefrom.

(*d*) Methodical disposition of the sick and wounded, so as to assure the retention of those effective on the firing line and to relieve the fighting force of the noneffective.

(*e*) Transportation of the sick and wounded.

(*f*) Preparation and preservation of individual records of sickness and injury, in order that claims may be adjudicated with justice to the State and to the soldier.

(*g*) Prompt acknowledgment of all General, Special and Field Orders, to the proper authority.

INDIVIDUAL DUTIES.

The duties of the Surgeon General shall be the supervision and administration of the Medical Department, as provided in paragraph XII of this order.

The duties of the Chief Surgeon in the field shall be those prescribed in the Manual of the Medical Department, U. S. A., and such other duties as may be prescribed by proper authority.

The duties of the sanitary inspector are those prescribed in the Manual of the Medical Department, U. S. A., and in the Field Service Regulations, U. S. A., and such other duties as may be prescribed by proper authority.

The duties of medical officers on duty with regiments, battalions, batteries, troops of cavalry, signal corps companies, and companies of engineers, shall be those prescribed in the Manual of the Medical Department, U. S. A., and such other duties as may be prescribed by proper authority.

The duties of the commanding officer of a field hospital shall be those prescribed in the Manual of the Medical Department, U. S. A., and such other duties as may be prescribed by proper authority.

The duties of commanding officer of an ambulance company shall be those prescribed in the Manual of the Medical Department, U. S. A., and such other duties as may be prescribed by proper authority.

In addition to their duties for the care of sick and wounded, medical officers will act as sanitary advisers of commanders of troops. They will make recommendations relative to selection of camp sites, report on water supply and other sanitary requirements, and shall make frequent inspections and subsequent recommendations.

All medical officers, addressing official communications to the Adjutant General, will forward same through the office of the Surgeon General. When in the field, through the office of the Chief Surgeon.

All requisitions for medical supplies will be forwarded through the office of the Surgeon General, who will approve or disapprove their issue to proper authority. When in the field, these requisitions will pass through the office of the Chief Surgeon.

All preceding orders, conflicting with the provisions of this order, are hereby revoked.

By order of the Commander in Chief: R. L. LEINSTER,
The Adjutant General.

STATE OF NORTH CAROLINA,
ADJUTANT GENERAL'S DEPARTMENT,

GENERAL ORDERS NO. 11. RALEIGH, June 19, 1911.

I. In connection with the target practice and camp of instruction of the several regiments of infantry, as provided in General Orders, No. 8, C. S., regimental commanders will require all field, staff, and line officers and non-commissioned staff officers to fire and qualify with rifle and revolver in special Course "C," and all enlisted men to fire and complete the marksman's course in special Course "C" with rifle.

II. No sighting shots will be allowed during the target practice, except at the five-hundred-yard firing point.

III. Before leaving home station, each company commander will prepare a list of members of his company, and immediately after arrival in camp will call upon the statistical officer for sufficient supply of score-cards and prepare same in accordance with printed instructions thereon—one for each member of company present for duty.

To insure prompt and efficient service in making provision for range and pit officers, scorers and target tenders, so far as practicable, complete companies will be detailed.

IV. The Regimental Adjutant will furnish the chief range officer with a copy of all details not later than 8 p. m. of the day preceding the firing for which the details were made. He will require these details, in charge of a commissioned officer, to report to the chief range officer at such time and place as the latter shall direct.

V. The statistical officer on duty with each regiment will submit report to this office, giving a complete record of all firing, duly certified by the proper officer, at the close of each regimental encampment.

VI. The senior officer or noncommissioned officer present will be held responsible for the conduct of troops of their respective organizations, while traveling and in camp.

By order of the Commander in Chief: R. L. LEINSTER,
The Adjutant General.

STATE OF NORTH CAROLINA,
ADJUTANT GENERAL'S DEPARTMENT,

GENERAL ORDERS NO. 12. RALEIGH, June 21, 1911.

I. The following scores made by winning teams in rifle competition held in pursuance of General Orders, Nos. 4 and 6, are announced:

Company team match, held at Raleigh, April 18-20, highest aggregate score, 1090.

Won by Company B, Third Infantry, Raleigh.

Company team match, held at Goldsboro, April 25-27, highest aggregate score, 1080.

Won by Company L, Second Infantry, Lumber Bridge.

Company team match, held at Gastonia, May 3-5, highest aggregate score, 1066.

Won by Company K, First Infantry, Asheville.

Regimental team match, held at Raleigh, June 5-7.

Company L team, Second Infantry, Lumber Bridge, 1169.

Company K team, First Infantry, Asheville, 1167.

Company B team, Third Infantry, Raleigh, 1121.

II. A protest was filed against certain members of the team of Company L, Second Infantry, on account of noncompliance with regulations relative to enlistments. After investigation, it was found that enlistment papers for four members of this team had not reached the Adjutant General's office—two original enlistments and two re-enlistments. When this fact was called to the attention of the Commanding Officer, Company L, Second Infantry, duplicate enlistments and re-enlistments were forwarded to this office and a sworn statement as to the previous service of the four members of the team against whom protest had been filed, and with the further statement that enlistments for these members of the team had been forwarded through the proper military channels.

While not unmindful of the neglect of responsible officers in this case in not forwarding enlistments in accordance with regulations, and being satisfied that no wrong or deception was intended by the commanding officer of Company L, Second Infantry, it is deemed for the best interests of the service that the trophy be awarded to the team making the highest score in the competition, held at Raleigh, June 7, 1911.

Therefore the Dupont Trophy is herewith awarded to Company L, Second Infantry, Lumber Bridge, N. C., for the year 1911.

III. The protest mentioned herein should serve a good purpose in calling the attention of organization commanders and responsible officers to the necescity of forwarding enlistment papers promptly.

IV. The attention of all officers is invited to Sections 4896 and 4912 of the Military Code, relative to enlistments, and may be found on pages 18 and 22, Regulations, North Carolina National Guard.

By order of the Commander in Chief: R. L. LEINSTER,
The Adjutant General.

STATE OF NORTH CAROLINA,
ADJUTANT GENERAL'S DEPARTMENT,

GENERAL ORDERS NO. 13. RALEIGH, 28 June, 1911.

I. The several divisions of the Naval Brigade will cruise aboard the U. S. S. *Elfrida* and the U. S. torpedo boat *Dupont* for summer exercises and instruction on the following dates:

July 19-26, inclusive,	Third Division, on *Elfrida*.
	Fifth Division, on *Dupont*.
July 27-August 3, inclusive,	Fourth Division, on *Elfrida*.
	Seventh Division, on *Dupont*.
August 9-16, inclusive,	Second Division, on *Elfrida*.
	Sixth Division, on *Dupont*.

II. The Commanding Officer, Naval Brigade, will issue such orders as are necessary to carry out the routine ship duties and for record target practice by each division in accordance with instructions of the U. S. Navy Department.

III. The general scope of the work for each Division will be prescribed by the Commanding Officer of the Naval Brigade. Battalion and Division Commanders are enjoined to carry out the duties assigned to their respective commands, to the end that the instructions given can be thoroughly understood and the greatest benefit derived therefrom.

IV. The senior officer or petty officer present will be held responsible for the conduct of the enlisted men, both aboard ship and on shore leave.

V. Upon completion of the summer exercises, a full report of same will be submitted by the Commanding Officer of the Naval Brigade to this office.

By order of the Commander in Chief: R. L. LEINSTER,
The Adjutant General.

STATE OF NORTH CAROLINA,
ADJUTANT GENERAL'S DEPARTMENT,

GENERAL ORDERS NO. 14. RALEIGH, 17 August, 1911.

I. The following named officers and enlisted men will constitute the team to represent the State of North Carolina in the National Matches at Camp Perry, Ohio, 1911:

PRINCIPALS.

Capt. C. I. Bard................................Company K, First Infantry.
Capt. J. H. Koon...............................Company F, First Infantry.

Sergeant W. S. Newton........................Company A, First Infantry.
Sergeant J. C. McClure........................Company H, First Infantry.
Sergeant J. H. Brown........................Company K, First Infantry.
First Lieut. S. E. Malone....................Company D, Second Infantry.
Second Lieut. O. C. Jones....................Company E, Second Infantry.
Corporal Ralph Wade........................Company D, Second Infantry.
Private H. L. Best..........................Company C, Second Infantry.
First Lieut. E. B. Parrish...................Company B, Third Infantry.
Sergeant J. T. McAdams......................Company I, Third Infantry.
Private J. A. Moorefield......................Company G, Third Infantry.

ALTERNATES.

Capt. J. B. Malloy..........................Company L, Second Infantry.
Sergeant H. C. Simons........................Company D, Third Infantry.
Sergeant R. C. Wray...........................Company G, Third Infantry.

TEAM OFFICERS.

Team Captain, Brig. Gen. R. L. Leinster..............The Adjutant General.
Team Coach, Lieut. Col. J. Wash Bizzell..............Ordnance Department.
Team Spotter, Capt. R. G. Gladstone............Company G, Third Infantry.
Team Surgeon, Capt. F. J. Clemenger......................Medical Corps.

The above named officers and enlisted men will report to the Adjutant General in Raleigh, August 19th, prepared to leave for Camp Perry, Ohio, on S. A. L. train No. 84, due to leave Union Station at 12:40 a. m., August 20th, arriving at Camp Perry, Ohio, August 21st, and remaining in camp until the morning of August 31, 1911.

II. Previous instructions to members of the team relative to equipment to be carried must be strictly adhered to.

By order of the Commander in Chief: R. L. LEINSTER,
The Adjutant General.

STATE OF NORTH CAROLINA,
ADJUTANT GENERAL'S DEPARTMENT,

GENERAL ORDERS NO. 15. RALEIGH, 26 September, 1911.

I. In accordance with request of the War Department, dated Washington, September 11, 1911, the following system for recruiting the several organizations of the North Carolina National Guard to war strength is herewith adopted:

The First Lieutenant of each company, battery, troop of cavalry, signal corps company, company of engineers, ambulance company, and field hospital, is herewith designated as its recruiting officer; and when a local organization is called into the service of the United States the recruiting officer will at once begin to recruit the same up to war strength. When a local organization goes to the State mobilization camp, the recruiting officer will remain behind with a detail of two enlisted men and continue recruiting, forwarding all recruits to the State mobilization camp.

The recruiting officer and his party will rejoin the proper organization before the latter leaves the mobilization camp.

Each regiment and separate battalion will, before it leaves the State, establish a recruiting party to recruit for its organization during the continuance of the war.

A general recruiting party for all the militia organizations of the State will be maintained at the State mobilization camp, the personnel of the recruiting party to be announced when the service requires.

All recruits will be forwarded through the State mobilization camp, where they will be thoroughly examined physically, armed and equipped, and instructed as far as time permits.

All recruiting officers will keep themselves thoroughly informed of all the requirements of their office, and will by application to the Adjutant General of the State secure the necessary blank forms to be used in recruiting service.

The minimum enlisted strength of militia organizations, before they will be accepted into the service of the United States, is as follows:

AMBULANCE COMPANY.

Sergeants, first class	2
Sergeants	7
Privates, first class, and privates	34
Total enlisted (minimum)	43

One captain and four first lieutenants of the Medical Corps are usually assigned to duty with an ambulance company.

FIELD HOSPITAL.

Sergeants, first class	3
Sergeants	6
Privates, first class, and privates	24
Total enlisted (minimum)	33

One major and four captains or four first lieutenants of the Medical Corps are usually assigned to duty with the Field Hospital.

COMPANY OF ENGINEERS.

First sergeant	1
Quartermaster sergeant	1
Sergeants	4
Corporals	6
Cooks	2
Musicians	2
Privates, first class	21
Privates, second class	21
Total enlisted (minimum)	58

The maximum enlisted strength of a company of engineers may be as high as 164, as prescribed in section 11 of the Act of Congress approved February 2, 1901.

SIGNAL CORPS COMPANY.

Sergeants, first class	5
Sergeants	5
Corporals	10
Cooks	2
Privates, first class	18
Privates	18
Total enlisted (minimum)	58

The normal quota of commissioned officers for a company of the signal corps is one captain and two first lieutenants. The grade of second lieutenant is not authorized for the signal corps. At least two-thirds of the officers and enlisted men of a company should be expert telegraphers and electricians.

INFANTRY.

Captain	1
First lieutenant	1
Second lieutenant	1
First Sergeant	1
Quartermaster sergeant	1
Sergeants	4
Corporals	6
Cooks	2
Musicians	2
Privates	42
Total enlisted (minimum)	58

The maximum enlisted strength of a company of infantry may be as high as 150, as prescribed in section 10 of the Act of Congress, approved February 2, 1901.

CAVALRY.

Captain	1
First lieutenant	1
Second lieutenant	1
First sergeant	1
Quartermaster sergeant	1
Sergeants	4
Corporals	6
Cooks	2
Farrier	1
Horseshoer	1
Saddler	1
Trumpeters	2
Privates	39
Total enlisted (minimum)	58

The maximum enlisted strength of a troop of cavalry may be as high as 100, as prescribed in section 2 of the Act of Congress, approved February 2, 1901.

COAST ARTILLERY.

Captain	1
First lieutenant	1
Second lieutenant	1
First sergeant	1
Quartermaster sergeant	1
Sergeants	4
Corporals	6
Cooks	2
Mechanics	2
Musicians	2
Privates	45
Total enlisted (minimum)	63

The maximum number of enlisted men in a company of coast artillery may be varied according to the service a company may possibly be called upon to perform.

By order of the Commander-in-Chief: R. L. LEINSTER,
The Adjutant General.

STATE OF NORTH CAROLINA,
ADJUTANT GENERAL'S DEPARTMENT,

GENERAL ORDERS No. 16. RALEIGH, September 29, 1911.

I. The following named officers and enlisted men of the North Carolina National Guard qualified in the classes indicated, during the target practice season, 1911:

GENERAL STAFF.

R. T. Daniel	Major	Pay Department	Marksman
Z. P. Smith	Captain	Ordnance Department	Marksman

FIRST BRIGADE STAFF.

A. C. House	First Lieut.	Aide	Marksman

FIRST INFANTRY.

FIELD AND STAFF.

J. T. Gardner	Colonel	Marksman.
L. W. Young	Major	Marksman.
J. F. Roberts	Captain	Marksman.
R. R. Morrison	Captain	Marksman.
A. W. Freeman	Lieutenant	Marksman.
W. J. Hill, Jr.	Lieutenant	Marksman.
Hall Morrison	Lieutenant	Marksman.
W. H. Hendley	Sergeant Major	Marksman.

COMPANY A.

R. P. Benfield	Sergeant	Marksman.
S. R. Bolch	Private	Marksman.

L. M. Bolch	Sergeant	Marksman.
W. V. Bowman	Sergeant	Marksman.
W. L. Church	Corporal	Marksman.
F. R. Davis	Private	Marksman.
W. A. Elrod	Private	Marksman.
R. P. Hawn	Private	Marksman.
W. H. Link	Private	Marksman.
W. S Newton	Corporal	Expert rifleman.
W. M. Sigmon	Private	Marksman.
Ray Travis	Private	Marksman.
H. R. Triplett	Corporal	Marksman.
W. B. Witherspoon	Musician	Marksman.
I. E. Williams	Cook	Marksman.

COMPANY B.

A. L. Bulwinkle	Captain	Marksman.
W. H. Badger	Private	Marksman.
W. S. Barfield	First Lieutenant	Marksman.
C. C. Craig	Second Lieutenant	Marksman.
P. K. Gilbert	Corporal	Marksman.
R. C. Gilbert	Artificer	Marksman.
W. L. Glover	Private	Marksman.
C. L. Hoard	Private	Marksman.
W. H. Little	Private	Marksman.
D. H. Penly	Private	Marksman.
R. C. Penly	Private	Marksman.
Grover C. Page	Sergeant	Marksman.
G. W. Short	Private	Marksman.
V. B. Short	Private	Marksman.
H. B. Stowe	Private	Marksman.

COMPANY C.

H. S. Beck	First Sergeant	Marksman.
S. C. Bodenhamer	Private	Marksman.
R. W. Bryant	Private	Marksman.
M. P. Children	Sergeant	Marksman.
C. W. Clodfelter	Sergeant	Marksman.
S. C. Crater	Private	Marksman.
Thos. Crews	Private	Marksman.
J. H. Evans	Private	Marksman.
W. D. Hicks	Corporal	Marksman.
W. A. Holder	Second Lieutenant	Marksman.
R. E. Marshall	Private	Marksman.
E. F. Reavis	Corporal	Marksman.
J. F. Reavis	Private	Marksman.
E. F. Rutledge	Private	Marksman.
E. S. Shore	Private	Marksman.
J. G. Wooten	Corporal	Marksman.

COMPANY D.

E. C. Bradley	Private	Marksman.
L. E. Broom	Private	Marksman.
L. B. Crayton	Private	Marksman.
G. C. Crowell	Private	Marksman.
W. P. Dunn	Private	Marksman.
J. S. Gattis	Private	Marksman.
R. C. Huddleston	Cook	Marksman.
Rufus M. Johnston	Second Lieutenant	Marksman.
L. Justice	Private	Expert rifleman.
L. M. Moore	Private	Marksman.
John Moyle	Sergeant	Marksman.
F. G. Mullis	Private	Marksman.
B. S. McCorkle	Artificer	Expert rifleman.
John A. Parker	Captain	Marksman.
C. P. Phifer	Private	Marksman.
E. E. Phifer	Corporal	Marksman.
O. K. Phifer	Private	Marksman.
J. M. Phillips	Corporal	Marksman.
C. C. Porter	Corporal	Marksman.
J. L. Smith	Private	Marksman.
D. W. Smith	Private	Marksman.
Norman Vann	Private	Marksman.

COMPANY E.

James Carter	Private	Marksman.
J. E. Deitz	Captain	Marksman.
Iva R. Elam	Private	Marksman.
Paul P. Foster	Private	Marksman.
Sam Hart	Private	Marksman.
Orin N. Honeycutt	Corporal	Marksman.
Ralph Honeycutt	Private	Marksman.
Ace Johnson	Musician	Marksman.
Kent B. Johnson	Musician	Marksman.
Flake T. Lyarly	Private	Marksman.
Neal P. Miller	Private	Marksman.
Oscar Mills	Sergeant	Marksman.
Erwin S. Millsaps	Private	Marksman.
C. Dunlap Morris	Private	Marksman.
Wm. Ramsey	Private	Marksman.
Davidson Ross	Corporal	Marksman.
Walter E. Sherrill	Corporal	Marksman.
C. H. Turner	First Lieutenant	Marksman.
Thurman Warren	Private	Marksman.
W. E. Warren	Sergeant	Marksman.
Rathy Warren	First Sergeant	Marksman.

COMPANY F.

F. T. Bourne	Private	Marksman.
J. D. Bourne	Corporal	Marksman.

W. A. Britt.................First Sergeant...............Marksman.
J. C. Duncan................Private ....Marksman.
C. H. Felmet................Lieutenant ....Marksman.
W. B. Gragg.................Private ....Marksman.
E. H. Henderson.............Corporal ....Marksman.
E. F. Jones.................Sergeant ....Marksman.
J. H. Koon..................Captain ....Expert rifleman.
W. H. Moody.................Cook ....Marksman.
F. S. Murdock...............Corporal ....Marksman.
W. E. Nix...................Private ....Marksman.
C. P. Pressly...............Private ....Marksman.
W. R. Robinson..............Corporal ....Marksman.
R. C. Woody.................Corporal ....Marksman.
R. C. Young.................Private ....Marksman.

COMPANY G.

George Borders..............Private ....Marksman.
Robt. Crowder...............Sergeant ....Marksman.
Sidney Elliott..............Corporal ....Marksman.
J. E. Fisher................Private ....Marksman.
J. Frank Jenkins............First Lieutenant.............Marksman.
J. S. Jenkins...............Private ....Marksman.
Yates Kendricks.............Private ....Marksman.
Branton Lawrence............Private ....Marksman.
George Moore................Sergeant ....Marksman.
J. S. Mull..................Private ....Marksman.
Eura McSwain................Private ....Marksman.
Chas. P. Roberts............Second Lieutenant ....Marksman.
Roy Stockton................Private ....Marksman.
Albert Turner...............Private ....Marksman.
Giles Webb..................Sergeant ....Marksman.
Zellie Whitaker.............Private ....Marksman.
Harry Woodson...............Corporal ....Marksman.

COMPANY H.

Alf. C. Arrington...Marksman.
Henry Barnes..Marksman.
Marion Blanton..............Private ....Marksman.
Vernon Brady................Private ....Marksman.
Marle B. Brendle............Private ....Marksman.
Grover Burnett..............Private ....Marksman.
Chas. M. Francis............Private ....Marksman.
Henry Gaddy.................Private ....Marksman.
Neil Gaddy..................Private ....Marksman.
Joshua Hardy ....Private ....Marksman.
Jas. H. Howell..............Captain ....Marksman.
Julius Hoyle................First Lieutenant.............Marksman.
Walter Hyatt................Private ....Marksman.
Carl Miller.................Private ....Marksman.

Henry Miller	Private	Marksman.
Joe McClure	Private	Expert rifleman.
Forest B. Platt	Private	Marksman.
Sam Robinson	Private	Marksman.
John Scater	Private	Marksman.
Francis Willard	Private	Marksman.

COMPANY I.

W. C. Albright	Corporal	Marksman.
J. S. Bolton	Private	Marksman.
R. A. Blizard	Sergeant	Marksman.
G. A. Bowman	Private	Marksman.
T. W. Bray	Private	Marksman.
O. Bunker	Private	Marksman.
A. D. Coleman	Private	Marksman.
W. A. Cox	Corporal	Marksman.
J. N. Cox	Private	Marksman.
J. H. Cox	Private	Marksman.
J. T. Gant	Sergeant	Marksman.
J. H. Gwyn	Second Lieutenant	Marksman.
R. L. Hayman	Private	Marksman.
W. A. Jackson	Captain	Marksman.
Pete Jones	Sergeant	Marksman.
Sam Lowery	Private	Marksman.
Fred Pruitt	Corporal	Marksman.
J. E. Pyrdle	Private	Marksman.
A. L. Riddle	Private	Marksman.
H. Stanley	First Lieutenant	Expert rifleman.
J. R. White	Private	Marksman.
E. L. Wilkinson	Sergeant	Marksman.

COMPANY K.

C. I. Bard	Captain	Expert rifleman
J. M. Bradford	Corporal	Marksman.
J. H. Brown	Sergeant	Expert rifleman
C. W. Byerly	Private	Marksman.
Will Coleman	Corporal	Marksman.
G. M. Cowan	Sergeant	Marksman.
H. D. Duckett	Private	Marksman.
B. E. Goodlake	Private	Marksman.
Cleve Holcombe	Corporal	Marksman.
Fred Jones	Private	Marksman.
J. W. Kesterson	Sergeant	Marksman.
E. A. Ledford	Private	Marksman.
A. E. Mitchell	Sergeant	Marksman.
D. S. Murdock	Sergeant	Marksman.
Chas. McMahone	Private	Marksman.
J. P. Patton	Private	Marksman.
L. D. Purland	Private	Marksman.
J. J. Riggsby	Private	Marksman.

Joe Sprouse	Sergeant	Marksman.
Roy Wright	Private	Marksman.

COMPANY L.

C. E. Clark	Private	Marksman.
E. L. Ennis	Private	Marksman.
Thos. I. Graham	Private	Marksman.
J. B. Kluttz	Private	Marksman.
Arter Lentz	Corporal	Marksman.
A. T. Miller	Musician	Marksman.
F. Y. McConnell	First Lieutenant	Marksman.
R. C. Thompson	Second Lieutenant	Marksman.
J. M. Whitley	Private	Marksman.
John M. Young, Jr.	Private	Marksman.

COMPANY M.

S. J. Best	Private	Marksman.
W. E. Bowman	Corporal	Marksman.
E. P. Carpenter	Captain	Marksman.
Carson Burns	Corporal	Marksman.
R. C. Crouch	Cook	Marksman.
Ken W. Kurlee	Private	Marksman.
C. B. Dare	Musician	Marksman.
J. J. Griffith	First Lieutenant	Marksman.
W. M. Guyer	Private	Marksman.
Ernest E. Hampton	First Sergeant	Marksman.
R. D. Hayworth	Musician	Marksman.
T. L. Hilton	Private	Marksman.
J. O. Pike	Corporal	Marksman.
M. B. Shiplett	Second Lieutenant	Marksman.
J. W. Welch	Corporal	Marksman.

FIRST INFANTRY—PISTOL FIRING.

J. T. Gardner	Colonel	Marksman.
R. R. Morrison	Captain	Marksman.
J. F. Roberts	Captain	Marksman.
R. H. Morrison	Lieutenant	Marksman.
J. H. Koon	Captain Co. F	Marksman.
W. A. Jackson	Captain Co. I	Marksman.
C. I. Bard	Captain Co. K	Expert.
W. S. Barfield	Lieutenant, Co. B	Marksman.
C. H. Turner	Lieutenant, Co. E	Marksman.
J. B. Hoyle	Lieutenant, Co. H	Marksman.
J. H. Gwynn	Lieutenant, Co. I	Marksman.
H. Stanley	Lieutenant, Co. I	Marksman.
M. B. Shipley	Lieutenant, Co. M	Marksman.
J. H. Brown	First Lieutenant	Expert.
J. B. Taylor	Sergeant Major	Marksman.

SECOND INFANTRY.

Field and Staff.

C. B. Elliott	Major	Marksman.
E. H. Lewis	Sergeant Major	Marksman.
T. S. Pace	Major	Marksman.
S. Cohen	Captain	Marksman.

Company A.

F. M. Carlisle	Second Lieutenant	Marksman.
W. B. Barnes	Private	Marksman.
M. Bass	Private	Marksman.
D. B. Carlisle	Sergeant	Marksman.
W. H. Hackney	Sergeant	Marksman.
B. F. Lane	Private	Marksman.
— — Rosenbloom	Private	Marksman.
F. A. Williams	Sergeant	Marksman.

Company B.

A. L. C. Hill	Captain	Marksman.
J. I. Brown	First Lieutenant	Marksman.
J. O. H. Taylor	Second Lieutenant	Marksman.
E. A. Faulkner	Private	Marksman.
J. A. Faulkner	Private	Marksman.
W. O. Faulkner	Private	Marksman.
G. V. Gray	Sergeant	Marksman.
David Hill	Private	Marksman.
B. F. Hughes	Corporal	Marksman.
J. A. Jackson	Sergeant	Marksman.
G. F. Marshburn	Private	Marksman.
V. B. Sutton	Sergeant	Marksman.
R. I. Sutton	Corporal	Marksman.
Paul Wallace	Cook	Marksman.

Company C.

J. S. Lewis	Captain	Marksman.
H. L. Daughtry	First Lieutenant	Marksman.
T. A. Avent	Corporal	Marksman.
H. L. Best	Private	Expert rifleman
N. D. Gwaltney	Sergeant	Marksman.
T. E. Hinton	Corporal	Marksman.
C. G. Inscore	Private	Marksman.
W. F. Jones	Corporal	Marksman.
Paul Merritt	Private	Marksman.
L. A. Pittman	Corporal	Marksman.
W. H. Riley	Private	Marksman.
Paul Viverette	Private	Marksman.
J. D. Winstead	Sergeant	Marksman.

COMPANY D.

S. E. Malone	First Lieutenant	Expert rifleman
G. C. Dorr	Second Lieutenant	Marksman.
C. E. Aycock	Sergeant	Marksman.
B. E. Barnes	Private	Marksman.
J. H. Capps	Private	Marksman.
B. W. Cox	Sergeant	Marksman.
J. H. Game	Quartermaster Sergeant	Marksman.
C. M. Gurley	Private	Marksman.
M. Hinnant	Corporal	Marksman.
H. Hinnant	Private	Marksman.
J. E. Parker	Private	Marksman.
M. Lynch	Private	Marksman.
R. A. Pearce	Cook	Marksman.
R. H. Perry	Corporal	Marksman.
G. L. Pittman	Sergeant	Expert rifleman
H. M. Powell	Private	Marksman.
T. F. Rackley	Corporal	Marksman.
S. G. Rackley	Corporal	Marksman.
N. M. Stafford	Private	Marksman.
A. M. Tyner	Private	Marksman.
Ralph Wade	Corporal	Expert rifleman
Jas. Williford	Private	Marksman.

COMPANY E.

A. O. Clement	Captain	Marksman.
B. F. Adams	First Lieutenant	Marksman.
O. C. Jones	Second Lieutenant	Expert rifleman
Chas. Adams	Corporal	Marksman.
W. H. Adams	Sergeant	Marksman.
A. B. Combs	Sergeant	Marksman.
J. B. Dunn	Private	Marksman.
L. T. Glisson	Private	Marksman.
Albert Lee	Private	Marksman.
R. P. Satterfield	Sergeant	Marksman.
F. L. Vaughan	Corporal	Marksman.
R. Warrick	Private	Marksman.

COMPANY F.

Paul Watson	Captain	Marksman.
D. R. Culbert	Corporal	Marksman.
R. D. Florence	Private	Marksman.
W. R. House	Private	Marksman.
J. M. Hudson	Private	Marksman.
G. T. Hall	Private	Marksman.
N. S. McNeill	Corporal	Marksman.
J. L. McFayden	Private	Marksman.
Lee Pittman	Musician	Marksman.
J. H. Tindall	Private	Marksman.

COMPANY G.

R. B. Cowell	Captain	Marksman.
W. B. Foreman	Corporal	Marksman.
E. H. Hobbs	Private	Marksman.
G. L. Hodges	Sergeant	Marksman.
G. Langley	Private	Marksman.
W. B. Whitley	Private	Marksman.
J. E. Williams	Private	Marksman.
Ray Woolard	Private	Marksman.

COMPANY H.

C. M. Faircloth	Captain	Marksman.
W. T. Beaman	Corporal	Marksman.
F. M. Bennett	Musician	Marksman.
O. R. Bizzell	Sergeant	Marksman.
W. H. Boyette	Cook	Marksman.
G. B. Cooper	Sergeant	Expert rifleman
J. P. Eldridge	Private	Marksman.
W. L. Gilbert	Private	Marksman.
J. I. Gainey	Corporal	Marksman.
W. A. Hawley	Private	Marksman.
L. G. Honeycutt	Private	Marksman.
J. S. Howard	Corporal	Marksman.
Anson Jackson	Private	Marksman.
E. F. Kennedy	Private	Marksman.
A. H. Kerr	Private	Marksman.
D. T. O'Quinn	Corporal	Marksman.
W. M. Page	Private	Marksman.
Eddie Warren	Private	Marksman.
C. B. Weeks	Quartermaster Sergeant	Marksman.
C. W. Westbrook	Private	Marksman.
H. T. Wynne	Private	Marksman.

COMPANY I.

W. S. Privott	Captain	Marksman.
E. L. Gray	Sergeant	Marksman.
R. K. Hall	Cook	Marksman.
R. I. Morris	Sergeant	Marksman.
C. L. Jones	Cook	Marksman.
G. R. Nixon	Private	Marksman.
W. B. Rea	Private	Marksman.
Ermon Simpson	Private	Marksman.
J. F. White	Quartermaster Sergeant	Marksman.

COMPANY K.

C. F. Batts	Captain	Marksman.
Geo. I. Allen	Quartermaster Sergeant	Marksman.
J. E. Beland	Private	Marksman.
H. C. Hales	Private	Marksman.

H. B. Lewis	Private	Marksman.
B. C. Newsom	Private	Marksman.
J. G. Overman	Private	Marksman.
C. E. Riley	Fifth Corporal	Marksman.
G. D. Strickland	Private	Marksman.
Joe Toney	Sergeant	Marksman.
C. F. Webb	Cook	Marksman.
J. W. Williamson	Private	Marksman.
B. H. Winborne	Musician	Marksman.

COMPANY L.

J. B. Malloy	Captain	Expert rifleman
J. L. Shaw	Second Lieutenant	Marksman.
D. A. Barlow	First Lieutenant	Marksman.
G. H. Beard	Corporal	Marksman.
L. E. Campbell		Marksman.
L. M. Currie	Sergeant	Marksman.
W. H. Freeman	Private	Marksman.
A. M. Hall	Corporal	Marksman.
J. E. Hall	Private	Marksman.
J. D. Jackson	Private	Marksman.
E. A. McGilvary	Private	Marksman.
J. T. McRainey	Private	Marksman.
D. W. Williford	Private	Marksman.

COMPANY M.

D. C. Parker	Captain	Marksman.
J. M. Riley	First Lieutenant	Marksman.
J. W. Bain	Corporal	Marksman.
R. C. Godwin	Private	Marksman.
W. D. Holland	Corporal	Marksman.
A. J. Holmes	Private	Marksman.
D. Johnson	Private	Marksman.
Manly Jones	Private	Marksman.
H. K. Matthews	Private	Marksman.
L. E. McKay	Sergeant	Marksman.
L. G. McLamb	Private	Marksman.
R. W. Warren	Private	Marksman.

SECOND INFANTRY—PISTOL FIRING.

H. C. Bragaw	Colonel	Marksman.
C. B. Elliott	Major	Marksman.
T. S. Pace	Major	Expert.
S. Cohen	Captain	Marksman.
S. P. Clark	Second Lieutenant	Marksman.
A. L. C. Hill	Captain, Co. B	Marksman.
J. I. Brown	First Lieutenant, Co. B	Expert.
A. E. Dixon	Second Lieutenant, Co. C	Marksman.
H. L. Doughtry	Lieutenant, Co. C	Expert.
G. C. Derr	Lieutenant, Co. D	Marksman.

A. O. Clement..............Captain, Co. E..................Sharpshooter.
B. F. Adams................Lieutenant, Co. E..............Expert.
O. C. Jones..................Lieutenant, Co. E..............Expert.
R. B. Cowell.................Captain, Co. G.................Marksman.
C. M. Faircloth.............Captain, Co. H.................Expert.
G. K. Hobbs.................Lieutenant, Co. H..............Marksman.
J. B. Malloy.................Captain, Co. L.................Marksman.
J. M. Riley..................Lieutenant, Co. M..............Marksman.
S. E. Malone................Lieutenant, Co. D..............Expert.
H. L. Best..................Private, Co. C..................Marksman.
W. G. Barnes................Lieutenant, Co. K..............Marksman.

THIRD INFANTRY.

FIELD AND STAFF.

S. W. Minor.................Lieutenant Colonel..............Marksman.
A. McCullen.................Captain ....Marksman.
C. J. Smith..................Captain ....Marksman.
S. E. Winston...............First Lieutenant...............Marksman.
Willis Holding..............Sergeant Major.................Marksman.

COMPANY A.

Wade H. Phillips............Captain ....Marksman.
R. F. Chitty.................First Lieutenant...............Marksman.
W. K. Perrell................Private ....Marksman.
K. L. Ritzell.................Private ....Marksman.
B. R. Yarborough............First Sergeant.................Marksman.

COMPANY B.

W. F. Moody.................Captain ....Expert rifleman
E. B. Parish.................First Lieutenant...............Expert rifleman
W. C. Holder................Second Lieutenant.............Marksman.
L. A. Allen..................Private ....Marksman.
A. P. Arnold.................Private ....Marksman.
T. J. Barefoot...............Private ....Marksman.
C. F. Cutts..................First Sergeant.................Marksman.
A. R. Chalmers..............Private ....Marksman.
C. B. Crabtree...............Musician ....Marksman.
W. F. Dannilley..............Private ....Sharpshooter.
M. L. Hagwood..............Private ....Marksman.
R. Holderfield...............Sergeant ....Sharpshooter.
P. S. Hunter.................Corporal ....Marksman.
G. W. Hunt..................Private ....Marksman.
R. G. Justice................Private ....Marksman.
L. N. Layton................Corporal ....Marksman.
R. E. Lee...................Corporal ....Marksman.
B. S. Parker.................Sergeant ....Marksman.
H. N. Parish.................Corporal ....Marksman.
J. A. Pennington............Private ....Marksman.
Jack Russell.................Art. ....Marksman.

R. H. Riddle	Private	Marksman.
H. C. Simons	Sergeant	Expert rifleman
J. W. Williams	Sergeant	Marksman.
E. L. Bridgers	Private	Marksman.

COMPANY C.

O. L. Kimball	Private	Marksman.
O. E. Murphey	Private	Marksman.
C. E. Hayes	Private	Marksman.

COMPANY D.

E. F. Collins	Private	Marksman.
C. E. Gilliam	Sergeant	Marksman.
Percy Gupton	Private	Marksman.
Ale Jones	Private	Marksman.
R. H. Jones	Corporal	Marksman.
E. I. Lancaster	Private	Marksman.
G. C. Lancaster	Private	Marksman.
J. J. Lancaster	Sergeant	Marksman.
E. S. Merritt	Sergeant	Marksman.
D. E. Radford	Private	Marksman.
J. T. West	Corporal	Marksman.

COMPANY E.

T. G. Stem	Captain	Marksman.
H. B. Arnette	Sergeant	Marksman.
W. H. Bowlings	Private	Marksman.
L. W. Bynum	Sergeant	Marksman.
L. C. Gooch	First Sergeant	Marksman.
J. H. Liner	Private	Marksman.
M. C. Parham	Corporal	Marksman.
Grady Ragland	Private	Marksman.

COMPANY F.

I. H. Kearney	Captain	Marksman.
E. M. Edwards	First Lieutenant	Marksman.
G. R. Holmes	Sergeant	Marksman.
L. B. May	Sergeant	Marksman.
I. Ayscue	Private	Marksman.
W. G. Wilder	Corporal	Marksman.
G. G. Cooper	Corporal	Marksman.
C. C. Kearney	Quartermaster Sergeant	Marksman.
C. J. Barrow	Corporal	Marksman.
B. P. Hinton	Private	Marksman.
B. H. May	Private	Marksman.
H. C. Hight	Private	Marksman.
J. R. Cooke	Corporal	Marksman.

COMPANY G.

R. G. Gladstone	Captain	Marksman.
R. G. Wray	First Sergeant	Expert rifleman

J. L. Beavers	Private	Marksman.
J. R. Gunn	Private	Marksman.
C. W. Huffines	Private	Marksman.
J. A. Moorefield	Private	Expert rifleman
W. H. Smith	Private	Marksman.
C. L. Tish	Musician	Marksman.
M. D. Watters	Private	Marksman.

COMPANY H.

J. C. Newell	Private	Marksman.

COMPANY I.

J. C. Freeman	Captain	Marksman.
W. B. Ellis	Private	Marksman.
Tom McAdams	Sergeant	Expert rifleman
B. C. Rogers	Sergeant	Marksman.

COMPANY L.

J. S. Burton	Sergeant	Marksman.
S. J. Crawford	Private	Marksman.
J. T. Fowler	Art.	Marksman.
E. O. Harris	Sergeant	Marksman.
M. C. Owens	Private	Marksman.
A. E. Perry	Art.	Marksman.
R. J. Westmoreland	Corporal	Marksman.

COMPANY M.

C. F. Bennett	Lieutenant	Marksman.
T. B. Edwards	First Sergeant	Marksman.
Frank Gallahughes	Private	Marksman.
O. L. Johnson	Private	Marksman.
Geo. Kerr	Private	Marksman.
E. F. Kerr	Corporal	Marksman.
W. J. Mitchell	Private	Marksman.

THIRD INFANTRY—PISTOL FIRING.

W. R. Miller	First Lieutenant	Marksman.
S. E. Winston	First Lieutenant	Marksman.
B. Durham	Captain	Marksman.
I. H. Kearney	Captain, Co. F	Marksman.
R. G. Gladstone	Captain, Co. G	Marksman.
J. H. Mobley	Second Lieutenant, Co. G	Marksman.
A. A. Russell	Second Lieutenant, Co. I	Marksman.
C. H. Newby	First Lieutenant, Co. L	Marksman.
M. B. Abernathy	Captain, Medical Corps	Marksman.
W. A. Holding	Sergeant Major	Marksman.

By order of the Commander in Chief:

R. L. LEINSTER,
The Adjutant General.

STATE OF NORTH CAROLINA,
ADJUTANT GENERAL'S DEPARTMENT,

GENERAL ORDERS No. 17. RALEIGH, 28 October, 1911.

I. In order to reward in a measure members of the North Carolina National Guard for long and faithful service, commencing January 1, 1912, and thereafter, service badges will be awarded to those officers and enlisted men whose names appear either on the active or retired list and who have been in the active military service of the State as herein specified:

To an officer or enlisted man who has performed honest and faithful continuous service for ten years or between ten and fifteen years, a bronze badge.

To an officer or enlisted man who has performed honest and faithful continuous service for fifteen years or between fifteen and twenty years, a silver badge.

To an officer or enlisted man who has performed honest and faithful continuous service for twenty years or between twenty and twenty-five years, a silver badge with one silver bar.

To an officer or enlisted man who has performed honest and faithful continuous service for twenty-five years, a gold badge; and for every five years additional service, a gold bar will be added.

In computing service, war service in the Army or Navy of the United States or Confederate States will be considered as continuous service within the meaning of this order.

To secure a badge, written application must be made to the Adjutant General setting forth date of original enlistment or commission and record of service.

By order of the Commander in Chief: R. L. LEINSTER,
The Adjutant General.

STATE OF NORTH CAROLINA,
ADJUTANT GENERAL'S DEPARTMENT,

GENERAL ORDERS No. 18. RALEIGH, 6 November, 1911.

I. Section 25c, North Carolina National Guard Regulations, which was added to the regulations by General Orders, No. 9, A. G. O. N. C., Raleigh, May 11, 1909, is hereby revoked, and the following substituted therefor:

Section 25c, Regulations, N. C. N. G.—The commanding officer of each company and band of infantry will make out on blank forms furnished by the Adjutant General's Department monthly report of drills and inspection, and forward copy of same to the regimental adjutant on or before the fifth day of each month for the month preceding. Regimental adjutants will consolidate these reports on blanks furnished by the Adjutant General's Department and forward to the regimental commander, who will sign report and forward same to the Adjutant General not later than the fifteenth day of each month.

The commanding officer of each company of Coast Artillery will forward monthly report of drills and inspection to the Adjutant of the Coast Artillery Corps, who will consolidate the reports and forward to the Commanding Officer, Coast Artillery Corps, who will sign same and forward to the Adjutant General by the fifteenth of each month.

The commanding officer of each company and detachment of sanitary troops will forward monthly report of drills and inspection to the Surgeon General not later than the tenth day of each month.

The commanding officer of each division of Naval Militia will forward monthly report of drills and inspection to the chief of staff, Naval Brigade, who will consolidate the reports and forward report, properly signed by the commanding officer, Naval Brigade, to the Adjutant General not later than the fifteenth of each month.

By order of the Commander in Chief:

R. L. LEINSTER,
The Adjutant General.

STATE OF NORTH CAROLINA,
ADJUTANT GENERAL'S DEPARTMENT,

GENERAL ORDERS, NO. 19. RALEIGH, 14 November, 1911.

I. In accordance with Section 4853 of the Military Code, the new Infantry Drill Regulations, approved by the War Department, August 19, 1911, are hereby adopted for the government of the North Carolina National Guard.

II. The new Infantry Drill Regulations require First Sergeants to be armed with sabre and revolver. Until sabres and revolvers can be issued, First Sergeants will at all formations wear belt and bayonet.

III. So much of the Infantry Drill Regulations of 1904 covering the use of the present pack will continue in force until the new Infantry pack can be issued, which will likely be a year or more.

By order of the Commander in Chief:

R. L. LEINSTER,
The Adjutant General.

STATE OF NORTH CAROLINA,
ADJUTANT GENERAL'S DEPARTMENT,

GENERAL ORDERS NO. 20. RALEIGH, 28 November, 1911.

I. The Secretary of War has ruled that the title to all arms, uniforms, and other equipment issued to the Organized Militia from funds appropriated by Congress for arming and equipping the Militia rests in the United States, and that a State has no insurable interest in the property. In view of this decision of the Secretary of War, it is not deemed necessary that organization commanders have Government property insured, and it is left optional with company and detachment commanders as to whether they will have State or Company property insured.

II. All orders and parts of orders in conflict with the above are hereby revoked.

By order of the Commander in Chief:

R. L. LEINSTER,
The Adjutant General.

STATE OF NORTH CAROLINA,
ADJUTANT GENERAL'S DEPARTMENT,

GENERAL ORDERS NO. 21. RALEIGH, 6 December, 1911.

Upon completion of the company school course in Infantry Drill Regulations, an examination will be held by a board of officers. The board will be appointed and questions will be sent out from this office at the proper time.

The examination will be of two parts: Practical, with a weight of 25%; theoretical, with a weight of 75%.

The final mark given will be the average of the marks of the members of the board, who will mark independently.

Upon completion of the examination, the president of the board will certify the marks to the regimental commander, who will furnish each one passing with a grade of 75% or more the following certificate:

Date..............................

Name ....Rank ....Reg........Co......

has successfully passed the examination covering pages.........to........

Infantry Drill Regulations, 1911, with a grade of........%.

(Signature)..............................

This certificate will exempt holder from examination for promotion in the subject-matter covered by the examination during the time such manual shall continue to be the authorized text.

Company commanders who act as instructors for at least five-sixths of the recitations of their company during the course will be given a certificate of proficiency, which shall exempt them likewise from future examination for promotion in the subject-matter covered by the course.

By order of the Commander in Chief: R. L. LEINSTER,
The Adjutant General.

STATE OF NORTH CAROLINA,
ADJUTANT GENERAL'S DEPARTMENT,

GENERAL ORDERS No. 22. RALEIGH, 18 December, 1911.

I. There shall be kept on file in field desk of every organization a large envelope, which shall be labeled "War Plans Envelope," and in which shall be filed all orders, instructions and necessary forms which relate to action in case of mobilization for U. S. service.

II. State inspectors will see that the "War Plans Envelope" file is kept up to date.

III. At present the following orders, instructions and forms should be in this envelope:

A copy of G. O. No. 15, A. G. O. N. C., 1911.
A copy of G. O. No. 126, War Department, 1911.
A copy of letter of instructions for "War Plans Envelope."
Sufficient enlistment blanks to permit the recruitment of organization to war strength.

By order of the Commander in Chief: R. L. LEINSTER,
The Adjutant General.

STATE OF NORTH CAROLINA,
ADJUTANT GENERAL'S DEPARTMENT,

GENERAL ORDERS NO. 23. RALEIGH, 30 December, 1911.

I. The following extracts taken from the reports of the Inspector General and the Assistant Inspector General for the current year are published for the information of all concerned. Colonel Thomas Stringfield, Inspector General, made the inspection of all organizations mentioned herein except the First and Second Companies, Coast Artillery Corps, which were inspected by Lieutenant Colonel H. D. Harper, Assistant Inspector General. Responsible officers are directed to note deficiencies reported and advise this office what corrective measures have been taken.

By order of the Commander in Chief: R. L. LEINSTER,
The Adjutant General.

1911 NOTES ON INSPECTION.

FIRST REGIMENT, N. C. N. G.

COMPANY A.

Officers present, 3; enlisted men present, 37; absent, 11; present and absent, 48; aggregate, 51.

This company is getting along fairly well. The facilities for the storage of the property were adequate, but the storeroom was not arranged in a way so as to facilitate the verification of property. The property room was very well cared for and in good condition. The property room needs more shelves, so the property can be stored neatly. With more attention paid to details by the officers, this company could be made one of the best in the Guard. Money value of property lost or not accounted for, $37.16.

COMPANY B.

Officers present, 2; enlisted men present, 43; absent, 5; present and absent, 48; aggregate, 50.

This company executed the manual of arms fairly well. Owing to the number of recruits, this organization did not make as good showing this year as it did last in drill and discipline. The company has moved headquarters from Dallas to Gastonia, and on that account a great many of the old men had been discharged and recruits enlisted to fill the vacancies. Efficiency of officers and men good and the property is well cared for. Money value of property lost or not accounted for, $57.95.

COMPANY C.

Officers present, 3; enlisted men present, 42; absent, 2; present and absent, 44; aggregate, 47.

Physical appearance, drill, and discipline very good. The men had not been properly instructed in the nomenclature of the rifle. The general condition of the company continues very satisfactory. The property was in good condition and properly arranged in lockers and packed neatly on shelves in the storeroom. Officers and noncommissioned officers are efficient, and a most commendable military spirit prevails. Money value of property lost or not accounted for, $58.81.

COMPANY D.

Mustered out and not inspected.

COMPANY E.

Officers present, 3; enlisted men present, 43; absent, 5; present and absent, 48; aggregate, 51.

The company has made substantial improvement in personnel, drill, and discipline. Improvement noted in armory, especially in the quartermaster room. The property was well arranged in storeroom, but the lockers were not arranged as systematically as they should be. The men were not well acquainted with the nomenclature of the rifle. Rifles and equipment in very good condition. Money value of property lost or not accounted for, $41.53.

COMPANY F.

Officers present, 2; absent, 1; enlisted men present, 37; absent, 8; present and absent, 45; aggregate, 48.

This company is getting along fairly well. The property is not all kept in the armory, as required by the regulations. In personnel, drill, and general appearance this company continues satisfactory. The men were not well acquainted with the nomenclature of the rifle. The quartermaster sergeant keeps no record of the property. Money value of property lost or not accounted for, $100.82.

COMPANY G.

Officers present, 3; enlisted men present, 44; absent, 6; present and absent, 50; aggregate, 53.

In general appearance, personnel, drill, discipline, and care of property this company continues in a very satisfactory condition. The company has moved into a new armory, which is furnished by the city and is quite an improvement over the old one; and with very little expense it could be made very attractive to the men. The property was in much better shape and better cared for than in former years. Money value of property lost or not accounted for, $88.76.

COMPANY H.

Officers present, 3; enlisted men present, 46; absent, 3; present and absent, 49; aggregate, 52.

In general appearance, personnel, drill, discipline, and care of property this company continues in a very satisfactory condition. The men should be more thoroughly instructed in the care and nomenclature of the rifle. The uniforms and equipment were not arranged with any system. The property is in good condition and well cared for. There was one gun carelessly lost by a private and should be paid for by him. Money value of property lost or not accounted for, $51.34.

COMPANY I.

Officers present, 3; enlisted men present, 37; absent, 3; present and absent, 40; aggregate, 43.

The general condition of this company continues satisfactory. Uniforms and equipment in lockers were arranged systematically and in such a manner as to facilitate the inspection and verification of property. Drill exercises consisted of the manual of arms and loading and firing, which was very snappy and good. The property was in good shape and well cared for. The officers are active and efficient. Money value of property lost or not accounted for, $15.27.

COMPANY K.

Officers present, 3; enlisted men present, 34; absent, 11; present and absent, 45; aggregate, 48.

The general appearance, personnel, drill, and discipline of the company continues in a very satisfactory condition. The rifles were in excellent condition, as were also the uniforms and equipment. The organization has a good armory and the books and records are well kept. The men were not acquainted with the nomenclature of the rifle. Money value of property lost or not accounted for, $118.85.

COMPANY L.

Officers present, 3; enlisted men present, 41; absent, 6; present and absent, 47; aggregate, 50.

The company continues in a very satisfactory condition. The armory and quartermaster room was in excellent condition. The property is kept in the armory and was well arranged for inspection. The officers and noncommissioned officers are active and efficient, and show much interest in the organization. The men should be more thoroughly instructed in the nomenclature of the rifle. Money value of property lost or not accounted for, $19.80.

COMPANY M.

Officers present, 3; enlisted men present, 45; absent, 7; present and absent, 52; aggregate, 55.

The general condition of the company continues very good. The new room for storage of property is quite well arranged for protection of the property and equipment not in use, all of which is kept in a very satisfactory manner by the quartermaster sergeant, who appears to be an efficient man. Officers and men show interest in the organization and the people of High Point seem to be proud of the company. Money value of property lost or not accounted for, $70.50.

SECOND REGIMENT, N. C. N. G.

COMPANY A.

Officers present, 3; enlisted men present, 37; absent, 3; present and absent, 40; aggregate, 43.

The general condition of this company continues satisfactory. Uniforms and equipment in lockers not arranged with any system. Men did not know nomenclature of rifle; noncommissioned officers not well instructed. A few men did not know how to load rifle. The company was just in the midst of moving into a new armory, which will be a great improvement over the old one. Reading room and club features connected with new armory, and captain says personnel much improved. Drill and discipline only fair. Money value of property lost or not accounted for, $73.13.

COMPANY B.

Officers present, 3; enlisted men present, 47; absent, 4; present and absent, 51; aggregate, 54.

This company has greatly improved over former inspection; in fact, it is in the best condition in my experience as inspecting officer. The quartermaster room was well arranged and in excellent condition; property in lockers should be so arranged as to expedite its verification. The addition of the quartermaster room made quite an improvement in the appearance of the armory. The general proficiency of the company in the various drills is very good; officers active and efficient. Money value of property lost or not accounted for, $48.35.

COMPANY C.

Officers present, 3; enlisted men present, 43; absent, 9; present and absent, 52; aggregate, 55.

The company is getting along very well. The guns are kept clean except a few dirty in the bore. The quartermaster room was dirty and the property was not arranged with any system. The general appearance very good, and most of the men knew nomenclature of rifle very well. The armory was in excellent condition. The officers are well informed, and there is great interest in the organization. Money value of property lost or not accounted for, $70.16.

COMPANY D.

Officers present, 3; enlisted men present, 47; absent, 3; present and absent, 50; aggregate, 53.

There has been very much improvement in the company over last year. The property was well cared for and in excellent condition. The men were well acquainted with the nomenclature of the rifle. In general appearance, personnel, drill, and discipline this company was in every way up to its usual standard of efficiency. The officers are competent and enthusiastic. Money value of property lost or not accounted for, $33.62.

COMPANY E.

Officers present, 3; enlisted men present, 54; present and absent, 54; aggregate, 57.

This company has made improvement. The property room was neat and everything arranged so as to facilitate the inspection and verification of property. The men did not know nomenclature of rifle very well. The armory was in excellent condition. Books and papers were well kept and the company is well officered; the captain enthusiastic and a willing worker. Money value of property lost or not accounted for, $45.50.

COMPANY F.

Officers present, 3; enlisted men present, 41; absent, 8; present and absent, 49; aggregate, 52.

In general appearance, personnel, and care of property this company has made marked improvement over former inspections. There is a lack of systematic arrangement of the equipment in the lockers and of property in the storeroom, but it was all properly packed away and fairly well protected. It was evident that the quartermaster sergeant had worked faithfully to improve conditions, but lacked proper arrangement to show best results. All of the property is not kept in the armory, but the new captain says that next year will find everything in first-class condition. The men did not know nomenclature of rifle. The officers are capable and interested, and under them, I believe, the company will advance in drill and efficiency. Money value of property lost or not accounted for, $61.00.

COMPANY G.

Officers present, 2; enlisted men present, 37; absent, 5; present and absent, 42; aggregate, 44.

This company is getting along fairly well, but is not improving as it should. The property was in very good condition, but too much was crowded in the lockers. At present there is much need of system to be inaugurated in this command, which will undoubtedly be accomplished when the officers, who are new to their positions, get more familiar with the affairs. The men did not know nomenclature of rifle very well. Money value of property lost or not accounted for, $77.52.

COMPANY H.

Officers present, 2; absent, 1; enlisted men present, 43; absent, 3; present and absent, 46; aggregate, 49.

At inspection the company showed to excellent advantage, both as to general appearance and knowledge of their duties. The men were well acquainted with nomenclature of rifle. The property was in excellent condition, well cared for, and systematically arranged for inspection. The books and papers are very well kept and the company excellently officered and maintain a very satisfactory standard of discipline and efficiency. Money value of property lost or not accounted for, $2.67.

COMPANY I.

Officers present, 2; absent, 1; enlisted men present, 41; absent, 2; present and absent, 43; aggregate, 46.

The personnel and general appearance is good. The noncommissioned officers are deficient in instructions. The men did not know the nomenclature of the rifle; the property is not all kept in the armory, as required by the regulations. The quartermaster room was much improved and the property well arranged—better care taken of it than in former years. Drill and discipline only fair. Money value of property lost or not accounted for, $82.89.

COMPANY K.

Officers present, 3; enlisted men present, 38; absent, 7; present and absent, 45; aggregate, 48.

Uniforms and equipments thrown into lockers without any system. The property is not all kept in the armory, as required by the regulations. The discipline was poor, as the men talked and cheered in ranks; drill in close order and extended order very good. The men did not know nomenclature of the rifle. Owing to the changes in officers from year to year, the company was not in a position to make as good showing as it otherwise would. The property not issued is stored in a fairly orderly manner, but somewhat mixed and without system. Money value of property lost or not accounted for $286.81.

COMPANY L.

Officers present, 3; enlisted men present, 43; absent, 7; present and absent, 50; aggregate, 53.

The general appearance was very good and soldierly. The uniforms and equipment shown on the men were in excellent condition. The storeroom as improved makes the arrangement for the care and protection of property very satisfactory. Owing to lack of time, the company only drilled in the manual of arms and firings, which was very good. The men should be more thoroughly instructed in the nomenclature of the rifle and noncommissioned officers' school should be more regularly held. Money value of property lost or not accounted for, $78.83.

THIRD REGIMENT, N. C. N. G.

COMPANY A.

Officers present, 3; enlisted men present, 41; absent, 1; present and absent, 42; aggregate, 45.

In personnel, drill, discipline, and general appearance, this company continues very satisfactory. The property is well cared for and in excellent condition. The quartermaster room was neat and clean and the property was so arranged as to be easily verified, and everything went to show that there was much interest in the organization. Money value of property lost or not accounted for, $36.64.

COMPANY B.

Officers present, 2; absent, 1; enlisted men present, 42; absent, 21; present and absent, 63; aggregate, 66.

This company continues in a very satisfactory condition. The property was in good condition and well cared for. The men were very good in the nomenclature of the rifle. The quartermaster room was in very good condition, but there was too much property in the quartermaster room to be readily verified at inspection. General efficiency very good. Money value of property lost or not accounted for, $16.65.

COMPANY C.

Officers present, 2; absent, 1; enlisted men present, 40; absent, 16; present and absent, 56; aggregate, 59.

In personnel and general appearance this company has improved very much over last inspection. The organization has secured a new armory, which can be made very satisfactory if the space is properly utilized. The men are permitted to carry some of the property out of the armory, and consequently there is considerable shortage. The captain should be required to obey the regulations in regard to keeping property in the armory. The men were not instructed in the nomenclature of rifle. The officers can make this company one of the best in the regiment. Money value of property lost or not accounted for, $180.24.

COMPANY D.

Officers present, 3; enlisted men present, 44; absent, 8; present and absent, 52; aggregate, 55.

This company has improved in personnel and general appearance over previous years. The captain has secured a new quartermaster room and is moving the property not in use into it, which will add greatly to the convenience as well as giving adequate storage for all property. The men should be more thoroughly instructed in the nomenclature of the rifle. The general proficiency of the company in the various drills is good. The books and records could be improved. Money value of property lost or not accounted for $42.56.

COMPANY E.

Officers present, 3; enlisted men present, 35; absent, 12; present and absent, 47; aggregate, 50.

This company shows a steady improvement over previous years. Property was in good condition and the quartermaster room was neat and clean and everything arranged so as to facilitate the verification of property. Drill in close and extended order fair. Men did not know nomenclature of rifle. The officers are interested, and under them, I believe, the company will continue to improve. Money value of property lost or not accounted for, $127.17.

COMPANY F.

Officers present, 3; enlisted men present, 45; absent, 2; present and absent, 47; aggregate, 50.

The company is getting along nicely. Nearly all the men were present at inspection, several of them coming a considerable distance and at great personal inconvenience and expense. Instruction in the several forms of drill received proper attention, as was manifested by the proficiency therein of the officers and men. This company needs a new armory very much; the one occupied at present being entirely unsuited for the purpose. I was told by the captain that arrangements had been made by which the company would soon get a new armory. The officers and noncommissioned officers are enthusiastic and informed. Money value of property lost or not accounted for, $9.58.

COMPANY G.

Officers present, 3; enlisted men present, 36; absent, 5; present and absent, 41; aggregate, 44.

The general appearance shows steady improvement over previous years. The men were soldierly and the appearance of the State property was most commendable. The personnel, drill, discipline, and general efficiency continue very satisfactory. The men should be more thoroughly instructed in the nomenclature of the rifle. The company is well officered and a splendid military spirit prevails. Money value of property lost or not accounted for, $88.09.

COMPANY H.

Officers present, 3; enlisted men present, 26; absent, 18; present and absent, 44; aggregate, 47.

This company does not show any improvement, but, on the contrary, the whole appearance of this command indicated a laxity of discipline, and it is certainly not efficient as at present constituted. The property is allowed to be taken out of the armory, and as the captain lives some distance out of town, he doesn't seem able to keep up with it. The guns were in fair condition, but the meat cans and the whole mess kit were dirty and rusty. I was told by the captain that the company did not get the proper encouragement or support from the citizens of the town and it was hard to keep the company up to a proper standard. Unless marked improvement is shown in a very short time, it would be for the best interest of the service to muster out this company. Money value of property lost or not accounted for, $122.97.

COMPANY I.

Officers present, 3; enlisted men present, 39; absent, 6; present and absent, 45; aggregate, 48.

Great improvement in the company over any previous inspection. The appearance was soldierly and pleasing, and care of equipment most marked. The lockers and quartermaster room were in excellent condition. The officers and noncommissioned officers are interested and painstaking and a most commendable military spirit prevails. Money value of property lost or not accounted for, $22.31.

COMPANY K.

Officers present, 2; enlisted men present, 24; absent, 2; present and absent, 26; aggregate, 28.

The expiration of enlistment of a number of the men and the refusal of most of them to reënlist, leaves this company far below the legal minimum strength, and from what I could learn from talking with the officers, they had doubts as to whether the company could be recruited in Weldon. Enthusiasm is evidently at a very low ebb and the citizens seem to have lost interest in its organization. Unless the company can be recruited in a very short time, I question the advisability of continuing it longer in the service. Money value of property lost or not accounted for, $71.77.

COMPANY L.

Officers present, 3; enlisted men present, 34; absent, 6; present and absent, 40; aggregate, 43.

This company is getting along fairly well, but it lacks the proper military spirit. It is evident that there were a large number of recruits in rank and the inspection was unsteady. The lockers and quartermaster room were in excellent condition and everything so arranged as to facilitate the verification of property. Drill and discipline only fair.. Men did not know nomenclature of rifle. The company is to move into a new armory, and it is hoped that the change will put new spirit in the organization and prove beneficial. Money value of property lost or not accounted for, $54.99.

COMPANY M.

Officers present, 3; enlisted men present, 34; absent, 5; present and absent, 39; aggregate, 42.

General condition of this company continues very good. Uniforms and equipments in lockers were not arranged with any system. The quartermaster room was in excellent condition, and everything so arranged as to facilitate the verification of the property. Some property is taken from the armory, which should not be allowed. The books and papers are very well kept. The officers and noncommissioned officers are progressive, enthusiastic, and popular, which keeps the company up to its usual standard of efficiency. Money value of property lost or not accounted for, $175.57.

BAND, FIRST INFANTRY, N. C. N. G.

This band is in excellent condition; property well cared for and in good condition; lockers neat and clean; quartermaster room in good condition. The musicians appear to be well instructed and to understand their duties, but require further instructions in the school of the soldier. Most of the instruments are old, but clean and well cared for.

BAND, SECOND INFANTRY, N. C. N. G.

This band has made great improvements in general appearance and personnel. The property is well cared for and in good condition, but is not all kept in the armory, as required by the regulations. The musicians are very well instructed and seem to understand their duties, but need more instructions in the school of the soldier. The instruments were fairly well cared for and in fair condition.

BAND, THIRD INFANTRY, N. C. N. G.

Physical appearance of men good. The property is in good condition and well cared for, but it is not all kept in the armory, as required by regulations. The quartermaster room was in very good condition. The musicians appear to be well instructed and understand their duties, but should have more instructions in the school of the soldier. Instruments clean and well cared for.

FIRST COMPANY, C. A. C.

Judging from the Inspector General's repart of last year, this company has not improved. There seems to be no love for the captain by the men. The organization is still intact and can be made an excellent company. I recommend that the appropriation be allowed.

SECOND COMPANY, C. A. C.

No recommendations for this company. It was the best the Inspector ever saw in this State. I recommend that the appropriation be allowed.

THIRD COMPANY, C. A. C.

The company has made improvement over last year in general appearance, personnel, and drill. The property was much better cared for and the quartermaster room was in good shape and everything well arranged for inspection. Some of the hats were mashed out of shape by being carried to the camps in dress-suit cases. The officers are energetic and efficient.

FOURTH COMPANY, C. A. C.

The company is just moving into a new armory and did not have property arranged as it should have been. There is ample room for the proper arrangement and storage of all the property, and the captain should be required to keep the property in the armory to prevent loss and shortage. The books and papers are only fairly well kept. Nomenclature of rifle poor.

FIFTH COMPANY, C. A. C.

This company since being transferred to the C. A. C. has improved very much. The officers are efficient and have the proper military spirit to make this one of the best companies in the Guard. The property was in good condition and well cared for, except meat cans, knives and forks dirty and rusty. Men did not know nomenclature of rifle. The company should have haversack hooks and canteen straps.

Circulars

STATE OF NORTH CAROLINA,
ADJUTANT GENERAL'S DEPARTMENT,

CIRCULAR No. 1. RALEIGH, January 14, 1911.

I. The following notes on conditions of organizations made by the Inspector General during the inspection of the North Carolina National Guard for the year 1910 are published for the information and guidance of all concerned.

II. Commanding and responsible officers will take the necessary steps to correct any deficiencies that may exist.

By order of the Commander in Chief: R. L. LEINSTER,
Adjutant General.

FIRST INFANTRY.

COMPANY A.

Officers present, 1; officers absent, 1; enlisted men present, 34; absent, 6; present and absent, 40; aggregate, 42.

The captain resigning just before the inspection, and the first lieutenant not being present, left the company in command of the second lieutenant, who did all he could to make the company show to advantage. The property was only fairly well kept and in fair condition. The personnel appears to be very good, and with more attention paid by the commissioned officers will develop into a number one organization. Money value of property lost or not accounted for, $96.23.

COMPANY B.

Officers present, 3; enlisted men present, 46; absent, 9; present and absent, 55; aggregate, 58.

This company, which has been in the service only a short time, is very well drilled and made a most satisfactory showing. The property is well cared for and in good condition. The efficiency of the officers justifies the hope that this company will be made one of the best in the Guard. Money value of property lost or not accounted for, $6.57.

COMPANY C.

Officers present, 3; enlisted men present, 42; absent, 4; present and absent, 46; aggregate, 49.

This company continues to improve both in drill and discipline. The property was in good condition and well cared for. The company is well officered and a most commendable military spirit prevails. This organization should be furnished the O. D. uniform as soon as possible. Money value of property lost or not accounted for, $27.01.

COMPANY D.

Officers present, 3; enlisted men present, 44; absent, 5; present and absent, 49; aggregate, 52.

This company is being neglected. The captain does not devote the necessary time and attention to its management nor to the study of the drill regulations. The property is not well cared for and a great deal lost. A part of the property looked as if it had been purposely torn. Unless there are changes made and great improvement in condition in a very short time, the company should be mustered out of the service. Money value of property lost or not accounted for, $177.60.

COMPANY E.

Officers present, 3; enlisted men present, 47; absent, 2; present and absent, 49; aggregate, 52.

There has been very much improvement in this company in the past year, both as to drill and discipline. The company has moved into a new armory, which is a great improvement over the old one; the property in the quartermaster's room was in excellent condition, but the lockers were too much crowded. Apparently there was much more interest taken in company affairs by officers and men. Money value of property lost or not accounted for, $136.53.

COMPANY F.

Officers present, 3; enlisted men present, 41; absent, 2; present and absent, 43; aggregate, 46.

The company's captain resigned a short time before inspection, leaving the organization in a very bad condition; much property left out of armory and a great deal lost; guns and equipments were left in a dirty and rusty condition. Maj. W. G. Smith, retired, was placed in command, and in a short space of a few weeks looked up a good deal of the property and had same returned to the armory, and had guns and equipments in excellent condition for inspection. The organization as turned over to the new captain was in a very good condition. I believe under the present officers the company bids fair to be one of the best in the Guard. There was an inexcusable loss of property, evidently due to the previous captain's administration, that should call for action of higher authorities.

COMPANY G.

Officers present, 3; enlisted men present, 44; absent, 6; present and absent, 50; aggregate, 53.

The company has improved very much in general appearance, personnel, drill, and discipline over last year. The property was well arranged and in good condition, but there was too much loss of property. The recruits had not been drilled and instructed in nomenclature of rifle; officers active and efficient. Money value of property lost or not accounted for, $111.65.

COMPANY H.

Officers present, 3; enlisted men present, 43; absent, 3; present and absent, 46; aggregate, 49.

Appearance, personnel, drill, and discipline very much improved over last year; the property is well cared for and in good condition; the property loss is very small in this company. It speaks well for the organization. Money value of property lost or not accounted for, $3.32.

COMPANY I.

Officers present, 2; enlisted men present, 45; absent, 1; present and absent, 46; aggregate, 48.

This company had made improvements over last year in discipline and drill; the property was very well cared for and in good condition. The officers are interested and painstaking and should in a very short time have the company up to the highest standard of discipline and efficiency. Money value of property lost or not accounted for, $52.03.

COMPANY K.

Officers present, 2; enlisted men present, 37; absent, 6; present and absent, 43; aggregate 45.

This company has made marked improvement over last year in personnel, general appearance, discipline, and drill. The property is in much better condition, and shows more care taken of it. The captain is taking constant interest in the organization. Should appoint two musicians. The company has quite a number of blue uniforms that are too small for use. Money value of property lost or not accounted for, $56.98.

COMPANY L.

Officers present, 3; enlisted men present, 49; absent, 9; present and absent, 58; aggregate, 61.

This company has made much improvement over former inspections; the discipline and drill were very satisfactory, and demonstrated the fact that this is one of the best and most efficient companies in the Guard. The officers are well informed and there is great interest in the organization. The property is well cared for and in excellent condition. Money value of property lost or not accounted for, $20.70.

COMPANY M.

Officers present, 3; enlisted men present, 39; absent, 14; present and absent, 53; aggregate, 56.

In general appearance, personnel, drill and discipline this company has made marked improvements over former inspections. Property in good condition and well arranged in storeroom, but is not looked after as closely as should be. There is too much loss of property. Officers active and efficient, and a most commendable military spirit prevails. Money value of property lost or not accounted for, $106.63.

BAND.

Enlisted men present, 24; absent, 2; present and absent, 26; aggregate, 26.

This band is in excellent condition, property well cared for and in good condition; lockers neat and clean. Property room in good condition; a good organization. Money value of property lost or not accounted for, $57.44.

SECOND INFANTRY.

COMPANY A.

Officers present, 2; absent, 1; enlisted men present, 36; absent, 4; present and absent, 40; aggregate, 43.

This company shows improvement in personnel and general appearance over last inspection; the property is in good condition, but there is too much loss of property. There is much room for improvement in drill and discipline. Men did not know nomenclature of rifle; noncommissioned officers not well instructed. Captain thinks there will be much improvement in another year. Money value of property lost or not accounted for, $114.85.

COMPANY B.

Officers present, 3; enlisted men present, 45; absent, 3; present and absent, 48; aggregate, 51.

This company has greatly improved in personnel and general appearance. The great loss of property, I was informed, was due to former officers, who did not keep property in armory. I should think that a great deal of the property could be found by making the proper search. Captain very energetic, but men lack individual instruction. Money value of property lost or not accounted for, $226.18.

COMPANY C.

Officers present, 3; enlisted men present, 38; absent, 11; present and absent, 49; aggregate, 52.

This company has only been in service a short time and is very well drilled, and made a most satisfactory appearance at inspection. The men were fairly well acquainted with the nomenclature of the rifle. Did not comply with General Orders No. 3. The property is in good condition and well cared for. The officers are active and efficient. Money value of property lost or not accounted for, $8.84.

COMPANY D.

Officers present, 3; enlisted men present, 27; absent, 15; present and absent, 42; aggregate, 45.

This company is not up to its usual standard of efficiency. All the property had not been kept in the armory, as required by regulations, and was not arranged as systematically as at former inspection. The quartermaster's room should be made larger and the leaks in the armory should be repaired to prevent damage to property. Money value of property lost or not accounted for, $89.57.

COMPANY E.

Officers present, 3; enlisted men present, 53; absent, 5; present and absent, 58; aggregate, 61.

This company has made improvement. The property was in excellent condition and well cared for. The property room was neat and everything arranged so as to facilitate the inspection and verification of the property. Noncommissioned officers and men were well instructed in the nomenclature of the rifle, and military spirit is very strong in this company. Money value of property lost or not accounted for, $35.77.

COMPANY F.

Officers present, 3; enlisted men present, 47; absent, 3; present and absent, 50; aggregate, 53.

The captain does not obey the regulations in keeping the property in the armory. There was an inexcusable shortage of property, which should not be allowed. Very little if any attempt had been made to have property arranged for inspection as ordered. Unless there is more attention paid to the care of the property, and the men not allowed to carry property off, I doubt very seriously the advisability of continuing this company in the service. Money value of property lost or not accounted for, $197.

COMPANY G.

Officers present, 2; absent, 1; enlisted men present, 37; absent, 4; present and absent, 41; aggregate, 44.

In personnel, drill and discipline this company continues most satisfactory; but there is too much loss of property. Property crowded in lockers and not properly arranged in storerooms for inspection. The company is well officered and an excellent military spirit is maintained. Captain was absent. Money value of property lost or not accounted for, $142.36.

COMPANY H.

Officers present, 2; absent, 1; enlisted men present, 46; absent, 4; present and absent, 50; aggregate, 53.

At inspection the company showed to excellent advantage, both as to physical appearance and knowledge of duties. Noncommissioned officers were well instructed. The property was in very good condition and well taken care of. The company is well officered and in excellent condition. Money value of property lost or not accounted for, $4.74.

COMPANY I.

Officers present, 3; enlisted men present, 38; absent, 8; present and absent, 46; aggregate, 49.

This company has not improved as it should. Only about one-half of the men knew different parts of rifle. Drill and discipline poor. Company could not execute squads right correctly. Did not comply with General Orders No. 3. The property was in good condition and well cared for. Money value of property lost or not accounted for, $38.05.

COMPANY K.

Officers present, 3; enlisted men present, 42; absent, 1; present and absent, 43; aggregate, 46.

Through recent change in the officers of the company and the resignation of the captain, it was not in position to make as good showing as it did last year. The showing made at inspection was very satisfactory, as the men drilled well and the discipline was very good. Company does not comply with paragraph 28, Organized Militia Regulations. Did not comply with General Orders No. 3. Money value of property lost or not accounted for, $64.40.

COMPANY L.

Officers present, 3; enlisted men present, 47; absent, 3; present and absent, 50; aggregate, 53.

This company has made improvements over last year in discipline and drill as well as the care of property. The property is well cared for and in good condition. The company did not comply with General Orders No. 3. All the property is kept in the armory. Did not separate serviceable and unserviceable property. Improvements noted as having been made in the Quartermaster's storeroom. Money value of property lost or not accounted for, $21.16.

COMPANY M.

Officers present, 3; enlisted men present, 33; absent, 12; present and absent, 45; aggregate, 48.

This company is being neglected. The Captain does not give necessary time and attention to its management nor the study of the regulations. Property is not kept in armory. There is a great loss of property and the property is not looked after properly. The citizens of the town and county do not give the company their moral or any other kind of support. Unless there is a great improvement in a short while I recommend, for the best interest of the service, that this company be disbanded. Money value of property lost or not accounted for, $227.06.

BAND.

Enlisted men present, 19; absent, 1; present and absent, 20; aggregate, 20.

This band has made improvement in general appearance, but they do not take care of their property. The bin in which the property is kept was dirty and in disorder; did not look like it had been cleaned in a year. Did not comply with General Orders No. 3. There was no system of any kind. They make very good music. Money value of property lost or not accounted for, $105.13.

THIRD INFANTRY.

COMPANY A.

Officers present, 3; enlisted men present, 36; absent, 7; present and absent, 43; aggregate, 46.

This company has made improvement over last year in drill and discipline. The property is in good condition and well cared for. The company complied with General Orders No. 3, and it also complied with paragraph 28, Organized Militia, in that it has its full quota of noncommissioned officers. Money value of property lost or not accounted for, $41.12.

COMPANY B.

Officers present, 3; enlisted men present, 52; absent, 2; present and absent, 60; aggregate, 63.

The company shows improvement over last year; all property in good condition and well cared for; guns not clean. Complied with General Orders No. 3, and complied with paragraph 28, Organized Militia Regulations, in that it has its full quota of noncommissioned officers and men. The company has improved in discipline and drill. Money value of property lost or not accounted for, $97.40.

COMPANY C.

Officers present, 3; enlisted men present, 45; absent, 5; present and absent, 50; aggregate, 53.

This company has not improved; in fact, it is going down hill. The property is not kept in the armory and a great deal is lost. The men were not familiar with the guns. Discipline and drill only fair. Did not comply with General Orders No. 3, and does not comply with paragraph 28 of Organized Militia Regulations, in that there are only five corporals. Unless there is great improvement in the conditions the company should be mustered out of the service. Money value of property lost or not accounted for, $136.74.

COMPANY D.

Officers present, 3; enlisted men present, 44; absent, 7; present and absent, 51; aggregate, 54.

This company is getting along very well, but it is not improving as much as it should. The property is fairly well cared for, but all of it is not kept in the armory all the time. Did not comply with General Orders No. 3. Men did not know nomenclature of rifle very well. Drill and discipline only fair. Money value of property lost or not accounted for, $63.71.

COMPANY E.

Officers present, 2; absent, 1; enlisted men present, 38; absent, 8; present and absent, 46; aggregate, 49.

This company is getting along very well. The property is very well cared for and in good condition. Very few of the men know nomenclature of rifle. Did not comply with General Orders No. 3. Drill and discipline only fair. Noncommissioned officers were not propertly instructed. Money value of property lost or not accounted for, $52.05.

COMPANY F.

Officers present, 3; enlisted men present, 50; total men present, 50; aggregate, 53.

This company is getting along very well and making satisfactory improvement in discipline and drill. The property is well cared for, and there is very little loss of property. The company is well officered and the men make a very good military appearance. Money value of property lost or not accounted for, $3.36.

COMPANY G.

Officers present, 3; enlisted men present, 34; absent, 10; present and absent, 44; aggregate, 47.

This company has made improvement. The personnel, drill, discipline, care of property and general efficiency continue most satisfactory. The officers and men show constant interest in the organization, and the company makes a creditable military appearance. Money value of property lost or not accounted for, $46.35.

COMPANY H.

Officers present, 3; enlisted men present, 42; absent, 6; present and absent, 48; aggregate, 51.

This company has made substantial improvement over last year, and bids fair to make a good organization if it keeps up the improvement. Property is not all kept in the armory, as required by the regulations, and that accounts for the loss of property. Did not comply with General Orders No. 3. Money value of property lost or not accounted for, $121.40.

COMPANY I.

Officers present, 3; enlisted men present, 27; absent, 17; present and absent, 44; aggregate, 47.

This company has not improved as it should. The property is not all kept in the armory, as required by regulations, and as a consequence there is a great loss of the same. The attendance was poor, but it was a very bad night for inspection. The property in the armory was well arranged. Money value of property lost or not accounted for, $237.24.

COMPANY K.

Officers present, 3; enlisted men present, 39; absent, 3; present and absent, 42; aggregate, 45.

This company has made marked improvement in drill and discipline. The property is well cared for and in good condition. The organization is well officered, and the men made a soldierly appearance. Much interest is shown in the company by the citizens of the town. Money value of property lost or not accounted for, $5.11.

COMPANY L.

Officers present, 3; enlisted men present, 39; absent, 2; present and absent, 41; aggregate, 44.

This was the first appearance of this company for inspection, having been organized since last inspection. The property is well cared for and in good condition, and the showing the company made was most commendable and satisfactory. Money value of property lost or not accounted for, $3.48.

COMPANY M.

Officers present, 3; enlisted men present, 43; absent, 5; present and absent, 48; aggregate, 51.

This company has made improvement in drill and discipline. The lockers were overcrowded, and the Quartermaster's room was dirty and in disorder. There is ample room for storing all of the property and it should be systematically arranged. Men were well acquainted with nomenclature of rifle. Money value of property lost or not accounted for, $40.28.

BAND.

Enlisted men present, 21; absent, 3; present and absent, 24; aggregate, 24.

This band continues in a most satisfactory condition. Property kept in much better shape than last year and better cared for. The organization has built new lockers and is better prepared to care for the property. This is a very good band.

FIRST COMPANY, C. A. C.

Officers present, 3; enlisted men present, 35; absent, 5; present and absent, 40; aggregate, 43.

This organization is getting along very well. The general appearance, personnel and discipline very good. The men did not know nomenclature of rifle. Did not comply with General Orders No. 3. General efficiency of company very good. Money value of property lost or not accounted for, $25.08.

SECOND COMPANY, C. A. C.

Officers present, 3; enlisted men present, 35; absent, 8; present and absent, 43; aggregate, 46.

In general appearance, drill, and discipline this company made an excellent appearance. The lockers were dirty and in disorder. There was such an accumulation of old property that there was not room for it. The company does not comply with paragraph 32, Organized Militia Regulations. Money value of property lost or not accounted for, $10.49.

THIRD COMPANY, C. A. C.

Officers present, 3; enlisted men present, 34; absent, 15; present and absent, 49; aggregate, 52.

This company has not made the improvement it should in the past year. The men did not know the nomenclature of rifle. Drill and discipline only fair. The armory was not as neat as it should be and the lockers were in disorder. Money value of property lost or not accounted for, $63.78.

FOURTH COMPANY, C. A. C.

Officers present, 2; absent, 1; enlisted men present, 42; absent, 16; present and absent, 58; aggregate, 61.

This company is getting along fairly well. The noncommissioned officers lack proper instructions, and the men did not know nomenclature of rifle. Property was in good shape and well arranged for inspection, but there was too much loss of property. Money value of property lost or not accounted for, $188.19.

FIRST HOSPITAL CORPS.

Officers present, 1; enlisted men present, 10; absent, 1; present and absent, 11; aggregate, 12.

This hospital corps has improved. Have moved into a new armory and are well located. The room is amply large for the storage of all the property. A great many of the drugs are very old, inert and not fit for use. Money value of property lost or not accounted for, $47.01.

THIRD HOSPITAL CORPS.

Officers present, 1; enlisted men present, 10; absent, 2; present and absent, 12; aggregate, 13.

This hospital detachment has not improved over last year, but continues in a good condition. The property was in very good shape and very well taken care of. Great many of the drugs are very old, inert and not fit for use. Money value of property lost or not accounted for, $32.81.

BATTERY A, FIELD ARTILLERY.

Officers present, 4; enlisted men present, 52; absent, 11; present and absent, 63; aggregate, 67.

There has been improvement in the care of property, and all of the property is in much better shape than last year; but I am of the opinion that unless the appropriation be greatly increased that it will never amount to much as a battery. I think it would be best to change this organization into an infantry company or to a coast artillery corps company, for as it is now it is of no use to the State or the United States.

UNIFORMS.

The issue of the new olive drab uniform was made during the year, and it was gratifying to note the increased pride the men were taking in their general appearance. It was noticeable from captain to private by the neat appearance of the men at inspection. The khaki uniforms in a great many instances have not been cleaned and were in a dirty condition. A good many of the companies have profited by previous criticisms and had their uniforms properly cleaned. More attention should be paid by the officers to the care of clothing not in use to prevent loss and damage by moths.

PROPERTY ACCOUNTABILITY.

Some officers responsible for public property do not fully appreciate their responsibility, and have not properly maintained the system of keeping records of property in their charge. The property book furnished is in many cases not properly kept, and in some cases not kept at all. I learned that in some instances the enlisted men were allowed to carry public property away to their homes, and in some cases it was not returned. By such methods a considerable amount of property is lost. The shortage of property in a great many companies is excessive, and is a reflection not only upon the efficiency of the officers, but the personnel of the company as well.

Immediate steps should be taken by all officers, who have so much shortage of property, to effect a prompt adjustment, and an effort should be made to instill into the enlisted men proper ideas of the care of public property.

MILITARY COURTESY AND DISCIPLINE.

The absence of saluting officers by enlisted men was very noticeable. This, I think, was due to the large number of recruits found in each command. That the majority of the men are willing to learn, and attentive, is an evidence of the general good discipline maintained. There are many instances in which the salute was incorrectly given. The error can not properly be attributed to the men, but the officers responsible for their instruction.

GALLERY PRACTICE.

All of the companies in the Guard have the Gallery Practice Outfit, and most all of them have short indoor ranges; and the men as a whole seem to take great interest in gallery shooting, but are not as fully instructed in the aiming and sighting as they should be. More attention to the details of aiming and firing should be paid, so the soldier, after being thoroughly drilled on the indoor ranges, can go out on the target range and make good scores; and it would save a lot of ammunition, which in many cases is needlessly expended.

ARMORIES.

Most of the changes and improvements in the different armories will be found under notes on inspection. In order for the better care of property it will be necessary for some of the companies to make improvement in their property rooms. The appearance of moths in most of the armories should be looked after and prevented from getting in the new olive drab uniforms.

ARMS AND EQUIPMENT.

Rifles as a whole were in excellent condition. The care, condition and appearance of property issued was shown to be in the best condition within my knowledge as inspecting officer. I am glad to say that there are only a few of the company officers who do not compel the men to take the proper care of the rifles. One of the most important things for an infantry soldier to learn is how to keep his rifle in perfect condition.

BOOKS AND PAPERS.

Several of the companies are very efficient in keeping books and papers, but there are a great many that are incomplete in regard to system. Some companies have introduced the card system, which is very good. The correspondence book is not kept by all the companies as it should be, and more attention to bookkeeping should be required, but I am glad to say that there is much improvement along this line.

DRILL.

Close order drill in some companies very good; in others only fair, and in some very poor. The same condition existed in extended order drill. A great many company commanders evidently have not read the drill regulations governing inspections, consequently they were at a loss to know what to do after marching their companies to place of inspection. This statement does not apply to all company commanders by any means, as some of them had their companies well in hand and gave them proper commands in every instance. The officers, with a few exceptions, are competent, but it is useless to try to conceal the fact that some of them are not diligent in the performance of their duties.

STATE ARSENAL.

Since last inspection the property from the old State Arsenal has been moved into a new and modern building and is in charge of Col. Thos. R. Robertson, Chief of Ordnance, who has everything pertaining to his department in excellent condition. The books pertaining to this department were in excellent condition, and the property was so arranged as to facilitate the filing of requisitions with the least possible delay. Receipts for all property which had been issued were properly filed.

To the officers of the North Carolina National Guard I am under many obligations for courtesies shown me during my tour of inspection. I am also under obligations to Lieut. C. M. Butler, U. S. A., for much valuable information and assistance.

Very respectfully, THOS. STRINGFIELD,
Col. and I. G., N. C. N. G.

STATE OF NORTH CAROLINA,
ADJUTANT GENERAL'S DEPARTMENT,
CIRCULAR No. 2. RALEIGH, February 18, 1911.

Referring to General Orders No. 1, current series, providing for the inspection of the organization of the North Carolina National Guard, the attention of company commanders is especially directed to the necessity for having rifles and accoutrements perfectly clean and neat.

To have this property in excellent condition will add very much to an organization's efficiency record.

By order of the Commander in Chief: R. L. LEINSTER,
Adjutant General.

STATE OF NORTH CAROLINA,
ADJUTANT GENERAL'S DEPARTMENT,
CIRCULAR No. 3. RALEIGH, February 22, 1911.

The following report of Lieutenant Shaw, U. S. Navy, of duty in connection with the summer cruise of the North Carolina Naval Militia, on board the U. S. ships *Elfrida* and *Dupont*, is published for the information and guidance of all concerned.

By order of the Commander in Chief: R. L. LEINSTER,
The Adjutant General.

I reported on July 6, 1910, to the Commanding Officer of the North Carolina Naval Militia on board the *Elfrida*, and was informed that the original plan conveyed in an order of the Adjutant General, for each of the five divisions to cruise one week, beginning July 1, had been changed. The next cruise planned was for the Windsor Division, beginning July 13. On July 12 the Commanding Officer of the Windsor Division telegraphed that his division could not cruise. His explanatory letter to Commander C. D. Bradham was to the effect that his men would not leave their business unless assurance was given that pleasure would be combined with duty. He referred to the discomforts of the *Prairie* cruise two years ago, which he said had nearly broken up his organization.

The Elizabeth City and Plymouth Divisions were the first to cruise. The *Elfrida* was sent to Plymouth and the *Dupont* to Elizabeth City, and the divisions came on board on July 24. Both ships then returned to New Bern to take part in the Bi-centennial Celebration, remaining there from July 25 to 30. On July 26 the crews paraded as infantry, and during the week a routine of ship drills was carried out. On board the *Dupont* the Elizabeth City Division showed an excellent spirit, taking up the unfamiliar and unattractive work of a torpedo boat with intelligent interest.

The Adjutant General inspected the ships on July 26.

The divisions returned to their home cities on July 30, and the ships returned to New Bern.

The next cruise was with the New Bern Division, August 8 to 15, on board the *Elfrida*. During this week an attempt was made to set up a target on poles on one of the shoals of Pamlico Sound. This was found impracticable on account of hard bottom. A temporary range was buoyed out and a small rectangular target rigged on a raft. Sub-calibre practice was carried on and two pointers fired eight rounds each from the three-pounder. These shots were more to test the gun and mount and to demonstrate the working of the gun than for pointer-training. Instruction was given in bore-sighting, safety precautions, methods of training and target practice work in general. During this cruise we swung ship and the officers were instructed in navigation as opportunity offered. The week's work of the New Bern Division was the most practical of the summer.

The Oriental Division failed to make the summer cruise.

As to the discipline and efficiency of the Naval Militia, the divisions that I accompanied were good considering the adverse conditions which exist. They lack training as a naval force and too much attention is given to military drill. The State pays the Naval Militia twenty-five cents a drill for infantry drill in the armories. The only money provided for the cruise is an appropriation to pay for subsistence. This does not tend to encourage the interest of the militiamen in their duties on shipboard. One officer expressed his views in about these words: "We must have a military company here on account of the large negro population, so I joined the Naval Militia, but I don't know anything about a ship."

Since the service is voluntary and without pay there is no way to compel the members to perform duty. In several instances it was necessary to hire men to take the ships from port to port. For the same reason, no pay, it is difficult to maintain discipline after getting a crew on board. It is not to be wondered at that a man rated as a seaman, for instance, should not care to spend his vacation in doing the work of a fireman without compensation, or in doing other ship duties that are purely hard work.

From what I saw during my tour of duty and from talks with militia officers, I have the following suggestions to offer:

(1) That the Naval Militia when serving on board ship be paid, as is the case with the organized militia on land, so that the men would be bound as to an employer.

(2) That officers and petty officers be required to qualify by examination for their rank or rating. Of course they could not be expected to pass a rigid examination in advanced subjects, but they should be required to show their ability to command and instruct men and an aptitude for their position. My point is illustrated by the case of a chief gunner's mate who was so gun-shy that he would not stay near a three-pounder gun when it was being fired. Qualification by examination would naturally follow if the recommendation in regard to pay were ever carried out.

(3) That the summer cruises in all cases be made on board ships of the fleet, where militia officers and men come in contact with the regular service. I do not consider the *Elfrida* of much value for a cruise of instruction, nor is a torpedo boat suitable for that work. These vessels can be used for drills during the year, but the other plan is much better for cruises.

(4) That measures be taken to have the militia exercise in naval matters in preference to infantry drill, to impress upon them the idea of becoming a reserve for the Navy to serve on board ship in time of need, not an organization for suppressing local disorder, or for parade purposes.

(5) That records of service of members of the Naval Militia be kept, and an effort made to keep in touch with the men who have had this training after they remove to places other than the one in which they served.

I think the Naval Militia is of prospective worth to the Government, serving with the regular naval force on board large ships. If they were to be called upon, they would be available at short notice and would arrive on board outfitted and partially trained. But in order to have a valuable reserve they should be put on a business footing, the Government and the militia contracting for service and compensation.

STATE OF NORTH CAROLINA,
ADJUTANT GENERAL'S DEPARTMENT,

CIRCULAR No. 4. RALEIGH, March 10, 1911.

With a view to holding target practice and rifle and revolver competition by teams consisting of one commissioned officer and nine enlisted men from each company of the several regiments of infantry during the month of April, company commanders are urged to hold gallery and outdoor target practice as often as practicable, to the end that the men may be ready to give the best results at shooting.

Company teams of the First Regiment will hold target practice on the range at Gastonia, N. C.; company teams of the Second Regiment on the range at Goldsboro, N. C., and the company teams of the Third Regiment on the range at Raleigh, N. C.

Pay, transportation and subsistence will be allowed officers and men who attend this target practice.

The Dupont Trophy will be competed for, and several other prizes will be offered, both for teams and individuals.

Orders setting forth the details of the target practice and the competitive shoot will be issued in due time.

By order of the Commander in Chief: R. L. LEINSTER,
The Adjutant General.

STATE OF NORTH CAROLINA,
ADJUTANT GENERAL'S DEPARTMENT,

CIRCULAR No. 5. RALEIGH, May 26, 1911.

The following reports of inspection by officers of the Regular Army, on the organizations of the North Carolina National Guard, are published for the information and guidance of all concerned:

Camp Glenn, Morehead City:

The field ranges in store are in a very rusty and dirty condition. They should be cleaned and greased or in some way protected from the action of the salt air.

Detachment Hospital Corps, Kinston:

Enlisted men are permitted to take property to their homes.

Detachment Hospital Corps, Charlotte:

Property is not properly cared for; men do not show the results of proper instruction; there is general lack of interest in the organization.

Coast Artillery Corps:

Headquarters: Paper work poor. No satisfactory system of keeping records. Several complaints received in regard to failure to keep up necessary official correspondence with companies, and in delay in acting on applications for discharge.

First Company: Paper work poor. Rifles only fair; improperly cleaned.

Fourth Company: Paper work poor. Property poorly stored, although ample means are available. Considerable property in possession of enlisted men and could not be produced by the Company Commander at inspection. A second counting of uniforms, after night inspection of company, was necessary in order to determine actual shortage of property.

First Infantry:

Headquarters: Enlisted men are permitted to take property to their homes.

Band: The uniforms and instruments are used in playing at hotels and in civil parades. Many of the instruments are obsolete and badly worn.

Company A: Rifles dirty, improperly cleaned. Bayonet slings rusty.

Company E: Rifles improperly cleaned.

Company G: Rifles dirty. Bayonets dirty and rusty. Improperly cleaned.

Company H: Rifles improperly cleaned. Rifling at muzzle worn.

Company L: Rifles injured by cleaning from muzzle instead of breech. Rifling near muzzle worn.

Company M: Rifles dirty and improperly cleaned.

Second Infantry:

Band: Property permitted to be carried home by enlisted men and used for non-military purposes. Instruments show careless handling.

Company A: Rifles—considerable rust in bores.

Company B: Property permitted to be carried home by enlisted men.

Company C: Rifles—some rust in bores.

Company D: Armory—old roof leaks. Property permitted to be carried home by enlisted men.

Company E: Rifles—marks on stocks show careless handling.

Company F: Property permitted to be carried home by enlisted men. Rifles—bores filled with rust.

Company G: Rifles—bores filled with rust.

Company I: Property permitted to be carried home by enlisted men. Rifles—bores filled with rust.

Company K: Property permitted to be carried home by enlisted men. Rifles—considerable rust.

Third Infantry:

Band: Property permitted to be carried home by enlisted men and used for non-military purposes.

Company B: A few articles permitted to be carried home by enlisted men. Rifles—bores filled with rust.

Company C: Property permitted to be carried home by enlisted men. Rifles—small amount of rust.

Company D: Property permitted to be carried home by enlisted men. Rifles—considerable rust in bores.

Company E: Rifles—considerable rust in bores.

Company F: Property permitted to be carried home by enlisted men. Rifles in poor condition except a few. All filled with rust and show lack of proper oiling and cleaning.

Company G: Armory—some leaking.

Company H: Property permitted to be carried home by enlisted men. Rifles—considerable rust in bores.

Company I: Property permitted to be carried home by enlisted men. Rifles—some rust in bores.

Company K: Property permitted to be carried home by enlisted men.

Company L: Armory—only fair protection from theft. Property permitted to be carried home by enlisted men. Rifles in poor condition.

The attention of all officers is invited to Part III, Regulations N. C. National Guard, relative to public property. Article XXX of said Regulations covers the care and custody of public property and must be adhered to.

Too much stress can not be laid on the necessity of keeping arms and accoutrements neat and clean, and officers are enjoined to give more attention to the care of the rifle and articles of equipment.

Where armory facilities are inadequate for the proper protection and care of property, organization commanders will take steps at once to remedy these conditions, or public property will be withdrawn and no further property issued until a suitable place for the care and protection of property is obtained.

The criticisms of the Inspecting officers for the United States relate chiefly to the condition of arms and the matter of allowing property to be carried home by enlisted men.

Rifles should be kept clean by the frequent and proper use of "Three-in-One" oil and Metallic Fouling Solution, when necessary.

Allowing Government property to be carried home by enlisted men is contrary to the regulations governing the North Carolina National Guard, and responsible officers are charged with correcting this infraction of Regulations.

By order of the Commander in Chief:

R. L. LEINSTER,
The Adjutant General.

STATE OF NORTH CAROLINA,
ADJUTANT GENERAL'S DEPARTMENT,

CIRCULAR NO. 6. RALEIGH, September 9, 1911.

The following scores made by the members of the rifle team representing the State of North Carolina in the National Matches at Camp Perry, Ohio, August 28 and 29, 1911, are published for the information of the North Carolina National Guard:

	200 Yds. S. F.	200 Yds. R. F.	600 Yds. S. F.	1000 Yds. S. F.	Skirmish	Total
Private John A. Moorefield, Company G, Third Infantry	43	48	43	37	83	254
First Sergeant James H. Brown, Company K, First Infantry	42	46	43	39	79	249
Sergeant James T. McAdams, Company I, Third Infantry	38	41	43	34	78	234
Captain J. H. Coon, Company F, First Infantry	40	36	42	36	68	222
Sergeant Wm. S. Newton, Company A, First Infantry	40	43	48	33	49	213
First Lieutenant S. E. Malone, Company D, Second Infantry	42	35	39	32	64	212
Corporal Ralph Wade, Company B, Second Infantry	34	40	43	35	60	212
First Lieutenant E. B. Parish, Company B, Third Infantry	36	32	43	44	49	204
Private Henry L. Best, Company C, Second Infantry	37	38	38	33	53	199
Captain Charles I. Bard, Company K, First Infantry	40	33	33	36	38	180
Sergeant J. C. McClure, Company H, First Infantry	35	42	39	28	36	180
Captain John B. Malloy, Company L, Second Infantry	37	29	40	22	46	174
Totals	464	463	494	409	703	2,533

By order of the Commander in Chief:

R. L. LEINSTER,
Adjutant General.

STATE OF NORTH CAROLINA,
ADJUTANT GENERAL'S DEPARTMENT,

CIRCULAR NO. 7. RALEIGH, 7 November, 1911.

To insure a knowledge of the new Infantry Drill Regulations, the following progressive course of instruction is prescribed for all infantry companies for the period from November 15, 1911, to June 30, 1912:

Lesson and drill sheets will be forwarded from this office about the fifteenth of each month.

To make a soldier that is fitted to go into battle as a private, requires a minimum of seven hundred and twenty hours of progressive instruction. The average service of National Guardsmen of this State is not over four years. It is therefore readily seen that the company commander, who desires during the average term of service to graduate men who are fitted for battle, must devote to instruction—

Two hours drill forty-eight weeks a year,
Two hours school twelve times a year, and
Thirty-six hours instruction at annual camp.

A total of one hundred and fifty-six hours instruction a year. This is a minimum; many States require more. It is hoped and believed that live, wide-awake company commanders interested in the service and desiring to have a good company will have at least this amount of instruction.

NUMBER OF RECITATIONS.

A minimum of one each month, preferably during the first seven days.

LENGTH OF RECITATION.

A minimum of one and one-half hours at each meeting.

WHO WILL ATTEND.

The instructor will be the ranking officer on duty with each company.

All officers and noncommissioned officers are required to attend this instruction; not more than four privates may, on approval of the company commander, be permitted to attend. It is recommended and urged that each captain select four of the most promising privates for attendance at this school, with a view to placing those who complete the course successfully on a list of eligible privates from which future vacancies in the grade of corporal may be filled.

At the end of the course an examination will be held, the questions for which, together with instructions, will be sent out from the office of the Adjutant General in due time.

The following lesson sheets attempt to indicate the paragraphs containing changes from old drill regulations and to give the instructor such other hints as may be practicable; but the success of the school will depend entirely upon the energy and ability of the company commander:

LESSON I.

Pages 7 and 8, and Paragraphs 1-47.

Note the changes from 1904 I. D. R. in paragraphs 10, 16, 19, 21, 22, 27, 28, 29, 39.

Note paragraph 40, first two lines, in connection with lines 1 and 2, page 163.

Officers and noncommissioned officers should be able to understand and use the military terms given on pages 7 and 8.

The following paragraphs contain general information to be read and understood but not necessarily memorized: 1, 2, 3, 4, 5, 6, 31, 32, 35, 36, 41, 45, 46.

The general rules for drills and formations, paragraphs 8 to 30, inclusive, are most important. Much weight should be given and their principles thoroughly learned.

Signals are most important and should be absolutely learned by every officer and noncommissioned officer, and later taught to the men in the company. The whistle and arm signals, paragraphs 42 and 43, are especially important. Each man should be thoroughly practiced until he knows these signals like his A. B. C's.

DRILL SCHEDULES.

For the Period December 1st to June 30th.

The following is considered the minimum amount of drill which a company ought to have during this period. It is recognized that companies which have proper zeal and military spirit will spend more time in military instruction than here laid down.

Each drill night should be divided into two periods; the first half should be devoted entirely to instruction in the movements prescribed by the following drill sheets; the second half of the drill will be used by the captain on the work his company needs most.

Drill nights not herein provided for to be used in work at the discretion of the captain.

GENERAL RULE: At least ten minutes of every drill should always be devoted to squad drill, each squad being commanded by its corporal or other noncommissioned officer, the whole being under the close and active supervision of the officers. Thus, and thus only, will you train your noncommissioned officers to exercise command and be of real assistance to you. Lieutenants should be allowed to drill the company occasionally, but under the close and personal supervision of the captain. A captain who turns his company drill over to some one else and leaves the armory can not expect to have even a fairly efficient military organization.

DRILL NO. I.

Paragraphs 41 to 44, Inclusive.

Have a musician blow the following calls, repeating them until most of the men know them. The company being in line, have the musician blow the call and ask some one what it is; then reverse the process, name the call, and ask some one to whistle it:

1. Attention.
2. Attention to orders.
3. Forward march.
4. Halt.
5. Double time march.
6. To the rear march.
7. Commence firing.
8. Cease firing.
9. Fix bayonets.
10. Charge.
11. First call (Parade, Gd. Mt., Rev. retreat).
12. First call for drill (Drill call).
13. Assembly.
14. Reveille.
15. Sick call.
16. Fatigue call.

Teach the whistle signals until all men in the company obey instantly the long blast and the short blast of the whistle. This is considered so important that the War Department has ordered all officers and sergeants to be equipped with whistles. All companies of this State will be furnished same without requisition as soon as they can be obtained. In the meantime it is very essential that the captain be equipped with a whistle.

Teach the men the arm signals of paragraphs 43. As these have already been given in school, you should have a competent corps of assistant instructors. Therefore, divide the company into small squads and have a noncommissioned officer in charge of each squad to instruct it in arm signals. At first the instructor makes the signal and asks a man to name it, then names a signal and has a man make it. After the signals are learned in this way the squad should be drilled by signals frequently. The noise of battle at present makes the voice of even the company commander practically impossible to be heard on the firing line. All commands and instruction must be made by whistle signals and arm signals (the trumpet is reserved for the use of the higher commanders). The great importance of these signals is therefore apparent. They can not be learned too thoroughly.

FLAG SIGNALS.

It is extremely desirable to have two men in each company who are expert in flag signaling. This work would take considerable time in addition to regular drills, but could be learned at home. In case any company has one or two volunteers for this work, the code will be furnished on application.

DRILL NO. II.

Paragraphs 41 to 44, Inclusive.

The subject of signaling is considered so important that Drill No. II will include a review of the subject-matter of Drill No. I.

LESSON IN FIRST AID TO THE WOUNDED.

In a modern battle each soldier will carry a bandage (first aid packet). A knowledge of first aid to the wounded will save many men's lives in the next war; it may save yours. In most cases you will get the first aid you yourself can furnish, and no more. It is therefore urged that an arrangement be made with some local friend in the medical profession for a lesson in first aid to the wounded, to cover the following points:

1. The difference between the color of artery and vein blood.
2. The difference in flow of artery and vein blood.
3. How to stop an artery wound in one of the extremities.
4. How to stop a vein wound in one of the extremities.
5. Illustrate 3 and 4 by particular supposed cases of wounds: (*a*) in the hand; (*b*) in the forearm; (*c*) in the scalp; (*d*) in the cheek or jaw; (*e*) in the foot; (*f*) in the thigh.
6. How to improvise and apply a splint to a broken leg or arm.
7. How to lift and carry a wounded man with least pain to him.

By order of the Commander in Chief: R. L. LEINSTER,

The Adjutant General.

STATE OF NORTH CAROLINA,
ADJUTANT GENERAL'S DEPARTMENT,

CIRCULAR NO. 8. RALEIGH, 8 November, 1911.

I. The attention of organization commanders is invited to Regulations, North Carolina National Guard, requiring the annual report of drills, target practice, and field instruction to be forwarded to the Adjutant General not later than the 15th of December of each year. This report should be made out full and complete and in accordance with printed instructions thereon. To comply with the requirements of the War Department, at least two-thirds of the strength of the company should be present for drill or target practice not less than twenty-four times per year.

II. The attention of all accountable officers is invited to the necessity for having annual return of property made out and forwarded to the Quartermaster General, Henderson, N. C., not later than December 1st. This return should be made out full and complete and in accordance with printed instructions thereon. To insure consolidated report and return being forwarded to the War Department on time, it is essential that officers responsible forward report or return on dates above specified to the Adjutant General or Quartermaster General, as the case may be.

By order of the Commander in Chief: R. L. LEINSTER,
The Adjutant General.

CORRESPONDENCE SCHOOL

NORTH CAROLINA NATIONAL GUARD.

Course 1911-12, December 1 to April 30, Inclusive.

Map Reading and the Handling of a Battalion on the March, in Attack, Camp and Outpost, and in Defense.

Abbreviations:

S.—Military Map Reading, Sherrill, 1909.
F. S. R.—Field Service Regulations, 1910.
I. D. R.—Infantry Drill Regulations, 1911.

Frequent references will be given in the various problems to the paragraphs of the authorized manuals where information asked for can be obtained. Their thorough study is urged.

It is expected that each officer will take the problems or questions and study them in connection with the references given. Consultation and discussion may also be had with others. No written notes should be made at this time. Twenty-four hours after an officer has satisfied himself that he can give a correct solution to the problem, he may write out his solution without again referring to notes or text-book. The solution will be returned to this office within ten days of receipt of the problem, accompanied by the following certificate:

"I certify on my personal honor that I have written the enclosed solution without having received assistance, either personal or written, within a period of twenty-four hours of the writing of the solution.

(Signature)..................................

It is desired that sufficient time elapse between the study of the problem and the writing of the solution to insure that what is written is what the officer actually knows, and not mere copy work.

Problems will be mailed between the 1st and 10th of each month. They should be solved and returned within ten days of date of receipt. All solutions will be examined and returned to the officer with the next problem.

A map will accompany each problem. Necessary marks may be placed on the map, which may be returned as a part of the solution.

Number your answers to correspond with the number of the question answered.

When the answer is indicated on the map it will be sufficient to say so, *i. e.*, Q. No. ....—Answer indicated on map.

Sign and date each answer sheet, and the map if returned.

Notations on maps may be in ink or pencil, using any color but red.

Assume all trees to be thirty feet high.

Spaces on map without conventional signs indicate short grass.

PROBLEM No. 1—MAP READING.

When asked to indicate anything on the map, place the number of the question on the map at the desired point and surround it by a circle; thus: Q. 1—Indicate on the map (a) an orchard, (b) trees, etc. Find an orchard on the map, mark it 1a and surround with a circle.

Q. 1.—Indicate on the map the following: (a) cut, (b) fill, (c) barbed wire fence, (d) smooth wire fence, (e) hedge fence, (f) orchard, (g) woods, (h) vineyard, (i) improved road, (j) unimproved road, (k) railroad, (l) bridge. (S., page 32.) (These may all be found on the western half of the map.)

Q. 2.—What is the scale of this map? (S., page 10, 3d.) (b) How far is it from 64 to 17, via the 64-14-16-Frenchman-17 road? (S., 1st under par. 15 and par. 16.)

Q. 3.—Indicate the magnetic north on the map. (S., par. 28-29.) The magnetic north is shown by the half arrowhead; the true north by the full arrowhead.

Q. 4.—About what degree of slope is found on the west side of Sentinel Hill, between contours 950 and 1000 feet? (b) Between contours 900 and 950 feet? (c) What is the practicability of these slopes for infantry? cavalry? wagons? (S., page 17, last three lines.) Compare the distances between the contours with the length of the contour intervals on the scale at the top of the map. (S., par. 19.) (F. S. R., page 223.)

Q. 5.—If you had to occupy Sentinel Hill, facing west, with a battalion, where would you put it? (S., par. 44.) (F. S. R., pars. 274, 276, 277, 278.)

Q. 6.—On the road from 15 to 17, western central part of the map, indicate when the road is up hill, level, or down hill, by dotted, solid, or dash lines respectively. (Ground between two consecutive contours of the same elevation is assumed to be level. Make your indications just off and to the north of the road.)

Q. 7.—Indicate on the map your route from Frenchman to the house about one hundred yards west of Moss, such that you would not be seen by a man standing on the ground at 17. Travel by road where possible. (S., pars. 42, 43.)

Q. 8.—You are on hill "A," about 1,675 yards northwest of Frenchman. Indicate on the map by solid lines the crests of three ridges which run from this hill south and southeast to the creek. Indicate on the map by dotted lines two valley lines running from this hill generally south to the creek. (S., par. 20, a and b.)

Q. 9.—You are commanding the support of an advance guard consisting of one battalion, marching from Frenchman to 17. Indicate on the map the route of your extreme western patrol or patrols from Frenchman to the point where it would cross the 19-17-15 road. (F. S. R., pars. 104, 106.)

Q. 10.—You are commanding a harassing patrol of two squads with orders to delay the march of a battalion of the enemy which is advancing from the west along the 36-38-30-28-24 road (southwestern part of map). State what steps you would take between 30 and 28 to carry out your orders. Give detailed description of just what your patrol would do.

STATE OF NORTH CAROLINA,
ADJUTANT GENERAL'S DEPARTMENT,

CIRCULAR No. 9a. RALEIGH, 10 December, 1911.

The following lesson, No. II, is herewith prescribed for infantry companies for the month of January, 1911. Lesson III will be sent out about January 15, 1912.

By order of the Commander in Chief: R. L. LEINSTER,
The Adjutant General.

LESSON II.

Paragraphs 48 to 92, inclusive.

Note changes from 1904 I. D. R., paragraphs 51, 56, 57, 65, 67, 68, 69, 75, 76, 78, 89.

The following paragraphs should be read and understood, but not necessarily committed to memory: 48, 49, 50.

See that each man can execute properly, as well as explain, the paragraph on which recitation is made. When the paragraph is very important, see that all can execute the movement, especially where there is a change from the 1904 I. D. R.

Read paragraphs 758 to 765 in connection with paragraph 58.

Note in paragraph 72 that the "turn to the right on the balls of both feet" takes the time of one step or count.

Study the second part of paragraph 75 and paragraph 100 in connection with paragraphs 98 and 99. This is especially important for the first sergeant. "Inspection arms" is absolutely and always the first command after assembly, and paragraph 100 the last command before dismissal. Do not confound this "inspection arms" with "prepare for inspection." See paragraph 745.

Note at the command "(1) At trail, forward; (2) March," the trail is not taken until the command "March."

Note the general rule for trail arms under "Sixth" in paragraph 75.

All the general rules, paragraphs 75 and 76, are most important.

"First," under paragraph 76, in connection with paragraph 78, changes position of the thumb of the left hand so that it now grasps the piece at "Present arms," including the sling in the grasp of the hand.

Paragraph 89 changes the method of coming to "Left shoulder, arms," from the right shoulder. The movement now goes from right shoulder to "Port," and then to the left shoulder, making four counts for the movement, and five counts from left shoulder to right shoulder.

DRILL No. 3.

Paragraphs 48 to 67, inclusive.

To be given after Lesson II has been taught in the school.

(Without arms.)

Insist at all times that each man stand in position of pragraph 51, when at attention. Nothing looks worse or shows *lack of discipline* so much as men in line moving their head or hand.

For this drill, divide the company into squads under noncommissioned officers. Officers and extra noncommissioned officers should actively supervise.

See that the men know the difference between "Dismissed" and "Fall out"; between "Rest" and "At ease."

Practice paragraphs 53, 54, 55, 56, and 57 until each man can execute movements correctly and promptly. Repeat each movement several times before passing to the next. Quality, not quantity, is the object sought. Have an awkward squad and place in it, as they develop, the backward men. Insist that each man should be able to perform or execute each movement before "letting up" on him.

Note that officers and enlisted men now have the same about face, paragraph 57. One of the most common faults at the last camp was a failure or inability of officers to execute the about face. The ability to repeat and write paragraph 57 will not enable an officer to execute the about face without practice. Nothing will take the place of this repetition in this or any other movement.

Insist on a smart salute (paragraph 58) properly made. Note that the plane of the palm of the hand is perpendicular to the plane of the forehead and not parallel to it. The hand should be held at salute until it is returned or the superior has passed. This rule now holds good in the case of both officers and enlisted men when saluting a superior. Proper saluting is the outward sign of inward grace and spells discipline.

Practice "(1) Forward, (2) March," paragraph 62, until ever man steps out *together, thirty inches*, at the command *March*. Then give the command "Halt," and see that every man in the company takes just exactly one step of thirty inches after the command "Halt," then places "the first foot by the side of the other." A very common mistake is for a man to take a short step, this last step, or to take even two short steps after the command "Halt" is given. For example, say the command "Halt" be given as the right foot strikes the ground; there should thereafter be only two sounds heard in the armory, namely, that of the left foot being planted thirty inches in advance and that of the right foot being planted by the side of the left. Do not quit "Forward, march" and "Halt" until they are executed exactly by every man in the company.

Note that to resume full step (paragraph 67) the command is now "Forward, march."

DRILL No. 4.

Paragraphs 68 to 73, inclusive.

(Without arms.)

Insist strictly on the position of the soldier when men are at "Attention."

For this drill, again divide the company into squads as in Drill 3. Officers should actively and personally supervise, passing from squad to squad, correcting movements, privately advising the noncommissioned officer in charge of the squad of his own mistakes of command, and occasionally taking personal command of a squad for a moment for purposes of illustration and instruction.

Note that the side-step and back-step are executed "At trail" without command.

If the command "Halt" be given as the left foot strikes the ground, paragraph 70 is plain in its application; but in halting from "Right step," if the command "Halt" be given as the right foot strikes the ground, plant the left as in marching (by the side of the right), then raise the right foot, as in mark time, and replace it. This completes the halt in two counts.

In marching by the flank (paragraph 71), insist on the turn being *square.* No break in the cadence is made by facing to the right or left. The face and the step off in the new direction together take just the time of one count.

In "(1) To the rear, (2) March," the turn "On the balls of both feet" takes the time of one whole count—no more and no less.

In change step, note that the *same foot* is advanced on the two consecutive counts after the command "March."

DRILL No. 5.

Nomenclature and Care of Rifle.

(With arms.)

Divide the company into squads as in Drill 4.

Insist strictly on position of the soldier when men are at "Attention." Give "At ease" when possible during explanations.

It is not necessary that privates should know the name of every part given on the plate facing page 26, but have each man take his rifle and see that he knows the use of, and can point out to the instructor, the following parts:

1. Safety lock. (Positions "On" and "Off.")
2. Cut off. (Positions "On" and "Off.")
3. Cocking piece.
4. Firing pin rod.
5. Firing pin sleeve.
6. Striker.
7. Extractor.
8. Magazine.
9. Magazine spring.
10. Bolt stop spring.
11. Floor plate.
12. Floor plate catch.
13. Fixed base.
14. Leaf.

15. Windage screw.
16. Slide screw.
17. Teach how to remove the bolt.

Now assemble the company and see that each man understands the following points on the care of his rifle. (These points should be covered beforehand in the school under Lesson II.)

(*a*) It should be treated at all times with the care due a fine machine. The rifle is not intended as a club and should not be used as such. Never jam it down on the ground in coming to the "Order arms"; but lower it gently without making any noise.

(*b*) Never clean the bore with a rod from the muzzle. Always remove the bolt and clean from the breech.

(*c*) As the bore of the rifle is manufactured with great care in order that a high degree of accuracy may be obtained, it should be carefully cared for. The residuum from smokeless powder tends to rust the bore, and should therefore be removed as soon after firing as possible. The following method has been practiced for years at the Springfield Armory with good results: Using the cleaning rod and small patches of cloth (Canton flannel is best), clean the bore thoroughly with patches soaked in a saturated solution of soda and water; then thoroughly dry the bore and remove the soda solution by the use of dry patches, and finally oil the bore with patches soaked in cosmic oil. Twenty-four hours after this first cleaning the bore should be again cleaned as described above, as it has been found that the powder gases are probably forced into the texture of the steel and will, if the second cleaning be not resorted to, cause rusting, no matter how thoroughly the bore may have been cleaned the first time.

(*d*) The bore should always have a light coating of cosmic oil, which should be cleaned out just before firing.

(*e*) Cosmic oil should be applied to all metallic surfaces to prevent rusting, when arms are stored, and not used for an appreciable length of time.

(*f*) Keep several greasy rags, on which has been placed a slight amount of sperm oil, and pass one over the metallic part of each rifle *immediately after every drill.*

(*g*) *Leather Equipment.*—Never permit leather to get so dry that it cracks. To oil equipment, take a damp sponge, squeeze nearly dry, rub it on castile soap to form a thick lather, apply the lather to surface of the leather, and let it stand until dry; when dry, remove with a clean, damp sponge; spots particularly soiled may be rubbed with a moist soaped cloth. While the surface of the leather is still slightly moist from the above process, apply a very little neatsfoot oil with a cloth slightly moistened with the oil. After the oil has been applied the leather should be left for some time, a day if possible, and then thoroughly rubbed with a coarse dry cloth until the surface is clean. This treatment is all that is necessary to keep leather in excellent condition. Two or three times a year is generally enough under ordinary conditions. If a polish only of personal leather equipment is desired, the dressing supplied by the Ordnance Department should be used, applied in the same way as tan shoe dressing; this, however, does not take the place of the oiling process described above, but is in addition to it.

Take up the work for the last half of the drill period.

Pass greasy rag over metal parts of rifle after the drill.

DRILL No. 6.

Paragraphs 77 to 92, inclusive.

(With arms.)

Insist strictly on the position of the soldier when the men are at "Attention." Give "At ease" when possible, during explanations.

Divide the company into squads as in Drill No. 4.

Insist that each movement of the manual be executed with snap, and that there be a distinct pause between each movement. The whole movement should be executed in the cadence of quick time; each individual part should be *completed* on the count. If some men commence the motion on the count and others complete it on the count, the effect will be ragged.

The first part of each drill and manual of arms should be "By the numbers," to insure correctness in details of each motion. This should be followed by drill (without the numbers) in order to get the cadence. There should be absolutely no sound of the rifle striking the floor when it is brought to the order. This rule is general.

There are two changes in the Manual from the 1904 I. D. R. Paragraph 78 says: "Grasp rifle with left hand at the balance." Paragraph 76, first, prescribes that the left thumb clasps the piece, including the sling in the grasp of the hand. Therefore at the "Present arms" the left thumb grasps the piece, and the sling is included in the grasp of the hand.

Paragraph 89, last four lines, prescribes that in coming from the right shoulder to the left shoulder, the rifle should be carried first to "Port arms" and then to the left shoulder; therefore at present this movement will take four counts.

If all the men of a company execute one movement of the manual it is very hard to tell just who is responsible for a slight raggedness of movement; but if several movements of the manual be combined into one consecutive movement, the sum of a slight error will soon be great enough to throw the man making it completely out of cadence. His error is brought home to him most forcibly, and can be corrected. The very best training for cadence in the manual of arms is to have such a series executed in succession at one command. The following has been tried most successfully:

THE FIRST SERIES.

The captain commands, "First series, present arms." The men execute the following in twenty consecutive counts:

Present arms. Two counts.
Order arms. Two counts.
Port arms. One count.
Order arms. Two counts.
Right shoulder arms. Three counts.
Order arms. Three counts.
Left shoulder arms. Three counts.
Order arms. Four counts.

THE SECOND SERIES.

The captain commands "Second series, present arms." The men execute in fourteen straight counts:

Present arms. Two counts.
Port arms. One count.
Right shoulder arms. Three counts.
Left shoulder arms. Four counts.
Order arms. Four counts.

Either of these series will obtain the object sought—regular cadence. They may be combined into a single series, and will thus embrace nearly every movement in the manual of arms. When a man is out of cadence, have him come to the order and remain there until the series is completed.

Note the points emphasized in Drill No. 3, under paragraph 62. Now that the soldier has a rifle, teach him to come to the order from the right shoulder in three counts, after the halt (paragraph 62) is completed, making five counts after the command "Halt." Also see that he comes to the right shoulder from the order during the first three counts after the command "March," simultaneously with the first three steps.

Take up the work for the last half of drill period.

Pass greasy rag over metal parts of rifle after drill.

Report of Chief of Ordnance

RALEIGH, N. C., December 1, 1911.

THE ADJUTANT GENERAL, *State of North Carolina.*

SIR:—I have the honor herewith to submit my annual report for the year ending November 30, 1911.

As you well know, the actual work rendered by this Department yearly is restricted to the supervision of target practice on the State Range, adjacent to Camp Glenn, during the annual encampments of the Infantry regiments. It is a matter of general congratulation that such satisfactory results are produced by these target competitions, as the Guard grows older and better, and there can be no doubt that the records, before a great while, will show a long roster of marksmen, sharpshooters, and expert riflemen. It is hard to conceive of anything in a soldier's line of duty deserving of more constant attention than persistent, increasing target practice.

The State Range, and its equipment and appurtenances, are in good condition at the present time. Some grading is necessary in front of the southern end of the butts, in order to remove a slight obstacle to the line of sight. Attention is also invited to the need of replenishing or renewing a part of the range equipment, which will be more clearly pointed out in a supplemental report, and authority will be requested to enable this Department to act in the premises. It is thought advisable also to suggest that a Surveying Officer examine and pass upon a lot of abandoned target equipment, with the view of getting the same regularly condemned and dropped.

The undersigned, pursuant to orders heretofore issued, remains in charge of the Military Supply Depot at Raleigh, both as custodian of all the State's military property stored therein, and duly vested with authority from the office of the Adjutant General to fill all requisitions for supplies. This latter duty not only involves great responsibility and labor, but means much to the life of the Guard. Unless a soldier is kept armed and uniformed up to the best attainable standards his efficiency can not be maintained in a way to promote the interests of the service. Every effort is made along this line to comply as far as practicable with all requisitions for supplies, and everything is issued properly as requested when the necessary stock is in hand.

Unfortunately it sometimes happens that due care is not taken of military property when turned over to individuals or organizations, and it is a fact that there is often a lack of that feeling of responsibility for government property when received, that should exist in the minds of responsible officers. If possible a more rigid system of accountability should be devised, to the end that military clothing especially be better preserved.

The storage facilities of this Depot are deemed ample for present purposes, and every article of military property in my charge is safely cared for and protected. Books of account are kept for the entry of all issues on requisition, and all official transactions are recorded as directed in orders. The business of this Depot has been conducted in that manner since April 3, 1909, the date of my assignment to this duty.

Very respectfully, THOS. R. ROBERTSON,
Colonel and Chief of Ordnance.

Register of the National Guard of North Carolina

COMMANDER IN CHIEF,

GOVERNOR WILLIAM WALTON KITCHIN.

BRIGADIER GENERAL R. L. LEINSTER, ADJUTANT GENERAL.

PERSONAL STAFF OF THE COMMANDER IN CHIEF.

Name	Office	Rank	Date of Rank	Residence
Alex. J. Feild	Private Secretary	Colonel	Jan. 29, 1909	Raleigh.
Charles E. Johnson	Aide de Camp	Colonel	Jan. 29, 1909	Raleigh.
Henry A. Grady	Naval Aid	Colonel	Jan. 29, 1909	Clinton.
H. Montague	Aide de Camp	Colonel	Jan. 29, 1909	Winston-Salem.
Finlay L. Williamson	Aide de Camp	Colonel	Jan. 29, 1909	Burlington.
C. B. Armstrong	Aide de Camp	Colonel	Jan. 29, 1909	Gastonia.
Albion Dunn	Naval Aid	Colonel	Aug. 4, 1910	Greenville.
John C Mills	Aide de Camp	Colonel	July 31, 1911	Rutherfordton.

GENERAL STAFF.

ADJUTANT GENERAL'S DEPARTMENT.

Name	Office	Rank	Date of Rank	Residence
R. L. Leinster	Adjutant General	Brig. Gen.	Nov. 1, 1910	Raleigh.
Alfred Williams	Asst. Adjt. Gen.	Colonel	Jan. 24, 1901	Raleigh.
Gordon Smith	Asst. Adjt. Gen.	Major	Nov. 18, 1910	Raleigh.
S. G. Brown	Asst. Adjt. Gen.	Major	Nov. 17, 1910	Greensboro.
A. A. Hicks	Asst. Adjt. Gen.	Major	April 1, 1909	Oxford.
E. A. Daniel, Jr.	Asst. Adjt. Gen.	Major	April 1, 1909	Washington.
W. A. Foil	Asst. Adjt. Gen.	Major	April 1, 1909	Concord.

QUARTERMASTER GENERAL'S DEPARTMENT.

Name	Office	Rank	Date of Rank	Residence
Francis A. Macon	Q. M. General	Brig. Gen.	Feb. 1905	Henderson.
Wyndham E. Gary	Asst. Q. M. Gen.	Lieut. Col.	June 10, 1903	Henderson.
H. S. Leard	Asst. Q. M. Gen.	Major	May 20, 1910	Raleigh.
Mark W. Williams	Asst. Q. M. Gen.	Major	April 3, 1909	Charlotte.
J. S. Poythress	Asst. Q. M. Gen.	Major	May 20, 1910	Henderson.
J. W. Dalton	Asst. Q. M. Gen.	Major	April 3, 1909	Winston-Salem.
J. L. Currin	Asst. Q. M. Gen.	Captain	Aug. 1, 1905	Henderson.

INSPECTOR GENERAL'S DEPARTMENT.

Name	Office	Rank	Date of Rank	Residence
Thos. Stringfield	Inspector Gen.	Colonel	Jan. 2, 1907	Waynesville.
Henry D. Harper	Asst. Insp. Gen.	Lieut. Col.	April 1, 1909	Kinston.
H. B. Parker	Asst. Insp. Gen.	Major	April 1, 1909	Goldsboro.
J. D. Gwynn	Asst. Insp. Gen.	Major	April 1, 1909	Reidsville.
J. P. Meadows	Asst. Insp. Gen.	Major	April 1, 1909	Roxboro.
Wm. Badham	Asst. Insp. Gen.	Major	April 1, 1909	Edenton.
J. C. Michie	Asst. Insp. Gen.	Major	April 1, 1909	Durham.

COMMISSARY DEPARTMENT.

Name	Office	Rank	Date of Rank	Residence
Wyatt L. McGhee	Com. General	Colonel	Jan. 12, 1905	Franklinton.
R. H. Reinhardt	Asst. Com. Gen.	Major	April 15, 1909	Lincolnton.
I. W. Little	Asst. Com. Gen.	Major	April 15, 1909	Wilmington.
C. A. Hunt	Asst. Com. Gen.	Major	April 15, 1909	Lexington.
Roger Gant	Asst. Com. Gen.	Major	April 15, 1909	Oxford.

ENGINEER'S DEPARTMENT.

Name	Office	Rank	Date of Rank	Residence
Jacob L. Ludlow	Chief of Engineers	Colonel	Jan. 12, 1905	Winston-Salem.
R. S. Neal	Asst. Chief Eng.	Lieut. Col.	April 1, 1909	Washington.
Quint E. Smith	Asst. Chief Eng.	Major	Feb. 1, 1908	Concord.
Robt. M. Coburn	Asst. Chief Eng.	Major	April 1, 1909	Raleigh.
J. C. Mintz	Asst. Chief Eng.	Major	April 1, 1909	Shallotte.
Thos. B. Whitted	Asst. Chief Eng.	Major	April 15, 1909	Charlotte.
W. W. Peirce	Asst. Chief Eng.	Major	Feb. 20, 1907	Goldsboro.
N. R. Morgan	Asst. Chief Eng.	First Lieut.	July 28, 1911	Goldsboro.

PAY DEPARTMENT.

Name	Office	Rank	Date of Rank	Residence
S. W. Cooper	Paymaster Gen.	Colonel	Sept. 8, 1910	Fayetteville.
Raleigh T. Daniel	Asst. P. M. Gen.	Major	Feb. 24, 1905	Weldon.
R. G. Allsbrook	Asst. P. M. Gen.	Major	April 3, 1909	Tarboro.
E. G. Sherrill	Asst. P. M. Gen.	Major	April 3, 1909	Greensboro.
M. L. Cannon	Asst. P. M. Gen.	Major	July 1, 1909	Concord.
Dixon V. Conn	Asst. P. M. Gen.	Captain	Oct. 19, 1911	Raleigh.

ORDNANCE DEPARTMENT.

Name	Office	Rank	Date of Rank	Residence
Thos. R. Robertson	Chief of Ordnance	Colonel	Mar. 26, 1903	Raleigh.
J. W. Bizzell	Ordnance Officer	Lieut. Col.	April 20, 1910	Goldsboro.
J. B. Thomas	Ordnance Officer	Major	April 3, 1909	Louisburg.
A. K. Powers	Ordnance Officer	Major	April 3, 1909	Burgaw.
J. Leigh Skinner	Ordnance Officer	Major	April 3, 1909	Raleigh.
L. B. Bristol	Ordnance Officer	Major	July 19, 1909	Statesville.
Thos. Orrell	Ordnance Officer	Major	June 30, 1910	Wilmington.
R. G. Gladstone	Ordnance Officer	Major	Feb. 19, 1912	Reidsville.
Z. P. Smith	Ordnance Officer	Captain	June 10, 1911	Raleigh.
York Coleman	Ordnance Officer	First Lieut.	May 27, 1910	Rutherfordton.

JUDGE ADVOCATE GENERAL'S DEPARTMENT.

Name	Office	Rank	Date of Rank	Residence
A. C. Davis	Judge Adv. Gen.	Colonel	April 3, 1909	Goldsboro.
V. C. Bullard	Asst. Judge Advocate General.	Lieut. Col.	April 3, 1909	Fayetteville.
T. A. Lyon	Asst. Judge Advocate General.	Major	April 3, 1909	Elizabethtown.
J. D. Proctor	Asst. Judge Advocate General.	Major	April 3, 1909	Lumberton.
A. P. Godwin	Asst. Judge Advocate General.	Major	April 3, 1909	Gatesville.
Elijah Moffitt	Asst. Judge Advocate General.	Major	April 3, 1909	Asheboro.

MEDICAL DEPARTMENT.

Name	Office	Rank	Date of Rank	Residence
S. Westray Battle	Surgeon General	Colonel	July 1, 1909	Asheville.
Philip J. Macon		Lieut. Col.	July 1, 1909	Warrenton.
E. B. Glenn		Major	Feb. 24, 1905	Asheville.
A. R. Winston		Major	Mar. 24, 1905	Franklinton.
J. V. McGougan		Major	July 1, 1909	Fayetteville.
H. I. Clark		Major	Feb. 21, 1910	Scotland Neck.
Claud L. Pridgen		Major	Sept. 25, 1911	Kinston.
F. J. Clemenger		Major	Sept. 26, 1911	Asheville.
E. C. Boyette		Captain	Nov. 22, 1906	Charlotte.
M. B. Abernethy		Captain	May 18, 1908	Reidsville.
Wm. C. Horton		Captain	Sept. 26, 1911	Raleigh.
H. A. Newell		1st Lieut.	April 21, 1910	Louisburg.
A. K. Tayloe		1st Lieut.	July 15, 1910	Washington.
Hubert B. Haywood, Jr.		1st Lieut.	Mar. 30, 1911	Raleigh.
Ralph S. Stevens		1st Lieut.	June 2, 1911	Raleigh.
Edwin F. Fenner		1st Lieut.	July 8, 1911	Henderson.
W. Myers Hunter		1st Lieut.	July 10, 1911	Charlotte.
Arthur F. Reeves		1st Lieut.	June 24, 1911	Asheville.
Reuben A. Campbell		1st Lieut.	Sept. 25, 1911	Statesville.

FIRST BRIGADE.

Name	Office	Rank	Date of Rank	Residence
B. S. Royster	Brig. Commander	Brig. Gen.	April 1, 1909	Oxford.
S. G. Brown	Asst. Adjt. Gen	Major	Nov. 17, 1910	Greensboro.
J. W. Dalton	Chief Q. M.	Major	April 3, 1909	Winston-Salem.
Roger Gant	Chief Commissary	Major	April 15, 1909	Oxford.
Jno. C. Michie	Inspector	Major	April 15, 1909	Durham.
J. B. Thomas	Ordnance Officer	Major	April 15, 1909	Louisburg.
R. T. Daniel	Paymaster	Major	Feb. 24, 1905	Weldon.
J. D. Proctor	Judge Advocate	Major	April 3, 1909	Lumberton.
J. Leigh Skinner	Inspector S. A. P.	Major	April 23, 1909	Raleigh.
H. I. Clark	Surgeon	Major	Feb. 21, 1910	Scotland Neck.
Henry T. Osborne	Aide de Camp	1st Lieut	Jan. 9, 1911	Oxford.
Arthur C. House	Aide de Camp	1st Lieut	Jan. 27, 1911	Weldon.

FIRST INFANTRY.

FIELD AND STAFF.

Name	Office	Rank	Date of Commission	Residence
J. T. Gardner	Colonel	Colonel	Jan. 30, 1905	Shelby.
J. C. Bessent	Lieut. Col	Lieut. Col.	Oct. 7, 1907	Winston-Salem.
R. L. Flannigan	Major	Major	July 20, 1899	Statesville.
D. D. Parks	Major	Major	Aug. 12, 1907	Mount Airy.
L. W. Young	Major	Major	Dec. 7, 1907	Asheville.
W. R. Minter	Chaplain	Captain	July 1, 1907	Lincolnton.
W. R. Robertson	Adjutant	Captain	June 1, 1904	Charlotte.
J. F. Roberts	Commissary	Captain	May 15, 1905	Shelby.
J. D. Lineberger	Quartermaster	Captain	Nov. 15, 1905	Shelby.
R. R. Morrison	Inspector S. A. P.	Captain	Mar. 30, 1911	Mooresville.
A. W. Freeman	Bat. Adjutant	1st Lieut	Dec. 12, 1899	Waynesville.
Joe Hill	Bat. Adjutant	1st Lieut.	Aug. 2, 1901	Concord.
H. A. Millis	Bat. Adjutant	1st Lieut.	June 25, 1909	High Point.
P. W. Eshelman	Bat. Quartermaster and Com.	2d Lieut.	June 16, 1905	High Point.
J. H. Gwyn	Bat. Quartermaster and Com.	2d Lieut.	Mar. 9, 1910	Mount Airy.
R. H. Morrison	Bat. Quartermaster and Com.	2d Lieut.	June 1, 1908	Stanley.

FIRST INFANTRY—COMPANIES.

Name and Station of Company	Name of Officer	Rank	Date of Rank
A Hickory Rifles, Hickory.	G. W. Payne W. C. Keever G. L. Huffman	Captain 1st Lieut. 2d Lieut.	April 8, 1910 April 8, 1910 April 8, 1910
B Gastonia.	A. L. Bulwinkle W. S. Barfield C. C. Craig	Captain 1st Lieut. 2d Lieut.	Feb. 20, 1909 Mar. 21, 1911 Mar. 21, 1911
C Forsyth Riflemen, Winston.	J. G. Wooten J. A. Stith Wm. A. Holder	Captain 1st Lieut. 2d Lieut.	Jan. 17, 1908 Nov. 14, 1904 Jan. 4, 1909
D Hornet's Nest Riflemen, Charlotte.	John A. Parker W. F. Robertson R. M. Johnston	Captain 1st Lieut. 2d Lieut.	April 5, 1909 July 18, 1911 Mar. 6, 1911
E Iredell Blues, Statesville.	J. E. Deitz C. H. Turner Neal Garrison	Captain 1st Lieut. 2d Lieut.	Jan. 27, 1902 Oct. 3, 1900 May 4, 1906
F Blue Ridge Rifles, Asheville	J. H. Koon E. F. Jones Carl H. Felmet	Captain 1st Lieut. 2d Lieut.	May 27, 1910 Oct. 20, 1911 Mar. 5, 1910
G Cleveland Guards, Shelby.	O. Max Gardner J. F. Jenkins Chas. P. Roberts	Captain 1st Lieut. 2d Lieut.	June 13, 1907 June 13, 1907 April 23, 1910
H Richland Rifles, Waynesville.	J. H. Howell J. B. Hoyle Geo. F. Plott	Captain 1st Lieut. 2d Lieut.	April 28, 1910 Oct. 19, 1903 April 28, 1910
I Blue Ridge Guards, Mount Airy.	W. A. Jackson Hiram Stanley Frank Walker	Captain 1st Lieut. 2d Lieut.	Oct. 7, 1906 Mar. 29, 1910 Feb. 9, 1912
K Asheville Light Infantry, Asheville.	C. I. Bard D. E. Penland J. B. Taylor	Captain 1st Lieut. 2d Lieut.	Nov. 11, 1905 June 6, 1910 Oct. 5, 1911

FIRST INFANTRY—COMPANIES—CONTINUED.

Name and Station of Company	Name of Officer	Rank	Date of Rank
L Cabarrus Black Boys, Concord.	Louis A. Brown Eugene C. Barnhardt, Jr. Robt. C. Thompson	Captain 1st Lieut. 2d Lieut.	Mar. 19, 1908 Dec. 30, 1911 Oct. 19, 1909
M High Point Rifles, High Point.	E. P. Carpenter J. J. Griffith M. B. Shiplett	Captain 1st Lieut. 2d Lieut.	Feb. 9, 1909 Jan. 26, 1911 Jan. 26, 1911

SECOND INFANTRY.

FIELD AND STAFF.

Name	Office	Rank	Date of Commission	Residence
H. C. Bragaw	Colonel	Colonel	Dec. 4, 1902	Washington.
J. Van B. Metts	Lieut. Colonel	Lieut. Col.	Feb. 22, 1907	Wilmington.
C. B. Elliott	Major	Major	Dec. 4, 1902	Edenton.
T. S. Pace	Major	Major	Dec. 4, 1902	Wilson.
W. C. Rodman	Major	Major	Mar. 26, 1908	Washington.
Hugh H. Murray	Adjutant	Captain	June 22, 1909	Wilson.
Nathaniel Harding	Chaplain	Captain	Aug. 16, 1884	Washington.
S. Cohen	Insp. S. A. P.	Captain	Mar. 31, 1903	Goldsboro.
J. N. Pearce	Quartermaster	Captain	May 4, 1905	Wilson.
F. L. Black	Commissary	Captain	April 13, 1908	Charlotte.
W. L. Barlow	Bat. Adjutant	1st Lieut.	July 7, 1910	Tarboro.
Donald J. Murray	Bat. Adjutant	1st Lieut.	Jan. 26, 1909	Wilson.
R. Graham White	Bat. Adjutant	1st Lieut.	April 5, 1909	Edenton.
J. T. Lumley	Bat. Quartermaster and Com.	2d Lieut.	July 7, 1910	Goldsboro.
W. H. Herring	Bat. Quartermaster and Com.	2d Lieut.	April 14, 1909	Clinton.

SECOND INFANTRY—COMPANIES.

Name and Station of Company	Name of Officer	Rank	Date of Rank
A Edgecombe Guards, Tarboro.	Paul Jones J. A. Jenkins F. M. Carlisle	Captain 1st Lieut. 2d Lieut.	Feb. 9, 1906 July 4, 1906 July 11, 1910
B Kinston Rifles, Kinston.	A. L. C. Hill J. I. Brown J. O. H. Taylor	Captain 1st Lieut. 2d Lieut.	April 14, 1909 Sept. 24, 1908 April 24, 1909
C Rocky Mount.	J. S. Lewis H. L. Daughtry Bruce Q. Nabers	Captain 1st Lieut. 2d Lieut.	Feb. 18, 1909 Jan. 9, 1911 Feb. 21, 1912
D Goldsboro Rifles, (First Organization), Goldsboro.	E. A. Simkins S. E. Malone G. C. Derr	Captain 1st Lieut. 2d Lieut.	Jan. 28, 1909 Jan. 28, 1909 Jan. 28, 1909
E Goldsboro Rifles, (Second Organization), Goldsboro.	A. O. Clement B. F. Adams Zeno G. Hollowell	Captain 1st Lieut. 2d Lieut.	Jan. 9, 1911 Feb. 21, 1911 Dec. 17, 1911
F Fayetteville Light Infantry, Fayetteville.	Paul Watson A. R. Williams A. G. Murchison	Captain 1st Lieut. 2d Lieut.	Feb. 4, 1911 Dec. 14, 1908 Feb. 4, 1911
G Washington Light Infantry, Washington.	R. B. Cowell B. B. Ross A. C. Hoyt	Captain 1st Lieut. 2d Lieut.	Jan. 9, 1911 Jan. 9, 1911 Mar. 21, 1911
H Sampson Light Infantry, Clinton.	C. M. Faircloth G. K. Hobbs N. F. Whitfield	Captain 1st Lieut. 2d Lieut.	Feb. 3, 1905 July 1, 1910 July 1, 1910
I Edenton Light Infantry, Edenton.	W. S. Privott W. A. Barrow Jno. G. Wood, Jr.	Captain 1st Lieut. 2d Lieut.	June 1, 1909 June 24, 1909 Oct. 12, 1909
K Wilson Light Infantry, Wilson.	C. F. Batts S. P. Clark W. E. Dunn	Captain 1st Lieut. 2d Lieut.	April 17, 1910 March 5, 1912 March 5, 1912

SECOND INFANTRY—COMPANIES—CONTINUED.

Name and Station of Company	Name of Officer	Rank	Date of Rank
L Lumber Bridge Light Infantry, Lumber Bridge.	J. B. Malloy D. A. Barlow J. L. Shaw	Captain 1st Lieut. 2d Lieut.	Oct. 13, 1906 Oct. 13, 1906 June 22, 1909
M Dunn Light Infantry, Dunn.	J. L. Hines W. A. Jackson Geo. P. McKay	Captain 1st Lieut. 2d Lieut.	Oct. 5, 1911 Feb. 13, 1912 Feb. 13, 1912

THIRD INFANTRY.

FIELD AND STAFF.

Name	Office	Rank	Date of Commission	Residence
J. N. Craig	Colonel	Colonel	Dec. 4, 1902	Reidsville.
S. W. Minor	Lieut. Colonel	Lieut. Col.	Mar. 28, 1903	Durham.
C. L. McGhee	Major	Major	Dec. 4, 1902	Franklinton.
J. J. Bernard	Major	Major	Dec. 4, 1902	Raleigh.
R. M. Albright*	Major	Major	Dec. 4, 1902	Raleigh.
A. McCullen	Chaplain	Captain	Dec. 1, 1898	Washington.
Don. E. Scott	Adjutant	Captain	Feb. 5, 1910	Graham.
R. W. Morphis	Commissary	Captain	July 30, 1903	Reidsville.
Baxter Durham	Quartermaster	Captain	Feb. 24, 1910	Raleigh.
C. J. Smith	Insp. S. A. P.	Captain	Jan. 16, 1909	Henderson.
S. E. Winston	Bat. Adjutant	1st Lieut.	Jan. 10, 1903	Youngsville.
W. R. Miller	Bat. Adjutant	1st Lieut.	July 6, 1906	Raleigh.
Henry J. Hervey	Bat. Adjutant	1st Lieut.	Feb. 14, 1911	Raleigh.
R. T. Burton	Bat. Quartermaster and Com.	2d Lieut.	July 6, 1910	Reidsville.
W. C. Harris	Bat. Quartermaster and Com.	2d Lieut.	May 11, 1910	Raleigh.
S. L. Rotter	Bat. Quartermaster and Com.	2d Lieut.	Mar. 14, 1908	Raleigh.

THIRD INFANTRY—COMPANIES.

Name and Station of Company	Name of Officer	Rank	Date of Rank
A Lexington Rifles, Lexington.	W. H. Phillips J. A. Leonard Joseph Farabee	Captain 1st Lieut. 2d Lieut.	June 29, 1907 Nov. 18, 1911 Oct. 20, 1911
B Raleigh Light Infantry, Raleigh.	W. F. Moody E. B. Parrish W. C. Holder	Captain 1st Lieut. 2d Lieut.	May 15, 1904 June 19, 1911 Aug. 19, 1911
C Vance Guards, Henderson.	R. J. Jones W. H. Jenkins, Jr. Bennett P. Rose	Captain 1st Lieut. 2d Lieut.	Aug. 22, 1911 Aug. 22, 1911 April 27, 1910
D Louisburg Rifles, Louisburg.	C. H. Banks J. A. Turner S. P. Boddie	Captain 1st Lieut. 2d Lieut.	April 24, 1909 April 24, 1909 July 4, 1911
E Granville Grays, Oxford.	Thaddeus G. Stem E. E. Fuller E. L. Parham	Captain 1st Lieut. 2d Lieut.	May 11, 1910 May 11, 1910 June 4, 1910
F Franklin Guards, Franklinton.	I. H. Kearney E. M. Edwards G. L. Cook	Captain 1st Lieut. 2d Lieut.	Feb. 21, 1905 Nov. 15, 1911 Nov. 15, 1911
G Reidsville Rifles, Reidsville,	W. B. Millner J. H. Mobley C. T. Somers	Captain 1st Lieut. 2d Lieut.	Feb. 27, 1912 Feb. 27, 1912 Feb. 27, 1912
H Warren Guards, Warrenton.	Frank Rose F. P. Wiggins W. H. Burroughs	Captain 1st Lieut. 2d Lieut.	Dec. 5, 1911 April 21, 1908 Jan. 25, 1909
I Holt Guards, Burlington.	J. C. Freeman A. A. Russell Freeman Neese	Captain 1st Lieut. 2d Lieut.	April 2, 1906 Dec. 11, 1911 Dec. 11, 1911
K Asheboro.	E. L. Auman Houston B. Hiatt Geo. R. Ross	Captain 1st Lieut. 2d Lieut.	Nov. 9, 1911 June 16, 1910 Nov. 9, 1911

THIRD INFANTRY—COMPANIES—CONTINUED.

Name and Station of Company	Name of Officer	Rank	Date of Rank
L Thomasville Blues, Thomasville.	W. O. Burgin C. H. Newby H. S. Williams	Captain 1st Lieut. 2d Lieut.	April 5, 1909 Sept. 5, 1911 Sept. 5, 1911
M Durham Light Infantry, Durham.	S. C. Chambers Chas. F. Bennett Walter E. Page	Captain 1st Lieut. 2d Lieut.	Mar. 16, 1909 Jan. 9, 1909 June 12, 1911

CAVALRY.

Name and Station of Company	Name of Officer	Rank	Date of Rank
Troop A Lincolnton	Wm. A. Fair John O. Shuford Robt. S. Reinhardt, Jr.	Captain 1st Lieut. 2d Lieut.	Feb. 17, 1912 Feb. 17, 1912 Feb. 17, 1912

COAST ARTILLERY CORPS.

FIELD AND STAFF.

Name	Office	Rank	Date of Commission	Residence
Max L. Barker	Major	Major	Jan. 12, 1909	Salisbury.
L. M. Dodamead	Adjutant	Captain	June 16, 1905	High Point.
W. D. Marrow	Art. Engineer	Captain	Jan. 14, 1909	Greensboro.
Walter R. Cox	Quartermaster	Captain	Sept. 26, 1909	Salisbury.
C. L. Shaver	Ordnance Officer	1st Lieut.	July 5, 1910	Salisbury.

COAST ARTILLERY—COMPANIES.

Name and Station of Company	Name	Rank	Date of Commission
First Company, Coast Artillery. New Bern.	R. Hunter Smith	Captain	July 27, 1911
	W. R. Pate	1st Lieut.	July 27, 1911
	G. A. Farrow	2d Lieut.	Aug. 3, 1911
Second Company, Wilmington.	Edwin A. Metts	Captain	Sept. 24, 1908
	P. L. Cantwell	1st Lieut.	Mar. 9, 1909
	J. B. Lynch	2d Lieut.	Mar. 9, 1909
Third Company, Greensboro.	E. D. Kuykendall	Captain	Mar. 4, 1908
	R. W. Brewer	1st Lieut.	Mar. 23, 1909
	C. D. Smith	2d Lieut.	Mar. 23, 1909
Fourth Company, Salisbury.	Marion F. Hatcher	Captain	Mar. 5, 1912
	John H. Miller	1st Lieut.	Mar. 5, 1912
	Chas. L. Coggin	2d Lieut.	Jany. 26, 1912
Fifth Company. Charlotte.	W. M. Robey	Captain	June 7, 1910
	C. B. Ross	1st Lieut.	May 4, 1909
	Claude E. Hobbs	2d Lieut.	June 1, 1911
Sixth Company, Hendersonville.	Rolla V. Ladd	Captain	Mar. 8, 1912
	Thos. V. Lyda	1st Lieut.	Mar. 8, 1912
	James H. Maxwell	2d Lieut.	Mar. 8, 1612

NAVAL BRIGADE.

COMMANDER AND STAFF.

Name	Office	Rank	Date of Rank	Residence
Thomas C. Daniels	Commanding	Captain	Mar. 30, 1904	New Bern.
F. H. Shipp	Chief of Staff	Lieut. Com.	July 5, 1909	New Bern.
E. Ellis Williams	Chief Engineer	Lieut. Com.	Mar. 24, 1906	New Bern.
R. DuVal Jones	Surgeon	Lieut. Com.	Feb. 22, 1907	New Bern.
C. W. Hollowell	Paymaster	Lieut. Com.	Feb. 9, 1910	Elizabeth City.
A. T. Willis	Signal Officer	Lieutenant	Nov. 14, 1908	New Bern.
C. F. Smith	Chaplain	Lieutenant	July 6, 1908	Elizabeth City.
W. J. Jackson	Aid	Lieut. J. G.	June 1, 1907	Plymouth.
John B. Green	Aid	Lieutenant	May 22, 1911	New Bern.

FIRST BATTALION.

Name	Office	Rank	Date of Rank	Residence
C. D. Bradham	Commanding	Commander	May 11, 1904	New Bern.
W. G. Dixon	Navigator	Lieutenant	July 5, 1909	Oriental.
R. Barcliff	Engineer Officer	Lieutenant	July 5, 1909	Oriental.
J. F. Patterson	Surgeon	Lieutenant	Feb. 20, 1908	New Bern.
J. S. Claypoole	Paymaster	Lieutenant	Feb. 9, 1910	New Bern.
W. E. Smith	Asst. Engineer	Lieut., J. G.	July 20, 1904	New Bern.
J. E. Bunting	Gunnery Officer and Adjutant.	Lieut., J. G.	July 5, 1909	Wilmington.

FIRST BATTALION—DIVISIONS.

Division and Name	Rank	Date of Rank	Residence
SECOND DIVISION:			
C. J. McSorley	Lieutenant	May 24, 1904	New Bern.
Geo. T. Bowden	Lieutenant, J. G.	Aug. 1, 1911	New Bern.
L. G. Mann	Ensign	Aug. 1, 1911	New Bern.
SIXTH DIVISION:			
Chas. L. Morton	Lieutenant	Nov. 27, 1911	Washington.
Wm. B. Harding	Lieutenant, J. G.	Nov. 27, 1911	Washington.
Herman Carrow	Ensign	Nov. 27, 1911	Washington.

SECOND BATTALION.

Name	Office	Rank	Date of Rank	Residence
J. L. Phelps	Commanding	Commander	Feb. 15, 1908	Creswell.
	Navigator	Lieutenant		
Brad. Sanders	Engineer Officer	Lieutenant	July 5, 1909	Elizabeth City.
A. W. Disosway	Surgeon	Lieutenant	Feb. 20, 1908	Plymouth.
Clarence Latham	Paymaster	Lieutenant	June 4, 1908	Plymouth.
J. C. B. Ehringhaus	Gunnery Officer	Lieut., J. G.	Oct. 13, 1910	Elizabeth City.

SECOND BATTALION—DIVISIONS.

Division and Name	Rank	Date of Rank	Residence
THIRD DIVISION:			
F. M. Dunston	Lieutenant, J. G.	Sept. 17, 1909	Windsor.
S. W. Kinney	Ensign	June 12, 1911	Windsor.
FOURTH DIVISION:			
W. R. Hampton	Lieutenant	July 15, 1910	Plymouth.
J. S. Norman	Lieutenant, J. G.	Mar. 30, 1910	Plymouth.
FIFTH DIVISION:			
J. Kenyon Wilson	Lieutenant, J. G.	Nov. 22, 1911	Elizabeth City.
Geo. F. Pappendick	Ensign	Nov. 22, 1911	Elizabeth City.
SEVENTH DIVISION:			
W. B. Hudson	Lieutenant	Aug. 15, 1910	Hertford.
H. T. Shannonhouse	Lieutenant, J. G.	Aug. 15, 1910	Hertford.
R. T. Brinn	Ensign	Nov. 25, 1910	Hertford.

Retired Officers

	Retired Rank.	
A. L. Smith	Brigadier-General	Charlotte
F. A. Olds	Brigadier-General	Raleigh
W. A. Bobbitt	Brigadier-General	Kinston
W. B. Rodman	Brigadier-General	Charlotte
W. C. Jones	Brigadier-General	Wilmington
Jno. F. Bruton	Brigadier-General	Wilson
Walker Taylor	Brigadier-General	Wilmington
Robt. S. Young	Brigadier-General	Concord
Jno. A. Pollock	Brigadier-General	Kinston
T. J. Winston	Colonel	Durham
Thos. C. James	Colonel	Wilmington
Chas. H. White	Colonel	Wilmington
Leo D. Heartt	Lieutenant-Colonel	Raleigh
P. T. Jones	Lieutenant-Colonel	Henderson
W. F. Robertson	Lieutenant-Colonel	Wilmington
Chas. S. Jordan	Lieutenant-Colonel	Asheville
A. H. Harris	Lieutenant-Colonel	Wilmington
White G. Smith	Lieutenant-Colonel	Asheville
J. M. Campbell	Lieutenant-Colonel	Asheville
N. Anderson	Lieutenant-Colonel	Wilson
H. M. Chase	Lieutenant-Commander	Wilmington
B. F. Payne	Major	Raleigh
E. R. MacKethan	Major	Fayetteville
Robt. S. Stuart	Major	Asheville
A. J. Ellington	Major	Reidsville
W. T. Whitten	Major	Raleigh
Jas. F. Jordan	Captain	Raleigh
J. K. Tew	Captain	Goldsboro
R. H. Dowdy	Lieutenant	New Bern